The Politics of Reforming School Administration

Education Policy Perspectives

General Editor: Professor Ivor Goodson, Faculty of Education, University of Western Ontario, London, Canada N6G 1G7

Education policy analysis has long been a neglected area in the UK and, to an extent, in the USA and Australia. The result has been a profound gap between the study of education and the formulation of education policy. For practitioners, such a lack of analysis of new policy initiatives has worrying implications, particularly at a time of such policy flux and change. Education policy has, in recent years, been a matter for intense political debate – the political and public interest in the working of the system has come at the same time as the breaking of the consensus on education policy by the New Right. As never before, political parties and pressure groups differ in their articulated policies and prescriptions for the education sector. Critical thinking about these developments is clearly imperative.

All those working within the system also need information on policy-making, policy implementation and effective day-to-day operation. Pressure on schools from government, education authorities and parents has generated an enormous need for knowledge amongst those on the receiving end of educational policies.

This series aims to fill the academic gap, to reflect the politicalization of education, and to provide the practitioners with the analysis for informed implementation of policies that they will need. It offers studies in broad areas of policy studies, with a particular focus on the following areas: school organization and improvement (David Reynolds, University College, Cardiff, UK); social analysis (Professor Philip Wexler, University of Rochester, USA) and policy studies and evaluation (Professor Ernest House, University of Colorado at Boulder, USA).

The Politics of Reforming School Administration

The 1988 Yearbook of the Politics of Education Association

Edited by

Jane Hannaway

Stanford University

and

Robert Crowson

University of Illinois at Chicago

The Falmer Press
(A member of the Taylor & Francis Group)
New York • Philadelphia • London

UK   The Falmer Press, Falmer House, Barcombe, Lewes, East Sussex, BN8 5DL

USA   The Falmer Press, Taylor & Francis Inc., 242 Cherry Street, Philadelphia, PA 19106-1906

First published 1989

Library of Congress Cataloging in Publication Data is available on request

ISBN 1 85000 456 0
ISBN 1 85000 457 9 (pbk.)

Typeset in 11/12pt Bembo by
Chapterhouse Typesetting Ltd, Formby, Lancs

Jacket design by Caroline Archer

Printed in Great Britain by Taylor & Francis (Printers) Ltd, Basingstoke

The **Politics of Education Association (PEA)** promotes the development and dissemination of research and debate on educational policy and politics. **PEA** brings together scholars, practitioners, and policy-makers interested in educational governance and politics; is affiliated as a Special Interest Group with the American Educational Research Association (AERA); and meets each spring in conjunction with AERA's annual meeting. The annual membership dues for **PEA** are $US20.00. Members receive a copy of the annual Yearbook and the *Politics of Education Bulletin*, which includes news on member activities and occasional short scholarly pieces. Membership dues should be sent to Robert Wimpelberg, **PEA** Treasurer, Department of Educational Leadership, University of New Orleans, New Orleans, LA 70148, USA.

Contents

Introduction

About the Editors and Contributors

Jane Hannaway is an Associate Professor in the School of Education at Stanford University. She previously taught at Teachers College, Columbia University and the Woodrow Wilson School of Public and International Affairs, Princeton University. She has published in policy and management journals and her book, *Managers Managing: The Workings of an Administrative System* is forthcoming shortly from Oxford University Press. Her PH D is from Stanford University.

Robert L. Crowson is a Professor in the College of Education at the University of Illinois (Chicago). His specialty in research and teaching is organizational theory and policy analysis in education. He has received a Fulbright Grant for research in West Germany, and is co-author of *Principals in Action* and *Managing Uncertainty*. His PH D in Educational Administration is from the University of Chicago.

Samuel B. Bacharach is a Professor and former Chairperson in the Department of Organizational Behavior, School of Industrial and Labor Relations and Professor of Education, Cornell University. He is also a Senior Research Consultant at Organizational Analysis and Practice, Inc., Ithaca, New York, with whom he has consulted to the National Educational Association and has consulted on numerous school improvement projects in various states. He also serves on an advisory committee to the Holmes Group, and has written in the fields of organizational behavior and education. Among his recent publications are papers on merit pay, teacher evaluation, career ladders, and school-site management. Most recently he has served as guest editor for a special issue of *Educational Administration Quarterly* on 'Educational reform: social change or political rhetoric?'

Joseph J. Blase is an Associate Professor of Educational Administration at the University of Georgia. He received his PH D from Syracuse University in 1980. His research focus has been upon the worklives of teachers, particularly ethnographic studies of teacher stress and teacher socialization. Recent inquiry into the micropolitics of the school is represented in publications titled 'The politics of favoritism: a qualitative analysis of the teachers' perspective (*Educational Administration Quarterly*, 1988), and 'The everyday political perspectives of teachers' (International Journal of Qualitative Studies in Education, 1988).

H. Dickson Corbett is Co-director of the Applied Research Project at Research for Better Schools, Philadelphia. His research focuses upon contextual influences on the implementation of educational policies, programs, and practices at the local level. Recent publications include *School Context and School Change* (1984) and *Change and Effectiveness in Schools: A Cultural Perspective* (1988).

Deborah J. Eaker is completing a PH D in the Social Foundations of Education at The University of North Carolina (Chapel Hill). She is also currently editing a book, *The Social Construction of the Health Professions*. Her major areas of research interest include sociology of education and medicine, qualitative research methodology, and feminist critical theory.

Richard F. Elmore is a Professor of Education and Political Science at Michigan State University, and Senior Research Fellow with the Center for Policy Research in Education. His current research is focused on the effects of state and local politics on the structure and content of public schooling and on policies directed at the labor market and educational problems of disadvantaged youth. His doctorate in policy is from the Graduate School of Education, Harvard University.

Susan H. Fuhrman is a Research Professor at the Eagleton Institute of Politics, Rutgers University and Director of the Center for Policy Research in Education (CPRE), a consortium of Rutgers, The State University of New Jersey, Michigan State University, Stanford University, and the University of Wisconsin-Madison. Dr Fuhrman is the author of numerous articles, research reports, and monographs on educational policy and finance. She was a consultant to the Ford Foundation's program on educational management and finance for ten years; and she also currently serves as a school board member in Westfield, New Jersey.

Rick Ginsberg is an Associate Professor in the Department of Educational Leadership and Policies at the University of South Carolina. He serves as secretary of the Politics of Education Association and is on the editorial board for *Urban Review*. He is co-editor of *Southern Cities, Southern Schools* (forthcoming, Greenwood Press), a series of historical essays examining urban school reform in the south. He received his PH D in Administrative, Institutional and Policy Studies at the University of Chicago.

Amy Gutmann is Andrew W. Mellon Professor of Politics and Director of the Program in Political Philosophy at Princeton University. Her most recent book is *Democratic Education* (Princeton University Press, 1987). She is also author of *Liberal Equality*, co-editor of *Ethics and Politics*, and editor of *Democracy and the Welfare State*, Gutmann serves on the Board of Directors of the Salzburg Seminar and the Executive Board of the Center for Policy Research in Education. Her PH D in Political Science is from Harvard University.

Susan Moore Johnson is an Associate Professor of Administration, Planning, and Social Policy at the Harvard Graduate School of Education. A former school teacher and administrator, she conducts research about schools – how they work and how they might be improved. She is the author of *Teacher Unions in Schools* (1984), and is presently completing a book about the school as a workplace for teachers.

David Marsh is an Associate Professor at the University of Southern California where he conducts research on school reform and local change processes. He has recently completed major studies on the California School Improvement Program, staff development practices in California, and high school reform strategies on which this article was based. He is currently studying middle school reform in California and has been chair of the AERA/SIG on research utilization the last two years.

Douglas E. Mitchell is a Professor of Education and Director of the California Education Research Cooperative at the University of California, Riverside. Education policy at the state and local levels has been the main focus of his research. In addition to a ten year interest in labor relations, he has studied issues of social science utilization, state legislative decisionmaking, teachers' unions, and citizen influence in the schools. His most recent books are *Work Orientation and Job Performance: The Cultural Basis of Rewards and Incentives* (co-authored with Flora Ida Ortiz and Tedi K. Mitchell) and *The Changing Idea of a Teachers' Union* (co-authored with Charles T. Kerchner).

George W. Noblit is an Associate Professor of Social Foundations at The University of North Carolina at Chapel Hill. After receiving his PH D in Sociology from the University of Oregon (1973), he was assistant then associate professor of sociology at Memphis State University (1973–79) and Senior Fellow at the National Institute of Education (1978–79). His most recent book, *Meta-Ethnography* (1988), combines his interests in qualitative research and sociology of education.

Allan Odden is a Professor in the School of Education at the University of Southern California and Director of the Southern California Policy Analysis for California Education (PACE) Center. He formerly was Director of Policy Analysis and Research and Director of the Education Finance Center at the Education Commission of the States. In 1979–80, he was President of the American Education Finance Association. His research interests include school finance, state education policy, and policy implementation.

Joseph B. Shedd is Director of the Educational Systems Division, Organizational Analysis and Practice, Inc., of Ithaca, New York, and principal consultant to a five-year New Jersey State Education Department project that aims to enhance labor-management cooperation in school systems throughout that state. His research and writing includes studies of compensation, career development, working conditions, and collective bargaining in public education. With Samuel Bacharach and David Lipsky, he is the author of *Paying for Better Teaching: Merit Pay and Its Alternatives*.

Gary Sykes is an Assistant Professor in the Department of Educational Administration, College of Education, at Michigan State University. His interests include policy analysis, and the study of teaching and school reform. His is currently working both with the Holmes Group and the National Board for Professional Teaching Standards.

Scott D. Thomson is Executive Director of the National Association of Secondary School Principals. He has also been a former teacher, principal, and local school district superintendent. His doctorate in education is from Stanford University. Thomson additionally serves as a member of the Board of Directors for the National Merit Scholarship Corporation and the Board of Trustees of the College Board.

Bruce L. Wilson is Co-Director of the Applied Research Project at Research for Better Schools, in Philadelphia. His current research addresses the impact of the external environment and internal organizational conditions on the operation of schools. His most recent publication is *Successful Secondary Schools*, 1988.

Robert K. Wimpelberg is the Associate Dean of the College of Education, Associate Professor of Educational Administration, and Director of the Louisiana LEAD:UNO Principals' Center at the University of New Orleans. His primary research interests include the national commission reform process and the effects of school reform on the work of principals and teachers. He is the lead author of 'Sensitivity to context: the past and future of effective schools research' in *Educational Administration Quarterly*, forthcoming.

1 Introduction and overview: the politics of reforming school administration

Robert Crowson and Jane Hannaway
University of Illinois at Chicago and Stanford University

Introduction

'Why is it', asked Mr Hennesey, 'that a rayform administration always goes to th' bad?'

'I'll tell ye', said Mr Dooley. 'I'll tell ye ivrything an' I'll tell ye this. In th' first place 'tis a gr-reat mistake to think that annywan ra-ally wants to rayform. Ye niver heerd iv a man rayformin' himsilf. He'll rayform other people gladly. He likes to do it. But a healthy man'll niver rayform while he has th' strenth. A man doesn't rayform till his will has been impaired so he hasn't power to resist what th' pa-apers calls th' blandishments iv th' timpter. An' that's thruer in politics thin annywhere else.'
(Finley Peter Dunne as 'Mr Dooley', 1902)

Many of the reforms on the mind of Chicago's turn-of-the-century humorist, Mr Dooley, are long forgotten. Others, however, were successful enough to be considered part-of-the-problem in public schooling today. Taking education out of politics, consolidating schools and centralizing managerial authority, establishing businesslike efficiency in school administration, and training persons to serve professionally in the special role of school executive – these were among the key objectives of eductional reformers some eight decades ago. While times have changed, and new reform is replacing the old, the questions raised by Mr Dooley are disturbingly modern. Does anyone *really* want to reform? Are we busy reforming other people gladly but not ourselves? Will we resist reform so long as we have the 'strength'?

Educators, and especially educational administrators, do not stand unaccused of a propensity to resist reform. They have been 'reformed' before. From *Laggards in our Schools* (Ayres 1909), through an efficiency movement, a human relations period, McCarthyism, decentralization experiments, Sputnik, teacher-proof curricula, and Federal 'intervention-ism', public education has experienced waves of criticism over the years, complete with strident voices clamoring for 'something-to-be-done' about the schools.

Some educators may cynically claim that 'this wave too shall pass', or may just as cynically note that many of today's proposals do little more than de-reform the efficiency-minded accomplishments of an earlier time. Other persons, familiar with the profession, might caution that change does not come easily to school administration. Indeed, the role of educational administrator is even (at least in part) describable as a protector of tradition, a stabilizer amidst ambiguity, a source of safe and cautious leadership during turbulent times (Tyack and Hansot 1982). Naturally conservative in approach, wary of 'politics', and mindful of their extremely tenuous controls over day-by-day events – the nation's educational administrators tend to be 'gray personages' (March & March 1977) – hard-working, stick-to-the-last types rather than outspoken, charismatic seekers of a changed educational order. Finally, a last group of observers might claim that at last the collective managerial 'will' has now been sufficiently impaired not only to demand but to pave the way for meaningful reform in school administration. An outpouring of reform reports, long-range plans, prescriptive pieces of state legislation – even, amazingly, a heavily intellectual best-seller on lost values by a University of Chicago professor – all combine to suggest that today's reform effort just might have a bit more staying power to it than movements in the past.

Background

Administrative reform of an earlier, turn-of-the-century era sought to centralize authority in the hands of managerial professionals – people who were trained to run educational organizations 'scientifically', in businesslike fashion, free from all political intrusions (Callahan 1962, Tyack 1974). An administrative hierarchy along corporate lines would have clear, top-down decisional responsibility for all staff assignments, resource allocations, procedural rules, and programmatic objectives. Strong, professional, school administration would be accompanied by a well-delineated and sharply limited role for the local school board – recognizing a policy role for the board but the ownership of a separate policy-into-practice role for administrators, reflective of their distinctive training and expertise (Peterson 1985, Spring 1986).

This 'scientific management' period of reform responded to complex societal forces of population growth, urbanization, immigration, industrialization, and technological change in America (Silver 1979). Interestingly, however, as is true for most reforms of significance, the turn-of-the-century reform movement simultaneously retained a key aspect of an earlier, nineteenth century view of administrative purpose in education – the view that educational leaders also act importantly as 'managers of virtue' for society (Tyack and Hansot 1982). Despite an increasingly complex urban-industrial environment, a preservation of the reputedly 'small town' qualities of moral earnestness, upstanding character, rural conservatism, banker-like respectability, even (usually Protestant) piety – has continued to be a much-expected characteristic of the school administrator. As Tyack and Hansot (1982: 249) note: 'The public-school system is probably the closest Americans have come toward creating an established church.'

The role of educational administrator continues, late in the twentieth century, to reflect both its scientific management and its managers-of-virtue roots. On its 'efficiency' side, educational administration has evolved over the remainder of this century into a much specialized career, served by hundreds of university training programs and rather powerful professional associations. The pedagogical philosophies thought to be 'best' for the training of administrators have changed over time (e.g., the human relations period followed by the theory movement); nevertheless the commonalities of course offerings, degree and certification requirements, state codes, and pathways into the profession (e.g., classroom teaching as a prerequisite) across the nation are remarkable (Cooper and Boyd 1987). No less remarkable are the common norms and values of the profession. A separation of functions between school board (policy) and administrator (implementation), expectations of professional autonomy (unencumbered by parental intrusion) in running the school system, a distrust of conflict and the political fray, and recurring admonitions to seek firm administrative control over their almost-determinedly uncontrollable enterprises – these are central ingredients in a professionally normative dimension of school administration.

On its small town-virtues side, educational administration clings with ideological fervor to canons of local control; to a commitment-generated sense of almost patriarchal responsibility for the educational workplace (e.g., 'my schools', 'my teachers', 'my kids'); and to a battle-hardened image of the job as guardian of community decency, discipline, decorum, and diligence. From this perspective, the profession (particularly among superintendents) continues rather unchangedly a demography of white, male, Protestant, and a tendency toward conservative, placebound, stick-to-the-last, practicality while on the job (March and March 1977, Tyack and Hansot 1982, Cunningham and Hentges 1982). Despite a continuing fascination with 'consideration' as well as 'initiating structure', and with the ideographic as well as the nomothetic, the normative world of the local administrator has tended more toward the general-in-charge image of 'trustee', as defined by Dale Mann (1976), than the guided-by-others concept of 'delegate' administrator.

Interestingly, today's press toward the reform of educational administration threatens to turn-on-its-head much of this decades-long accommodation between nineteenth- and twentieth-century perspectives. Put simply, it is now at the state level that a new 'morality' of public, not professionally mandated excellence is to be found. Conversely, it is at the local level that attention is being given to a new professionalization in school administration. Among the states, a tradition of university – and association-dominated authority over professional preparation, poorly monitored, is encountering increasing legislative prescriptiveness vis-a-vis administrator training and on-the-job performance, more closely monitored. A state-level morality of mandated excellence and standardized (curriculum, evaluation, etc.) requirements is replacing the historically loose federation of profession-centered controls and the even looser constraints traditionally placed by state upon locality. Alternatively, at the local level a culture of professional administrator-in-charge and administrator as guardian of local virtue is threatened by demands for a shared and collaborative professionalism, with participative leadership in place of Moses-like commandments. The reform agenda is replete with proposals for a radical restructuring of teacher-administrator relationships – away from 'strong' principals toward a school-site environment of enhanced teacher participation, teacher control of curriculum, peer evaluation, and collegially shared leadership. The suggestion is that a new spirit of professionalism should characterize the management of schools, with much greater autonomy and 'involvement' for teachers, replacing a currently over-managed educational enterprise (see Holmes Group 1986, CFEE 1986). Increasingly, local districts under experimentation are now attempting a bottom-up approach to improvement – with a 'school site management' philosophy of grassroots' authority over budgetary allocations, curricula, teacher assignments, and performance measures (Pierce 1977, NCEEA 1987).

In short, normative imperatives are now centrally of state concern while a decentralized and under-managed professionalism is the local thrust. The old, old tradition of state authority but defacto local control is pressured by the rediscovered bureaucratizing power of the state mandate. The tradition of local control, in turn, finds itself up-ended by debureaucratizing pressures toward the establishment of enhanced employee participation and autonomy (Cuban 1988). The conflicts embedded within such simultaneous trends have been analyzed by Arthur Wise (1988). On the one hand, reflecting a distrust of local educators, is the growing imposition of state controls over school curricula, achievement standards, teacher evaluation, staff development, and administrative roles. On the other hand, the reform-minded assertion of power by educators (and some like-minded policy makers) seeks to bring decision making more fully into the hands of a newly professionalized community of local educators, promising improvement through decisions 'made closest to the prople to be served'. Caught in the middle, of course, notes Wise (1988), are the administrators – pulled at the same time upwards toward state mandates and downwards toward collegial/parental expectations.

The issues

Political issues abound in this topsy-turvy push toward reform. Of initial (and fascinating) political interest must be an exploration of the key issues surrounding the fact that the two major strains of administrator reform are impacting education *simultaneously*. States have been influenced by a school effectiveness literature which suggests the value of strong administrative leadership with high expectations for instructional quality, a steady monitoring of student performance, and the enforcement of an orderly/secure school environment (Odden 1987, Murphy 1987). With reform-minded fervor, state school codes have increasingly demanded instructional quality – placing heavy, top-down emphasis upon the separate districts and the schools to supervise teachers closely, standardize curricula, measure student outcomes regularly, and hold personnel publicly accountable for performance against statewide and national norms.

State legislation directed toward the reform of educational administration and the organization of schooling has been wide-ranging. Principals have been ordered by state law to spend more of their time directly evaluating the classroom performance of teachers. Administrative preparation and certification standards/procedures have been revised. Pupil assessment and promotion policies have been tightened, with increased control transferred to the state. Clear indications of curriculum priority statewide (e.g., mathematics and science, reading improvement programs, substance abuse programs) have been newly legislated. Local administrative discretion has been reduced through legislation requiring highly specific administrative actions (e.g., criminal background investigations of prospective employees, prohibitions against the 'social promotion' of pupils, requirements for uniform pupil testing at specified grade levels). Beyond state law, considerable normative pressure has been placed upon educational administration by way of reform-minded reports (e.g., NCEE 1983) to tighten degree standards, cut 'frills', return to basics, revive a 1950s-style secondary education, and press hard toward quality in classroom teaching.

Much of the state-level and 'at risk'-oriented pressure has now been labeled a first wave of reform, and is further characterized as a 'top-down' approach to school change. A second wave, described as more bottom-up in orientation (Shanker 1988) is (at least in part) a reaction to basic, first-wave assumptions about education (e.g., what 'really' needs to be done to correct deficiencies in school quality). Additionally, the second wave is a movement within the profession itself (e.g., its associations, key interest groups, the academic community) to address the 'deeper structures' (Tye 1987) of reform in education, as well as to do battle professionally about basic directions of change. With the second wave, the 'honeymoon is over' in the school-improvement debate, writes Dale Mann (1988). Teachers are reaching for more control, citizens and politicians are exploring anew the break-up of school bureaucracies, those who train administrators and those who train teachers are blaming one another, the professional associations are warring with the academics, and top-down supporters are battling bottom-up enthusiasts over the consequences of reform implementation (Mann 1988, Cuban 1988a, McNeil 1988). Theorists and practitioners, administrator associations and teacher associations, state mandates and local traditions, public expectations and professional interests, legislators and executives, building administrators and classroom teachers – all are embroiled, sometimes heatedly and nearly always confusingly, in an energetic search for school improvement, a search filled with images of new accommodations, altered alliances, changed working relationships, revised operating procedures. In short, the two waves of reform in education have now reached a point of debate (and by no means consensus) wherein it is timely to undertake both a reappraisal of and renewed attention to the political side of educational administration. The old, old political question of who gets what, when, and how (Lasswell 1936) has been raised anew in the management of public education.

Overview of the Yearbook

The chapters in this second Yearbook of the Politics of Education Association have been selected to examine the politics of reforming school administration from both top-down and bottom-up perspectives. The chapters of the Yearbook are arranged in three parts. In Part 1, state-level reform initiatives are examined, with legislation-into-practice questions about the impact of reform upon local schools and local administrators. Part 2 explores the micro-politics of reform within schools, for it is ultimately within this context (the 'deep structure of schooling') that basic changes in educational administration will have to occur. Finally, as a central issue in Part 3, the politics of reforming the profession itself is addressed – exploring the actors, the interests, and the incentives involved in a heated, contemporary debate regarding the training of the nation's cadre of school administrators.

Part 1: The politics of state reform implementation

Of critical, initial concern in the politics-of-reform debate must be the basic question of how successful/unsuccessful is the implementation of state (top down) reform legislation. Studies of the reform-scuttled-by-practice genre have become common reading in the implementation literature (Murphy 1971, Weatherly 1979, Pressman and Wildavsky 1973). Nevertheless, recent examinations of policy-into-practice find that over time most governmental programs do receive a modicum of local acceptance (Kirst and Jung 1982, Peterson *et al*. 1986, Rabe and Peterson 1988). However, as Odden and Marsh point out in this volume: 'Claiming that programs get implemented is not the same as claiming that they "work".' Furthermore, the 'work' demanded of modern-day reform goes far beyond the past implementation of categorical grant programs or the provision of new services to a previously under-served clientele. Local education authorities are now being asked by their states to change organizationally and to alter time-honored (and time-bound) practices of curriculum and instruction (see Cuban 1984, 1988a). The demands are greater, the reforms are more all-encompassing, and the interplay between state-level and site-level appears to be more complex.

The critics of top-down as a strategy toward reform are many. A common argument is that legislated packages of educational reform to date have essentially, and conservatively, left the existing organizational structures, norms, relationships, and governance mechanisms of the public schools quite well intact (Elmore 1987, Chubb 1988, Cuban 1988b). Indeed, argues Cuban (1988b: 230), first-order changes may act paradoxically to strengthen organizational stability. They tend to be structural in nature and are easily monitored (e.g., mandating staff development programs, minimal competency testing for prospective teachers, student dropout projects). However, they may also create new, supportive political constituencies (e.g., staff development professionals, dropout prevention spokespersons) and may become embedded within existing organizational arrangements (e.g., adding to bureaucratic specialization and rigidity). Thus, the reforms could add to difficulties in the deeper, 'innercore' of second-order reform – the alteration of teacher-administrator relationships, classroom instruction practices, and procedures for school-site governance.

In this Yearbook the debate over the success of top-down, or state-legislated reform is by no means brought to an end. Findings thus far regarding state reform implementation differ; and these differences are highlighted informatively in four of the Yearbook's contributions.

In chapter 2, Robert Wimpelberg and Rick Ginsberg analyse the effect that national commissions and their reports, particularly the NCEE report *A Nation at Risk*, have on the policy making process. While education commissions do not prescribe solutions to problems, the authors argue that commissions do more than provide symbols of concern. They create a sense of crisis which 'pushes' people into action and they also shape the policy agenda by legitimizing certain routes to reform.

The top-down approaches discussed in the other three chapters of this section describe more direct routes to reform than the commission approach. In Chapter 3, Allan Odden and David Marsh sends a message to skeptics of top-down reform initiatives. They review the literature on the implementation of education programs and set forth a conceptual framework for analyzing both the macro and the micro dimensions of implementation. They use their framework to study SB 813, California's comprehensive education reform package, and conclude that successful implementation was characterized by reforms that were simultaneously top-down and bottom-up. They were initiated at the state level in a top-down manner and implemented within districts at the school level with the active bottom-up involvement of school site administrators and teachers.

In Chapter 4, H. Dickson Corbett and Bruce Wilson describe the consequences at the local level of states' using mandated minimum competency testing as a policy lever. The authors are less sanguine than Odden and Marsh about the benefits of at least some top-down reforms. Their analysis of the implementation of testing programs in two states suggests that state mandated testing is, indeed, a very powerful direct top-down lever that affects the behavior of district administrators and teachers, but not necessarily in ways that are productive. Administrators and teachers reported they felt pressure to improve test scores even when it meant suspending their own best professional judgments about teaching and learning.

In Chapter 5, Susan Fuhrman cautions us not to overgeneralize. What top-down means in one state could very well be very different from what top-down means in another state. Fuhrman argues that, despite striking similarities in reforms across states, a state's political culture and history significantly affect the course of reform it takes. She makes the point by analyzing specific reform policies and their early implementation in six states.

Part 2: The school-site politics of reform

Schools are 'small polities', writes Elmore (1987), with critical questions regarding the structure and exercise of authority to be found at the intersection between reform policy and changed conditions of teaching/learning (see also Sarason 1971, Hoyle 1986). Although a new teacher-involved professionalism is at the center of such reform-mindedness, a larger question of bottom-up change versus the top-down strategies of state mandates is presented. From 'school-site management', to 'participative management' (Shanker 1988), to schools as 'living laboratories for reform' (Futrell 1988) – the sense is that meaningful change begins at the grassroots level of interacting teachers, building administrators, parents, and children. Changes at the bottom of the organizational hierarchy, in the form of a participatory professionalization of the school-site, are claimed to give promise of a more lasting and more productive route toward reform than that emanating from distantly imposed state mandates, test-driven 'competencies', and tightened supervision/certification standards.

However, curiously under-investigated to date, and therefore of inadequate guidance in reform, are answers to many enduring questions of professionalism in education-e.g., the degree to which teachers are actually willing to engage in participative management; the constraints surrounding enhanced collegiality among schoolteachers; and the strains in school-site governance flowing out of separate representational roles among teachers, administrators and parents. Such questions as these are at the heart of second-wave reform. And, they are essentially unanswered. As Lieberman (1988) notes, the move to professionalize teaching will inevitably conflict with existing authority relations and with the current bureaucratic orientation of schools. Other conflicts can be expected along traditional lines of union and management, old guard and 'young reformer', change-radically and change-minimally types, child-first advocates and subject-first defenders.

Amidst an array of political perspectives and interests, where does change start? With efforts to build a sense of 'collegueship' among teachers, breaking down that which tends to keep teaching professionals isolated from one another? With structural alterations in mechanisms for school-site governance, including increased parental participation, budgetary autonomy, enhanced teacher-reward power, and greater teacher-control of working conditions? With from-the-beginning changes in the training/socialization of both teachers and administrators, training both in shared leadership and shared visions for school improvement? The probable answer: Reform starts at each of these points of intervention, all at once – with, as a consequence, an intriguing albeit confusing kaleidoscope of reform arguments, solutions, exposes, and examinations.

Four of the chapters in the Yearbook provide, collectively, a beginning assessment of the politics accompanying school-site administrative reform. In chapter 6, Gary Sykes and Richard Elmore examine the relationship between the role an administrator plays and the context in which he or she operates. They make the argument that administrative behavior is largely a function of its context and that significant reforms in administrative behavior will emerge only when there are significant institutional reforms. Exhortations for better performance, behavioral prescriptions for managerial success and externally-generated regulations will have little value, indeed they may be counter-productive, within existing structures. The last section of their chapter identifies ways in which schools could be restructured that would lead to different conceptions of management's role in education and presumably also to more effective schools.

Two of the chapters in this section that look closely at the dynamics within schools, particularly the interchange between administrators and teachers, support the view that restructuring schools may indeed be necessary for true educational reform. Both the chapter by Susan Moore Johnson and that by Joseph Blase argue that principals, sometimes unknowingly, have a very large influence on the behavior and attitudes of teachers at work. Johnson interviewed a number of teachers reputed to be excellent about their jobs. Among other things, she found that they sought professional feedback, but saw little correspondence between their own professional values and those of their formal supervisors. While they expressed little interest in assuming administrative roles themselves, many felt blurring the lines between administrators and teachers, or as Sykes and Elmore put it letting 'structure follow technology', might provide them with a more professionally engaging environment. Blase also notes the division between principals and teachers in his chapter. He claims teachers feel very vulnerable to criticism, particularly in schools with authoritarian principals. In such schools they are likely to develop a protectionist stance concealing problems and conforming to directives even when they compromise their professional judgements. Principals who manage school in a more participatory style elicit more productive responses from teachers, but Blase fears that the top-down performance and accountability demands now being placed on schools may lead to more controlling and authoritarian type principals.

Accountability is a theme that runs through most of the chapters in this volume. George Noblit and Deborah Eaker deal with it directly in their chapter. They claim that evaluations flourish during periods of accountability. But, contrary to the thinking of many, evaluations are not politically neutral. Evaluation designs, they explain, define social relations among relevant parties and imply very different political strategies.

Part 3: The politics of reforming the profession of school administration

Much of the discussion at the micro-level, regarding changed relationships between teachers and administrators, is wrapped within a third issue of considerably broader scope. Included within the politics of reforming school administration is the key question of reform in administrator preparation. The education of administrators is 'an American tragedy', writes Richard Gibboney (1987). Administrator preparation programs have had a 'managerial obsession', saturated with courses in administrative techniques and technical 'efficiency', which are still little disguised in their modern-day equivalents of assessment centers, skills development programs, and instructional leadership seminars (Gibboney 1987, also Peterson & Finn 1985 and Hoyle 1985). In sentiments echoed by Cuban (1988b), schools have somehow been viewed by administrators as enterprises rather than as centers for learning (Gibboney 1987). Somehow, 'teaching and administering have become divorced from one another over the last century' (Cuban 1988b).

The nation's school administrators have been pointedly accused of being 'out of step with the general public', with 'their heels dug in' on issues of school reform (Feistritzer quoted in Rodman 1988). Discovered under survey to be disproportionately white, male, and aging; found to be well satisfied with their jobs and insulated from the public; and accused of being thoroughly out-of-synch with the nation's concerns over school quality – America's educational administrators themselves, in association, charge that many of the most severe critics of school quality have a seriously limited knowledge of administrative practice, hold sharp biases against (or have at least a mistrust of) administrators, and have abandoned earlier efforts within the professoriate to link effectively with practice. A 'mandarin class' of reformers (e.g., deans of colleges of education), unfamiliar with the complicated world of administrative practice, has become itself a central part of the problem (Thomson 1988). Proposals for the reform of school administration have included suggestions for a National Policy Board on Educational Administration, separate state licensure boards with authority to establish/enforce standards of admission and professional practice, and (highly controversial) the elimination of administrator preparation programs ('mediocre programs in academically weak institutions') among some 300 institutions of higher education (NCEEA 1987). Meanwhile, state legislatures have forged ahead with much-tightened procedures for administrator certification as well as fully spelled-out "competencies" that administrator candidates are expected to acquire during their period of University preparation. Additionally, critics of administrator preparation provide evidence that current graduate training in educational administration tends to be both weak as well as wrong-headed (Peterson and Finn 1985, Cooper and Boyd 1987, NCEEA 1987, AACTE 1988). Indications are that the 'best and the brightest' among the nation's educators do *not* move into administration; that admission standards for school administrators-to-be are often embarrassingly low; that programs of preparation and certification frequently lack structure, sequencing, and focus; and that far too many programs of weak quality turn out far too many underprepared administrators (Cooper and Boyd 1987, NCEEA 1987, Griffiths 1988).

An even deeper criticism of administrator training finds programs of University preparation to be abysmally out-of-touch with practical reality. For example, administrator training, and the field of school administration in general, reflect a gender bias of substantial magnitude. Within a profession employing large numbers of women, working in institutional settings often referred to as 'women's workplaces', the representation of women in administrative positions is decidedly minimal (Ortiz and Marshall 1988). Ortiz and Marshall (1988: 123-126) argue that four themes in the development of educational administration reflect its history as a field for men. *First*, teaching occupied more by women than men, has become identified over time as a separate profession from administration, occupied in turn by more men than women. Women teach and men supervise; consequently, two professional roles with more intrinsic commonalities than differences have nevertheless reached for separate, often antagonistic identities. *Second*, the development of school administration has been hardened in its separation from teaching – through its search for 'businesslike' professionalism represented in scientific-management and hierarchical control ideologies. Goals of efficiency, standardization/uniformity of performance, and organizational control *can* be pursued as managerial roles distinct from teaching and learning. *Third*, access into administrative careers has been much characterized by a process of sponsorship rather than open competition – tending to produce 'just-like-us' recruits (effectively excluding women and minorities) who are mentored/socialized into the dominant themes of efficiency and control. *Fourth*, the development and transmission of knowledge has similarly emphasized a separation of teaching from administration, producing a conventional managerial wisdom disconnected from issues of instruction, social issues, and gender.

Against this backdrop, three of the Yearbook's chapters examine issues related to the politics of reforming the school administration problem. The chapter by Douglas Mitchell and the chapter by Samuel Bacharach and Joseph Shedd both deal with union issues. Both authors claim that unions are in a state of flux, redefining their role in public education and the nature of their relationship with schools and school districts. As the union role becomes redefined so too will the role of administrators and the day-to-day working relationships between administrators and teachers. Many of the old labor-management distinctions implied by the current industrial model of union relations may become obsolete. The Mitchell chapter suggests twelve policy options that would modify union relations in ways that would better reflect the role of teachers as professionals in public organizations. The Bacharach and Shedd chapter identifies factors that influence the evolution of union policy and suggests where labor-management relations is probably heading.

The chapter by Amy Guttman completes this section. It is a relective chapter identifying principles upon which the proper role for educational professionals should be judged in a democratic society. In a sense, it is a real 'back to the basics' chapter. It asks not what is politically expedient or feasible for any particular interest group, but rather what is good for our society.

Researchers, mainly academics, who sit safely on the sidelines observing and commenting on the reform scene and the place of administrators in the reforms, wrote most of the chapters in this volume, The final chapter is an exception. It is a commentary written by Scott Thompson, who is the executive director of a major professional association serving school administrators. His chapter provides an assessment from the point of view of frontline education managers of the reforms and of the analysis in this volume by academics.

References

American Association of Colleges for Teacher Education (1988) Report (Washington, DC: AACTE).

AYRES, L. P. (1909) *Laggards in our Schools: A Study of Retardation and Elimination in City School Systems* (New York: Charities Publication Committee).

CALLAHAN, R. E. (1962) *Education and the Cult of Efficiency* (Chicago: University of Chicago Press).

CARNEGIE FORUM ON EDUCATION AND THE ECONOMY (1986) *A Nation Prepared: Teachers for the 21st Century* (New York: CFEE).

CHUBB, J. E. (1988) 'Why the current wave of school reform will fail', *The Public Interest*, pp. 28-49.

COOPER, B. S. and BOYD, W. L. (1987) 'The evolution of training for school administrators', in J. Murphy and P. Hallinger (eds.) *Approaches to Administrative Training in Education* (Albany: SUNY Press), pp. 3-21.

CUBAN, L. (1984) *How Teachers Taught* (New York: Longman).

CUBAN, L. (1988a). 'A fundamental puzzle of school reform', *Phi Delta Kappan*, 69(5), pp. 340-344.

CUBAN, L. (1988b) *The Managerial Imperative and the Practice of Leadership in Schools* (Albany: SUNY Press).

CUNNINGHAM, L. L. and HENTGES, J. T. (1982) *The American School Superintendency 1982: A Summary Report* (Arlington, VA: American Association of School Administrators).

DUNNE, F. P. (1963) *Mr Dooley on Ivrything and Ivrybody* (New York: Dover).

ELMORE, R. F. (1987) 'Reform and the culture of authority in schools', *Educational Administration Quarterly*, 23(4), pp. 60-78.

FEISTRITZER, C. (1988) 'Profile of school administrators in the US', (Washington, DC: National Center for Education Information).

FUTRELL, M. H. (1988) Speech to National Press Club, Washington, DC as reported by L. Olson, *Education Week*, 6 April, pp. 1,26.

GIBBONEY, R. A. (1987) 'Education of administrators: an American tragedy', *Education Week*, 16 April, p. 28.

GRIFFITHS, D. (1988) 'Educational administration: reform PDQ or RIP', Invited Address, Annual Meeting of the American Educational Research Association, New Orleans, 7 April.

HOLMES GROUP (1986) *Tomorrow's Teacher* (East Lansing, MI: Holmes Group).

HOYLE, E. (1986) *The Politics of School Management* (London: Hodder & Stoughton).

HOYLE, J. R. (1985) 'Programs in educational administration and the AASA Preparation Guidelines', *Educational Administration Quarterly*, 21(1), pp. 71-93.

KIRST, M. W. and JUNG, R. (1982) 'The utility of a longitudinal approach in assessing implementation: a thirteen year view of Title 1, ESEA', in W. Williams (ed.) *Studying Implementation: Methodological and Administrative Issues* (Chatham, NJ: Chatham House).

LASSWELL, H. D. (1936) *Politics: Who Gets What, When, How* (New York: McGraw-Hill).

NATIONAL COMMISSION ON EXCELLENCE IN EDUCATIONAL ADMINISTRATION (1987) *Leaders for America's Schools* (Washington, DC: NCEEA, University Council for Educational Administration).

LIEBERMAN, A. (1988) 'Teachers and principals: turf, tension, and new tasks', *Phi Delta Kappan*, 69(9), pp. 648-653.

MANN, D. (1988) 'The honeymoon is over', *Phi Delta Kappan*, 69(8), pp. 573-575.

MARCH, J. C. and MARCH, J. G. (1977) 'Almost random careers: the Wisconsin School Superintendency, 1940-1972', *Administrative Science Quarterly*, 22(3), pp. 377-409.

MCNEIL, L. M. (1988) 'Contradictions of control, part 3: contradictions of reform', *Phi Delta Kappan*, 69(7), pp. 478-485.

MURPHY, J. T. (1971) 'Title 1 of ESEA: the politics of implementing federal education reform', *Harvard Educational Review*, 41 (1), pp. 35-63.

MURPHY, J. (1987). 'The instructional leadership role of the school administrator: an analysis', unpublished paper, University of Illinois at Urbana-Champaign.

NATIONAL COMMISSION OF EXCELLENCE IN EDUCATION (1983) *A Nation at Risk: The Imperative for Educational Reform* (Washington, DC: US Government Printing Office).

ODDEN, A. (1987) 'School effectiveness, backward mapping, and state education policies', in J. J. Lane and H. J. Walberg (eds.) *Effective School Leadership: Policy and Process* (Berkeley: McCutchan), pp. 33-61.

ORTIZ, F. I. and MARSHALL, C. (1988) 'Women in educational administration', in N. Boyan (ed) *Handbook of Research on Educational Administration* (New York: Longman), pp. 123-141.

PETERSON, K. D. and FINN, Jr., C. E. (1985). 'Principals, superintendents, and the administrator's art', *The Public Interest*, Spring, pp. 42-62.

PETERSON, P. E. (1985). *The Politics of School Reform, 1870-1940* (Chicago: The University of Chicago Press).

PETERSON, P. E., RABE, B., and WONG, K. K. (1986). *When Federalism Works.* (Washington, DC: Brookings Institution).

PIERCE, L. C. (1977) 'School Site Management', an occasional paper, Aspen Institute Program in Education for a Changing Society (Cambridge, MA: Aspen Institute for Humanistic Studies).

PRESSMAN, J. and WILDAVSKY, A. (1973) *Implementation* (Berkeley: University of California Press).

RABE, B. G. and PETERSON, P. E. (1988) 'The evolution of a new cooperative federalism', in N. Boyan (ed.) *Handbook of Research in Educational Administration* (New York: Longman), pp. 467-485.

RODMAN, B. (1988) 'Administrators seen to be out of step with general public', *Education Week*, 7(17), pp. 1,23.

SARASON, S. B. (1971) *The Culture of the School and the Problem of Change* (Boston: Allyn & Bacon).

SHANKER, A. (1988) Speech to National Press Club, Washington, DC., as reported by L. Olson, *Education Week*, 6 April, pp.1,26.

SILVER, P. F. (1979) 'Administrator preparation', in H. E. Mitzel (ed.) *Encyclopedia of Educational Research*, 5th edition, vol. 1 (New York: The Free Press), p.49.

SRING, J. (1986) *The American School, 1642-1985* (New York: Longman).

THOMSON, S. D.(1988) 'The parting of deans and administrators', *Education Week*, 7(16), pp. 48,36.

TYACK, D. B. (1974) *The One Best System* (Cambridge: Harvard University Press).

TYACK, D. and HANSOT, E. (1982) *Managers of Virtue: Public School Leadership in America, 1820-1980* (New York: Basic Books).

TYE, B. B. (1987) 'The deep structure of schooling', *Phi Delta Kappan* 69(4), pp. 281-284.

TYLER, R. W. (1987) 'Education reform', *Phi Delta Kappan*, 69(4), pp. 277-280.

WEATHERLY, R. A. (1979) *Reforming Special Education: Policy Implementation from State Level to Street Level* (Cambridge, MA: The MIT Press).

WISE, A. E. (1988) 'Legislated learning revisited', *Phi Delta Kappan*, 69(5), pp. 329-333.

2   *The national commission approach to educational reform*

Robert K. Wimpelberg
University of New Orleans

Rick Ginsberg
University of South Carolina

In 1988, five years after the release of the landmark report, *A Nation at Risk*, US Secretary of Education William Bennett evaluated the impact of this, the most heralded national commission study of American schools. Although he acknowledged that some progress had been made, he concluded that 'the absolute level at which our improvements are taking place is still unacceptably low' ('Reform' 1988: 1). Further, he was puzzled by the slow pace of improvement, believing that the ingredients needed to upgrade schools are not mysterious. In his follow-up evaluation Bennett recommended a number of specific changes: strengthening the curriculum, providing equal opportunity, fostering an 'ethos of achievement', recruiting and rewarding talented teachers and principals, instilling accountability in the schools, increasing parental choice, and focusing spending on classroom resources rather than on administrative and other support services.

Secretary Bennett's analysis unwittingly reflected the universal status of the national commission report as a species of policy documents that can trace its roots back to the Common School Era (Ginsberg and Wimpelberg 1988). First, commission reports seldom have much direct, sustained impact on schools and classrooms; second, they recur *in perpetuum*, nevertheless; and, third, commission advocates insist – in the face of apparent counter-evidence – that generic school improvement is a reasonably straightforward, specifiable, and achievable condition (Ginsberg Wimpelberg 1987). The study of national commission reports on educational reform suggests that they function more in keeping with the image of 'trickle down' change, in which recommendations for innovations are filtered unevenly downward from the federal through to the state and local units of governance. On occasion, changes at the bottom may only remotely resemble the concepts originally preferred at the top. Certainly, as a call to arms, reform reports like *A Nation at Risk* produced by the National Commission on Excellence in Education (NCEE) may inspire widespread discussion and debate. Nevertheless, such reports historically lack the necessary ingredients to cause substantial changes in practice.

The fact of the matter is that the national commission process persists as a genre of policy influencing activity. In this chapter we scrutinize it from three angles. First, we sketch out the characteristics of the education commission phenomenon, showing the generalizability of Bennett's observations carried backward across ninety years of reports. Second, we explore the imagery of 'trickle down' as a means of understanding commission reporting methods by deriving it from the partial applicability of two other less effective images: report-as-blueprint and report-as-ceremony. We support the 'trickle down' interpretation by documenting the clear desire of commission members – in this care, from the NCEE – to stir up more than a debate while they stop short of prescribing uniform school solutions. Finally, given that we cannot substantiate commission effects in terms of their technical modifications in classrooms, we look to the commission report as a vehicle for influencing policy agendas. Here we place it in the context of commission efforts across several fields, including education, health policy, and race relations.

Ninety years of commission activity

Historically, national commissions have been a popular mechanism in education, bringing together panels of experts to grapple with an urgent problem identified by a mobilizing constituency, agency of government, or privately organized group. The panel typically considers a store of data, collected with varying degrees of control or rigor, and then offers recommendations that it thinks would ameliorate the condition. Beginning in the 1890s the National Education Association appointed several committees to study an array of educational issues. Documents like that issued by the first NEA commission widely known as the *Report of the Committee of Ten* (Committee on Secondary School Studies 1893) signaled the dawn of an era of commission type activity in education. During the twentieth century literally thousands of local, state, and national commission style reports have been produced. In our analysis of fourteen major reports published from 1893 to 1983 (Ginsberg and Wimpelberg 1987), we derived four themes which characterize the commission approach.

First, the commission is a persistent vehicle for reform attempts, having an impressive longevity that spans ninety years. Reports carrying titles like *The Committee of Ten* (Committee on Secondary School Studies 1893), *The Cardinal Principles of Education* (Commission on the Reorganization of Secondary Education 1918), *The Eight Year Study* (Progressive Education Association 1942), the 'Conant Report' (Conant 1959), and *A Nation at Risk* (NCEE 1983) are popular examples which reflect the reform mood of their particular times. While the kinds of sponsoring organizations for these and other reports has shifted away from the professional education groups, best exemplified by the NEA, and the membership of the commission panels is now much more inclusive of business, political, and non-educational academic interests than ever before, the popularity and frequency of the commission approach has not waned.

A second theme consistent in all the reports we reviewed is the very general manner in which commissions tend to cast their recommendations for change. Whether it was the Committee of Ten (Committee on Secondary School Studies 1893) urging high schools to adopt one of four curricula that would 'help prepare students for life's work', the Educational Policies Commission (1937) report on the functions of schooling which called for 'developing the mind, spirit, and body of students through social, practical and fine arts training', or *A Nation at Risk* (NCEE 1983) appealing for 'grades to be indicators of academic achievement', reports usually fashion their recommendations for change with too little detail about the reform intention for practitioners to clearly understand the pedagogical outcomes that comissioners might have wanted. Peterson (1985) believes that commissions discuss reform at such an abstracted level because it makes it easy for members to agree on the broader goals of schooling without having to undertake the potentially devisive exercise of specifying the policies and mechanisms which might implicate particular classifications of personnel or program sponsors as inadequate. The effort to avoid more detailed specification sidesteps the possibility of offending important interest groups who might weaken the critical support network which commissions of ten believe is necessary to sustain the change process they are starting. Finally, the technology of commission work is such that the relatively small number of meetings which commissioners hold does not allow for careful social scientific inquiry into problems. Thus, cause and effect relationships are difficult to pinpoint, and proposals for change have to be laid out in abstracted form.

The third issue typical of the national commission process is a close relative of the second theme: namely, that commission reports never attend to the important topic of implementing the changes they propose. The developing body of literature on change (for example Fullan 1982, Berman and McLaughlin, 1976) reveals that innovation is a complex and confounded process in education, characterized by a greater degree of pessimism than positive potential. People who have studied change processes identify a wide array of conditions which can have an impact on successful implementation. Loucks and Hall (1979), for example, see change in educational settings as a multi-staged process that often requires special assistance (resources or coaching) and ample time so that new instructional behavior and curricular content can become integrated into classroom and school routines. Other students of change implementation discuss variables like incentives for structures, availability of change agents, and support and commitment as necessary ingredients (Fullan 1982). These factors, like others, are hard to specify through the commission process because the source of change is so removed from those who would manage the implementation. The one kind of assistance that an external and removed agent like the commission can provide in some cases is financial, yet in the typical case, once their reports are written, commissions only have money left to disseminate their recommendations. And detailing the exact methods by which other agencies or professional groups could enact the commission's non-specific recommendations constitutes an understandable, yet weakening, characteristic of the reporting process.

The final aspect of the fourteen commission reports we analyzed was the degree to which their recommendations appeared to have an impact on school districts and schools. Despite the popularity of many of the reports – captured in their wide distribution and the considerable public attention they often garner – the actual impact the reports have on schools and classrooms appears to be small. This is the conclusion common in the extant follow-up literatures that have reviewed commission effects (Ginsberg and Wimpelberg 1987). Some changes in line with report recommendations may take place over time, but tracing a path back to a reform commission report is difficult. In fact, some have wondered about a chicken-and-egg effect, hypothesizing (and even documenting) that certain commission recommendations for change actually pick up on ideas already in the general public discussion or propose innovations already in place (Peterson 1985, Wimpelberg and Ginsberg 1985b). The most common conclusion of all, however, is that commission reports simply get ignored – put on the shelf – and this result is readily understandable to the policy analyst who notes that American education is, at best, a loosely a coupled system from the national level, (at which the commissions we are reviewing operate) to the classroom (Guthrie 1985).

On this important point, an analysis of the staying power of educational reform by Kirst and Meister (1985) is helpful. The most stringent criteria are met by reforms in policies that: (1) promote change in organizational structure; (2) classify pupils; (3) change certification regulations; or (4) establish compensatory rights and procedures (Kirst and Meister : 179–180). Clearly, none of these conditions is met by reform recommendations that are characterized as general in nature, making no reference to specific identifiable populations of students, and lacking prescriptive implementation. The one element common to the commission reports of the 1980s, like *A Nation at Risk* (1983), that meets the spirit and perhaps the letter of condition (3), 'change in certification regulations', is the call for new graduate requirements that specifies the number of courses in different subject matters that would be required.

Earlier analysis: prescription and ceremony

We know that historically commissions have maintained wide appeal. Their popularity persists despite the fact that commissions make only very general suggestions to resolve the problems they identify, and they offer little assistance with the difficult process of implementation. Commission acitivity also continues in the void of documented evidence of change in school practice that can be attributed to their published reports.

So why does the commission process persist? Two common formulations for explaining this phenomenon can be expressed, on the one hand, as the rational, structural, or diagnostic/prescriptive approach and the symbolic or ceremonial approach, on the other hand (Deal 1985, Wimpelberg and Ginsberg 1985a). It is our contention that neither the prescriptive nor the ceremonial analysis is satisfying in the long run, however, aspects of the two meld in an interesting third conceptualization – 'trickle down' – which is the subject of the next section.

The rationalistic and prescriptive view emphasizes certain elements in the commissions process more than others, namely, expert panels that are called together to address identified (and presumably solvable) problems. Using an information base of scholarly papers and authoritative testimony, the panel identifies the elements basic to the problem it is empowered to study and makes recommendations for change that are presumed to function as solutions directly deduced from the analysis of the problem confronted.

This interpretation is most easily cast aside on the basis of our growing knowledge of commission procedures. There is seldom little more than a semblance of scientific inquiry associated with the process. In fact Harnischfeger and Wiley (1976) argue that rigorous data analysis is anathema to commission processes since they are typically political undertakings designed to conform *a priori* positions. Further, the difficult cause-and-effect relationships between educational practice and desired educational outcomes make the scientific model even less promising in a procedure that is short-lived and carried out by representatives who may have little or no experience with scientific argument and rigor.

The second line of reasoning is more powerful but still insufficient in explaining the commission phenomenon. It stresses the symbolic or ceremonial character of group activity. Deal (1985) applied this analysis to the modern educational commission, likening the process to ancient tribal ceremonies which send cultural signals to the populace. Thus, commission reports are not seen as rational documents prepared to shape schools in well-defined ways but rather are ceremonies whose dramatic appeals should revitalize and strengthen our interest in schools. Once performed, these episodes of theater lead an alerted and aroused public to re-shape educational practices at state and local levels closer to the points of practice.

Such an argument is plausible and offers an explanation for the longevity and uniformity of the commission approach. The general nature of recommendations, the lack of attention to implementation, and the minimal direct impact of the reports are more easily understood if the commission process is viewed as ceremony rather than blueprint making. Yet, problems remain. The symbolic/ceremonial thesis leaves open the question of intent – do commission members and sponsors themselves intend to be thespians in a dramatic production rather than architects of change? Given that commission members are usually professionals whose time is scarce and given that policy interests may be known before these persons join a panel (Plank and Ginsberg 1988), it is unlikely that commission members intend to be mere actors in a theatrical performance. These conditions, however, do not obscure the fact that some ceremonial gesturing inevitably follows the release of commission reports. Yet, as our data on limited impact implies and as most students who have tried to find a copy of any but the most popular commission reports know, the vast majority of reports are characterized by obscurity, suggesting that the ceremony they may play out is empty and without practical effect, indirect or otherwise.

Trickle down

We turn to the imagery portrayed in the economic concept known as 'trickle down' in order to capture the strengths of the competing rationalistic and ceremonial interpretations (Ginsberg and Wimpelberg 1987). Supply-side economics calls for tax cuts and incentives, couped with tight monetary controls and reduced government spending, to stimulate expansion of the private sector. Supply-side economics was intended to reduce inflation, balance the federal budget, increase output of goods and services, and expand employment opportunities. Critics referred to it as 'trickle down' economics to express the idea that lessening economic constraints on the wealthy – by moving away from federal policies of redistribution – was assumed to carry eventual benefits in expanded job opportunities and salary levels for the general populace.

Without examining the strengths or weaknesses of supply-side economics, it is the underlying assumptions of this trickle down thesis that help to explain the commission process in educational reform. To be sure, commissions do not purposely benefit one class of schools more than another, although their common focus on public schools may be thought to tacitly exempt the efforts of private schools from criticism. Further, Clark and Astuto (1987) take note of the values shift in the most recent commission era, fueled by *A Nation at Risk*, that moved from equity as a basis for federal policy intervention to excellence and standards setting, an observation that has class implications. If it is an appropriate analogy, trickle down in educational reform policy emphasizes a different 'class' of educational conditions in the same way that economic trickle down gives initial advantage to holders of capital over labor.

What we find most alike about the commission process in education and trickle down in economic policy making is that strong dramatic gestures (if not policies) are adopted at an upper, federal level of government, and are intended to filter down through the state, district, school, and classroom layers of school organizations. At times, national commissions direct their reform recommendations at discrete levels of political or administrative governance, yet before any recommendation can be converted into state or district policy, it must at least provoke discussion, be modified to fit state or local contexts, and be cast in regulatory language that can lead to monitoring and enforcement (Kirst and Meister 1985).

Ultimately, the trickle down image captures an interplay between prescription and ceremony. In contrast to be ceremonial interpretation in which higher level actors may help create an atmosphere in which local officials can accomplish individualistic reform (Deal 1985), the trickle down thesis allows that commission sponsors and commission members have, to some degree, a set of parameters for what counts as legitimate and substantial points of attack in educational systems. As we shall explore more fully later, commissions may have their most potent effects through the function of setting the political agenda and providing policy alternatives. In the imagery of trickling down, the 'water' that leaves the commission pail must still be 'water' after it has filtered through the layers of sediment and reached the subterranean level of school and classroom. It gets there, however, as so many discrete drops and not as a powerful stream. A good example from this decade's commission activity is the commonality of curriculum elements (usually in the form of graduation requirements) and differentiated teacher pay plans (usually based on performance criteria) that run through many of the reports of the early 1980s. These elements, with some variance in specification and approach, are those most frequently found in state and local policy changes related to education (Plisko and Stern 1985).

To some degree, the commission reform process is an act of faith predicated upon pronouncements that are made with enough strength and drama that they may survive in spirit, if not in letter, the process of trickle down. Only recommendations made in nonspecific language can be supported in this process, and attention to implementation at the national level is inappropriate because of the sequence of modifications implied in the filtering process. The motivations of commission members to produce some rather specific changes in educational outcomes, then, are dampened by the political and structural realities of the vertical loose coupling inherent in state level autonomy and the ideology of local control. That poses a real dilemma for the role of the commission member that can be compromised by an anticipation that national pronouncements may only have a third or fourth generation effect on the behavior of school teachers and principals and may constitute a mere local shadow of the original national intent.

This observation raises yet another interesting and largely unexplored aspect of the commission process: namely, the intentions that commission members brought to their work, the expectations placed upon them by their organizers, and the signs that commission organizers and members alike use to judge the effectiveness of their enterprise. The question of intentionality is critical to the usefulness of the concept of 'trickle down' as an interpretive vehicle. For 'trickle down' to be a helpful notion in the analysis of the national commission process, commission members must come close enough to a prescriptive impulse so as not to accept just *any* state or local changes as valid and reformative. At the same time they must stay clear of the requirement that state and local agents read report recommendations as blueprints for replication in a manner that would verge on a national or central restructuring of education akin to those governance systems common outside North America.

The intentions of commission members

A limited number of sources of data are available on the specific operation of the National Commission on Educational Excellence in producing its report, and we draw on them to develop this topic. We cannot know the extent to which the activities of the NCEE may stand as proxy for other national commissions; few students of the process have taken the care or had the opportunity to 'go back stage'. However, there are some patterns of discernible commonalities with at least one other commission (Peterson 1985).

Ginsberg and Wimpelberg (1986) surveyed the eighteen members of the NCEE in order to obtain insight into the processes that lead to the drafting of its report and construction of its recommendations. More recently, papers donated to Brown University contained early report drafts, staff memoranda, letters and related materials ('Inside *A Nation at Risk*' 1988). These data reveal that the idea of spearheading a movement to reform schools grew among the commissioners as they interacted in repeated sessions, face-to-face. Most of the members had strong concerns about educational inadequacies before they convened, so they shared their sponsors' conviction that a reformist message was timely. In similar fashion, data were collected that supported commissioners *a priori* points of view, without scrutiny for completeness or validity, confirming the judgement by Harnischfeger and Wiley (1976) cited earlier. Beliefs overwhelmed inquiry to the extent that commissioners refused to agree with staff members who argued for a more balanced treatment of issues. Instead, consensus on an unequivocal message was the commission's ultimate goal and moral suasion from the 'bully pulpit' (Jung and Kirst 1986), dressed in the trappings of scientific inquiry, was its adopted medium.

In the Ginsberg and Wimpelberg (1986) survey of NCEE members, an understanding of commission process was approached through four topics: the commission's purposes and goals; its process for producing the final report; members' opinions and activities subsequent to the proceedings; and their reactions to published criticisms of *A Nation at Risk*. NCEE commissioners were in agreement that schooling was in need to reform and they generally assumed that they were picked as panelists primarily: (1) because they represented important constitutencies; or (2) because their past experiences and comments on education signaled to the US Department of Education (the convener of the NCEE) their interest in change. Commissioners' prior sense of urgency and conviction appear to have affected the particular recommendations that were incorporated in the report.

In the process of drafting its report, commissioners had varying degrees of involvement and were unable to negotiate a complete agreement on many specific proposals. Nevertheless, they were unanimous in their conviction that the final product should allow them to 'put one face forward'. Our findings are supported by the retrospective comments of Milton Goldberg, Executive Director of the NCEE, who explained that 'when the commission decided, finally, that they wanted to produce a fairly brief, hard-hitting report, that communicated a central message to the American people . . . then everything else became, if you will, peripheral'. He commented further that issues 'fell-out' if they were too complicated or might detract from the central themes ('Inside *A Nation at Risk*' 1988: 22–23). Our survey and the Brown University papers both show that the final report followed a series of drafts which were presented to the commission as a whole by staffers and individual commission members, after which a single commissioner wrote the version that would be adopted as the formal and final published presentation of the commission's work.

The Brown University papers reveal that a balanced presentation of issues was often consciously ignored and that a number of issues of interest to specific staffers or commissioners were completely dropped in favor of putting forth a small, succinct document with an uncomplicated message. One staff member explained that, in the process, there developed 'a classic split between the researchers – who wanted to be sure that more data, more refinement, more sides of an issue, more *caveats* were displayed . . . ' and those who were involved in administering the commission so that its work could be completed expeditiously. Another staffer said that early staff drafts were criticized for presenting 'too much of a balanced view' ('Inside *A Nation at Risk*' 1988: 22). In the end, mention of disadvantaged children, gifted and talented students, increasing federal involvement, or attaching price tags to the recommendations were issues that were ultimately excluded. As a staff member concluded, 'the basic determination that the commission made was that if at all possible, it would issue a unanimous report, and that it may have to sacrifice attention to some issues in order to gain it' ('Inside *A Nation at Risk*', 1988: 23).

The Ginsberg and Wimpelberg (1986) survey concluded that commissioners were generally pleased with the final report and proud of their accomplishment. Although one commissioner lamented the fact that simple solutions were presented for complex problems, most agreed with the commissioner who said that 'the data have been a catalyst to motivate creative dialogue and spur constructive reform' (p. 17). In their opinions about the style of the report, commissioners hammered at the need to get people to act. This was variously expressed as the need 'to get people interested in education' by 'mak[ing] it easily understood by the public'. In somewhat more grandiose terms, one commissioner emphasized the need 'to get the attention of all who cared about our country'. The compulsion to get attention, according to another commissioner, led the NCEE to review national reports issued over the last 40 years in order to isolate those that 'caused the most stir or generated the most interest. We then fashioned our report in such a manner' (p. 18).

The intensions that commissioners carried into their service on the NCEE may be assessed through their reactions to criticism levied against the conclusions in *A Nation at Risk*. The survey asked NCEE members to respond to seventeen specific and substantive criticisms gathered from published sources (Ginsberg and Wimpelberg 1986). With near unanimous consistency, commissioners labelled 16 of the 17 criticisms unfounded. Only on the complaint that the NCEE report focused too little attention on elementary education did the commissioners agree that criticism was warranted.

In their defense of *A Nation at Risk* we get an ironic reversal of the distinction between 'fact' and 'belief'. During the deliberative phase of the NCEE's work, commissioners admit to having suppressed staff and researcher efforts to present a more balanced ('factual') view of American education in favor of evidence that confirmed their belief in a state of crisis. Yet, in response to those who found the report lacking in its balance, one commissioner's captures a general reaction:

> I feel that some of the criticisms are not based on the material contained in the report but on someone else's ideas about it, without actually reading the document. But, nonetheless, criticism is offered as fact. (p. 22)

Another theme that comes through in reactions to criticism is a resentment that the commission's 'missionary' efforts were not fully appreciated. 'Missionaries for the children of this nation' was the phrase one member used to characterize the dedication and motivation of the NCEE. We get the image of true believers who set out to open the eyes of the blinded masses to the bedevilment that has been visited upon their schools. However, when critics faulted the effort for its excessive zealousness, most members of the NCEE defended their pronouncements as factual and realistic, and, on the counter offensive, dismissed the critics as biased.

By whatever measures of intentionality and purpose, then, we conclude that members of the NCEE pitched their work as simultaneously prescriptive and ceremonial. They wanted to spur on the local debate by heightening sensitivity to the condition of the schools: 'The reform movement is forcing school districts to discuss their education program and face some of the problems that have been there for a while that no one admitted or wished to talk about' (p. 21). At the same time, the NCEE wanted to delimit the content for debate to certain subject areas and specific structural elements of schooling.

Educational commissions and the policy process

The chance to excite and bound a debate is the desired outcome of trickle-down reform. Commissioners knew they could not manipulate classroom innovations, but they were not satisfied with leaving the substance of reform totally open to idiosyncratic responses from state and local units. NCEE members clearly endorsed the sense of urgency that lead the US Department to bring them together in the first place.

With these observations as background, it becomes apparent that national commissions in education serve a generic purpose shared by commissions in other public arenas – namely, to influence the policy agenda at a time of crisis. What causes the commissions in differing policy fields to diverge, however, is the relationship of the commission to the origins and nature of crisis.

Polsby (1984) describes a crisis as 'some notable, well publicized, exogenous event . . . demanding quick decisions'. The crisis approach is 'characterized by short elapsed time between identification of a problem and enactment of a measure to meet the problem' (p. 168). Polsby argues that there is a common political strategy in America used when politicians need to coerce feelings of urgency because of their own ready-made policy alternatives. Such maneuvers require the creation of an atmosphere conducive to the pursuit of specific policy measures different from those currently in effect.

The most important dimension of crisis for the commission process is whether the commission is empanelled to respond to a situation widely perceived to have crisis status of whether the commission functions in a dual capacity – first, to create or heighten the sense of crisis and then respond to it. Each of these polar positions, we proffer, is associated with a correspondingly divergent means of commission response, ranging from the purely cere-monial to the effort to assure an audience that prescriptive remedies have, in fact, already solved the problems at issue. Further, we posit that the positioning of a commission on the factors outlined above will depend upon the perceived (or real) relationship between the crisis and the health, welfare, and safety of the public. Finally, the variety of areas of policy substance addressed by the national commission process – at least as they have been reviewed in the literatures on public policy – separate education from health care, social unrest (race riots), and nuclear disaster (Three Mile Island) along the several dimensions of analysis. This set of propositions is presented in figure 1.

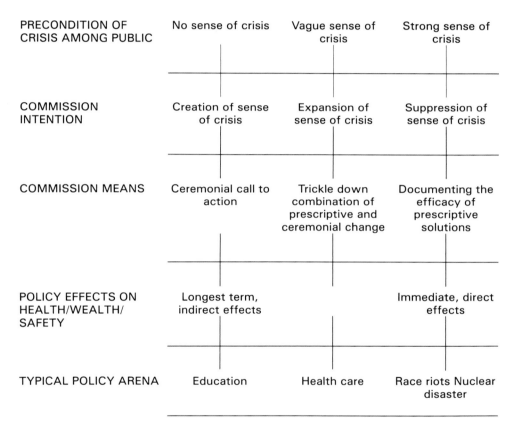

PRECONDITION OF CRISIS AMONG PUBLIC	No sense of crisis	Vague sense of crisis	Strong sense of crisis
COMMISSION INTENTION	Creation of sense of crisis	Expansion of sense of crisis	Suppression of sense of crisis
COMMISSION MEANS	Ceremonial call to action	Trickle down combination of prescriptive and ceremonial change	Documenting the efficacy of prescriptive solutions
POLICY EFFECTS ON HEALTH/WEALTH/SAFETY	Longest term, indirect effects		Immediate, direct effects
TYPICAL POLICY ARENA	Education	Health care	Race riots Nuclear disaster

Figure 1. Commission effects on policy agendas: precondition of crisis and commission response.

Most national education commissions are proactive policy shapers, by nature. They tend to be called into service at a time when social, economic, or political problems are heightened in the public consciousness, but the causes are typically not attributable with any certainty or direct logic to inadequacies in the educational systems among the states. The national education commission typically sets about to draw or cement a connection between the social malaise and education in order to move the more proximal units of educational governance into action. Given that its function is largely exhortatory, the education commission's means will play heavily on symbols and dramatic language.

Political scientists have clarified the means of moving from crisis to policy considerations in ways that are particularly helpful in our discussion. Cobb and Elder (1972), for example, refer to 'the policy agenda' as 'a general set of political controversies that will be viewed at any point in time as falling within the range of legitimate concerns needing the attention of the policy' (p. 14). Similarly, Kingdon (1984) sees the agenda as that list of subjects or problems to which governmental officials and people outside of government are paying some serious attention at any given time. The agenda setting process narrows the conceivable subjects to the set that actually becomes the focus of attention. Thus, the agenda setting process resembles what Cronbach (1982) sees as the divergent and convergent stages of evaluation – where all possible issues are considered, then, through prioritization, those actually to be dealt with are identified.

For Kingdon (1984) there are focusing events, crisis, and symbols, which open policy windows. These are opportunities for advocates of proposals to push their pet solutions or attention to specific problems. Regarding the need for focusing events, Kingdon explains that 'problems are not always self-evident by the indicators . . . . They often need a little push' (p. 99). We suggest in our approach to policy agenda setting that the need for advocate-made focusing events will depend, in part, upon the public's sense of the relationship of the policy area to concerns about health, welfare, and safety.

Cobb and Elder (1972) support and elaborate this schema when they identify the prerequisites for attaining access to the policy agenda. For Cobb and Elder, the key ingredients of concern to the policy activist are widespread attention to or awareness of an issue, shared concern that action is necessary, and the shared perception that the matter is appropriate for governmental action. 'For an item or issue to acquire public recognition', they explain, 'its supporters must have either access to mass media or resources necessary to reach people' (p. 86). The size of the audience is critical to the success that an issue will have in reaching the policy agenda, and five characteristics that affect the audience are identified:

1. Concreteness: The more ambiguously an issue can be defined, the greater its likelihood of reaching an expanded audience. Everyone may be able to find a cause in a broadly stated campaign.
2. Social Significance: The more socially significant an issue is defined to be, the greater the likelihood of expansion.
3. Temporal Relevance: The more an issue is defined as having immediate importance, the greater the chance of expansion.
4. Complexity: The more non-technical an issue is defined to be, the greater its possibility of expanding to a larger audience.
5. Categorical Precedence: An issue defined as lacking a clear precedent is more likely to expand.
(Cobb and Elder 1972: 112–122)

The activities of national education commissions are more easily understood against the backdrop of the Cobb and Elder formulation. Given the importance of reaching the policy agenda and the need to expand the issue audience, the intent of commissions to be 'crisis creators' becomes understandable. By defining the current state as grim, by offering their proposals as a 'last hope', by avoiding scientific processes and difficult implementation issues, and by suggesting only general recommendations, the education commission fulfills four of the methods of expanding an issue – the key prerequisites to attaining policy agent status. Most important, because so few people attribute to education a direct and immediate relationship to the conditions of health, welfare, and safety in society, the national commission in education must work with special diligence upon the agenda setting processes related to audience arousal and expansion.

These characteristics and necessities of the education commission become even more clear when they are contrasted with the functioning of commissions in other policy arenas. We find that many commissions outside education do not work to create crisis in order to expand their audiences, but rather hope to quell public discontent so that an item gets *removed* from the policy agenda. It is our observation that the 'suppressive commission' comes into play when the policy issue is already perceived by the public to be at crisis status and is thought to endanger the health, welfare or safety of the populace. Two studies give us insight into commissions that worked under these kinds of policy conditions: Alford's (1975) research on the New York City health care system and Lipsky and Olsen's (1977) investigation of the race riot commissions.

Alford (1975) reviewed over twenty studies of the health care system in New York and found that the commission format was a standard response to a sense of crisis in the health care field. He argued that the commission-as-policy-response was utilized for political reasons to display governmental concern with a problematic situation when the prospects of finding a new or innovative intervention that could work were felt to be minimal. Alford concluded that commissions 'produce public quiescence in the face of deeply imbedded structural problems' (p. 101).

Lipsky and Olsen (1977) reached similar conclusions in their study of race riot commissions. First, they found that the commission formulation was the typical political response to racial disorders in this century in the United States. In the face of social unrest, the commission investigates the conditions and extent of violence and develops reform proposals. Most important: the commission reassures the public that problems are being addressed. 'In a period of high tension, public officials give the appearance of taking corrective steps without making binding commitments' (Lipsky and Olsen 1977: 76–77). In the end, Lipsky and Olsen argue that commissions 'provide a forum for debating controversial racial issues without forcing any public official or city agency to do anything about those issues' (p. 363).

The commission-as-issue-queller gives policy makers some breathing room to allow the storm of controversy to blow over and, in time, pass out of public view. President Carter's blue-ribbon commission to investigate the Three Mile Island nuclear power plant disaster alerted the public that something was being done about a direct and immediate threat to their health and safety, and, upon the release of its report, the controversy subsided. The commission's recommendations – whatever they were – became moot in terms of the policy agenda. Viewed in this way, the non-education commission serves the function of buying time during which the state of crisis can become relaxed. It is also important to note that buying time is essential when the necessary actions of government to remedy a situation are unclear, either because the cause-and-effect relationships are not well enough understood or because the level of government at which the commission is empanelled has no legal or natural jurisdiction in the controversy.

Conclusions

The national commission process in education is a mode of policy activity that is only recently getting scholarly attention. We have reviewed the study of this phenomenon both over the sweep of its near-century of existence and with concentration on the intensity of recent activity to expose the configurations and generalizations already perceptible in the national commission model when it undertakes a reform mission in education.

We have also sketched a short-hand schema related to the commission's role in setting policy agendas. This discussion, we hope, may initiate and promote more detailed comparative studies of commission functions across several policy arenas. It can also lead to the cross-cultural study of the purposes and procedures of national commissions in an inter-national context. While individual case studies are much easier to find than ever before (see, for example, Dockrell 1987 and Gumbert 1988), no systematic effort that we know of has been exerted to pull into a common and uniform framework the analysis of prototype national education commissions as they function in different nations. In comparative studies across policy fields and across countries, we see a great potential for the students of education and public policy to understand a phenomenon that we can safely predict will re-emerge with constant regularity.

References

ALFORD, R. (1975) *Health Care Politics* (Chicago: University of Chicago Press).

BERMAN, P., and McLAUGHLIN, M. W. (1976) 'Implementation of educational innovations', *Educational Forum*, 40, pp. 345-370.

CLARK, D. L. and ASTUTO, T. A. (1986) 'The significance and permanence of changes in federal educational policy', *Educational Researcher*, 15.

COBB, R. W. and ELDER, C. D. (1972) *Participation in American Politics* (Baltimore: Johns Hopkins University Press).

COMMISSION ON THE REORGANIZATION OF SECONDARY EDUCATION (1918) *Cardinal Principles of Secondary Education*, Bulletin 1918, no 35 (Washington, DC: Government Printing Office).

COMMISSION ON THE REORIENTATION OF SECONDARY EDUCATION (1937). *Functions of Secondary Education* (Washington, DC: National Education Association).

COMMITTEE ON SECONDARY SCHOOL STUDIES (Committee of Ten) (1893) *Report of the Committee on Secondary School Studies (National Education Association)* (Washington, DC: Government Printing Office).

CONANT, J. B. (1959) *American High School Today* (New York: McGraw-Hill).

CRONBACH, L. J. (1982) *Designing Evaluations of Educational and Social Programs* (Berkeley, CA: McCutchan).

DEAL, T. E. (1985) 'National commissions: blueprints for remodeling or ceremonies for revitalizing public schools?' *Education and Urban Society*, 17, pp. 145-156.

DOCKRELL, W. B. (1987) 'The impact of Scottish national surveys of achievement on policy and practice', *Educational Evaluation and Policy Analysis*, 9, pp. 274-282.

EDUCATIONAL POLICIES COMMISSION (1937) *Unique Functions of Education in American Democracy* (Washington, DC: National Education Association).

FULLAN, M. (1982) *The Meaning of Educational Change* (New York: Teachers College Press).

GINSBERG, R., and WIMPELBERG, R. K. (1986). 'Examining the reform commission process: the National Commission of Excellence in Education Responds', paper presented at the annual meeting of the American Educational Research Association, San Francisco.

GINSBERG, R., and WIMPELBERG, R. K. 'An assessment of twentieth century commission reports on educational reform', in C. Willie and I. Miller (eds.), *Twentieth-Century Theories of Education* (Westport, CT: Greenwood Press), in press.

GINSBERG, R., and WIMPELBERG, R. K. (1987) 'Educational change by commission: Attempting "trickle down" reform', *Educational Evaluation and Policy Analysis*, 10, pp. 344-360.

GUMBERT, E. B. (ed.) (1988). *Making the Future: Politics and Educational Reform in the US, England, the Soviet Union, China, and Cuba* (Atlanta: Center for Cross-Cultural Education, Georgia State University).

GUTHRIE, J. W. (1985) 'The educational policy consequences of economic instability: the emerging political economy of American education', *Educational Evaluation and Policy Analysis*, 7, pp. 319-332.

HARNISCHFEGER, A., and WILEY, D. (1976) 'The teaching-learning process in elementary schools: A synoptic view', *Curriculum Inquiry*, 6, pp. 5-43.

'Inside *A Nation at Risk*: a view from the cutting room floor' (27 April 1988), *Education Week*, pp. 1, 22–23.

JUNG, R., and KIRST, M. (1986) 'Beyond mutual adaption, into the bully pulpit: recent research on the federal role in education', *Educational Administration Quarterly*, 22(3),pp. 80-109.

KINGDON, J. (1984) *Agendas, Alternatives and Public Policies* (Boston: Little Brown).

KIRST, M. W., and MEISTER, G. R. (1985) 'Turbulence in America secondary schools: what reforms last', *Curriculum Inquiry*, 2(15), pp. 169-186.

LIPSKY, M., and OLSEN, D. (1977) *Commission Politics* (New Brunswick, NJ: Transaction Books).

LOUCKS, S., and HALL, G. (1979) 'Implementing innovations in schools: a concern based approach', paper presented at the meeting of the American Educational Research Association, San Francisco.

NATIONAL COMMISSION ON EXCELLENCE IN EDUCATION (1983) *A Nation at Risk: The Imperative for Educational Reform* (Washington, DC: Government Printing Office).

PETERSON, P. E. (1985) 'Did the education commissions say anything?' *Education and Urban Society*, 17, pp. 126-144.

PLANK, D. N., and GINSBERG, R. (1988) 'Catch the wave: Reform commissions and school reform', paper presented at the annual meeting of the American Educational Research Association, New Orleans.

PLISKO, V. W., and STERN, J. D. (eds) (1985) *The Conditions of Education: 1985 Edition* (Washington, DC: Government Printing Office).

POLSBY, N. W. (1984) *Political Innovation in America: The Politics of Policy Initiation* (New Haven: Yale University Press).

PROGRESSIVE EDUCATION ASSOCIATION (1942) *The Eight Year Study*.

'Reform: plaudits for staying power, prescriptions for new directions', (4 May 1988), *Education Week*, pp. 1, 20-21.

WIMPELBERG, R. K. and GINSBERG, R. (1985a) 'Reviewing the critiques of reform commissions', *Politics of Education Bulletin*, 12(1), pp. 10–13, 16.

WIMPELBERG, R. K. and GINSBERG, R. (1985b) 'Are schools districts responding to *A Nation at Risk*?' *Education and Urban Society*, 17, pp.186-203.

3 Raising the stakes in statewide mandatory minimum competency testing*

H. Dickson Corbett and Bruce Wilson
Research for Better Schools, Philadelphia

One manifestation of educational reform in this decade has been the use of statewide, mandatory, high stakes tests – particularly in certifying professionals and encouraging student attainment of certain minimum competencies. The level of the stakes associated with a test is the extent to which test performance is perceived by students, teachers, administrators and/or parents to be 'used to make important decisions that immediately and directly affect them' (Madaus 1988:86). In the case of minimum competency testing (MCT) – the type of statewide testing with which this chapter is concerned – connecting test results to student promotion or graduation raises the stakes associated with the test and increases the seriousness with which educators and citizens regard the state's program. Whether the ensuing activity at the local level reforms systems for the better remains unanswered, and consequently so does the advisability of a state's use of higher stakes as a policy lever to instigate that activity.

This chapter looks specifically at two states' mandated MCT programs, discusses some of the effects on school districts associated with raising the testing stakes, and makes several recommendations regarding a state's use of stakes. The argument is that as the stakes of statewide MCT rise, the testing program is indeed taken more seriously at the local level, especially in terms of matching local objectives to those covered in the test and in terms of resequencing course content to insure that content contained on a test is covered in classrooms prior to the test. However, at some point during an increase in stakes, pressure on a district can intensify such that a shift in local focus occurs, and student performance on the test becomes an end in itself rather than merely an indicator of student attainment of broader learning outcomes. The consequence is that educators in the district begin to question whether their efforts to improve specific test scores are consistent with their interest in promoting student learning. The policy challenge is to encourage local attention to reform without instigating counterproductive responses.

Stakes and testing

The literature on the effects of various changes in state educational MCT testing policies is scant (Madaus 1988, Stake *et al.* 1987). But six investigations of high-stakes testing in general

*This publication is based on work sponsored, wholly or in part, by the Office of Educational Research and Improvement (OERI), Department of Education, under Contract Number 400-86-003. The content of this publication does not necessarily reflect the views of OERI, the Department, or any other agency of the US Government. Portions of this work were made possible through the co-operation of the Maryland State Department of Education (MSDE). The opinions expressed, however, do not necessarily reflect those of MSDE either.

provide at least a starting point for examining the topic. Relying heavily on anecdotes, testimony from public hearings, historical accounts, and an occasional international study, Madaus (1988:88-98) induces seven principles regarding the relationship between the level of stakes a test is perceived to have and the effects of the test on action at the local level:

- the power of tests and examinations to affect individuals, institutions, curriculum or instruction is a perceptual phenomenon: if students, teachers, or administrators believe that the results of an examination are important, it matters very little whether this is really true or false – the effect is produced by what individuals perceive to be the case;

- the more any quantitative social indicator is used for social decision-making, the more likely it will be to distort and corrupt the social processes it is intended to monitor;

- if important decisions are presumed to be related to test results, then teachers will teach to the test;

- in every setting where a high-stakes test operates, a tradition of past exams develops, which eventually de facto defines the curriculum;

- teachers pay particular attention to the form of questions on a high-stakes test, (e.g., short answer, essay, multiple choice), and adjust their instruction accordingly;

- when test results are the sole or even partial arbiter of future educational or life choices, society tends to treat test results as the major goal of schooling rather than as a useful but fallible indicator of achievement;

- a high-stakes test transfers control over the curriculum to the agency which sets or controls the exam.

This list emphasizes that stakes can become high not only when test results automatically trigger important consequences for students or the school system, but also when educators, students, or the public perceive that significant consequences accompany test results. Thus, an automatic triggering of consequences need not be formally built into the testing program for stakes to be high. Instead test results can cause the public to make an assessment of the quality of the school system that serves them, and this judgment in turn can lead to a conclusion that children's choices of post-secondary schooling or occupation have been affected. The product of this process is increased public pressure to improve test scores when the perception is that the system is likely to have a negative impact on those choices. Such was the case in Kentucky (Center for the Study of Testing, Evaluation, and Educational Policy 1986) and such was the case in one state to be discussed more fully later in this chapter.

Murnane (1987) identifies three common district responses to high-stakes conditions: excluding low-scoring children on some basis from taking the test, focusing instruction on the skills measured on the tests, and teaching test-taking skills. He notes, however, that

> . . . publicizing outcome data for individual schools and school districts may be a relatively effective strategy by which states and the federal government can persuade local school districts to concentrate on improving student learning. On the other hand . . . the responses of local school officials could result in improved average test scores without increasing student learning. In this case the publicized test scores provide misleading information and the responses by local officials reduce the effectiveness of the organizations that they lead. (p.105).

Thus, Murnane, like Madaus, argues that there is the potential for distorted, counterproductive local behavior under high stakes conditions.

Three empirical studies of district high-stakes testing programs also note the potential for similar effects. Polemini (1977) found test security in a large city's testing program to be a problem as local educators sought to obtain advanced copies of the test, primarily because they feared job accountability would be tied to results; First and Carenas (1986) claimed that districts excluded certain categories of students, particularly those who would likely do poorly, from the test-taking pool as a way to boost test results; and LeMahieu (1984) discovered that local, high-stakes tests could be beneficial, but great care had to be taken to avoid having staff make testing objectives the sole content covered in classes.

It would seem that high-stakes tests are at least taken more seriously, if not always productively, at the local level in terms of local staff perceptions that test results have to be addressed. Increasing the stakes, then, is a means of increasing the pressure on local systems to alter their operation. From the state perspective, such pressure is a critical ingredient in promoting successful improvement at the local level, according to findings from a ten-state study of state-initiated school improvement reported by Anderson *et al.* (1987). The same researchers also say that 'more important than the type of pressure was the fact that it existed' (Anderson *et al.* 1987:74). This chapter contains an argument to the contrary on this latter point: pressure via raised stakes encourages local action, but this action may be contradictory to the intended goals of reform.

The next two sections of this chapter discuss the effect of the level of MCT stakes on local action, first in terms of the seriousness with which districts regard the tests and then in terms of a shift in district focus from long-term learning objectives to short-term test score improvement.

Stakes and how seriously the program is taken at the local level

An important estimate of the seriousness with which a program is taken is the extent to which local activity is adjusted in response to the test. Results of a survey Research for Better Schools (RBS) conducted during the winter of 1986-87 in Pennsylvania and Maryland bear out the expectation that school districts in higher stakes testing situations make more adjustments in instruction and organization than those in lower stakes situations. A questionnaire that solicited information concerning the administration of the testing program, test uses, test impacts, and school system context was completed by a teacher, principal, and central office staff member in 277 of Pennsylvania's 501 districts and by three occupants of each position in 23 of Maryland's 24 systems. Below is a brief summary of the conclusions. (See Corbett and Wilson 1987 for a complete discussion of the study.)

The two states designed their testing programs such that there were at least four important differences. First, in Pennsylvania, failing students were identified and were supposed to receive remediation to be determined by the district. Students were not required to retake the test to the point of achieving a passing score. In contrast, Maryland made a passing score on all four tests a prerequisite for graduation. At the time this chapter was written, the first cohort of students required to pass all four were juniors. Thus, one year remained before the testing program reached its most stringent point. Special education students who did not meet this requirement could receive a certificate of attendance. Second, Pennsylvania students took their tests in the third, fifth and eighth grades. Maryland tested students beginning in ninth grade, although a practice test was administered in the middle school. Third, the legislature in Pennsylvania made a special appropriation to assist local remediation, whereas Maryland offered no financial assistance for this purpose. Fourth, Pennsylvania's test was a legislative response to the calls for educational reform that accompanied the reports from the commission and panels convened in the early 1980s. Although educators in the state suggested test objectives, commercial test publishers were invited to bid on a contract to provide the state's instrument. Maryland initiated a statewide curriculum improvement program several years prior to beginning the testing program, with the expressed purpose of anticipating the instructional quality necessary to perform well on the tests. Moreover, educators from around the state were selected by the SEA to provide input into the content and form of the tests.

Clearly, Maryland's program should have had a greater impact on its local systems than Pennsylvania's program, primarily because Maryland's policy insinuated itself into an important organizational event – graduation – and because preceding statewide improvement and actual test development activities engendered a cumulative anticipation of the day the tests would be put into place. According to the RBS survey, this proved to be the case. Essentially, in comparison with Pennsylvania, Maryland school systems focused more directly on improving their test scores, altered their curriculum to a greater extent (especially in terms of redefining course objectives and resequencing course content), and used the scores more often to compare school performances within the district as well as across school systems. Maryland educators also reported that students tended to take school more seriously, and those with special learning needs were better known and received more attention. At the same time, Maryland teachers were reported to be under greater stress, to have more paperwork, and to have experienced decreased reliance on their professional judgments than teachers in Pennsylvania. Regarding these last findings, interviews with Maryland educators subsequent to the survey revealed that these changes in teachers' work lives were largely concomitants of self-induced pressure to make sure that their students succeeded. That is, regardless of their personal and professional opinions about the tests, the fact was students had to pass, and teachers felt responsible to ensure that their students did so.

In addition to information concerning the above curriculum adjustments, the survey also asked respondents to assess whether the adjustments were for the better. The state-to-state differences were once again dramatic and consistent. In Maryland there was a much stronger feeling that the state mandated MCT program had narrowed *and* improved the curriculum in terms of both course objectives and the range of courses offered. Local educators explained that this assessment of the curriculum was the consequence of aligning the curriculum with test objectives. A clearer definition of what was expected to be covered represented an inprovement over rambling curriculum guides but at the same time did exclude some content that staff members previously had deemed worthy of inclusion. Up to a point, Maryland educators viewed a tighter curriculum as a better one; they worried, however, that the trend would lead to excessively basic course offerings.

Maryland educators also believed their systems had become more focused on testing than learning, and experienced a greater sense of discontinuity between the testing program and what they felt should be taught than did Pennsylvania educators. These latter two effects became exacerbated in the year following the survey. Those subsequent developments are the topic of the next section of the chapter.

Effects of raising the stakes

The survey discussed above presented a snapshot of the differences in educators' reactions to two state-mandated testing programs. The picture was taken in the late Fall of 1986 and the early Winter of 1987. Events in both states subsequent to the survey, however, had significant effects on educators' perceptions of the tests. In both states, the testing stakes increased – due to a brief public release of school district rankings based on test scores in Pennsylvania and to the approach of the time when Maryland students would be responsible for passing all four of the tests to graduate, two of which were particularly troublesome. Field interviews RBS conducted in eleven school districts in the two states during the Fall of 1987 as a followup to the survey elicited comments concerning the local effects of raising the stakes.

Pennsylvania

The key event in Pennsylvania was the publication of the results from the spring of 1987 test administration. Rather than the customary low-key sending of the scores to districts for each to handle as it saw fit, the event was orchestrated by the Chief State School Officer (CSSO). In a public media briefing, the CSSO provided documents that ranked school systems in the state from top to bottom in terms of the percentage of students who passed the cut-off point. A subpopulation of schools that had achieved a 100% passing rate despite a 'high risk' student population was singled out as being 'poised on the brink of excellence', and other subgroups of 'improving' schools were lauded. To cap off the presentation, the CSSO touted the tests as the best measure available to assess the effectiveness of Pennsylvania's schools. An immediate protest to this use of the scores arose from educators across the state and resulted in the withdrawal of the documents containing the rankings. This reaction was intelligible not only in terms of the conflict between the rankings and local views of the purposes of the testing program but also, as the chapter by Susan Furhman in this volume makes clear, in terms of the more subtle role the Pennsylvania SEA traditionally adopted in its interactions with districts.

The withdrawal of the rankings did not strike the event from either educators' or their communities' emotional record. Educators in three of the six Pennsylvania districts visited argued that the 'game' had now changed in their systems:

> The purpose of the test changed in September. It is no longer for remediation, but to rank order schools. [District 1 superintendent]

> The results should be between the state and the school district if the test is to help. When they release scores and say 58 kids need help, we can say we've already identified 40 of them. But the negativism starts; it starts [phone] calls and there is no question I now have pressure on me. [District 2 superintendent]

> The test was not all that important... But we might as well face up to it; with the publication of school by school results... one of the goals will be to raise the percentage above the cut score. [District 3 assistant superintendent]

Of the remaining three districts, one – an urban system – had 'bought into' the test early in the program and had already begun using the scores comparatively. In fact, interview subjects in this system, to a person, pointed with pride to several of the schools that had achieved 'high' passing rates relative to the student population they served. The visibility of the scores was already considerable in the community and the CSSO's actions contributed little additional publicity to how the schools were doing. In another district (which was rural), the community had taken little interest in the scores and, according to the superintendent, the system did not need to treat the test as other than a means of identifying students for additional instruction. In the third, an assistant superintendent claimed that 'the publication of scores was deplorable; it was never the intent to rank schools'. Nevertheless, the person asserted that the scores would be downplayed in the district as they had been in the past.

What really seemed to be changing for the first set of three districts in Pennsylvania was the stakes; they got higher, primarily through the increased visibility of score comparisons and the subsequent increased, albeit reluctant, acceptance of the scores as a benchmark – that is, as a widely recognized point of reference when discussing the performance of schools in the district and surrounding districts.

Staff in the three districts reported that they did not believe the tests to be particularly important educationally, and they did not embrace the tests as valid indicators of attainment. They nevertheless acknowledged that they already were or would soon be treating the scores more seriously than in previous years. As one disgruntled educator claimed, what once was an educational tool had now become a weapon.

A central office administrator in District 3 commented, 'The tests are not all that important. We use our own standardized testing program to modify instruction.' But since the publicity surrounding the scores had increased, more attention had been given to the tests. According to that administrator,

> One thing we did was to say 'here are the objectives on which the test was developed, look at them and see if they are being covered'. This didn't result in change but now that they [SEA] are publicizing the test scores more people who felt they could put the test aside will look at it and say not only have I covered it but do I feel the students will do well? Before I don't think there was as serious a reaction to analyze and interpret the schools' program as there probably is now.

Additional impetus for emphasizing test objectives in this same district came when a six percent difference in the number of students passing occurred between two middle schools in the system. Despite the fact that both had passing rates above 89%, the administrator went on to say:

> We couldn't come up with an answer [for the difference] although the lower [scoring] school said they didn't think they needed to take it seriously. My response is you'd better. We might as well face up to it. One of the goals is going to be to raise the percentage of students above the cut score; so if you're not now emphasizing the test, you'd better. It may not be a legitimate impact, but it is there. The danger is not keeping it in proportion. We need to understand what the tests' place is and that's the danger in how the results are now being emphasized and publicized.

In District 1, a problem arose when surrounding districts' scores matched those of the system, even though the Superintendent felt that its carefully and systematically developed curriculum far surpassed the offerings of those around them. The response?

> We don't believe in the tests that strongly, but we will be forced to see all material is covered before the tests. We definitely are going to do it. We won't be caught in the newspapers again. [superintendent]

The brunt of not 'getting caught' was placed on the reading program – a recently revised, developmental curriculum. The timing of the test administration required shifting the sequence of topics to be covered. An outraged reading co-ordinator responded,

> You have to alter a curriculum that is already working well and so [now] we can't follow the developmental process already established. Kids are already growing in a structured program; but it [pressure to change] comes from the board, community, and adverse publicity.

The superintendent empathized with the co-ordinator,

> I don't have much faith in the tests. I don't want to change the curriculum, and it's not a major revision, but we've got to do better. Still, it's not the right thing to do to anyone, I don't want to over-react, but I'm also going to have to spend time on things I shouldn't have to do: public relations, testing meetings – just to make the board feel comfortable. It'll never happen again when we see a worse district doing better than us.

The actions were to be undertaken in a context similar to District 3 where standardized tests had long been an integral part of school improvement.

> We feel you can't toy with nationwide standardized tests. That's what we believe in, and our performance has been very good. But over the next seven months, we'll be publishing more things about standardized tests and our interpretations of the [state] test scores.

District 2 administrators also indicated a preference not to alter a systematic process for addressing curriculum issues. The district took a cyclical approach, working on one content area at a time according to a long-established time frame. No longer. As the superintendent stated,

> We looked at a natural curriculum picture before September, but we will address state priorities because our scores were awful. We weren't surprised; the student population we serve is the same as those at the bottom, the big city populations. We will try to raise scores in the third, fifth, and eighth grades. It doesn't mean they'll be smarter.

Another central office administrator detailed the changes more specifically:

> We are building student anxiety, raising their level of concern. We don't want to do that with low esteem kids so we're talking out of both sides of our mouths for our own political needs. Also, changes in math will be addressed in the normal math curriculum cycle next year, but this year we'll go ahead and make the changes in 3rd, 5th, and 8th grades. Essentially, the [CSSO] just specified the 3, 5, and 8 reading and math curriculum. There is no local option because we have to spend more time on minimal curriculum than enrichment.

Once again, this district had relied on standardized tests in the past to gauge their instructional strengths and weaknesses. The assistant superintendent noted that,

> In the past we've had more of a focus on [standardized tests]. Now the focus has shifted dramatically because we're looking for higher scores in the 3rd, 5th, and 8th grades on the state tests. They'll have more of an impact than the standardized test.

Clearly administrators in these three districts were planning expedient strategies to improve the test scores, and just as clearly there was resentment to do so and a concern that what they were doing was compromising a standard of good professional practice. Essentially the message being given was that the test scores were becoming benchmarks for political reasons, namely to appease school boards and communities who had had the opportunity to see their schools compared to one another and their system compared to neighboring districts, and did not like what they saw. And no matter how district staff had portrayed their performance in the past, part of that portrayal in the future had to include the test scores. Staff, in other words, were beginning to use the tests as a reference for judging local effectiveness.

This development reflected obligation more than acceptance. Perhaps most revealing was the ubiquitous 'but' in their comments. Woven throughout the above passages were comments like 'normally we do that, *but* now we have to do this'. This syntactical form called attention to staff catching themselves in contradictions between what they publicly professed as good professional practice and what they found themselves actually doing. Put in terms of the dilemma Murnane (1987) stated, staff members were worried that specific attention to improving test scores would not improve learning.

Maryland

Maryland districts subsequent to the RBS survey seemed to be devoting more and more administrative and teacher time to devising strategies to improve scores on two of the tests and seemed to be using the scores more and more as benchmarks, resulting in augmented pressure on teachers to get students to pass. Although no single event had dramatically heightened the stakes of the tests, students soon would have to pass all four of the tests in order to receive a diploma. The pressure to improve the percentage of students passing the tests increased dramatically with each yearly test administration date.

In Maryland, not all four tests were regarded equally. Educators discriminated between the reading and math tests on one hand and the writing and citizenship ones on the other. The reading and math tests, in Maryland educators' minds, were adequate measures of basic competence in the respective content areas and covered objectives already well-entrenched in the curriculum. The curriculum development aspect of the state initiative began in the late seventies, and these two tests were the first to be developed, trial-tested, and implemented. Actual local curriculum and instruction changes had been in place for seven to nine years in some districts. By 1987, these adjustments had become institutionalized, to the point that interview subjects in four of the five districts argued that what was now routine was once novel.

> We made sure everything we tested was in the curriculum. But that was done eight or nine years ago. The changes were already made [well before the survey]. [Central Office Administrator]

> The [survey] mean [adjustments in curriculum and instruction] is skewed. Reading and math have been implemented for a while. [Teacher]

> The changes in my area would have occurred well in the past. [Teacher]

The upshot was that the two tests were no longer obtrusive.

> In reading, there probably hasn't been much change; the same in math. The scope and sequence were already complete and the content match was already there. [Principal]

> Math and reading teachers probably don't have much of a problem anymore. [Central Office Administrator]

Such was not the case for the writing and citizenship tests. Both generated considerable controversy. The writing test did so because staff viewed it as demanding a performance level well beyond that necessary to be minimally competent in writing. The citizenship test's controversial aspect centered around its requirement that students memorize information about local, state, and federal governments – information that even the teachers did not possess without special study. Fueling educators' concerns were the difficulties that a significant number of students were having in meeting the performance levels required by the two tests. Administrators, teachers with responsibilities in certain grades and in certain content areas, and special education teachers experienced growing pressure to improve the passing rate, adopting increasingly expedient methods of accomplishing this.

This 'concentrated' approach to improving test results was apparent in all five districts, especially in schools where the scores were lowest.

District 1 staff reported that considerable time was spent in preparation for the tests:

> We are concentrating more on basics. We are now spending from September to November on basic skills rather than on our developmental program. [Reading teacher]

Another person complained that the writing test's importance was getting out of proportion.

> The test has become the judge of the total system. [English teacher]

Schools with low scores seemed to be getting special attention, as indicated in the following comment:

> When the scores are low, [the poor performance] takes me into the school for the names of the kids who failed. There is no stroking in schools where scores have dropped. Everyone is sitting around with bated breath waiting for the test scores. [Central office administrator]

District 2 central office administrators agreed that the tests were assuming greater importance in the system, and the scores were a constant presence in their work.

> Of course the tests are benchmarks. I always say it's only one indicator but it is a benchmark. It's reality. [Central office administrator]

> The first question we ask is how we did relative to so and so. [Central office administrator]

> Today I have 105 seniors who haven't passed. My anxiety is higher. [Central office administrator]

One adminstrator believed the pressure was greatest on schools with low scores.

> I'm in the middle. I have no pressures at all. I know I'd feel uncomfortable on the bottom. [Principal]

District 3 seemed less consumed by the tests than other systems. Partly because of its small size, the burden of improving test performance fell on only a few shoulders. Moreover, the district had a history of deflecting the impact of state initiatives. Nevertheless, the tests had to be addressed.

> We're bucking the system here. Many districts moved Civics to the ninth grade and are testing for it in the tenth. We've had a program for a while in the twelfth grade. But it causes problems with no ninth grade civics class; we're interrupting classes to do a review. [Teacher]

> I'm right now panically [sic] moving toward the test. [Teacher]

District 4 teachers were concerned about the extent to which passing the test was becoming an expediency in the district.

> We realize a kid is taken out of science every other day for citizenship and will fail science to maybe pass the citizenship test. [Building administrator]

> We're just getting them to memorize facts until [the test is given]. [Teacher]

> I'm not opposed to the idea of testing. But I'm not sure we haven't gone overboard, the tail is wagging the dog. The original idea was that there were to be certain standards the *student* would have to meet, but if the student doesn't pass, people will ask what's wrong with the school and teachers. [Teacher]

These very targeted means for getting students to pass were acknowledged as a necessary evil:

> We've had to do things we didn't want to do. [Central office administrator]

Staff in District 5 reported increasingly frequent interactions concerning how students were doing relative to the tests' objectives. They faced heightened awareness of the scores.

> Teachers feel pressured to meet the superintendent's expected pass rate. [Central office administrator]

> In administrators' meetings the talk is about where we rank. Parents let you know. You see it in newspapers. [Principal]

The result was the adoption of very focused strategies to teach test objectives in the classrooms.

> Teachers feel jerked around. The test dictates what I will do in the classroom. [Teacher]

> If you deviate from the objectives, you feel guilty, especially if kids fail. [Teacher]

> We have materials provided by the county as 'quick help'. We were told 'here's how to get kids to pass the test fast'. They were good ideas but specifically on the test. For example, if the area in a rectangle is shaded, you multiply; if not, you add. [Teacher]

And in response to the above stream of comments, a teacher summarized,

> Talk about games and game-playing!

Reservations about strategies used to raise test scores were expressed in all five of the Maryland systems, just as they were in three of the Pennsylvania districts. As the importance of getting students to pass the tests heightened, local activity zeroed in more and more on the two troublesome tests, but in ways that produced the same linguistic qualifiers heard in Pennsylvania (most frequently 'but'). Nevertheless, improving results became superordinate to other job responsibilities for many Maryland district administrators and a subset of teachers. Most of their professional time became devoted to test-related activities, to the exclusion of other staff development and improvement initiatives. This shift in job orientation seemed more widespread across the districts in Maryland than in Pennsylvania.

Shifting the local focus

It is important to note that the stakes – the extent to which citizens and educators perceived that test performance would be used to make important decisions – increased in the two states for two different reasons: first the SEA's use of the test scores to make comparisons of districts' performances in Pennsylvania; and second the approach of the time when all four tests would serve as an obstacle to graduation in Maryland. The stakes increased in what were originally both low and high stakes situations. As they did so, public pressure on districts to improve their performance intensified – especially when a district's ability to improve seemed questionable (either because of the nature of the students or the nature of the test or both) and/or when the need to demonstrate improvement was immediate (e.g., to correct unfavorable comparisons with other districts or between schools within a district). Educators' concern shifted almost completely to influencing test performance in response. Put differently, a shift occurred in the manifestations of the seriousness with which the test was taken. The shift can best be described as a shift from a long-term focus to a short-term one, from using the test as one indicator among many to treating the next set of test results as the most important outcome of schooling.

Such a shift is a probable occurrence in most rising stakes testing situations. In minimum competency testing, where the results are formulated typically in terms of the percentage of students passing the test, little technical expertise is needed to interpret what the numbers are saying. Thus, the results easily become publicly accepted proxies for school performance. As the stakes associated with these readily intelligible numbers rise, the results also assume greater importance as statewide, standardized benchmarks – and such benchmarks can become effective levers with which to move a district. Primarily because the public, and to an extent district staff members, hold the system as somehow responsible for the performance of its students on the test, a need to gain control over activity that can influence those benchmarks is created. That is, the local community perceives the results as controllable, and the system undertakes an obligatory effort to do so. Moreover, students are the ones that directly suffer the consequences of failure in terms of being unable to graduate or move to the next grade, causing local educators to exert an even greater effort to improve student test performance. In the process, resources are drawn from other activities as staff members begin to analyze specific areas of student weakness on the tests and to develop materials directed specifically at improving performance. The more formidable overcoming student weakness appears to be and/or the more quickly improvement must be demonstrated, the more staff members devote their time to test-related activities.

Heightening this pressure to narrow the local focus is the cyclical nature of testing programs. The school year takes on a rhythmic quality with the tempo set by the test administration date. As the date approaches, activity directed toward improving performance becomes more frenetic. The test becomes foremost in at least the minds of the staff. The end result is that the major emphasis in the school becomes to improve the next set of scores rather than some longer-term, more general goal of improving student learning. Thus, the indicator of performance becomes the goal itself.

This recalls the dilemma stated by Murnane earlier: what if improving test scores does not improve student learning? Indeed, the key question in all of this discussion of stakes is, has learning improved or have only test results improved? The initial answer is that probably both occur. Focusing on improving the test scores of all students probably does result in improved performance in general. But this works only up to a point. As the stakes rise and the pressure to perform better intensifies, activity becomes so focused on improving test scores that long-term learning opportunities are subordinated to efficient short-term strategies to improve specific areas of weakness as indicated by the test. Educators themselves verbally demonstrate the point at which this shift occurs by the use of linguistic qualifiers.

Stakes and the politics of education

Perception. Pressure. Practice. This chapter's message is that the perception of increased stakes associated with a state minimum competency test leads to an intensification of the pressure on local educators to improve test scores, which in turn stimulates changes in local practice. Even though experts may regard some of these practices as appropriate (e.g., Popham *et al.* 1985), our research indicates that educators themselves feel uncomfortable about the long-term value of many of their responses to high stakes testing. Improving the test results tends to become and end in itself, instigating considerable activity to improve the performance of 'at risk' populations through quick, intense preparation for the 'day of the test'.

Much of the pressure instigating these practices comes from the local community – the newspaper, the school board, and parents. Actually these constituents seek to promote attainment of a desired level of an outcome rather than to encourage educators' engagement in specific practices. Nevertheless, demanding particular levels of outcomes has been shown to be an especially effective means of exercising power over organizational action (Mintzberg 1983). Power, according to Mechanic (1962:351), is 'any force that results in behavior that would not have occurred if the force had not been present'. Given the statements of the local educators detailed above, it is reasonable to assume that they would not have engaged in many of the described practices in the absence of the community's pressure to improve test scores. Thus, outside influences became particularly potent factors in getting educators to behave in ways they ordinarily would not have.

In the specific instance with which this chapter is concerned, knowledge of local performance on the test was the means of empowerment for various local constituencies. The test scores served as proxies for the quality of local educators' instructional behavior. In other words, how well teachers and administrators were discharging their educational responsibilities became more visible through the windows of test results. Increased visibility of one's performance improves the ability of others to reinforce behaviour in accordance with expectations and to punish deviance (Merton 1968, Nyberg 1981). The information provided by the test enabled the community to determine whether its desired level of performance was being attained or not and, accordingly, whether to attempt to influence district behavior.

The level of the stakes associated with mandated tests is the trigger for motivating external use of test scores as a lever to affect local practice. The community has other 'objective' indicators available to it upon which to base judgments about district performance and subsequent influence attempts. Whether an effort to shape district behavior ensues would seem to be related in large part to whether that indicator is used to make important decisions; the higher the stakes, the greater the pressure will be to correct performance deficiencies – especially if improvement seems difficult or the need to demonstrate improvement is immediate.

High stakes statewide testing programs, then, can alter the political character of districts by increasing the probability that community elements can and will exercise influence. As Gutman's (1988) chapter in this volume explains, educators are accustomed to having to compromise the exercise of their professional judgment; citizen empowerment through their knowledge of test scores is just one of several barriers to the attainment of what she terms 'appropriate levels of educators' autonomy' – that is, autonomy that is neither so great as to shut out external influence altogether nor so insignificant as to make educators totally vulnerable to outside pressure. Johnson's (1988) chapter provides empirical evidence that teachers value highly this kind of 'appropriate' autonomy and concludes that the key ingredient of current teacher reform proposals, if they are to produce better places for teachers to teach and students to learn, is the emphasis on enabling teachers to gain more control over their work. It seems, however, that the effects of high stakes testing on local control of education that were described above would countervail the most promising outcome of efforts to reform teaching.

Policy makers may want to consider ways to minimize having one set of reforms negate another set. A significant step would be to lower the likelihood that scores alone will be perceived to affect important decisions. For example, if poor performance on the test triggered a district's engaging in a systematic, long-term improvement process rather than the denial of a symbol of progress like promotion or a diploma, then the direct consequences for students would be lower – as would the level of the stakes that the public probably would associate with the test. Likewise, creating alternative paths to graduation for seniors who fail a test (e.g., through teachers' and principals' certifying that a student demonstrated mastery of tested skills in homework or classwork) should accomplish much the same purpose. Doing the opposite, i.e., raising the stakes associated with a test, focuses attention solely on student performance and promotes the attainment of higher scores without improved learning. Such use of policy ultimately will undermine the very reforms it is supposed to encourage.

References

ANDERSON, B., ODDEN, A., FARRAR, E., FUHRMAN, S., DAVIS, A., HUDDLE, E., ARMSTRONG, J., and FLAKUS-MOSQUEDA, P. (1987) 'State strategies to support local school improvement'. *Knowledge: Creation, Diffusion, Utilization*, 9(1), pp. 42-86.

CENTER FOR THE STUDY OF TESTING, EVALUATION, AND EDUCATION POLICY (1986) 'An evaluation of the ICY essential skills tests in mathematics and reading' (Chestnut Hill, MA: Boston College).

CORBETT, H. D., and WILSON, B. L. (1987). 'Study of statewide mandatory minimum competency tests' (Philadelphia: Research for Better Schools).

FIRST, J. M., and CARDENAS, J. (1986) 'A minority view of testing'. *Educational Measurement: Issues and Practice*, 5(1), pp. 6-11.

FUHRMAN, S. (1988) 'State politics and education reform', in J. Hannaway and R. Crowson (eds), *The Politics of Reforming School Administration*. (London: Falmer Press).

GUTMANN, A. (1988) 'Democratic theory and the role of teachers in democratic education', in J. Hannaway and R. Crowson (eds), *The Politics of Reforming School Administration* (London: Falmer Press).

JOHNSON, S. (1988) 'Schoolwork and its reform', in J. Hannaway and R. Crowson (eds), *The Politics of Reforming School Administration* (London: Falmer Press).

LeMAHIEU, P. G. (1984) 'The effects on achievement and instructional content of a program of student monitoring through frequent testing', *Educational Evaluation and Policy Analysis*, 6(2), pp. 175-187.

MADAUS, G. (1988) 'The influence of testing on the curriculum', in L. Tanner (ed.), *Critical Issues in Curriculum: 87th Yearbook of the NSSE, Part I* (Chicago: University of Chicago Press).

MECHANIC, D. (1962) 'Sources of power of lower participants in complex organizations', *Administrative Science Quarterly*, pp. 349-364.

MERTON, R. (1968) *Social Theory and Social Structure* (Chicago: Free Press).

MINTZBERG, H. (1983) *Structure in Five: Designing Effective Organizations* (Englewood Cliffs, NJ: Prentice Hall).

MURNANE, R. (1987) 'Improving education indicators and economic indicators: the same problem?' *Educational Evaluation and Policy Analysis*, 9(2), pp. 101-116.

NYBERG, D. (1981) 'A concept of power for education', *Teachers College Record*, 82(4), pp.535-551.

POLEMINI, A. J. (1977) 'Security in a citywide testing program', *Journal of Teaching and Learning*, 2(3), pp. 34-40.

POPHAM, W. J., CRUSE, K. L., RANKING, S. C., SANDIFER, P. W. and WILLIAMS, P. L. (1985). 'Measurement-driven instruction: it's on the road', *Phi Delta Kappan*, 66(9), pp. 628-634.

STAKE, R., BETTRIDGE, J., METZER, D., and SWITZER, D. (1987) 'Review of literature on effects of achievement testing' (Champaign, IL: Center for Instructional Research and Curriculum Evaluation).

4   *State education reform implementation:*
a framework for analysis

Allan Odden and David Marsh
University of Southern California

During the past five years, comprehensive state education reform has dominated education policy. Spurred by the *Nation at Risk* (National Commission on Excellence in Education, 1983) report, states enacted sweeping reform programs designed to improve local schools (Education Commission of the States, 1984) and increased funding per pupil by nearly 20% after adjusting for inflation (Odden, 1987). In 1986, moreover, governors made education reform a top state policy issue for at least the next five years (National Governors Association, 1986).

This swift response to the imperative to strengthen the nation's education systems reflected a new capacity and will among state governments (Doyle and Hartle, 1985), leading toward state dominance of education policy leadership (Odden, 1986a). The rapid state response fit into no previous political science model of policy innovation, but reflected new political realities that fast and comprehensive action was required (McDonnell and Fuhrman, 1985).

Yet, there were critics. Peterson (1983), analyzing the *Nation at Risk* report and a similar report, *Action for Excellence* (Education Commission of the States, 1983) authored by state governors and legislators, argued that research supported neither the nature of the education problems these reports identified nor the types of solutions proposed and subsequently enacted by several states. Cuban (1984) seriously questioned whether *top-down* reform mandates could make *local* schools better, a view which reflected the sentiments of other political scientists as well as state and local education leaders.

This chapter responds to these education reform implementation skeptics by analyzing the implementation of one state's comprehensive education reforms within the framework of current political science theory and knowledge of government program implementation. The first section of this chapter traces the evolution of knowledge and theory about policy implementation and discusses their implications for analyzing the implementation and impact of state education reforms. The second section outlines in more detail a conceptual framework that combines macro- and micro-implementation issues, and section three reports the results of a study that used this framework to study the implementation of California's comprehensive education reform, Senate Bill 813. The final section presents conclusions and suggests how this study advances knowledge of the politics of government program implementation.

The evolution of implementation knowledge and theory

Research on government program implementation has evolved through several stages during the past two decades. The first two stages primarily addressed macro-implementation issues. They investigated how programs initiated at higher levels of government get implemented at lower levels. Stage one began with the expansion of intergovernmental grant programs in the 1960s and focused on early implementation problems and 'inherent conflict' in federal (or state) initiated but locally implemented programs. Research in stage two, conducted several years later, found that programs ultimately get implemented through a mutual adaptation process. Stage three has just begun. It is focusing on program quality issues and alternative frameworks for analyzing implementation issues, including initiatives that attempt to improve local systems rather than just create new categorical programs at the margin.

The first stage of implementation research

The first stage of implementation research, based mainly on late 1960s and early 1970s research on several programs (for education as well as several other functions), concluded that there was inevitable conflict between local orientations, values and priorities and state or federally initiated programs. New governmental programs met hostility at the local level. Most research showed that local governments had neither the capacity nor the will to implement initiatives designed by higher level governments (Murphy, 1971). The expectations and hopes of state and federal program designers were dashed on the shoals of local resistence and ineptness (Derthick, 1976, Pressman and Wildavsky, 1973). At best, higher level governmental programs created opportunities for continuous bargaining with local governments over the values, foci and substance of the new programs (Ingram, 1977). But according to theory at this stage, conflict would continue, bargaining would never abate and programs would rarely get implemented.

Thus, early implementation research showed that implementation problems not only emerged from faulty program design but also, and even more importantly, from the policy's relationship to the local institutional setting. Indeed, much early implementation research showed that local governments often used new program fiscal resources for purposes other than those for which the programs were designed (Murphy, 1971). As a result, regulations were developed to constrain aberrant local behavior and to force correct use of funds (Barro, 1978). Theories addressing both policy design (including needed regulations) and, in part, local institutional settings were developed to improve policy implementation (Sabatier and Mazmanian, 1979). Yet, conventional wisdom (still believed by many) held that ongoing and continuous conflict was inevitable, that higher level government programs simply did not work, and that local governments would never implement them faithfully.

The second stage of implementation research

Changes in understanding the workings of government program implementation began to emerge in the early 1980s, with publication of several studies that investigated more recent implementation of programs designed in the 1960s and early 1970s. These studies focused on program implementation after the initial start-up years and addressed the question of whether, after fifteen years of effort, programs in compliance with legislative design and accompanying regulations could be implemented.

Kirst and Jung (1980) produced the first second stage synthesis of federal education program implementation, focusing on Title I of ESEA. They claimed that research in the late 1970s showed that early Title I implementation problems had essentially abated by the late

1970s and that, by the close of the 1970s, local school districts had not only learned how to administer Title I in compliance with rules and regulations but also had even begun to sanction the education priorities embodied in Title I.

Their claim was substantially strengthened by publication of a series of research products that emerged from several federally sponsored studies. These research efforts, conducted between 1981 and 1983, investigated the state level interaction and local implementation of several similar federal and state categorical programs including compensatory education, special education, bilingual education, vocational education and other civil rights rules and regulations (Moore *et al.* 1983, Knapp *et al.* 1983). These studies found, at both state and local levels, that the federal (and state) programs: (1) were being implemented in compliance with legislative intent and accompanying rules and regulations; (2) were providing extra services to students who needed them and who probably would not get them if the state and federal programs did not exist; (3) did not cause curriculum fragmentation in local schools and, in fact, allowed local educators to create a set of relatively integrated services for eligible students; and (4) while creating some extra paperwork were, in the minds of local educators, worth while because they provided needed extra services.

A few years later, additional Title I (then changed to Chapter I of ECIA) research showed that even when rules and regulations were waived (but subsequently reinstated) state and local district implementation practices maintained faithfulness to their spirit and usually their letter as well (Farrar and Milsap, 1986). What these studies showed is that, over time, the grand expectations and rigid regulations of federal and state program designers were adapted to a program that could work locally, that local opposition was transformed into support for new program initiatives for targeted students, that local capacity was developed to run the programs in compliance with rules and regulations, and that eligible students were provided appropriate services (Jung and Kirst, 1986).

Peterson *et al.* (1986) produced the seminal stage two implementation book that provided both a new theory of program implementation and, to support the theory, empirical data for programs in education and for several other functions as well. Peterson *et al.* identified two types of higher level governmental programs – developmental and redistributive – and argued that the implementation process differed for each.

Developmental programs, such as community development, transportation, and in education, curriculum, instruction and vocational education, are those in which most local governments are involved anyway. Such federal and state programs substantially reinforce local initiatives and program priorities and provide extra resources for them, usually with marginal new program foci. Based on several case studies of such programs, Peterson *et al.* show that developmental programs typically get implemented fairly quickly and with a relatively uncontentious implementation process.

By contrast, redistributive programs such as compensatory education, special education and desegregation assistance in education require that local governments – school districts in the case of education – provide more service to some clients – students – than to others. Moreover, Peterson *et al.* report, most redistributive programs focus attention on groups of clients to whom local governments had not given extra attention before the higher level governmental intervention. Again through an analysis of multiple case studies, Peterson *et al.* conclude that redistributive programs experience a relatively contentious, initial implementation process but that, over time, they too get fully implemented in compliance with legislative intent, rules and regulations. Initial grandiose redistributive program goals and initial local resistance get 'worked out' through a 'mutual accommodation' process which produces a workable program for both local and higher level governments.

In short, Peterson *et al.* make two significant points. First, that most governmental programs eventually become implemented. Second, that the implementation process is different for developmental versus redistributive programs.

Hargrove (1983) moves beyond these authors and provides both a theory and empirical data for the politics of redistributive program implementation. But the important overall conclusion from stage two implementation research, as compared to stage one, is that higher level government programs eventually get implemented locally, that the initial conflict gets 'worked out' over time, and that the opportunity for 'bargaining' ultimately produces a workable program for both parties.

The third stage of implementation research

Claiming that programs get implemented, however, is not the same as claiming that they 'work', i.e., that they solve the problems for which they were created. Indeed, as stage two implementation research knowledge emerged so also did the realization that many programs were not having their desired impact. Students receiving extra services did better than similar students who did not receive services, but the impact was small and often eroded over time (Kennedy et al., 1986). Indeed, as the 1980s began, several analysts saw direct trade-offs between compliant implementation and program quality, or noted at least that efforts to develop rules and regulations to get programs 'in place' had overlooked issues of program substance, quality and impact (Elmore and McLaughlin 1981, Elmore and McLaughlin 1983, Hargrove 1983).

Thus, one imperative for stage three implementation research was to determine not only how to get programs implemented, but also how to make them effective. To improve education program quality, one general proposal was to integrate categorical program services more with the main or regular school curriculum program (Elmore and McLaughlin 1983, Odden 1986b).

More theoretically, two ideas have been proposed for structuring stage three implementation research. McDonnell and Elmore (1987), drawing on more general implementation research, suggest that new research should focus less on specific programs and more on policy instruments or 'implements' such as mandates, regulations, incentives, funds, etc. They argue that the underlying policy instruments used in any new program may be the most important elements for ultimate program impact and that more needs to be known about how different implements work across different program types, across different program functions, as well as across different program purposes within any particular function. Their research on current state education reform implementation is designed to provide more knowledge about the efficacy of various policy implements.

McLaughlin (1987) takes a different tack and suggests that program quality and impact issues are most promisingly analyzed by focusing on local, micro-implementation issues, and the connections between micro- and macro-implementation concerns. McLaughlin argues that program impact depends on focusing those who deliver services – teachers in education – on the substance of the particular program and in having those professionals apply state-of-the-art knowledge in the delivery of appropriate new services. McLaughlin sees this task as a micro-organizational/implementation issue that is informed more by the local educational change literature (Huberman and Miles 1984) than by political science literature. In this approach, she is reemphasizing earlier points made, in part, by Berman (1978).

Given the problem for which the program has been developed, the implementation issues are, according to McLaughlin: (1) what is known about effective practice at the service delivery level; (2) how can local practitioners be influenced to apply their energies and attentions to that problem; (3) what strategies can be used to make local practitioners expert in the effective practices they need to apply; and (4) how can higher level policy at the district, state and/or federal level be designed to help local practitioners put these practices into local use? Thus, McLaughlin suggests an approach closer to Elmore's (1979-80) 'backward mapping' than necessarily to a study of policy instruments, and offers an approach that emphasizes intra-organizational implementation issues and, thus, a local change orientation.

There is an additional issue, related to the nature of the program itself, to consider in deciding how to approach an analysis of education reform implementation. The 1980s education reforms are substantively different from the education reforms of the 1960s and 1970s. The earlier reforms targeted special programs to particular types of students. Even when there was overlap between the types of students who could be served in the various programs, the implementation issue was whether services could be delivered to the targeted students. Rarely did a categorical program from the 1960s and 1970s focus on the regular curriculum program, or the overall local education system. By contrast, current state education reforms were created to do just that, i.e., to improve the regular curriculum and instruction program – to change the quality of the local education system. As noted below, both the different nature of current education reforms and the evolution of implementation research shape how implementation and impact analysis should be conceptualized.

A conceptual framework that combines macro and micro implementation dimensions of school reform

Our conceptual framework for studying education reform implementation was based on six features of the policy implementation literature discussed above. These principles can be summarized as follows:

1. Education reform implementation research should integrate analysis of the content of the reform, the process of its implementation in the local setting, and its effects.

2. Education reform implementation research should focus on the influence of the reform on the overall local educational system as well as on the content, implementation process and more specific impacts.

3. Education reform implementation research should integrate a macro (state level) with a micro (district/school level) focus for analyzing the above issues.

4. Education reform implementation research should draw on the distinction between developmental and redistributive types of governmental programs.

5. Education reform implementation research should use recent research on the local change process and relate the results to the macro context, to the content of the reform and to the outcomes at the local level.

6. Education reform implementation research should identify several types of outcomes, including impacts on the individuals within local educational systems and impacts on the systems themselves.

The application of these design principles, then, constitute a conceptual framework for studying education reform implementation. This section presents additional detail of these design principles and how they were adapted for the study of education reform implementation in California.

Reform content and the local educational system

The goal of SB 813 was to improve local schools. In particular, it (like many other state reforms) was designed to improve: (a) the regular curriculum, (b) teachers' instructional strategies, and (c) schools as organizations. For example, under the curriculum category, California's reform included increased high school graduation requirements, model curriculum standards, new K-12 curriculum frameworks, revised tests emphasizing more content areas as well as thinking and problem-solving skills, and better textbooks. Under the instructional strategies category, California's reform included new approaches to teacher evaluation, a mentor teacher program focused on helping beginning teachers, and several new state staff development programs which often were complemented locally with additional inservice training thrusts. Under the improving schools category, California's program included school rewards for improving student achievement, a grant program for teachers to develop innovative programs, and new state recognition programs for exemplary schools. While SB 813 was not designed as an integrated and holistic program and this tri-partite categorization is an *ex post facto* creation, it nevertheless 'fits' with what policymakers hoped would happen as a result of enacting SB 813.

Given the comprehensive nature of California's (and many other states') education reform package, it was appropriate to study implementation *in toto*, i.e., the degree to which the reforms taken together improved local education systems (Knapp and Stearns 1986). Tracking individual pieces of the reform, the implementation strategy of the past, or even studying various implements, we felt, was off the mark.

Studies needed to capture the degree to which, and how, state education reform programs and policies became part of the local vision for education excellence. Further, the vision at the district and school level needed to be analyzed separately from state reform initiatives. Issues at this stage included both the degree to which state programs helped determine the substance of local visions of excellence, and how strong, *a priori*, local visions incorporated or wove into their fabric the substance of state initiatives.

The conceptual framework also had to allow for the possibility that the education reform vision might evolve even as the study was conducted. In particular, studies needed to differentiate between which 'phase' of reform was being studied. While there was no definitive definition of reform phases, four general phases could be conceptualized, and the study assumed that implementation might vary for each:

Phase 1 Higher standards, increased high school graduation requirements, basic skills tests, more traditional academic courses, more homework, a return to the 'traditional' good high school.

Phase 2 Better courses, new model curriculum standards, better textbooks, curriculum alignment, beginnings of new teacher roles, education program quality indicators, reduction in dropouts.

Phase 3 More radical curriculum change, curriculum integration across content areas, greater emphasis on writing and communication, higher order thinking skills, and problem-solving skills, broader uses of technology, interpersonal small group skills.

Phase 4 Teacher professionalism, teacher decision making, national standards board, career ladders, policy trust agreements to replace traditional collective bargaining, restructured schools, more parental choice, system incentives, merit schools.

This concept of the substance of reform had several implications for the study's design. First, the study was designed to analyze the linkage between the substance of reform, including the local reform vision, and the local implementation process. Second, the study defined different phases of California's reforms and analyzed somewhat separately the implementation processes for each phase. Third, the study examined the impacts of each phase on the three broad goals of reform described above.

To study the content of the reform and its relationship to the local education system, we identified the substance of the local education program and, in particular, the vision that local leaders had for improving their school systems. This vision was identified for both district and site leaders.

In a parallel fashion, we focused our study on the nature of each state policy initiative as it appeared in the local setting and on the relationships among these policy initiatives as they were implemented locally. Finally, we focused on the relationship of the state policy initiatives, individually and collectively, to the local educational vision and how the state reform content had influenced the local vision.

Linkage of macro and micro implementation

The conceptual framework also had to link state policy initiatives and influences to local implementation issues. Based on preliminary information about California's reform, we knew that SB 813 policy initiatives and influences were of several types. First, state policy initiatives and influences were likely to shape the content of the reform. For example, the content might be shaped through mandates such as higher graduation requirements and a requirement that districts compare their curriculum against state model curriculum standards. As described above, the reform content included changes in curriculum, instruction and school organization.

State policy and activity might also help districts and schools integrate dimensions of effective curriculum and instruction. At the state level, the model curriculum standards were closely aligned with the state textbook adoption criteria and the content of the state achievement testing program. The state activities could both encourage and prod districts to carry out more specific curriculum alignment within the content parameters of the state direction in curriculum.

Third, state policy was intended to shape implementation assistance provided to districts and schools. In some cases, the assistance was to be in the form of state incentives for districts to establish mentor teacher programs or to establish other forms of staff development. In other cases, the state mandated aspects of the local implementation process such as the requirement that local administrators must be certified by their local school board as being competent to evaluate teachers. The state also funded a set of regional curriculum centers which, in turn, were to provide implementation assistance to local districts on specific aspects of the reform.

Finally, state policy initiatives and activity were likely to influence local accountability for the success of the reform process. Schools were provided with site-specific data on a set of state-defined 'quality indicators' that included, for example, patterns of student enrollment in academically demanding courses, test results on the state achievement test and the national advanced placement tests, and drop-out and attendance rates. The State Department of Education developed techniques for comparing schools having similar socio-demographic student characteristics and encouraged both professional educators and the public to examine these indicators of school success. The State Department also revised a school recognition program that identified and rewarded highly successful schools.

We needed to examine the nature of these influences at the district and school levels. To accommodate these possible state influences, our study had to focus on the influence of these macro level issues on the content of the local reform and its implementation in the local setting.

Focus on developmental v. redistributive programs

The reforms were clearly developmental in nature. They bolstered activities in which local educators already were involved. As noted above, state education reforms sought to improve curriculum, instruction and schools as organizations and that is precisely what local educators, to greater or lesser degree, always had emphasized. Formal implementation, according to Peterson *et al.*, should therefore be relatively quick, relatively uncontentious, and generally faithful to rules and regulations. Evidence from several California studies conducted just two years after SB 813 was enacted produced data indicating that the major reform components were being formally implemented and were in compliance with rules and regulations (PACE 1985, Grossman *et al.* 1985, Swain 1985, Kaye 1985). Using Peterson *et al.*'s typology, the education reform program in California behaved like a developmental, rather than a redistributive effort.

Consequently, in anticipation that districts and schools were proceeding to implement the reforms rather quickly, the conceptual framework for the study had to focus extensively on the implementation process itself. Moreover, since recent perspectives on policy implementation promoted the view that reform content, implementation process, and effects needed to be examined, the study had to anticipate that implementation might have proceeded sufficiently that the relationship of content, implementation process and effects could be fairly assessed.

Local implementation factors

Recent policy implementation research discussions (McLaughlin 1987) emphasized the importance of implementation factors in local settings and their relationships to policy initiatives. To examine local implementation factors, we used the literature on local change processes, especially Fullan (1985), Huberman and Miles (1984) and Crandall *et al.* (1986). Whereas policy implementation research has tended to be limited to the local adoption process, the local change research has focused on processes after adoption. We used Huberman and Miles' depiction of four implementation stages: adoption, early implementation, later implementation and institutionalization.

Our study design included specific factors that the local change literature had identified as important in these implementation processes. We grouped these factors into the above four stages of implementation. The factors that have received the most attention are:

Selection of a high quality, proven effective program: Many specific education programs have been developed for a variety of educational problems, and have been proven effective in a number of different contexts. For most school problems, there are programs 'out there' that could remedy the problem. Developing one's own program is time consuming and costly and runs the risk of producing a 'dud'; teachers develop commitment only when the program 'works'. Thus, using a high quality, proven effective program that 'fits' the local school problem is assumed to increase the likelihood of a successful change effort. Several aspects of SB 813 and subsequent state department initiatives could be studied under this heading.

Top-down v. bottom-up initiation: While it is helpful if teachers can be and are involved in the initiation process, top-down initiation also has been found in recent studies to work (Yin and White 1984). The risk associated with bottom-up initiation is that a problem area could be selected which does not match with central office or state priorities; indeed, many failures of the organizational development approach to change is that top managers often ignore the issues selected or identified by those at the 'bottom'. The risk with top-down initiation is that teachers may never commit to trying or working on the change program. Recent research (Huberman and Miles 1984) concludes that top-down initiation can work if the area targeted for improvement concerns core educational issues such as curriculum, improved teaching and improved student performance; is followed immediately by heavy teacher involvement in determining implementation specifics; is accompanied by lots of technical assistance throughout the change process; and produces expected impacts on teachers and students.

Central office support: However initiated, Fullan (1985) reports that successful change efforts need top level central office support to move into the complete implementation and institutionalization stages. This support needs to be both symbolic and technical. It needs to include the provision of resources – money, people and time – and on-going 'staying power'. A districtwide or at least district-supported, school-specific plan for implementation is needed. A central office program coordinator is another tangible sign of central office support. Since institutionalization requires organizational and district structural change, at least to some degree, top district support and commitment is needed.

Principal support and preparation: Fullan (1985) adds that site principals also need to be both supportive of and knowledgeable about the change effort. Principals need to know the content of the change effort and need to develop skills for their roles in implementing that effort. The two are different and strongly related. Principals manage schools, allocate scarce school resources and identify school priorities. Schools also need long term implementation plans to carry out a successful change effort. Again, to enter the complete implementation and institutionalization stages, top support of site administrators is key.

Cross-role teams: Huberman and Miles (1984) found that teachers must be heavily involved in all details of implementing educational change. They are the technical experts and it is their lives that are affected. Cross-role teams are committees of teachers, department heads, site administrators and central office staff that plan, coordinate and even help manage implementation activities. Cross-role teams not only develop teacher-teacher collegiality but also teacher-administrator collegiality. Both provide the informal tight coupling associated with successful change efforts. All studies identified teams of administrators and teachers which worked on the specifics of site implementation as critical to both short and long term success. If initiation is top-down, cross-role teams are even more important and must begin work immediately after the start decision.

Training and assistance: Recent studies (Joyce and Showers 1988, Crandall *et al.* 1986, Huberman and Miles 1984) report that major change does not occur successfully unless there is substantial training and long term assistance, both technical and psychological. The assistance can be provided from within the school, from the district central office or by consultants outside the school. High quality, up-front training in the techniques needed to begin implementation is important. Follow-through training, ongoing assistance, observation, feedback and coaching, however, are the sine qua non of successful change efforts. Without follow-through assistance, mastery of new instructional strategies is unlikely to occur, and teacher commitment thus will not emerge. Follow-through assistance and training should be at least two to three times that of up-front or initial training. The types of assistance and training should change over time as the change effort moves through the various stages/phases of implementation.

Continued top leadership, support and pressure: Huberman and Miles (1984) give extensive emphasis to the idea that 'sticking with' the uneventful details of long term implementation requires 'staying power' and pressure. Gaining new expertise requires the expenditure of effort by teachers. Initial enthusiasm often wanes after the euphoria of initial implementation and the reality of hard work becomes apparent. Thus, school leaders need to keep the pressure on to continue the program, need themselves to stay heavily involved in implementation efforts, and need to be liberal in the provision of the supports and assistance teachers need to develop skills mastery. This is a critical stage for most change efforts. This type of staying power is possibly sustained by complementary central office and site administrator press. This type of formal tight coupling gives consistent messages to teachers about the priority of the change effort and its fit with strategic directions of the district and school.

Press for fidelity of implementation v. mutual adaptation: Huberman and Miles (1984) warn that high quality, proven effective programs can be 'watered' down under the guise of 'mutual adaptation'. But, to be successful, i.e., to produce the intended effects on student performance, all critical elements of proven effective programs need to be implemented. Press for fidelity, thus, is a new element of successful change efforts. Adaptation occurs but more in how the program fits within the school or district system; mutual adaptation of the 'dummying down' variety is associated with less successful implementation and few intended impacts on students and teachers.

Teacher effort, skill-mastery and commitment: Guskey (1986) and Huberman and Miles (1984) challenge the conventional wisdom, including the Rand study, that held that teacher commitment must be built 'up-front' usually by involving teachers in identifying the change focus, in selecting the change program and in developing materials. The argument was that this initial involvement developed teacher commitment to the change program itself. More recent change research found that teacher commitment often emerged at the end of the implementation cycle, when teachers gained mastery over the strategies needed to implement the new program and saw that the program improved student performance. This research suggested that teacher commitment came *after* mastery and *after* teachers saw that the program 'worked'.

    While the findings seemed in conflict, they differed only at the margins. First, all studies identified *teacher commitment as absolutely necessary* to successful educational change efforts. At the time of the Rand study (Berman and McLaughlin 1978), there were very few high quality, proven effective programs so teacher up-front involvement in identifying topics to work on and in developing materials was crucial to initiating change efforts. But Rand also found that teacher skills mastery and positive program effects on students were necessary for complete implementation and institutionalization.

    There also were two different kinds of commitment: commitment to try the new program and commitment to the new program. *Commitment to try* needed to be developed up-front; without it, teachers would not become engaged in trying to implement the program. This type of commitment was probably built through awareness sessions on what the program was and in responding to teachers' personal concerns about how the program might affect them individually. *Commitment to the program* usually emerged at the end of the implementation process as teachers developed the expertise needed to implement the new program and see that it, indeed, resolved the problem to which it was applied, i.e., that it 'worked'.

Outcomes

Recent research on educational improvement (Crandall *et al.* 1983, Anderson *et al.* 1987, Berman *et al.* 1984, and Marsh and Bowman 1988) had found that successful efforts produced both individual and system impacts. An approach for studying education reform, then, should include outcomes for individuals within the system (teachers, administrators and students), for the curriculum program (what is taught in the system), and for the school itself (the social organization within which learning and teaching occur).

Drawing on this research and our analysis of the intent of California's reform, we identified a list of outcomes which were assessed for each school site. Our study design included student outcomes such as achievement gains in reading and mathematics, improvement in attendance rates, changes in the treatment of students within schools and gains on proficiency (basic skills) tests. Teacher outcomes included changes in teacher practice and attitudes such as extent of content knowledge, ability to teach a traditional curriculum program, expertise in teaching higher order thinking skills and sense of professional efficacy.

Outcomes also included changes in administrator practice and school climate. Administrative practice outcomes included the ability of site and district leaders to set a vision for continued reform, to manage change, to provide clinical supervision and to manage improvements in curriculum and instruction. School climate outcomes included improvements in the ability of school site staff to develop a shared sense of vision, collegiality and mutual trust, focus of teacher talk on curriculum and instruction and the ability to carry out a school improvement process.

The study and selected findings related to the research design[1]

A sample of seventeen secondary schools was studied – 12 high schools and 5 middle or junior high schools. Only schools that were actively working to improve and that exhibited significant increases in student enrollments in academic courses were selected. If schools were actually improving, then questions could be posed about 'why?' and whether Senate Bill 813 had any influence on the changes. In some districts, a senior and a junior high school were included in the sample. Attention was paid to districts, as well as individual schools, because of a presupposition that school board policies and central office management activites could prove to be one important component of school change. Junior high schools and middle schools were selected in order to encompass the range of secondary schooling.

The selection process produced schools that reflected the geographic and urban-rural diversity of the state. The 17 schools also reflected the cultural and ethnic diversity of secondary students in California, as well as the range of distribution of these students in schools across the state. So while the study selected a purposive sample in terms of response to reform, the sample had characteristics representative of the state's geographic and demographic diversity. The hope was that if effective school implementation processes emerged, then the process variables could help guide district and state leaders in structuring effective reform in other schools across the state.

Data collection

Research teams studied specific districts and schools. Each team collected data at several different times during the 1986-87 school year, spending a total of at least 11 days in the field for each school. Three mechanisms were used to gather data. Each research team collected documents and other data reflecting school and district activity. Each team interviewed dozens of individuals at the district and school levels. Last, each team observed the interactions of education professionals among each other and with students at both the district and school levels. These documents, interviews, and observations were carefully coded and analyzed in case studies that addressed a detailed set of substance and process issues.

The fall round of data collection and case reporting focused on state policy initiatives and local reform visions; the winter round focused on the local implementation process, including the role of state programs in this process, and on the special student populations dimension of the study; and the spring round focused on outcomes for student, teachers, administrators and the school as an organization. A team of one or two data collectors visited each site (district and school) to interview, observe and examine materials before preparing case material that focused on both the specific features and the gestalt of interactions at the site.

To develop a common conceptual framework for understanding the study objectives and the intellectual substance driving the study, a long briefing document was prepared that reviewed the relevant literatures and detailed the intellectual assumptions of the study. The October training meeting and the January analytic meeting devoted considerable time to analysis and discussion of this intellectual material.

For each round of data collection, vast amounts of qualitative and quantitative data were gathered that described both the 'trees' and 'forest' of the focus of that round of data collection.

State program implementation and local reform vision: For round one, each site researcher produced qualitative data that answered, for each of 14 state policies, a series of detailed questions about the policy as implemented in the school, the process of implementation, linkage to school/district vision and other state policies, and perceptions of the policy's purpose and substance by teachers and administrators; the field report averaged about 50 pages. In addition, each site researcher prepared a case study of the school's overall response to reform, which provided integration across the individual state policies, and state and school visions.

The local implementation process: For round two, each site researcher produced another large report which answered detailed questions about the 26 implementation factors in the conceptual framework, factors shown by other research to be important in successful education program implementation. These factors were arrayed in a conceptual sequence of cause and effect through the stages of implementation, so the data not only describe the factors individually but also their role in the context of an implementation process. In addition, another case study described the site's overall implementation themes and discussed how the factors interrelated to produce successful (or unsuccessful) implementation.

Outcomes: For round three, a range of outcome data were collected including student performance outcomes, outcomes for teachers and administrators, outcomes for the curriculum program and outcomes for the culture and other aspects of the school as a social organization. On a scale of 0 to 100, researchers provided a rating for 1982, the year before reform, and for 1987, four years after reform. The difference indicated the amount of change for the variable. On a score from 0 to 6, researchers also indicated the degree to which SB 813 contributed to the change, with a 3 indicating no SB 813 impact, a score below 3 indicating a negative impact and a score above 3 indicating a positive impact.

Programs for special populations: Finally, an additional series of data describe the operation of four special needs, student programs – remedial, compensatory, limited-English proficient and at-risk of dropping out – and how these programs were or were not integrated with the overall improvement initiatives.

Other quantitative, CAP test score, descriptive and socio-demographic data of the schools and districts were also collected. The final data base was large, rich, diverse and unique.[2]

Data analysis

Studies of the implementation process have traditionally been hampered by weak data analysis techniques. A major advancement in data analysis techniques was achieved by Miles and Huberman (1984). Their approach emphasized using site researcher knowledge and conducting and portraying the data analysis in terms of display charts. Thus, data analysis was pursued in two primary ways: (1) identifying tentative themes in the analytic meetings which then were confirmed in the subsequent analysis of case studies; and (2) conducting inductive analysis of the case studies themselves. Within the analytic meetings, group process procedures were used to identify tentative themes in the findings. These themes were expanded in subsequent analytic memos in several ways: (a) memos written by the core team to capture and extend the ideas generated in the meetings, and (b) memos written by individual data collectors about their specific sites in relation to the ideas developed in the analytic meetings.

The inductive analysis of the case survey material took place in several phases. For each site, case study material consisted of: (a) descriptions of the nature of each state policy as implemented at each site and district, (b) a global report focusing on the district/school vision and initial implementation of the locally defined reform, (c) local implementation factors and approaches discussed first individually by each factor and then by the gestalt of these factors, (d) the nature of local programs serving four types of special populations and the relationship of these programs to the reform effort, and (e) ratings of outcomes regarding school climate, administrative practice, teacher practice and student accomplishment. Because the case study material was well organized and labeled, no within-site analysis was needed prior to commencing the cross-site analysis.

In the first phase of the cross-site analysis, extensive low inference descriptive information was assembled using the same descriptors for each site. Sites appeared as the columns of the display and were ordered by size of district. The steps in preparing these charts included generating the descriptors, summarizing the information for each site using these descriptors, and confirming this analysis first by a second analyst and then by the site researcher. The second phase of the analysis consisted of reducing the descriptive information to a high inference rating (such as high, moderate, low). For example, a high inference rating was prepared for each of the implementation factors identified in the conceptual framework.

The final phase of the analysis began by clustering sites according to their ratings or performance on selected outcomes. For example, schools were clustered according to their gains in reading and math achievement as assessed by their CAP score differences between 1983 and 1987. Next, the high-inference ratings of the implementation process (from the second phase of the analysis) were displayed for each of the schools in each of the clusters. Finally, the charts were analyzed to identify implementation antecedents related to: (a) CAP score gain, (b) organizational capacity gain (the combination of school climate and administrative capacity gain), and (c) extensive implementation of Phase three reforms. The entire set of displays for the first, second and final phase of the analysis appear in the complete report (Odden and Marsh 1987).

Empirical findings

Findings from the study (Odden and Marsh 1987, Odden and Marsh 1988) confirm the power of the above approach to researching education reform implementation. First, we found that all the major SB 813 programs had been implemented in a manner consistent with state policy and regulation. The study design let us trace the process of district and school level implementation that led to this result. The rapid implementation rate confirms the importance of the distinction between developmental and redistributive programs and the need for the study design to show how development programs (such as current state education reform) can be implemented, in this case, quickly and compliantly.

Second, we found that the state vision influenced the content of the local reform effort and that the local vision itself was systemic and focused on the core curriculum and instruction program. District leaders transformed the state technical core of curriculum and instructional elements into integrated, district visions of reform. 'SB 813 certainly did not cause the reform, but it sure helped', said one local superintendent. District leaders used the state curriculum and instructional elements because they believed that these represented important and substantively sound content. They also felt ownership of the reform process because they had initiated at least some action before SB 813. Further, district leaders tailored the state reform to local needs and priorities without destroying its essence. The content of the resulting local vision was a much more integrated, substantively rigorous, technical core of curriculum and instruction than districts had prior to 1983, and included a greater academic orientation than previously had been the case. These findings illustrate why it was important for the study to address the content of the reform at both the state and local levels.

Third, we found that the new district academically-oriented and cognitively-demanding curriculum was balanced at the site by a complementary school vision that focused on climate and often emphasized concern for students, self-esteem, teacher collegiality, and social responsibility. The school vision often fit the demographic or local school environment and made the more academically-demanding district program possible to implement. This finding fits with the strong role of school climate in other effective secondary school research. The study approach let us trace how the content of the reform was transformed and expanded at the site level.

Fourth, the local implementation process was a dynamic interaction of local factors influenced by state policy initiatives and activities. For example, the reform tended to be *initiated* in a top-down manner, characterized by increased state and district centralization of curriculum development and textbook selection but then *implemented* with extensive site-level teacher and administrator participation. Districts, site administrators and teachers seemed to be 'teaming' in ongoing reform development and implementation. The study design let us examine the important dynamics of top-down leadership and bottom-up teacher involvement in the local implementation process.

Fifth, while teacher involvement in implementation was important, so too was administrative leadership. New and instructionally oriented superintendents and principals played key roles in reform initiation in most districts and schools. Department chairs also played key roles and were becoming more critical to implementation at the site level. Moreover, it was important that the district leadership role not just be 'upfront' in proposing the directions for the reform, but continue throughout the entire implementation process in the form of ongoing coordination, leadership, pressure, and monitoring. The study design specifically focused data collection and analysis on understanding the dynamics of the local implementation process itself.

Sixth, state policy initiatives and activities influenced this local implementation dynamic through mandates, incentives and assistance. The final report of the study (Odden and Marsh 1987) describes these influences on the local reform process in more detail but several unexpected findings are reported here. First, the state testing program (CAP) had a substantial influence on site program design and planning. All sample schools were sensitive to the importance of CAP tests to school and district public image. Most site personnel were aware of the shift in focus of the test toward higher order thinking and problem-solving skills as well as the inclusion of a direct writing sample in the test. More importantly, most sites were planning curriculum revisions to address the new focus of the CAP exam. We concluded that we had found numerous examples of how a creative test was stimulating schools to make progressive changes in their curriculum.

Another unexpected finding was the extent to which state implementation assistance was also being transformed by the local reform agenda. For example, in the several years after 1983, the mentor teacher program in a district often had a diffuse focus. Individual mentors created and carried out isolated projects that typically had little lasting impact. More recently, district leaders have used the mentors in more strategic ways to assist in implementing major components of the district reform effort.

Finally, the study design allowed us to identify patterns of positive findings relating reform content and implementation process elements to various outcomes. For example, some sites made considerably more CAP score gains and/or had greater increases in their capacity for continuing the reform than did other of the sites studied. For both of these outcomes, higher gain sites had implementation patterns emphasizing elements portrayed by the conceptual framework such as: (1) clear and consistent district reform visions focused on improving basic skills; (2) more active use of cross-role teams and implementation plans; (3) stronger implementation coordination between the school and the district and among the departments in the schools; (4) greater use of initial training; (5) active administrator pressure and monitoring; (6) substantially more on-going assistance, both from district and school leaders; (7) stronger on-going administrative commitment and leadership; and (8) tight coupling between schools and their districts. Further, teacher effort, skill mastery and commitment at high gain schools were dramatically different than at low gain schools. The high gain schools had consistently high or modest ratings for teacher effort, skill mastery and commitment. In turn, low gain schools had consistently modest or low levels of teacher effort, skill mastery, and commitment. Importantly, high gain sites were not different from other sites in terms of school or student demographic variables.

Conclusions

We began by suggesting that stage three implementation research, especially for state education reform, should focus on the micro-implementation process, linkages between macro- and micro-implementation factors, and on the relationships between program content, local process variables, and impacts and effects. Our study followed those suggestions and used a research approach that let us: (1) learn about the content of reform and how state, district and site content elements interrelated; (2) learn about the dynamics of the local implementation process itself including the key elements of local implementation and how those local elements affected the extent of implementation of the various content elements; and (3) identify a range of effects – on students, teachers, administrators and schools as organizations – of both content and process variables.

The study results seem to support the usefulness of such a research approach. First, the study provides extensive detail on the content of reform at the state, district and site levels.

The study shows very clearly what 'it' was that local districts and schools implemented. Further, the study shows how the fragmentation of the state education reform package (a major problem noted by many analysts) was integrated into a cohesive and comprehensive curriculum and instruction vision that fit the local context, and how the schools then added cultural and climate components to this reform agenda. The results show, therefore, the need to analyze what reform is at the state, district and site level in order to determine whether apparent incoherence at the state level is an insurmountable problem or is transformed locally into something more powerful and organized, which generally occurred in the schools this study investigated. Further, the results show that while culture is important to local school improvement, both its definition and creation is a site issue and remains a site issue even when the substantive content is defined at levels above the site. Last, the study shows how the content of local reform is changing, and at least for the schools studied, seems to be moving beyond state defined content and into more complex curriculum and instruction including emphasis on thinking/problem solving skills and deeper content understandings.

Second, the study shows how several components of the local implementation process interact and complement each other. For example, the study shows how top-down initiation at the state, district and site levels was balanced by bottom-up involvement of teachers through cross-role teams active in the implementation process. As such, the study begins to outline the dimensions of appropriate system (district and school) leadership and teacher involvement, and how the two inter-relate. The findings suggest that both system leadership and teacher involvement are crucial, not either one or the other. Finally, the study shows how several important local process variables interact over time in a 'causal network of variables' to bring local reform visions to full implementation.

Third, the study documents implementation impacts beyond just improved student performance on achievement tests. While students in the schools studied improved their test scores at rates above the state average, the study also found positive impacts on teachers, administrators and schools as organizations. To those who felt student achievement gains might have to be 'traded-off' for teacher, administrator and organizational gains, the study found just the opposite. Further, the study found that the same local content and process factors that led to the greatest student achievement score gains also led to the greatest organizational and administrator expertise gains.

In addition, for those concerned that equity might be overrun in the new pursuit of excellence and tougher academic standards, the study also found that the needs of special student populations – the low achiever, the poor, the limited-English proficient (LEP) and the potential dropout – were being addressed by schools and districts. Indeed, the trend in the study seemed to be an increase in both the degree of services and the types of approaches used to provide them.

In addition, nearly all special student program goals were to move students into the mainstream. While there was variation in accomplishing these goals, the goals were to remedy academic deficiencies in order to equip students to function successfully in a regular curriculum program. Special program services tended to focus on basic skills of reading and mathematics, and usually did not include alternative pedagogical approaches to teaching higher level thinking skills. But, the curriculum in most special-needs programs had been aligned with the regular, core curriculum of the school, and had increased substantively in academic rigor, even though it was still somewhat less rigorous and demanding than the regular program. The students still may be at-risk, therefore, but they are receiving programs and services and are not being ignored.

Finally, the study documented an evolving reform agenda that is more complex than the traditional issues addressed in SB 813 and most other state education reforms. Most of the districts and schools studied were beginning to engage in more fundamental curriculum reform, with an emphasis on deeper content and higher level thinking skills, including new instructional strategies; further, this new curriculum was being proposed for all students, not just the top students. It is quite likely that successful implementation strategies for this new agenda will be different from those for traditional education reform. In particular, while the top-down nature of the 1983 varieties of education reform might have worked with teachers primarily involved in implementation specifics through cross-role teams, those specific mechanisms might not work with this more complex curriculum. Restructured curriculum, restructured schools and transforming teaching into a full profession, which seems to be today's reform agenda, might *by definition* need more decentralization and deregulation, and fewer top down mandates. The good news is that education reform content appears to be evolving to a more complex level. Successful implementation processes for this agenda, however, might be quire different from those found in this study.

Notes

1. A detailed description of the study, its methods and findings is available in Odden and Marsh (1987).
2. Several strategies were used to ensure that the data were of sufficient quality and were comparable across sites:

   1. use of very specific and uniform data collection instruments;
   2. obtaining data from a site both in terms of specific, highly-directive questions and topics, and in terms of more global, less-directive questions;
   3. use of multiple rounds of data collection;
   4. extensive data collector training that included procedures and formats for writing up the information.

   Additionally, post-data collection analytic meetings were held where data collectors pooled insights and refined their descriptions of local sites. All data collectors met for two-day analytic meetings in January after the first round of data collection in June after all data had been collected. An additional meeting of the PACE principals involved in the study was held in April. In several instances, all data collectors were asked to provide additional information about a specific topic, or to generate high-inference ratings for newly defined variables. The effect of these combined strategies was to greatly increase the quality and comparability of data from the sites.

References

ANDERSON, B. ODDEN, A. FARRAR, E. FUHRMAN, S. DAVIS, A. HUDDLE, E. ARMSTRONG, J. and FLAKUS-MOSQUEDA, P. (1987) 'State strategies to support local school improvement', *Knowledge: Creation, Diffusion and Utilization*, pp. 42–86.

BALDRIDGE, J. V. and DEAL, J.V. (eds.) (1975) *Managing Change in Educational Organizations* (Berkeley, CA: McCutchan).

BARRO, S. (1978) 'Federal education goals and policy instruments: an assessment of the "Strings" attached to categorical grants in education', in M. Timpane (ed.) *The Federal Interest in Financing Schools* (Santa Monica, CA: Rand Corporation).

BERMAN, P. (1978) 'The study of macro- and micro-implementation', *Public Policy*, 26 (2) pp. 157–184.

BERMAN, P. and MCLAUGHLIN, M. (1978) *Federal Programs Supporting Educational Change* (8 vols.) (Santa Monica, CA: Rand Corporation).

BERMAN, P. GJELTEN, T. CSEZAK, C. IZU, J. and MARSH, D. D. (1984) *Improving School Improvement: The Final Report of the Statewide Study of the California School Improvement Program*. Vol. II: Findings (Berkeley, CA: Berman, Weiler and Associates).

CRANDALL, D. AND ASSOCIATES (1983) *People, policies and practices: The chain of school improvement*, vol. 1–10 (Andover, MA: The Network).

CRANDALL, D. EISEMAN, J. W. and SEASHORE LOUIS, K. (1986) 'Strategic planning issues that bear on the success of school improvement efforts', *Educational Administration Quarterly*, 22 (3) pp. 21–53.

CUBAN, L. (1984) 'School reform by remote control: SB 813 in California', *Phi Delta Kappan*, 66 (3), pp. 213–215.

DERTHICK, M. (1976) 'Washington: angry citizens and an ambitious plan', In W. Williams and R. Elmore, (eds.) *Social Program Implementation* (New York: Adademic Press).

DOYLE, D. and HARTLE, T. (1985) *Excellence in Education: The States Take Charge* (Washington, DC American Enterprise Institute).

EDUCATION COMMISSION OF THE STATES (1983) *Action for Excellence* (Denver, CO: ECS).

EDUCATION COMMISSION OF THE STATES (1984) *Action in the States* (Denver, CO: ECS).

ELMORE, R. (1979-80) 'Backward mapping: implementation research and policy decisions', *Political Science Quarterly*, 94 (4), pp. 601–616.

ELMORE, R. and McLAUGHLIN, M. (1981) 'Strategic choice in federal policy: the compliance-assistance tradeoff', in A. Lieberman and M. McLaughlin (eds.) *Policymaking in Education* (Chicago: University of Chicago Press).

ELMORE, R. and McLAUGHLIN, M. (1983) 'The federal role in education: learning from experience', *Education and Urban Society*, 15 (3), pp. 309–330.

FARRAR, E. and MILSAP, M. A. (1986) *State and Local Implementation of Chapter I* (Cambridge, MA: ABT Associates).

FULLAN, M. (1982) *The Meaning of Educational Change* (New York: Teachers College Press).

FULLAN, M. (1985) 'Change processes and strategies at the local level', *The Elementary School Journal*, 85(3), pp. 391–421.

GROSSMAN, P. KIRST, M. NEGASH, W. and SCHMIDT-POSNER, J. (1985) *Curricular Change in California Comprehensive High Schools: 1982–83 to 1984–85* (Berkeley, CA: University of California PACE).

GUSKEY, T. (1986) 'Staff development and the process of teacher change', *Educational Researcher*, 15 (5) pp. 5–12.

HARGROVE, E. (1983) 'The search for implementation theory', in R. J. Keckhauser and D. Leebaert, (eds.) *What Role For Government?* (Durham, NC: Duke University Press).

HUBERMAN, M. and MILES, M. (1984) *Innovation Up Close* (New York: Plenum).

INGRAM, H. (1977) 'Policy implementation through bargaining: the case of federal grants-in-aid', *Public Policy*, 25 (4), pp. 499–526.

JOYCE, B. and SHOWERS, B. (1988) *Staff Development for Student Achievement* (New York: Longman).

JUNG, R. and KIRST, M. (1986) 'Beyond mutual adaptation, into the bully pulpit: recent research on the federal role in education', *Education Administration Quarterly*, 22 (3), pp. 80–109.

KAYE, L. (1985) *Making the Grade? Assessing School Districts' Progress on SB 813* (Sacramento: California Tax Foundation).

KENNEDY, M. BIRMAN, B. and DEMALINE, R. (1986) *The Effectiveness of Chapter I Services* (Washington, DC: US Department of Education).

KIRST, M. and JUNG, R. (1980) 'The utility of a longitudinal approach in assessing implementation', *Educational Evaluation and Policy Analysis*, 2 (5), pp. 17–34.

KNAPP, M. *et al.* (1983) 'Cumulative effects at the local level', *Education and Urban Society*, 15, (4), pp. 479–499.

KNAPP, M. and STEARNS, M. (1986) 'Improving systemwide performance: evaluation research and the state education reform programs', in J. Wholey, M. Abramson and C. Bellavita (eds.) *Performance and Credibility: Developing Excellence in Public and Non Public Organizations* (Lexington, MA: Lexington Books).

McDONNELL, L. and ELMORE, R. (1987) 'Getting the job done: alternative policy instruments', *Educational Evaluation and Policy Analysis*, 9 (2), pp. 133–152.

McDONNELL, L. and FUHRMAN, S. (1985) 'The political context of reform', in V. Mueller and M. McKeown (eds.) *The Fiscal, Legal, and Political Aspects of State Reform of Elementary and Secondary Education* (Cambridge, MA: Ballinger).

McLAUGHLIN, M. and MARSH, D. (1978) 'Staff development and school change', *Teachers College Record*, 80, pp. 69–93.

McLAUGHLIN, M. (1987) 'Learning from experience: lessons from policy implementation', *Educational Evaluation and Policy Analysis*, 9 (2), pp. 171–178.

MARSH, D. D. and BOWMAN, G. A. (1988) 'Building better secondary schools: a comparison of school improvement and school reform strategies in california', a paper presented at the annual meeting of the American Educational Research Association, New Orleans.

MILES, M. and HUBERMAN, M. (1984) *Qualitative Data Analysis* (Beverly Hills, CA: Sage).

MOORE, M. GOERTZ, M. and HARTLE, T. (1983) 'Interaction of federal and state programs', *Education and Urban Society*, 15 (4), pp. 453–478.

MURPHY, J. (1971) 'Title I of ESEA: the politics of implementing federal education reform', *Harvard Educational Review*, 41 (1), pp. 35–63.

NATIONAL COMMISSION ON EXCELLENCE IN EDUCATION (1983) *A Nation at Risk* (Washington, DC: GPO).

NATIONAL GOVERNORS ASSOCIATION (1986) *Time for Results: The Governors' 1991 Report on Education* (Washington, DC: NGA).

ODDEN, A. (1986a) 'When votes and dollars mingle: a first analysis of state reforms', *Politics of Education Bulletin*, 13 (2), pp. 3–8.

ODDEN, A. (1986b) 'How fiscal accountability and program quality can be insured for Chapter I', chapter prepared for a forthcoming book on new Chapter I policies.

ODDEN, A. (1987) 'State funding changes in the 1980', paper presented at the annual meeting of the American Educational Research Association, Washington, DC.

ODDEN, A. and MARSH, D. (1987) *How State Education Reform Can Improve Secondary Schools* (Berkeley, CA: University of California/PACE).

ODDEN, A. and MARSH, D. (1988) 'How comprehensive education reform can improve secondary schools', *Phi Delta Kappan*, 69 (7).

PETERSON, P. (1983) 'Did the education commissions say anything?' *The Brookings Review*, 3–11.

PETERSON, P. RABE, B. and WONG, K. (1986) *When Federalism Works* (Washington, DC: The Brookings Institution).

PRESSMAN, J. and WILDAVSKY, A. (1973) *How Great Expectations in Washington are Dashed in Oakland, or Why It's Amazing that Federal Programs Work at All* (Berkeley, CA: University of California Press).

POLICY ANALYSIS FOR CALIFORNIA EDUCATION (1985) *Conditions of Education in California: 1985* (Berkeley, CA: University of California/PACE).

SABATIER, P. and MAZMANIAN, D. (1979) 'The conditions of effective implementation: a guide to accomplishing policy objectives', *Policy Analysis*, 5, pp. 481–504.

SWAIN, C. (1985) *SB 813 and Tenth Grade Counseling: A Report on Implementation* (Berkeley, CA: University of California/PACE).

YIN, R. K. and WHITE, J. L. (1984) *Microcomputer Implementation in Schools* (Washington, DC: Cosmos Corporation).

5   State politics and education reform*

Susan H. Fuhrman
Center for Policy Research in Education, Rutgers University

The 1980s have been characterized as the decade of state education reform. Every state considered policies intended to increase academic rigor, improve the quality of the teaching force, and enhance knowledge about student performance. Most states enacted policies that entailed more state specification about curriculum, teacher credentialling and the assessment of student outcomes. Education was the most salient state political issue in the mid years of the decade; it dominated governors' state of the state messages between 1984 and 1988 and appropriated legislative agendas in those same years.

The amount of state activity related to education was so impressive and unprecedented that it is tempting to assume that the current reform movement is entirely unique. Never before had states made so many changes of education policy in such a short period of time. Certain facets of the movement, such as its sheer momentum and the rapidity with which various elements spread from state to state, so distinguish it from previous spurts of state-level education reform that it appears to resist analysis based on our knowledge of traditional state education politics (McDonnell and Fuhrman 1986). Specifically, it seems that this reform movement is peculiarly national in nature. The variation from state to state that so characterizes state politics and policymaking appears dwarfed by the similarities among states in the reform policies and process.

This article analyzes the process of reform and implementation in six states – Arizona, California, Florida, Georgia, Minnesota and Pennsylvania – arguing that state political culture and history are as important to the course of reform as previous research on state politics would lead us to believe. While the similarities from state to state are striking, the progress of reform policies is best understood in the framework of each state's history and culture. After a discussion of the aspects of the reform movement that make it appear uniquely national in nature, I briefly review the literature asserting the importance of state context in shaping policy and the policy process. I then turn to the reforms in the six states and examine the influence of context on the process that produced the reforms, the nature of specific reform policies and their initial implementation experience.

*This research was conducted as part of a five-year study of state-level reform conducted by the Center for Policy Research in Education (CPRE). CPRE is a consortium of Rutgers University. Michigan State University, Stanford University and the University of Wisconsin-Madison, funded by the Office of Educational Research and Improvement (OERI-G0008690011-88) to study state and local policies to improve schooling. This article draws on interviews and analyses conducted by the author and colleagues at Rutgers, the RAND Corporation and the University of Wisconsin between April 1986 and February 1988. State and local policymakers and practitioners in the six states, 24 districts and 59 schools were interviewed. The author acknowledges with gratitude the many insights contributed by colleagues who visited the various sites. However, the opinions expressed are those of the author and are not necessarily shared by CPRE or the US Department of Education.

The national nature of the reform movement

Several characteristics of the current reform movement suggest reason to expect considerable consistency from state to state in reform policies and policymaking. The targets of reform were common across states and there were noticeable patterns in the process that produced them.

First, the current reforms respond to an explicit national agenda. *A Nation at Risk* and the other reform reports enumerated the key themes of the reform movement: the link between education and economic productivity; the danger that American schools and students had gone 'soft' and the imperative for everyone in the system to work harder. Policymakers were exhorted to shore up student standards, particularly at the secondary school level; to tighten entry to the teaching profession; to lengthen the time spent in school; and to reward teacher and student performance. The commission reports diagnosed the problem and prescribed the treatment with some very specific suggestions about curricular and other reforms. The reports boosted the efforts of states that had already begun the process of increasing standards and revising teacher certification and encouraged others to start down the same road. They gave legitimacy to a set of policy options that became the currency of the reform movement.

Some of the policies suggested by the reports became so popular as to be virtually universal. For example, 45 states modified requirements for high school graduation, predominantly by increasing the total number and adding to specific requirements. Over three-fourths of the states increased math and science requirements, for example. Between 1980 and 1986, 19 states imposed a competency test requirement for admission to teacher education programs. In the same period, 29 states mandated an assessment prior to certification. By 1986, 46 states required one or the other, or both, types of teacher assessment (Darling-Hammond and Berry 1988). New student testing programs were also very common. Thirty-one new state testing programs began in the 1980s; and, between 1988 and 1990, 11 new programs will start. Only two states have no state-level testing program or provision (CCSSO 1988).

Not only did many states adopt similar policies, there were certain aspects of the reform process that were also parallel. In most states, for example, legislatures and governors played leading initiating roles. With the backing of business leaders, governors established commissions to devise reform recommendations; key legislators translated the recommendations into legislation and packaged the policies to aggregate support. Legislatures and governors, again typically with support from important business interests, came up with the resources to supplement state aid so that increases averaged 21% in the reform period (Odden 1987). Even in states where reform was accomplished more through regulation than legislation, state boards were encouraged in their efforts by knowledge of legislative and gubernatorial interest or by anxiety about legislative preemption. Chief state school officers sometimes made fundamental intellectual contributions, but did not typically exert public leadership or spark the reform efforts.

The leadership of general government was a common factor that crossed the states. So was the relatively unimportant role of education interest groups. Teacher associations were generally reactive. While often opposed to specific aspects of the new reforms, such as differentiated pay plans, or agnostic about others, such as increased student standards, they also knew that the reforms had strong public and elite support and that they were likely to be accompanied by increased state aid. They concentrated on modifying the elements they most opposed, but even that resistance was conducted quietly (McDonnell and Pascal 1988).

Similarly, groups representing administrators and school boards played secondary roles aimed at blunting aspects of the reforms seen as detrimental to local control. As associations they were represented on reform commissions and testified at hearings but did not feel influential. Individual administrators who chose to be proactive did what they could to assure that the state reforms would complement or support local initiatives (Fuhrman *et al.* 1988). But the associations were hampered by the need to represent all districts, including those that were way out ahead of new state reforms as well as those who would have difficulty addressing them.

Evidence about the popularity of certain reform policies combines with the recognition of similarities in the political landscape to create a sense of uniformity about the reform movement. It is tempting to focus on the parallels and consider this reform movement exempt from the variation that typically characterizes state politics. However, the literature on state context suggests a different conclusion: state context strongly shapes the process, nature and implementation of policies.

The importance of political context

The unique political context of each state is a distinct theme of research on state politics. Students of state politics are prone to assert that each state is different, in some senses a nation unto itself. The depth of this belief is exhibited by the words of the editors of a recent volume of state case studies who apologize for profiling political life in only 12 states: 'selecting fewer than all 50 states leaves something to be desired' (Rosenthal and Moakley 1984).

In analyzing the nature of the variation among states, many political scientists have embraced the notion of political culture. The concept has been variously defined but there is loose agreement on its major dimension: the orientation of citizens to government, including their basic expectations from and responses to authority (Almond 1956, Verba 1965, Patterson 1968). Elazar's application of political culture to states is perhaps the best-known use of the idea. He identifies and classifies states by three ideal types and hybrids: individualistic, where professional politicians dominate and government is limited; moralistic, where citizens believe in and turn to government to solve their problems; and traditionalistic, where an elite aimed at preserving tradition prevails (Elazar 1972).

The effect of political culture is widespread. It influences the kinds of people who seek and attain leadership roles; the manner in which people engage in leadership; the extent and nature of participation in politics; the nature of political parties and interest groups; and the distribution of authority and influence between branches, the public and private sector and the state and localities (Rosenthal and Moakley 1984). It can also produce policy differences. For example, political variables related to culture, such as state-local centralization, have been shown to influence expenditures on various state functions, independently of state economic factors (Sharkansky 1967).

Context, including political culture, is an important theme of research on policy implementation. For example, analysts have concluded that it is not fruitful to examine the implementation of programs or projects in isolation; they must be seen as part of the broader system. The supports, incentives and constraints that reside in the policy system influence the capacity and motivation of implementors (McLaughlin 1987).

Analysts of state education politics and policy have also recognized the significance of political context. The strength of local control norms, citizen support for public education and public support of equity goals affect the state role in the implementation of federal programs and state special need programs (McDonnell and McLaughlin 1980). Context, as defined as the distribution of power and the structure and function of various branches, agencies and groups, exerts a key influence on the state choice of mandates, inducements or other strategies to influence local behavior (McDonnell and Elmore 1987, McDonnell 1987).

In sum, the research on state politics in general and on education politics in particular sends a clear message. Political beliefs and behaviors vary significantly among the states. Those convictions and activities in turn shape the development and nature of policy including the translation of policy into practice. No two states are likely to have identical experiences. While patterns exist, variation in policy and process persists.

State context and reform

The six states reported on here were the subjects of a major five-year study of the implementation and effects of reforms in the area of student standards and curriculum and policies on teacher certification, retention and compensation. Arizona, California, Florida, Georgia, Minnesota and Pennsylvania were chosen because, in addition to representing regional differences, they also represented a range in both the scope and amount of reform undertaken as well as in their use of mandates, inducements and other strategies to address reform issues. Because we could observe specific reforms in different combinations in these states, we hoped to be able to untangle the effects of particular strategies. The sample was not chosen to provide examples of distinctive political cultures. However, the influence of state context on the progress of reform is so strong that, not surprisingly, by searching for states with different approaches to reform, we ended up with states that vary strongly in their political orientations and behaviors.[1]

In the following sections I examine the influence of political context on the process, nature and implementation of reforms in the six states. Specifically, I examine the fit between the process of reform and traditional political patterns related to the scope of policy activity, the participation of various actors, and the balance of power between the branches of government. I then turn to the specific reform policies in the states and explore the political factors, such as state trust in local officials, that influenced the particular strategies chosen. Finally I consider initial findings about the implementation of the reforms and indicate how politically-defined patterns of state and local capacity and influence are affecting the experience of reform policies.

State context and reform process

Despite the national momentum bolstering the reform movement, the manner in which the current reforms were fashioned in each of the study states is entirely consistent with and reflective of traditional education politics, and politics more generally, in those states. Those states which habitually resorted to large scale policy fixes continued that tactic; others who normally act more incrementally persisted in doing so. States that generally experience widespread participation by a variety of interests continued that pattern. The balance of power between branches of government that had developed over the years since reapportionment and the professionalization of legislatures and gubernatorial offices was evident in the current reforms, despite the tendency for both legislatures and governors to play a leadership role.

California's most visible reform effort was a major 1983 legislative package, Senate Bill 813. SB813 was a huge legislative parcel that incorporated over 80 separate reform items, including a mentor teacher and alternative route program, state graduation requirements and provision for state board definition of student competencies, incentives for a longer school day, increased beginning teacher salaries, and reforms in personnel management that made it easier to dismiss and transfer teachers. The bill was a 'big fix' that echoed earlier large-scale legislative initiatives, such as compensatory education legislation in 1964, early childhood education in 1972, school finance reform in 1972 and 1977, and school improvement in 1979. Like those earlier initiatives, the legislation exhibits the California legislature's penchant for innovation and for activism. The process of developing SB813 also manifests other aspects of California legislative politics: the tendency for ideas to develop quietly among sophisticated legislative staffers and members, often in consultation with key professional lobbyists who have longevity and expertise, and the emergence of skilled leadership within the legislature that orchestrates the reforms, grafting programs together so as to create a supportive coalition. In addition, a state surplus made it possible to inject money into a badly-under-funded system that was suffering from the combined effects of Proposition 13 tax limitation and the national recession. As in the past in California, money provided the immediate impetus for reform as well as the glue that held an omnibus package together (Elmore and McLaughlin 1982). In fact, the only major difference between the politics of SB813 and previous legislative reforms was the relative unimportance of educational interest groups. The major interests had formed a loose coalition that smoothed the way for school finance reform in the 1970s, submerging potential disagreements between wealthy and less wealthy districts and urban and non-urban districts. In the case of SB813, the groups were more reactive and considerably less pivotal.

The political scene in California is complex and crowded – dozens of staff, analysts, lobbyists, and interests vie for influence (Kirst 1981, Fuhrman and McDonnell 1985). In such a setting it is not surprising that SB813, as large as it was, is only part of the reform story, and maybe not the most important part.

Simultaneously, and using SB813 as leverage to the extent possible, Superintendent of Public Instruction Honig is leading an effort to align state-level testing, textbook selection and model curriculum standards around more rigorous academic content. Honig's grassroots campaign for office on the platform of school reform provided momentum for SB813 and his subsequent skillful public leadership on the issue of excellence has enhanced the potential of reform efforts. Many states have elected chief state school officers but in few are they as politically influential. Certainly Honig and his predecessor Wilson Riles have amplified the leadership potential of the office, but the position in and of itself carries significant promise. California's diversity, massive electorate and weak party system boost the importance of any state-wide elected official; only those who develop state-wide recognition are able to amass a sufficient power base to run for governor (Bell 1984). As a potential political threat to the governor, the chief state school officer has considerable sway.

Florida's reform was primarily a legislative effort, one that followed in the path of numerous previous legislative reforms, at the rate of about one major effort a session. Florida's legislature has dominated state education policymaking since the early 1970s. It has actively sought leadership, wresting initiative from the state department of education and passing programs that place the somewhat reluctant department in a more aggressive stance vis a vis local districts (Turnbull 1981). For example, in 1972, the legislature revised the school code. In 1973 it established a new school financing scheme which incorporated an equalization plan and a method for weighing pupils according to various educational needs. The legislature granted teachers the right to bargain collectively in 1974 and then turned to early childhood education in 1975. The Educational Accountability Act of 1976 established statewide assessment standards, student progression standards and a high school basic skills exit exam. In 1977 a compensatory education program was developed to provide remediation for those students having difficulty in meeting the standards established by the accountability act. At the close of the decade, the legislature turned back to personnel issues, addressing teacher certification and the method in which teachers were disciplined.

Like these previous undertakings, the development of the 1983 comprehensive education reform depended heavily on the leadership of the presiding officers of the House and the Senate. Speaker Lee Moffitt and Senate President Curtis Peterson each developed major sections of the package. The legislation's new initiatives in math, science and computer education derived from a task force established by Moffitt; increased graduation requirements as well as a provision for an extended day were first included in a bill called RAISE that Peterson, working with a long-time Senate education leader, Jack Gordon, had written. Despite rotating leadership, the Speaker and Senate President are powerful figures. They appoint all committee chairmen, including the rules chairmen who control bill flow, and refer all bills to committee. Because the majority caucus chooses future leaders in advance, as 'designates', leadership can work with their successors to shape future activities. Unlike many other states where party leaders defer entirely to education committee chairmen or other legislative education experts, the Florida presiding officers have played key roles in shaping education policy and in developing consensus that bridges the deep divisions, particularly between urban and rural interests, that characterize state politics (St Angelo 1984).

The Governor of Florida, Robert Graham, was also a key actor in the evolution of the 1983 reform. It was a Graham commission that recommended much of what the Senate later incorporated into the RAISE bill; he also championed the master teacher program feature of the reform. Graham's activity can be traced to his own leadership in the field of education when he served in the legislature. In fact, so important is the legislature's leadership role in education that it functions as an incubator for education leaders throughout Florida government. Both the previous and current elected commissioners of education were legislative education leaders; numerous top department of education positions have gone to legislative staffers (Turnbull 1981).

Georgia is another state that embarked on large-scale reform. Three factors about the process that led to the 1985 Quality Basic Education Act (QBE) are particularly reflective of Georgia politics in recent years. The first is that, like previous efforts to reform education from the state level, QBE was the product of gubernatorial initiative. The two major reform attempts prior to QBE, the Minimum Foundation Program of Governor Sanders and Jimmy Carter's Adequate Program for Education in Georgia were gubernatorially-initiated programs that attempted to tie school finance reform to substantive education changes. Both earlier assays failed for lack of funding, but they shaped expectations about education reform in Georgia. Georgians tend to anticipate little from government, expecting to work out their own problems in the private sector or through individual initiative. However, when an issue gets defined as a matter meriting state attention, the governor can be expected to play a major role. Georgia's governor may not look extremely strong on paper (only since 1976 can governors succeed themselves), but governors control the budget process and can dominate legislative deliberations through the use of floor leaders and through party allegiance in this predominantly one-party state.

Governor Harris set about education reform by establishing a commission, the Education Review Commission, to study developments in other states as well as the findings of education research and to recommend changes. The group was headed by corporate leaders and its deliberations were permeated by business concern about improving Georgia's competitive position and making schools attractive to corporate executives of firms that might choose to locate in Georgia. Business dominance would be expected in a state where the importance of multi-national companies to the economic and political scene grows steadily. Atlanta is home to several corporate giants, such as Coca-Cola, Southern Bell and Turner Broadcasting, whose influence accounts for all the attention to 'reform' in a state not previously known for its innovative spirit.

The development of QBE reflects Georgia's own unique political makeup in a third way. Although there was considerable behind-the-scenes vote soliciting and trading, QBE as embodied in the Commission's recommendations was shepherded through the legislature without amendment and passed unanimously. Such consensus politics is typical of Georgia where there is as much maneuvering, bargaining and compromise as anywhere but where it goes on largely out of the public eye. Perhaps, as Hepburn (1984) has suggested, the emphasis on consensus provides essential glue in a system so potentially ripe for schism. Georgia's deep racial, economic and geographic divisions could paralyze government if policymakers did not seek methods of minimizing conflict.

In contrast to California, Florida and Georgia, Pennsylvania is a state that attempted more incremental reform. It increased graduation requirements and stiffened the criteria for teacher certification through regular, periodic revision of the state code and avoided any big legislative fixes. The incremental approach and the dominance of reform by the state board regulatory process has several roots. Pennsylvania considers itself a very strong local control state and is loathe to undertake strong state-level initiatives. Policymakers also prefer to let the state board make changes in state code; they profess that regulation permits more flexibility than statute. The governor has particularly strong influence over the board as the chief state school officer is a political appointee who is part of his cabinet. Legislative comfort with state board activity was significantly enhanced after legislative chairs were included as members of that board and after legislative review of regulation was instituted earlier in the decade. Now the legislature tends to act as somewhat of a court of appeals (Katz 1981). When local districts, groups or interests are unhappy with state board action, or pending action, they petition the legislature. For example, in the case of graduation requirements, a bill to raise standards was introduced during the state board deliberations. The pending legislation encouraged the state board to act; when regulations encompassing most of bill's elements were adopted, the bill was dropped.

Arizona is another state that approached reform more incrementally. Its fundamentally conservative nature makes it hesitant about change, especially large-scale change. State politics are often about keeping the state role from growing, from impinging on the private sector economic development that has blossomed without intrusive state regulation (Peirce and Hagstrom 1983). Consequently, the state legislature did not pass Governor Babbitt's comprehensive education reform proposal, a 1984 package that combined increased funding for all levels of education, including post-secondary, with reforms like full-day kindergarten. The legislature had begun to deal with teacher quality issues in the early 1980s, first introducing and gradually expanding teacher testing, then eliminating the undergraduate education major for secondary teachers, then amending tenure to permit dismissal of teachers with due process. In 1985, it turned to the development of a career ladder. The progress of the career ladder reflects several aspects of the Arizona political scene: the more progressive stance of the State Senate; particularly the then Education Chair, Anne Lindeman, who drew on research and experience in other states to develop the program; the resistance of the rest of the legislature to making more education policy and particularly to spending more on education without ties to quality; the inability of the teacher's association to mount effective opposition in this essentially anti-union, non-collective bargaining state; and the governor's frustration about failure to increase state education spending. The career ladder was probably Arizona's most significant education reform, although proposed changes, such as vesting certification with local districts, may be more far-reaching.

Finally, Minnesota did not jump on the national reform bandwagon. It took its own unique approach to the educational problems other states were addressing through graduation requirements by concentrating on introducing choice through a post-secondary, and eventually, a high school, options program, and instituting improved performance measures. Minnesota's efforts reflect two salient features of its education politics: the tendency to allow local districts substantial leeway and the dominance of the legislature. The first feature accounts for Minnesota's limited use of regulation at the state level. Reluctance to constrain local behavior relates both to enormous pride in the achievement of its students who rank very highly in all measures of performance and attainment and to widespread trust in the good intentions and capacity of local officials. Minnesotans traditionally see government as a vehicle for achieving good; the early trust that was spawned in comfortable Northern Protestant homogeneity was rewarded by years of leadership that responded to the needs and problems of laborers and farmers. Because their elected officials were so responsive, the citizens forswore the initiative, referendum and other Populist/Progressive reforms, leaving responsibility 'squarely in the hands of the regularly elected legislature . . . still one of the most powerful and sensitive to public demand in the country today' (Peirce and Hagstrom 1982: 541). Legislative authority in Minnesota education politics can also be traced to the sizeable number of legislators who have specialized in education over a long time period.

This brief review indicates that the politics of reform in each state manifest distinctive themes: coalition politics in California; business dominance and consensus politics in Georgia; the influence of presiding officers in Florida; piecemeal, conservative politics in Arizona; gubernatorial and legislative delegation to the state board in Pennsylvania; and legislative dominance within the context of a relatively low-profile state role in Minnesota. Whatever similarities existed in factors such as the intellectual origins of reform and the roles of interest groups, the reform process reveals traditional political configurations in each state.

State context and reform policies

Several of the reforms apparent in the six states were common features of the reform movement in all states. Five of our six study states increased graduation requirements, just as 90% of all states did. The policy areas in which these states chose to act – student standards, teacher certification and compensation, student testing – were defined by the national commission reports. However, many of the specific policies and approaches adopted by the states are strongly reflective of their unique political contexts.

Georgia's experience provides several examples of the molding of reform to state context. The primary approach taken by QBE is to mandate local behavior, stipulating numerous activities and responsibilities. The statute provides for the establishment of a state-wide basic curriculum with competencies specified for each grade level; applies teacher tests and evaluative techniques previously applicable only to beginning teachers to veteran teachers; and substantially increases mandated student testing. Such strong state directives reflect distrust of the 186 local school systems, particularly the majority that have elected school superintendents, to respond to state leadership and bring education up to par with the expectations of the increasingly influential metropolitan Atlanta business elite. Suspicion of local education leadership was also fueled by the apparent, though little discussed, tendency of many local boards, especially in southern Georgia, to underinvest in improving the schooling of predominantly black, improverished populations. Doubts about local co-operation with QBE's provisions increased the support for a unique and potentially far-reaching monitoring system authorized in the legislation, an information management system that would provide extensive information on student, classroom, teacher and school progress to state-level officials. So concerned were the Governor and other leaders of the Education Review Commission about the intransigence of county education leadership that there was consideration of a constitutional amendment providing for the appointment of all school superintendents during the process of developing QBE.

The move to abolish the elected local superintendency was aborted, reflecting the historic strength of the county system in Georgia. Respect for county power is also exhibited in provisions of QBE that propose structural change in school districts. Unlike most of QBE's provisos, which are mandates in nature, the parts of the act relating to the formation of middle schools and to district consolidation provide explicit financial inducements to local districts. The state may stipulate the content of education or the skills of potential teachers, but it cannot yet direct local counties to change their structure or governance.

The Georgia reforms indicate that different kinds of policy change require different strategies in that state. Curriculum matters can be mandated, for example, while structural issues require an inducement approach. In California and Minnesota, there was more consistency in the choice of policy strategy or instrument. California's reforms, particularly those included in SB813, reflect a reality of California life. To mandate anything in California is almost prohibitively expensive because of the size of the system and the high portion of funding that comes from the state in the post-Proposition 13 era. The state is required to fully fund any mandates. Hence, California relies heavily on inducements to local districts. The mentor teacher program is open to districts and teachers who choose to participate; the minimum teacher salary program is also optional. The state also provided cash rewards for improvements in student performance on state testing.

Minnesota's approach to reform embodies its belief in the importance of government and governance. Perhaps only a citizenry so respectful of government could choose to alter education practice primarily through changes in governance structure, rather than by identifying particular curricular or instructional innovations. Minnesota's choice and testing programs both address the dimension of accountability. The PSOE and the new open enrollment choice program make the schools ultimately accountable to parents and students who can vote with their feet. The testing program grants more information to policymakers about student outcomes in the hope that the performance data would provide leverage for improved achievement. A number of the supporters of statewide testing hoped for uniform testing that would make comparison of districts possible; the current program falls short of that goal but still permits more extensive knowledge of outcomes.

The reforms in Pennsylvania were not only developed incrementally, they were also restrained in nature. As indicated previously, Pennsylvania's legislature is primarily reactive. It involves itself in programmatic education issues only when they are brought before it, by the board or department or by various interests who are nervous about executive policies. It tends to define most education issues as fiscal issues. The legislature also works hard to mute the divisiveness of party and region in this diverse, very partisan state, especially in the case of education (Katz 1981). The state aid program, the Equalized Basic Subsidy for Education (ESBE) was a carefully-designed, well-compromised formula that balanced disparate claims. Hence, when the education reforms related to teaching and student standards requirements were established by the state board, the legislature rebuffed gubernatorial efforts to develop categorical funding for these programs. Instead, it funnelled new money into the ESBE formula, which had been developed so painstakingly. By providing no funding explicitly linked to these new reforms, the state made a strong statement to local districts about the reforms: they were to be considered part of the continuing responsibility of districts to provide an appropriate education, not as something requiring extraordinary effort. This premise was reinforced by the failure of the state to furnish any additional state capacity to assist or monitor the activities of local districts. In fact, state agency staff was cut severely over this same period as part of Governor Thornburgh's general reduction-in-force effort, and the current administration has made no efforts to remedy the situation. An interesting exception to legislative refusal to consider categorical programs was the Testing for Essential Learning and Literacy Skills Program (TELLS), which is discussed at some length in the chapter by Corbett and Wilson (1988) in this volume. This testing and remediation program provided funds to districts to remediate student failure. In keeping with Pennsylvania politics, the cut-off scores permit Philadelphia to get the largest share without depleting all the funding available to other districts. Also, TELLS stops short of reporting school-by-school scores, a practice which is acceptable in California but not in the more locally-controlled Pennsylvania.

The reforms in Arizona and Florida are similarly strongly reflective of state context. Two features of Arizona's career ladder program indicate how closely it conforms to what is feasible within Arizona's political context, despite the extensive research on other state career ladder plans that informed its development. First, the program was created as a pilot program specifically because a full program would have bumped up against the state's constitutional limit on spending, a limit which symbolizes the state's belief in government restraint. The conviction that government should promote individual achievement (primarily by minimizing obstrusiveness) can be seen in the outcome emphasis of the career ladder program. The state explicitly requires that student performance be used as a criterion in teacher promotion. Florida's reform exhibits the extensive detail and specification, as well as the reliance on mandates, that have come to be commonplace in that state as the legislature has exerted more and more policy leadership. The reform statute enumerates the amount of time students should spend writing and limits the number of students teachers of writing may teach, spells out exactly what degree requirements are necessary for visiting scholars to schools in various disciplines, and has a host of other such stipulations.

State context appears to exert its strongest influence on the choice of policy strategy, such as the use of mandates or inducements, at least in the case of the current reforms where the substance of policy change (e.g. student standards, teacher certification) was defined by a clear national agenda. Therefore, while both Florida and California developed some sort of differentiated pay for teachers, Florida's master teacher program was statewide and criteria were specified at the state level and California's mentor teacher program was optional and left selection criteria to local districts. However, setting appears to affect some very specific and particular aspects of policy as well. Arizona's use of outcome measures in its career ladder seems consonant with its political culture just as Pennsylvania's abjuration of categorical funding is understandable given its complex politics.

State context and implementation

As initial efforts to implement the current reforms are undertaken, a number of patterns are emerging. Changes in graduation requirements are resulting in moderate modifications in course offerings and more coursetaking in academic subjects by middle and below average students (Clune 1988). Teacher policies, particularly statewide differentiated reward systems, are encountering greater problems in implementation, perhaps because of lack of knowledge about and agreement upon teacher evaluation criteria and procedures. School personnel do not report major implementation problems related to reforms, and there is evidence that, regardless of the specific state, many local districts are using the reforms creatively to address local needs (Fuhrman *et al.* 1988). The chapter by Odden and Marsh (1988) in this volume reinforces the latter point. However, state-to-state variation in implementation experience is as striking as the diffrences in policymaking process. Clearly, as implementation research has demonstrated in the past, context has a pronounced effect on the translation of policy into practice.

In Georgia, wide variation in local capacity may seriously diminish the impact of QBE. Georgia's consensus politics meant that QBE had to be a common denominator, in some senses. Its goals had to be achievable by the poverty-stricken, racially isolated districts in the South and acceptable to Atlanta and the fast-growing northern metropolitan suburbs. The ambitious monitoring and extensive testing provisions of QBE reveal awareness that the state must play a heavy hand to pull some of the most backward districts into the twentieth century. However, there are early indications that the bootstrapping approach may be encountering predictable problems. For example, a particularly disadvantaged district was finding new academic diploma graduation requirements irrelevant because so few students were in the academic track. On the other hand, higher capacity counties are chaffing under some of QBE's rigidity, such as a requirement in the revisor bill which later amended QBE to use the state teacher evaluation instrument, designed for beginning teachers, for career ladder advancement. That instrument is seen by some as too structured and supportive of a routinized and bureaucratized approach to teaching.

Minnesota's low profile state role has interesting implications for the implementation of state policies. Some effects are easily predicted. With the state relatively uninterested in monitoring or enforcement, considerable variability in local response would be expected. Districts that saw advantages in and were comfortable with state policies were more supportive and compliant. Those districts that saw little to gain tended to view new state policies as tangential and devoted little energy to them. However, the continued belief in the primacy of local districts appears to have another, more intriguing and challenging impact. Because the state does not articulate a strong role for itself, it tends to produce whatever education policy it does make in a rather uncoordinated, piecemeal manner. When several seemingly unrelated state policies converge on the local district, as they must ultimately, unforeseen pressures and problems may result. For example, the Post-Secondary Options Program and an assessment and remediation program, called the Assurance of Mastery Program, had different supporters and were aimed at different populations. Neither carried funding. They both required substantial amounts of guidance counselor time over approximately the same period. At the same time, as of early summer, 1987, the legislature was considering cuts to state support of counseling and guidance services.

The implementation of Arizona's career ladder pilot has taken a distinctive path. State-level implementation is entirely in the hands of the legislature. Initially, the state department of education was given the task of developing the Request for Proposals to which local districts interested in becoming pilots would respond. However, in a short period of time, the Senate staff took over the responsibility. From the Senate's point of view, the department may not have been sufficiently interested in a program it did not initiate. Some in the department, on the other hand, felt rushed by the Senate. Whatever the specifics of the legislative-department interaction on the career ladder, legislative distrust of the agency reflects the split that is prone to develop in a state with an elected chief state school officer of a different party than the legislature. In this case, the chief was a prominent Democrat, preparing to run for governor, and the legislature was Republican. At present, the legislature still runs the program, which has expanded in the number of pilot districts, even though an Attorney General's opinion holds that it is usurping executive authority.

The implementation of SB813 and the California state department's curricular reforms are affected by the enormous public interest accorded education. Public attention has been heightened by the grass-roots campaigns of Riles and Honig, concerns about taxation and spending, the tight relationship between perceived quality of schooling and real estate prices, uneven and sometimes enormous population growth, and concerns about educating the burgeoning number of school children of minority and immigrant background. The public scrutiny makes it possible for the state to rely heavily on jawboning to influence local behavior. A performance report card details achievement and attainment data for each school, and school officials know that realtors and citizens pay attention to the results. In such a climate, state tests and the curriculum objectives they test are likely to garner the attention of school personnel.

In Florida, a number of the more specific and directive aspects of the 1983 reform have been modified in subsequent years as implementation problems have arisen. An initial requirement for a 1·5 gradepoint average for graduation was delayed. The mandate for an extended school day was changed into an incentive program. The Master Teacher program ran into extensive administrative difficulties, some of them traceable to aggressive legislation that outstripped departmental capacity. There was also dissension about evaluation criteria and procedures. The legislature then developed an optional, locally-designed career ladder program which will take effect only if funding is provided by 1988. The penchant for tinkering, fine-tuning and modifying during the implementation process appears, at least partially, a predictable outgrowth of legislative specification, given the complexity of Florida and the diversity of local interests and capacity. If the initial legislation were less directive and more authorizing in nature, there would probably be less statutory revision during the implementation process.

Pennsylvania has also experienced tinkering and modification related to its 1984 reforms. In this case, local districts and interest groups unhappy with the reforms have gone back to the state to get them changed; they have bargained and mediated the implementation of reforms in keeping with the negotiation ethos that characterizes Pennsylvania politics. Two examples illustrate. First, it very quickly became apparent that new academic graduation requirements and simultaneouus new requirements for vocational education might conflict, with students and schools finding it hard to have time for both. Although some policymakers wanted to stand firmly behind the more academic and not permit the new requirements in math and science to be watered down, in the end a bargain was struck. As a result of negotiations between the General Assembly and the Department of Education, students are able to substitute as many as three credits of vocational education for academic credits where it is demonstrated that the vocational course content is comparable to the academic course. No one voices great concern about accounting or other similar business courses that have considerable academic content, but there are worries about courses like baking and cosmetology being approved as math and science substitutes. A second example concerns the revision of teacher certification regulations to require continuing professional development credits for certification renewal. Unable to modify this provision while the state board was considering it in 1984, teacher associations went to the legislature. Subsequent legislation succeeded in exempting teachers with masters' degrees from the requirement and permitted local districts to design their own continuing professional development plans provided that teachers would be represented on the committees developing the plans and pending submission of plans to the state.

The findings about implementation are preliminary; some of the reforms in these states were not yet even in effect as of this writing and others had just gotten underway. However, even these very tentative findings reinforce conclusions from previous research about the link between capacity and implementation. Resources, expertise and leadership play important roles in the translation of policy into practice. In turn, political setting influences capacity. Consequently, in relatively high local control states, like Arizona or Pennsylvania, state agencies are not active in implementation and are not receiving the resources to improve their capacity. Our examples illustrate that state politics also affects implementation in other, more subtle ways. Minnesota state policymakers do not see themselves as directive of local behavior and may fail to anticipate burdens to local districts. Pennsylvania districts that feel burdened seek to negotiate ways out of literal compliance. And California can rely considerably on public accountability to provide pressure for implementation. Whether these initial patterns are maintained as more reforms are phased in is an important question for future research.

Conclusion

This chapter has argued that state politics and culture are strong influences on the course of reform, even in the current setting that is characterized by the widespread adoption of similar policies by many states. Major areas of reform – standards for students and teachers, reward systems and assessment of outcomes – were common in the six states examined and in the nation more generally. Furthermore, many aspects of the politics of reform were comparable from state to state, particularly the leadership of governors and legislatures and the relative inactivity of interest groups. Patterns also exist in the initial implementation experience of districts, regardless of the state. Many student standards policies are rather readily adopted and a number of teacher programs, particularly differential pay systems, are encountering difficulties. However, important differences in the political cultures of the six states affect the progress of reform.

Three major areas of variation in the course of reform can be related to political context. First, the politics of reform initiation and enactment reflect politics as usual in the states in important ways. States that habitually resort to big legislative fixes in education continued to do so, and those packages were crafted in traditional ways, through coalition or consensus politics and strong leadership. States that normally act more incrementally maintained that approach. The locus of policy initiative among the branches of government was also in keeping with established patterns.

Second, the specific reform policies are shaped by state political culture as well as by the national reform agenda. Choices about strategy, such as the use of mandates or incentives, and about a number of particular aspects of new programs reflect key political realities, such as the balance of power between state and local districts.

Finally, states and districts are managing the implementation of reform in ways that might have been predicted from examination of political context. Local districts in one state are inclined to return to the state to bargain or mediate the impact of reform. In another, policymakers are continually fine-tuning the initial reform which was extremely specific. In others, factors such as high public visibility or extreme variation in district capacity are encouraging or impeding implementation.

A key implication of this analysis is the need to view policies as part of the larger setting in which they are initiated and implemented and to observe their progression over time. Policy evolves as local experience leads to modification at the state level or adaptation at the local level. Differences from state to state in policies that are normally similar at the point of initiation should become more pronounced over time, as context continues to exert its influence.

Note

1   In 1972 Elazar characterized the political cultures of the six study states as
     follows: Arizona – Traditionalist dominant, strong Moralistic strain; California
     – Moralist dominant, strong Individualistic strain; Florida and Georgia –
     Traditionalist dominant, strong Individualistic strain; Minnesota – Moralistic
     dominant; Pennsylvania – Individualistic dominant.

References

ALMOND, G. (1956) 'Comparative political systems', *Journal of Politics*, 18, pp. 391–409.

BELL, C. G. (1984) 'California', in A. Rosenthal and M. Moakley (eds.) *The Political Life of the American States* (New York: Praeger.)

CLUNE, W. H. (1988) The Implementation and Effects of High School Graduation Requirements: First Steps Toward Curricular Reform (New Brunswick, NJ: CPRE).

CORBETT, D. H. and Wilson, B. (1988) 'Raising the stakes in statewide mandatory minimum competency testing', in J. Hannaway and R. Crowson (eds.) *The Politics of Reforming School Administration* (London: Falmer Press).

COUNCIL of CHIEF STATE SCHOOL OFFICERS (1988) *Accountability Reporting in the States: Report of a Survey: 1987*, working draft (Washington, DC: CCSSO).

DARLING-HAMMOND, L. and BERRY, B. (1988). *The Evolution of Teacher Policy*, prepared for the Center for Policy Research in Education (Santa Monica, CA:RAND Corporation).

ELAZAR, D. (1972) *American Federalism: A View from the States* (New York: Crowell).

ELMORE, R. F. and McLAUGHLIN, M. W. (1982) *Reform and Retrenchment: The Politics of California School Finance*, RAND Educational Policy Study (Cambridge, MA: Ballinger Publishing Company).

FUHRMAN, S., CLUNE, W. H. and ELMORE, R. F. (1988) 'Research on educational reform: lessons on the implementation of policy', in *1988 Yearbook of the American Educational Finance Association* (Cambridge, MA: Ballinger).

FUHRMAN, S. and McDONNELL, L. M. (1985) *Mapping Instate Information Networks in Education Policy: An Exploratory Study*. (Alexandria, VA: National Association of State Boards of Education).

HEPBURN, L. R. (1984) 'Georgia', in A. Rosenthal and M. Moakley (eds.) *The Political Life of the American States* (New York: Praeger).

KATZ, E. (1981) 'Pennsylvania', in S. Fuhrman and A. Rosenthal (eds.) *Shaping Education Policy in the States* (Cambridge, MA: Institute for Educational Leadership).

KIRST, M. (1981) 'California,' in S. Fuhrman and A. Rosenthal (eds.) *Shaping Education Policy in the States* (Cambridge, MA: Institute for Educational Leadership).

McDONNELL, L. M. (1987) 'The instruments of State education reform', paper presented at The Western Political Science Association Annual meeting, Anaheim, California.

McDONNELL, L. M. and ELMORE, R. F. (1987) *Alternative Policy Instruments*, prepared for Center for Policy Research in Education (Santa Monica, CA: RAND Corporation).

McDONNELL, L. M. and FUHRMAN, S. (1986) 'The political context of education reform', in V. Mueller and M. McKeown (eds.) *The Fiscal, Legal, and Political Aspects of State Reform of Elementary and Secondary Education* (Cambridge, MA: Ballinger, pp.43–64.

McDONNELL, L. M. and McLAUGHLIN, M. W. (1982) *Educational Policy and the Role of the States*, prepared for the National Institute of Education (Santa Monica, CA: RAND Corporation).

McDONNELL, L. M. and PASCAL, A. (1988) *Teacher Unions and Educational Reform,* prepared for Center for Policy Research in Education (Santa Monica, CA: RAND Corporation).

McLAUGHLIN, M. W. (1987) 'Lessons from past implementation research', *Educational Evaluation and Policy Analysis*, 9, pp.171–178.

ODDEN, A. (1987) 'The economics of financing education excellence', paper presented at the American Educational Research Association Meeting, Washington, DC.

ODDEN, A. and MARSH, D.(1988) State education reform implementation: a framework for analysis, in J. Hannaway and R. Crowson (eds.) *The Politics of Reforming School Administration*. (London: Falmer Press).

PATTERSON, S. (1968) 'The political cultures of the American states', *Journal of Politics*, 30, pp.188–191.

PEIRCE, N. R. and HAGSTROM, J. (1983) *The Book of America: Inside 50 States Today* (New York: W. W. Norton.)

ROSENTHAL, A. and MOAKLEY, M. (1984) *The Political Life of the American States.* (New York: Praeger.)

SHARKANSKY, I. (1967) Economic and political correlates of states government expenditures: general tendencies and deviant cases, *Midwest Journal of Political Science* (Athens, GA: University of Georgia).

ST ANGELO, D. (1984) 'Florida', in A. Rosenthal and M. Moakley (eds.) *The Political Life of the American States.* (New York: Praeger.)

TURNBULL, A. (1981) 'Florida', in S. Fuhrman and A. Rosenthal (eds.) *Shaping Education Policy in the States* (Cambridge, MA: Institute for Educational Leadership).

VERBA, S. (1956) 'Comparative political culture', in L. W. Pye and S. Verba (eds.) *Political Culture and Political Development* Princeton, Princeton University Press. 391–409.

6   *Making schools manageable: policy and administration for tomorrow's schools*

Gary Sykes and Richard F. Elmore
Michigan State University

The title of this chapter sets forth our leading premise. If we are to see improvements in school performance then we must search for ways to make schools more manageable. We contrast this idea with the more common formulation of the problem in current research and policy, which is to fit people into institutions and roles as they now exist and exhort them to greater performance. Schools have their heroes and miracle workers, to be sure, but we doubt the prospects for a substantial increase in their numbers. We argue instead for changing institutions so that ordinary people may successfully carry out the extraordinary work of education.

This concern for institutions carries its own burden of skepticism. Since the inception of the Common School there has been no lack of effort to rethink and re-form the institution of schooling, and the contemporary romance with 'restructuring the schools' is but the lastest in a long line of efforts in our society to remake our institutions so they may better serve their fundamental purposes. The history of such efforts gives cause neither for optimism nor pessimism. Institution-changing is complex and difficult. Indeed change of any kind, whether attempted by individuals or institutions, is a painful and risky business that demands time and energy, as it increases uncertainty and anxiety. We believe, however, in encouraging some far-ranging efforts at inventing new forms of organization for the future. In taking this stand we do not wish to denigrate the many incremental reforms underway, but to argue that the organization and administration of schools is not so well settled as to preclude transforming experiments of various kinds. In this chapter we set forth a critique of how the problem of school administration typically is framed, we provide a perspective on school management, and we conclude with some themes for the next generation of policy and administration.

Framing the problem of school leadership

The way in which a policy problem initially is framed directs the search for solutions. Virtually all the research on administration and leadership in education focuses on the behavior of people, usually principals and teachers, performing institutionally prescribed roles within a fixed organizational structure. The leading premise of this research is that a certain kind of administrative behavior, often characterized as principals' 'instructional leadership', is positively – perhaps strongly – related to teacher satisfaction and student achievement. Yet the research raises a number of problems, not least of which is the persistent finding that principals who play the role of instructional leader are a relatively small proportion of all principals and that most principals, while they accept instructional leadership as an ideal, direct their attention to tasks unrelated to instruction and student performance (Crowson and Porter-Gehrie 1980, Leithwood and Montgomery 1982, Martin and Willower 1981).

From one perspective this observation is neither surprising nor particularly damning. As Larry Cuban (1988) most recently reminds us, teachers and administrators alike must manage three complex roles in their daily work: the instructional, the managerial, and the political. School principals must attend to imperatives from downtown and pressures from the community as they struggle to control the behavior of a school full of youngsters. Little wonder that pupil control is a longstanding subject of research in school administration (Packard 1988). Like most managerial work, running a school is multi-faceted and demanding, a three ring circus in which the hours of the day chase the tasks to be accomplished.

Yet the research also indicates that principals feel least competent around the role they regard as most important – the instructional role (Lortie et al. 1983). Many consequently disengage from this aspect of their work in favor of other duties. Hence there is a strong contradiction between the normative conception of leadership and administration in education and the actual behavior of educational administrators that has been a constant feature of the work since Elwood Cubberley founded the field in the 1920s: guilt over spending too much time on clerical tasks and non instructional work rather than supervision surfaced repeatedly after the 1920s in reports on the principalship. A common question asked of principals after they reported how much time they spent on administrative, supervisory, and other tasks was to list how they would prefer to spend their time. Four studies done in the 1920s, for example, asked principals what the *ideal* distribution of their time would be. In each case, elementary principals wished to spend more time with supervision than admini- stration. That pattern persisted in a massive survey of elementary principals in 1968 and for high school principals in 1978 (Cuban 1986: 111–12).

Research in the field appears to support the notion of herioc leadership, and with a few notable exceptions does not examine competing hypotheses about the direction or nature of causality between administrative behavior and school outcomes. The research is, for the most part, unidirectional, positing a line of force from administrative behavior to teacher behavior to student behavior; and unicausal, positing that administrators control the things for which they are nominally responsible, which in turn are assumed to influence teacher and student behavior. Such simple models poorly reflect the dynamics of organizational life (for review of more complex, non recursive and interactive models, see Pitner 1988).

· Educational administration, both as a field of professional study and of scholarly inquiry, is for the most part role-driven and predicated on the existing formal structure of relationships in schools. Professional study consists of preparing people for a narrowly constructed set of roles in a highly regulated occupational structure (teacher, principal counselor, central office administrator, etc.). Research consists of studying how people perform these prescribed roles. As a consequence, educational administration has been relatively impervious to alter- native models of schooling that question the formal structure of existing relationships in schools and to knowledge from other fields that does not accord with the conventional structure of schooling.

We argue for a new problem frame. Research and policy should turn the traditional focus inside-out: instead of concentrating on how people behave in received roles within a fixed structure, research should begin to create the roles and structures that support and encourage the educational practices that we want. 'Making schools manageable' captures this frame. Our leading premise is that too many schools today are not manageable if judged against our deepest educational ideals. Fitting people into impossible roles and structures, relying on their coping behavior, and lionizing their successes does not constitute an effective, long-term strategy for the improvement of schooling. Instead we must create conditions for the invention of new structures that enable the emergence of leadership on a broad basis.

This shift in problem frame poses new and potentially productive research questions about the relationship between behavior, structure, and performance in schools. It also poses a series of new policy issues. Since it is impossible to study structures that do not exist, and since the range of variation among existing structures is too narrow to make productive studies possible, policymakers will have to authorize new arrangements in order to increase our collective knowledge about making schools manageable. Before exploring the possibilities, we must more closely assess current research and thinking in the field.

An appraisal of the field of educational administration

Our premise, derived from a reading of research, is that enhancing the effectiveness of people in administrative roles in the present structure of schools will have very limited pay-off for improvements in the performance of schools. Yet the prevailing thrust of much thinking within educational administration is to identify success criteria based on study of 'outliers' (a statistical term indicating rare and isolated cases falling far off the regression line), then to generate prescriptions from such cases for the mainstream to emulate. Empirical work of this sort has been fruitful (for a review of this and related research, see Purkey and Smith 1983). We can indeed identify a set of attributes in the existing population of principals. But such procedures and results offer less than meets the eye.

It is virtually impossible to find a unique effect of instructional leadership on student performance because of multiple causality and weak specification of underlying models within the current research. Furthermore the very strategy of generating prescriptions from outlying cases suggests that most principals do not manifest the attributes of instructional leadership in their daily work. And, as Larry Cuban (1984) has argued, a list of attributes is not self-implementing. The current research leaves open how principals ought to go about transforming themselves into instructional leaders and their schools into winners.

A case can be made that while the norms of the field – what might be termed the ideology of school administration – exhort administrative engagement in instruction, the conditions of work and the attributes of people in administrative roles may promote disengagement. A variety of reasons for disengagement come readily to mind.

First, principals are, by role, generalists who must manage the work of specialists. This problem characterizes many organizations today, for we live in an age of specialization and professionalization. Many lines of work seek to professionalize and most professionals today, including doctors, lawyers, accountants, engineers, and others work in large-scale organizations. Sociologists have long noted tensions between bureaucratic and professional forms of control, but these have become endemic in our society. The drive to professionalize teaching parallels a broader movement within work organizations, and we have not yet evolved management strategies to accommodate a professionalized workforce (see for example, Raelin 1986 and Benveniste 1987, for discussion of these trends). Close observers of teaching (e.g., Lortie 1987, Darling-Hammond 1984) have described the status strain that exists between a well educated workforce imbued with the expectation of exercising professional autonomy in their work and a bureaucratic-regulatory approach to the management of educational institutions.

Principals are unprepared by education or experience to wield instructional authority over teachers who possess greater knowledge about teaching and learning. Perhaps in small elementary schools the principal can serve as master teacher exercising expert authority to direct and co-ordinate instruction, but in most other schools the principal manages a group of specialists: reading and special education, physics and chemistry, social studies and English, business education and shop, school nurses and social workers, and the list goes on. The principal is charged with instructional leadership but that is no more plausible than charging the chief administrator of a hospital with medical leadership across the entire spectrum of medical specialties.

A second factor complicating the direct exercise of authority over instruction is the typical span of control in many schools. Principals are expected to evaluate teachers annually in most districts, usually by means of classroom observations, but in many schools, the principal is hard-pressed to visit teachers in their classrooms for more than a brief period. Principals do not have the time to oversee instruction systematically. This means that teaching goes unappraised in many schools, while in others this function may be carried out by assistant principals, department chairs, team leaders, master teachers, and others. These patterns have been little studied so it is difficult to assess their relative effectiveness, and scant guidance exists on how principals might delegate authority yet retain influence overall for the school's academic mission. We suspect leadership in schools is more diffuse than popular images suggest; as we sketch out below, new structural arrangements could encourage multiple sources of initiative in schools without undercutting overall direction and purpose. A 'community of leaders', in Roland Barth's (1986) telling phrase, is an image with which we are sympathetic. These structural realities promote disengagement from the core work of schools but other factors abet this tendency. Schools have evolved into general purpose social agencies that dispense a variety of services while fulfilling a range of functions in communities. Principals can – and must – attend to dozens of problems and incidents each day that have little to do with the improvement of instruction. Just as some teachers avoid the intellectually demanding task of conveying academic knowledge in favor of social and emotional goals for students, so principals can avoid the perplexing aspects of their work by substituting attention to other matters. And, if truth be told, communities often value fielding winning teams and supplying entertainments over intense engagement with academic knowledge. So communities often do not press school administrators toward instructional improvement as the central mission of the school.

Further, administrator selection and credentialing processes, usually do not reward prior evidence of strong engagement with instruction. Indeed, rapidly achieving social distance from teaching is nearly obligatory for status and advancement in administrative careers, a tendency we suspect is deeply influenced by gender (Ortiz and Marshall 1988). The sexual division of labor in education has meant that women teachers work for male administrators whose paternalistic attitudes betray condescension toward teaching. The flight upward into administration is equally a flight *from* teaching, and the evidence suggests that few principals, in Deborah Meier's (1985) phrase, 'retain the teacher's perspective in the principalship'.

If school systems do not systematically select candidates with a history of strong involvement in and a concern for academics, neither do training programs systematically promote such an orientation to the work. Administrator training appears to be an unusually 'weak treatment' relative to professional preparation in other fields. It is most often a dilatory option, pursued on a convenience basis, part-time, on the margins of a workday. The collection of core courses is small, there is little attention to the clinical aspects of training, and almost no attention to professional socialization.

Furthermore, research indicates that leadership in schools (as elsewhere) is highly 'situational'; whether defined in terms of subordinate attitudes or organizational outputs, it varies with attributes of the workforce, the organization, and the organization's environment. Consequently, one would expect a weak relationship between general knowledge about administrative behavior and the actions required to make specific organizations work effectively.

Finally, in many locales, collective bargaining agreements have institutionalized conflict and distrust between administrators and teachers, disturbing efforts to exercise instructional leadership by either party. As Susan Johnson's (1983) research demonstrates, there is considerable variation across schools operating under the same contract in teacher-administrator relations, but the rise of militant unionism has introduced a new element into many schools that complicates the possibilities for cooperation. If some administrators work through and with the contract, others use it as an excuse for inaction and adversarialism.

The situation appears heavily overdetermined in favor of disengagement. Without countervailing pressures, many administrators pursue the path of least resistance, avoiding the school's central mission of teaching and learning. Much analysis of schools has explored the forces that drive teaching toward a bland mediocrity. We believe parallel processes work at the administrative level, implicating task and role structures, goal ambiguity and conflict, inadequacies of material and knowledge resources, and patterns of recruitment, training, and socialization.

This litany of woes may have a familiar ring in that most organizations and their role incumbents are oriented to maintenance, not change, while goal displacement is a commonplace feature of organizational life. We acknowledge that the tendencies described here have their counterparts in other kinds of organization, partaking, in Crozier's (1964) phrase, of the bureaucratic phenomenon. Little wonder that a burgeoning literature on the reform of management fills not simply the specialist jounals but popular bookstores. The Peters and Waterman (1982) phenomenon, not to mention the fascination with all things Japanese, bespeaks widespread dissatisfaction with management in both public and private sectors. School administration participates in this general problem and appears to be daunting work for even the most able and committed educator.

School administration as impossible work

Certain occupations involve impossible work, an observation that is not original with us. Writing in 1937, Sigmund Freud observed that analysis looked to be ' . . . the third of those "impossible" professions in which one can be sure beforehand of achieving unsatisfying results. The other two, which have been known much longer, are education and government.' 'People-changing' occupations in particular appear to be impossible. These include psycho-therapy and social work, teaching, public health care, forms of police work, and politics as vocation. We do not mean that such work cannot be accomplished, for people carry out responsibilities daily in such fields. Rather, the work involves ideals that admit no easy realization, the resources of knowledge, material, authority, and status typically are inadequate to the tasks, and the goals are often multiple, ambiguous, and conflicting. Successful practice in such fields involves great wisdom, skill, and dedication, for the coping behaviors that make such work manageable often undermine the ideals that inform such work (Lipsky 1980).

School administration is not the only field confronting these circumstances, but along with teaching it surely qualifies. Listen for a moment to a veteran elementary school principal reflecting on the qualities needed in her work. The scene is a university classroom for a graduate course on 'School Administration' taken by aspiring principals. She writes,

The professor is making *his* list of the qualities of a good principal. The eager aspirants are giving input. Democratic, visionary, decisive, energetic, calm, dispassionate, objective, approachable, intelligent, firm, supportive, honest, organized, disciplined, friendly, healthy, courageous, having a sense of humor, broad liberal education, excellent management skills, knowledgeable about latest research in education, good judge of character, able to relate to students, imaginative, creative, clear-thinking, wise, determined, patient, kind, respecting. (Carmichael 1985: 312)

She is coteaching this course with the professor, and as she watches him scribble this list on the board, she responds:

I suddenly felt a wave of electrical panic flow through my body. My God! That list is horrendous! I hardly have any of these qualities. I have some of them, but only some of the time . . . Tomorrow it would be my turn to present myself before the class and impart information about the 'good' school administrator. Six months from now I would return from sabbatical to my school and faculty and have to play this administrator role. Role, hell – it was a suit of armor. (ibid.)

Such existential testimony makes our point: the role is a suit of armor protecting the principal, perhaps, but weighing her down, rendering her inflexible and slow to respond. The formal expectations that operate on educational administrators, especially at the school level, amount to impossible work – building manager, instructional leader, buffer to the external environment, subordinate to the central office on standard operating procedures, and implementor of federal, state, and local policy. The research suggests that most building administrators adapt to impossible work by selecting and specializing, rather than by broadening their repertoire of skills, and that most district administrative structures adapt to building administrators' behavior by tolerating a wide range of discretion at that level.

Two perspectives in the recent literature on school administration mitigate the impossibilities of the work. One perspective explores 'substitutes for leadership', a variety of subordinate, task, and structural characteristics than can substitute for the direct effects of leader behavior (see, for example, Kerr and Jermier 1978, and Pitner 1986). These include, for example, the level of experience/training of subordinates and their professional orientation, task clarity and task-provided feedback, cohesive workgroups, spatial distance between superior and subordinates, and low leader position power.

The intent of this work has been to identify and obtain effect size estimates of the contingencies under which administrative leadership is not likely to make a difference in desired end-results such as commitment, motivation, or performance. Alternatively, however, this theoretical perspective suggests that organizational arrangements and structures may substitute for administrative control, obviating the need for heroic leadership. An implication of this work is that by attending to organizational arrangements, principals may exercise indirect leadership and so manage the dilemmas and difficulties of the position.

A second perspective portrays school administration as the humble, mundane, but necessary work of running a bureaucracy. Administrators may chafe at the dozens of inconsequential actions and decisions that absorb their daily attention, but these are not diversions from the 'real' work of school administration – they constitute the work of the school administrator. 'Elementary competence in organizational life is often underrated as a factor in managerial effectiveness when we write against the background of a concern for the great issues of leadership', notes James March (1978: 233). If the work appears impossible against our highest ideals, then against the quotidian realities of daily life, it appears to involve consistently doing a large number of little things well (see also Murphy 1988 for an expression of this perspective).

We acknowledge the wisdom of both these perspectives. Regardless of the structure, elementary competence will be necessary as will reliance on organizational factors such as the skill and experience of subordinates. However, our aim is to begin imagining how schools might come closer to realizing their central ideas. If one approach is to recruit, train, and socialize qualified individuals to fit the current institutional structure, another is to rethink elements of that structure in response to evidence that the institution itself impedes the performance of all those working within it – students, teachers, and administrators. We turn then to an exploration of some principles that might guide the reinvention of schools.

Organizing themes for the next generation of policy and administration

Leadership and administration in education is caught in a difficult bind. Administrators, particularly principals, are expected to play roles dictated by a formal structure, but which only a gifted few people can fulfill. Research reinforces this bind by studying how people perform in prescribed roles, finding, not surprisingly, that few are capable of meeting the full range of expectations dictated by the structure. State and local policymakers reinforce this bind by assuming that the structure is basically sound though the people in it may be flawed, and by relying on the formal chain of command for implementation. At the same time, policymakers make administrative work increasingly difficult by heaping greater and greater demands on administrators.

Administrators, like anyone confronted with similar problems, respond to the demands of impossible work by focusing on certain parts of the job and delegating or disregarding others. The most common pattern of adaptation to the demands of impossible work is for administrators to disengage from the core activities of schools – teaching, learning, and student performance – and to focus on peripheral matters, often constructing seemingly important roles for themselves in such areas as facilities, transportation, and food service management, public relations, and bureaucratic politics, unconnected to any explicit theory or understanding of teaching, learning, and student performance. ·

Because the roles that school administrators play are largely adaptations to externally-generated demands, administrators are usually not instrumental in the enactment of any explicit theory of teaching, learning, and student performance. If public schools fail, either by the criterion of client satisfaction or by falling short of expected performance on objective measures of achievement, retention, and engagement in learning, one probable cause is that administrative roles and organizational structure do not serve the core activities of the organization. On the contrary, the core activities of the organization are expected to conform to established structure and roles. An organization whose structure inhibits, rather than enabling, the accomplishment of its central tasks is an organization with a limited future.

Breaking this structural bind will require simultaneously 'unfreezing' structure, practice, research, and policy. If research and practice are to focus on something other than a monotonous recitation of marginal adaptations to impossible work, there will have to be a wider range of structures in which to work, study, and reflect. But state and local policy constrain the range of possible structures, limiting acceptable variations, for the most part, to those that leave traditional roles of teacher, student, parent, and administrator intact. It is impossible to practice in, to study, and to reflect upon structures that do not exist. So in order to break the structural bind researchers and practitioners will have to invent, and policymakers will have to authorize, new structures.

How might we go about unfreezing structure, practice, research, and policy in a way that demonstrates concern for the multiple purposes of public education and for public accountability? As a first step in this direction, we advance some operating principles for the next generation of policymaking and research on school organization and administration.

Principle 1: core technology drives structure

In the late 1970s, a major debate in the sociological literature on education revolved around the question of whether the formal organization of schooling exists to reinforce the core technology of schools – processes of teaching and learning – or to buffer that technology from an intrusive and disruptive social and political environment. This debate gave rise to a literature that characterized schools as 'loosely-coupled' systems (Weick 1976), with little direct oversight or management of teaching and learning, carefully maintained barriers to their external environment, and largely symbolic certification rituals designed to legitimate schools with their constituents (Meyer and Rowan 1977).

Lately, the debate has shifted to a more systematic examination of the possible connections, first, between core technology, structure, and management (Bossert *et al.* 1982) and second, between schools and their clients (Elmore 1987a, Raywid 1985). This new perspective suggests that the central problems of future research on school organization are problems of institutional design, or how to bring external incentives and internal structures into alignment with some definition of effective educational practice (Clune 1987, Gormley 1987, Brandl 1988). Some initial conceptual work has been done to unpack the domain of external incentives, by specifying the policy instruments that are typically used to influence schools and the expected effects of those instruments (e.g. McDonnell and Elmore 1987). Very little work has been done to define the possible ways in which competing theories of good instructional practice could be translated into different organizational structures (see, for example, Rowan, forthcoming).

The central principle of institutional design for future research and policymaking, then, would be something like, 'core technology drives structure'. That is, instead of inventing or reinforcing structures that are designed to buffer teaching, learning, and student performance from external influences, the problem is finding structures that reflect and reinforce competing theories of good teaching and learning. The degree to which these structures will buffer important aspects of teaching and learning from external influences will vary, depending, for example, on the extent to which a given theory of teaching and learning relies on client choice, parental involvement, or performance assessment as ways of connecting schools to their external environments. The objective of institutional design is explicitly to plan and implement school structures that represent very different views of the core technology, rather than trying to shoe-horn different views of core technology into a narrowly-defined structure.

For example, one plausible theory of teaching and learning might stipulate a high level of adult-student interaction and engagement in academic learning, a high level of teacher and student responsibility for results, teaching for conceptual understanding rather than drill and practice, and a high degree of parent involvement and reinforcement of student learning. Researchers and practitioners might be commissioned to design and implement a number of different settings in which these basic principles drive roles and structure. State or local policymakers might set certain minimum constraints – operating costs per pupil, development costs, duration of the development and implementation period, etc. – and then monitor the development of a range of organizational solutions to the problems posed by an explicit theory of teaching and learning. Some models, for example, might alter the mix of roles and responsibilities of practitioners within schools to increase adult-student interaction, by increasing the ratio of lower-cost personnel, introducing supervisory teaching roles, and lowering the ratio of administrative and support staff to instructional staff. Other models might take the existing mix of instructional roles as given and alter the use of time, focusing instruction on a few well-articulated content areas over longer periods of time, permitting more sustained interaction within a more conventional teacher-student ratio.

This example illustrates three consequences of letting core technology drive structure, rather than vice versa. First, establishing an instrumental relationship between structure, resources, practice, and performance requires *everyone* involved in the enterprise to think both educationally and managerially, educationally, because in order to let core technology drive structure, one has to have an explicit theory of instruction; managerially, because in order to translate a theory into an operating structure, within a set of resource constraints, one has to make explicit judgments about the most effective use of the key resources of the organization.

Second, letting core technology drive structure requires policymakers and administrators to assume very different roles. In their new roles, policymakers would set resource constraints, commission the design of new settings, hold researchers and practitioners to their espoused purposes and to some schedule of performance, and decide which ventures should be sustained and which should be abandoned. They would not mandate system-wide structures, instructional programs, monitoring systems, or even uniform standards of performance, except possibly to require that individual designs should include attention to these components. Some policymakers will see this new role as an opportunity to exert greater leverage over the system, some will see it as a threat to their traditional role.

A new relationship between core technology and structure also requires administrators to behave differently. Their role is not to 'run the school', whatever that means, or to buffer the school from a hostile or demanding environment, but to manage a development process, assuring that people assume responsibility for key design decisions, that operating details don't swamp the central ideas of the theory, that key managerial problems become someone's responsibility, and that commitments to policymakers are kept.

By the same token this new view requires teachers to behave differently. In the existing structure, teachers 'manage' the most valuable resource in the organization – interaction between themselves and students around learning tasks – without any explicit acknowledgement of their managerial role. Turning the relationship between structure and practice inside out requires not just acknowledging the central managerial role of teachers, but institutionalizing it. If teachers are to be expected to behave responsibly toward their management of the organization's main resource, then they have to be put in positions where they make individual and collective decisions about its use against constraints and expectations, just like any other manager, and then take responsibility for the implementation and results of those decisions.

An obvious criticism of increasing the importance of teachers' managerial roles in the worklife of schools is the perception that most good teachers do not want to manage (see, for example, Johnson [1988] in this volume). Teachers take their main satisfaction from interaction with students, evidence indicates, and they consider other responsibilities distractions from their most important work. The problem with this point of view, of course, is that teachers are already managers of the organization's most important resource, whether they want to be or not. The question, then, is not whether they are or should be managers, but how well they perform that role, whether they have the resources and formal authority to perform it effectively, and whether they do it in the service of some collective purpose or in the service of some individual, idiosyncratic purpose.

A third consequence of letting core technology drive structure is that traditional canons of school organization probably would be violated with great regularity. One such canon is the notion of an optimum size for all schools, regardless of instructional theory or practice. Typically, school size is dictated by some combination of administrative expedience and historical accident, elaborated at the secondary level by crudely developed notions of the economies of scale required for certain functions (gym, football teams, chemistry labs, and the like). If school size were driven by core technology, size would vary considerably, depending on what educators were trying to accomplish. One could imagine a secondary school, for example, based on a model of engagement that stipulates that every teacher should personally know and work with every student – a design that would require dramatic reductions in size. In order for such a design to work, policymakers and administrators would have to break the canon that every school has its own building, instead treating existing space as a flexible resource that can be divided and used in a variety of ways to accommodate different instructional designs. Such designs might also require schools to contract with other schools, or with private providers, for necessary functions that they do not want to provide for themselves – exotic languages, physical education, capital-intensive vocational or technical education, for example.

The principle 'core technology drives structure', then, requires a significant realignment of traditional relationships among policymakers, administrators, and teachers. It requires the creation of structures that reflect explicit theories of teaching and learning. These structures would probably look much different from the standard model. The principle requires a new division of labor within schools, since everyone in the organization has to think and act with both educational and managerial concerns in mind. And the principle requires a reexamination of the traditional canons of educational administration, letting such features as school size, program mix, and relationships among schools and other educational organizations be driven by instructional practice.

The effect of this realignment of responsibilities is to make the worklife of schools more complex in some respects. People in schools would have to think routinely about the relationship between their own work, the work of others, and some overall conception of what the school is trying to do. In this respect, schools would be more challenging places in which to work and manage.

On balance, though, schools would become more manageable. Holding the people who work in schools responsible for designing, implementing, and managing instructional programs eliminates many of the excuses that teachers and administrators now offer for failing to meet the public's expectations. If core technology is allowed to drive structure, then most of what educators currently regard as constraints to good teaching and learning – class size, schedules, paperwork, materials, middle management, and the like – can be attacked directly. If it's in the way, move it. If it can be put to better use, change it. People would be expected to manage their workplaces, they would be given the tools and responsibilities to manage them, and they would be evaluated on the basis of how well they manage.

Principle 2: uncouple leadership from role

A central problem with the current organization and management of schools, we have argued, is that formal structure assumes a coincidence of leadership with role that is largely unwarranted. Leadership is probably overrated as a *cause* of organizational performance (see Elmore 1987a Meindl *et al.* 1985). But to the degree that leadership does influence performance, structures should be flexible enough to capitalize on leadership where and when it occurs. This means uncoupling leadership from formal role.

If schools were given major responsibility for designing an instructional program and the organization to go with it, formal and informal leadership would emerge. The design of work, including leadership roles, would vary from one school to another. In some schools, the structure might look like an idealized form of the traditional one: a 'strong' principal who manages through a cadre of senior teachers. Other schools might adopt a 'managing partner' or 'head teacher' model, in which a senior teacher assumes lead management responsibility for the school, but maintains an involvement in practice (see Lorsch and Mathias 1987). Still other schools might adopt a 'hospital administrator' or 'building manager' model, in which major management decisions are made by a board (of teachers or of teachers and clients) and day-to-day oversight is done by an administrative officer, who might or might not be an educational professional. Still other schools might adopt a consumer co-operative model, in which a lay board with *ex officio* participation by educators makes major management decisions and day-to-day oversight is done either by a managing partner or an administrative officer.

These four models define managerial responsibility in quite different ways, and they offer very different opportunities for leadership. Competent teachers with little interest in daily management problems might gravitate toward the more traditional structure. Teachers with a well-developed sense of professional authority might gravitate toward the managing partner model. Teachers who want to exercise strong influence over their work but want to limit the demands that daily management makes on their practice might gravitate toward the building manager model. And teachers with a strong sense of client empowerment might gravitate toward the consumer cooperative model.

Leadership would emerge through a variety of channels in different organizational forms. The instructional leader envisioned by the literature on principals might emerge through the traditional structure, leaving some residual informal leadership to a cadre of teachers. The senior teacher who commands loyalty and support from his or her colleagues as *primus inter paras* might emerge in the managing partner model. A leadership clique, with mutual aims and interests, might emerge in the building manager model. And the consumer cooperative model would combine professional leadership with community leadership.

Uncoupling leadership from role probably would produce an even wider variation in managerial and leadership structures than those outlined above. This variability has several major advantages. It opens up opportunities for people to work in organizations that correspond to their view of professional responsibility and leadership. And it permits leadership structures that represent distinctive points of view about instructional practice.

Not the least of the advantages of uncoupling leadership from role is that it allows career structures to reinforce organizational performance. In the existing structure, people are selected for leadership positions on the basis of criteria that are largely irrelevant to organizational performance – credit hours of education completed, seniority, credentials, etc. The structure rewards people who seek refuge from the classroom and higher status in a bureaucratic hierarchy. These rewards have little to do with how well schools educate children. Uncoupling leadership from role allows policymakers to send a clear message to schools: reward people with ideas about teaching and learning and the organizational skills to put them to work.

The major disadvantage of uncoupling leadership from role, of course, is that it scares policymakers and central administrators who equate uniformity and control with quality. The allure of standardized models of organization is that they create the illusion of consistency and quality, even as they reward mediocrity.

From a policy perspective, it is more important that an organization *have a management structure and use it* than that every organization have the same structure. If schools can satisfy certain minimum requirements for specifying who represents the organization in key decision making forums, who is accountable for district- and state-level requests for plans and information, and what the school has to do to demonstrate stewardship and performance, then the form that the organization takes should be of little concern to district and state policymakers. It is possible to run an orderly and accountable system which has great diversity among its organizational units, if higher-level managers do not mistake uniformity for quality.

Principle 3: reduce the complexity of the authorizing environment

The most efficient form of regulation, when it works, is self-regulation (Bardach and Kagan 1982). Generally speaking, it is less costly and more effective to design institutions, and the incentives under which they operate, to reward people for doing the right thing, rather than punishing them for doing the wrong thing. Similarly it is better to design institutions so that people are encouraged to take responsibility for their own actions, rather than expecting others to evaluate and judge them. It is less costly and more effective, in general, to encourage invention and problem-solving directed at public objectives, rather than to require the performance of specific actions. The exceptions to these propositions are cases in which people have strong personal or material motivations to behave in anti-social ways.

When people generally want to do the right thing, but lack the knowledge, skill, or institutional capacity to do it, regulation is a very inefficient way of eliciting the desired response (Elmore and McLaughlin 1988). No amount of coercion can make people do the right thing if they lack the wherewithal. If they possess the wherewithal, coercion will make doing the right thing more difficult.

Regulation is a refined form of coercion, and coercion is costly. Its costs are reckoned both in terms of the direct costs of oversight, enforcement, and compliance, and in terms of the indirect costs of lost initiative, diffuse responsibility, and organizational complexity (McDonnell and Elmore 1987). Because coercion is costly, one can argue that there should be a 'rebuttable presumption' against its use (Schultze 1977).

It has been said of nineteenth century Prussian bureaucracy, to which public education bears an increasing resemblance, that its operating principle was 'that which is not required is prohibited'. Schools would perform better if the operating principle were instead 'that which is not required is permitted', and requirements were focused on areas where failure posed a genuine risk to adults and children in schools. A corollary of this principle is the Zen proverb, 'to control a cow, you must make a large pasture'.

Most state and local policies are predicated on the assumption that schools invariably will do the wrong thing unless they are told to do the right thing. Textbooks must be chosen from the approved lists, prescribed content must be covered by a prescribed time, certain test items must be administered at certain times to determine whether students have accumulated the required knowledge, subject matter must be allocated to prescribed times in a sequenced schedule, students who qualify for special treatment must be sorted and tracked in particular ways, teachers and principals must play prescribed roles within a well-defined authority structure, information on student progress must be provided in the prescribed form to middle managers at the district and state level, and students must advance through prescribed grade levels on a timetable dictated by the nineteenth century agricultural calender.

As we have noted earlier, these controls produce the opposite of their intended effect. The authorizing environment of schools – that collection of rules, processes, and hierarchical structures designed to control the behavior of people – is so crowded with requirements, and the enforcement of those requirements is so idiosyncratic, that school people are forced to sample and select in order to survive. Sampling and selecting produces coping skills among school administrators, and encourages organizational structures, which are designed more to keep an intrusive environment at bay, than to deliver a high quality education to students.

An important part of making schools manageable, then, is reducing the complexity of their authorizing environment, and an important part of that is introducing new principles of regulation. At present, the only constraint on new requirements is whether advocates can generate sufficient political support for their enactment. Once political support is established, new requirements are usually considered by policymakers to be 'free goods'. Under this system, new requirements can increase without regard for their cost or the capacity of schools to implement them.

One principle for rationing new requirements might be that any government – federal, state, or local – must calculate and pay the full cost – direct or indirect – of implementing any requirement they initiate. A second rationing principle might be that for any new regulation which survives the test of political support and cost, any school or district would be authorized to seek exemption before its implementation based on past performance and a plan of future action. A corollary of this principle might be that any school or district could seek a waiver from an established requirement based on past performance and a plan of future action. A third rationing principle might be that any time an existing requirement is amended, the whole body of requirements on that subject must be re-enacted. So, for example, any proposal to alter testing, curriculum, or textbook requirements on that subject would have to be reconsidered and re-enacted. A final rationing principle might be the introduction of four- or five-year sunset provisions for all non-constitutional state and local requirements governing public education, including curriculum, testing, credentialing, finance, and governance. In effect, if most of the authorizing enironment for public education were open for discussion and re-enactment at the state and local level every four or five years, policymakers would be forced to simplify in order to control their own agenda.

These principles all have the effect of significantly increasing the cost of initiating new requirements and introducing strong incentives to simplify existing requirements. In the absence of such measures, policymakers will continue to enact requirements as if they were costless and continue to wonder why those requirements have limited and sporadic effects. Simplifying the authorizing environment of schools would also have the effect of increasing the signal-to-noise ratio of messages coming from federal, state, and local sources about what schools are expected to do. Reducing the noise increases the likelihood that schools will attend to what policymakers think is important, rather than sampling and selecting from a welter of signals. Increasing the clarity of the signal also increases the likelihood that people will take responsibility for what they do – a basic condition of success for teaching and learning.

Principle 4: deepen public discourse on results

Public expectations about the outcomes of schooling constitute a critical factor in the authorising environment of school administrators, and create dilemmas that are difficult to manage. On one hand, evidence indicates that the public expects schools to pursue four broad goals with all children, that Goodlad (1984) characterizes as the intellectual, vocational, social, and personal. When forced to choose among these, the intellectual goal is most strongly emphasized, but large segments of the public are concerned about the other goals as well. On the other hand, a narrow range of indicators have dominated the public appraisal of schooling, These include drop out and absentee rates, enrollments in advanced courses, track placements, college attendance rates, and test scores that are norm and criterion-referenced. Such indicators have obvious face validity but soon displace attention to other outcomes and to the qualities of good schools.

Certain schools in our society are well-situated with respect to such basic indicators. Schools that serve affluent, educated populations enjoy a degree of 'social capital' (Coleman 1987), and often a level of resources, that is unavailable to schools serving disadvantaged communities. Such privileged schools fare well on the basic indicators and so are relatively free of public scrutiny. Schools serving less privileged communities confront a far more difficult task in measuring up on the basic indicators. When they fail to do so, the response most often has been to increase external regulation of curriculum and instruction.

A regulatory response to school failure has a number of virtues. Efforts to specify the curriculum and its outcomes serve to reduce uncertainty about the school's mission and to direct the work of educators. Evidence also suggests that the most powerful means for improving test scores is to teach what is tested, to align curriculum content with test content (Cohen 1987). In these senses, external regulation, whether from the state or the district level, can make schools more manageable by directing the productive processes of schooling to politically sanctioned ends, thereby reducing the ambiguity and instability so long associated with the goals of schooling in our society.

The implication accompanying this approach is that no fundamental restructuring of schools is necessary. Rather, what is needed are a series of technical adjustments in the regulatory framework of schooling and in the tools utilized to implement the state's directives.

We believe this approach is inadequate and insufficient. The inherent dangers are well known and bear brief mention (see also Corbett and Wilson [1988] in this volume). First, an emphasis on indicators of organizational performance, particularly when linked to rewards and sanctions, directs attention to the indicators not to the underlying purposes, goals, and mission of the organization. Test scores become the result, not learning; children become test takers not students; and counts come to dominate educator consciousness, not the deeper significance of their work. Second, what is not counted, measured, or tested gets overlooked and de-emphasized. Educators have many legitimate intentions for their students, but the accountability system focuses on a narrow band of outcomes, leaving a broader range of educational goals and purposes out of the account of successful schools. Educators, parents, and students can lose sight of education's liberal, democratic, and humane purposes in the face of accountability pressures.

A third objection is that teachers must be responsive to student diversity, providing learning experiences that accommodate a wide range of differences in prior knowledge, learning style and ability, interest, and socio-cultural background. A regulatory approach to teaching tends to produce a standardized pedagogy – all students moving at the same pace through the same material, with 'coverage' driving the instruction and the test driving the coverage. Operating within such constraints, teachers do not and cannot respond sensitively to students. They do not become students of children's learning, do not discover and invent ways to encourage and invite engagement. Again, the deeper ideals of education are too easily frustrated by accountability systems as sophisticated technically as they are crude educationally.

We also argue that educators must adopt an experimental stance toward their work, participating in the creation as well as the implementation of instructional and organizational innovations within schools. Improperly managed, accountability systems can create disincentives to innovate, because risk taking and entrepreneurship is punished. Healthy organizations create a dynamic balance between accountability and innovation, encouraging all workers to be innovative some of the time. Too many schools fail to encourage educators to be innovative, denying that professionals operate under twin imperatives: to produce results and to contribute improvements in producing results. External accountability typically concentrates on the former, ignoring the latter to the detriment of organizational and personal-professional growth.

Finally, accountability systems influence the motivation of professional workers, and the evidence suggests that reliance on extrinsic pressures alone produces neither commitment nor competence in teachers or students (see, for example Deci and Ryan 1985, and Fuller *et al*. 1982). Educators must have high expectations for students, but they must also tap intrinsic factors in learning (for a review of student motivation, see Brophy 1986). School climates must encourage engagement with challenging academic material, but provide genuine access and reward students for their efforts. The danger of accountability-driven education is that the motivational climate for teaching and learning becomes distorted. Students and teachers become alienated and disengage from real learning. They go through the motions; they are 'schooled', not educated. Sadly, substantial ethnographic evidence, particularly at the secondary level, exposes such perversions (see, for example, Cusick 1982, McNeil 1987, Powell *et al*. 1985, and Sedlak *et al*. 1986). Accountability pressures are not solely responsible for the contemporary pathologies of teaching and learning, but they contribute to school climates that are profoundly anti-educational.

If productive relations are to develop among school staffs, if schools are to be innovative in approaching problems of organization and instruction, and if more humane and sophisticated education is to take shape, then educational leaders must construct a public, appreciative framework for the schools that directs student and teacher engagement with academic work, promotes commitment and organizational effectiveness, and gives scope to schooling's broad purposes. This is an ongoing task in our society for Americans do not speak with one voice about their schools. The history of American education is a chronicle of disagreement and conflict over the purposes of schooling.

Educators must take responsibility for deepening the discourse about education's fundamental purposes and about the soundest ways to pursue them. Policymakers must welcome such discourse and allow educators room for invention and for the creation of strong and distinctive cultures. Schools cannot prove their excellence if they are overregulated, but they must be held to account as public trusts. This means that educators themselves must be willing to propose standards of good practice and norms of conduct against which they are willing to be judged. Such norms and standards must include reference to learning outcomes and other results of schooling, but also should encompass qualities of schools and of students' experiences within them.

If education's regulatory framework emphasizes certain measures that must be common to all schools, then policy and administrative practice also must encourage each school to cultivate idiosyncratic virtues, and to celebrate and make public its unique strengths and comparative advantages in serving students and communities. If policy explicitly encouraged and rewarded school-based approaches to excellence, then school leaders – teachers and administrators alike – could discover, develop, and share their strengths. But policy and practice must authorize such approaches to schools, and this requires a justifying public discourse that acknowledges the complexities of education in a diverse, democratic society, that celebrates the qualties of educational experiences as well as educational outcomes, and that maintains the necessary tension between shared standards and unique approaches to excellence.

A concluding note

We need finally to clarify our lead theme, making schools manageable. The prevailing tendency in educational policy and administrative practice today is to create rules, structures, and routines that increase control as they impoverish education. We cannot make schools manageable at the expense of our deepest ideals. We need instead visions of schools that provide hopeful, realistic prospects as they acknowledge the unavoidable dilemmas and complexities of the educational endeavour in a democratic society. As we search for more efficient and effective ways to organize and manage the work of teaching and learning through policy and administration, we constantly must consult purposes and ideals.

We have argued in this essay that the range of solutions to the management of education is too narrow, and that policy, research, and administrative practice each contributes to a status quo that ill serves many communities. Two tendencies capture the most prevalent approaches to reform. One is to study the successes under current forms of organization, then extrapolate policy and practice. The other is to increase the external regulation of the enterprise. Neither points the way to tomorrow's schools, neither creates the conditions for invention that will be necessary if American education is to contribute to an American Renascence. It is to encourage this spirit, to press the frontiers, that we set forth these observations and proposals.

References

BARDACH, E. and KAGAN, R. (1982) *Going by the Book: The Problem of Regulatory Unreasonableness* (Philadelphia: Temple University Press).
BARTH, R. (1986) 'The principal and the profession of teaching'. *Elementary School Journal*, 84(4), pp. 471–492.
BENVENISTE, G. (1987) *Professionalizing the Organization. Reducing Bureaucracy to Enhance Effectiveness* (San Francisco: Jossey Bass).
BOSSERT, S., DWYER, D., ROWEN, B. and LEE, G. (1982) 'The instructional management role of the principal', *Educational Administration Quarterly*, 18(3), pp. 34–64.
BRANDL, J. (1988) 'On politics and policy analysis as the design and assessment of institutions', *Journal of Policy Analysis and Management*, 7(3), pp.419–424.
BROPHY, J. (1986) 'On motivating students', occasional paper No. 101 (East Lansing, MI: Institute for Research on Teaching).
CARMICHAEL, L. (1985) 'Working within the authority pyramid: the principal as learner', *Education and Urban Society*, 17(3), pp. 311–323.
CLUNE, W. (1987) 'Institutional choice as a theoretical framework for research on educational policy', *Educational Evaluation and Policy Analysis*, 9(2), pp. 117–132.
COHEN, A. (1987) 'Instructional alignment: searching for a magic bullet', *Educational Researcher*, 16(8), pp. 16–20.
COLEMAN, J. (1987) 'Families and schools', *Educational Researcher*, 16(6), pp. 32–38.
CORBETT, H.D. and WILSON, B. L. (1988) 'Raising the stakes in statewide mandatory testing programs', in J. Hannaway and R. Crowson (eds.) *The Politics of Reforming School Administration* (London: Falmer Press).
CROWSON, R. and PORTER-GEHRIE, C. (1980) 'The discretionary behavior of principals in large-city schools', *Educational Administration Quarterly*, 16(1), pp. 45–68.
CROZIER, M. (1964) *The Bureaucratic Phenomenon* (Chicago: University of Chicago Press).
CUBAN, L. (1984) 'Transforming the frog into a prince: effective schools research, policy, and practice at the district level', *Harvard Educational Review*, 54(2), pp. 129-151.
CUBAN, L. (1986) 'Principaling: images and roles', *Peabody Journal of Education*, 63(1), pp. 107-119.
CUBAN, L. (1988) *The Managerial Imperative and the Practice of Leadership in Schools* (Albany: State University Press of New York).

CUSICK, P. (1983) *The Egalitarian Ideal and the American High School* (New York: Longman).

DARLING-HAMMOND, L. (1984) 'Beyond the commission reports: the coming crisis in teaching', R-3177-RC (Santa Monica: RAND Corporation).

DECI E. and RYAN, R. (1985) *Intrinsic Motivation and Self-Determination in Human Behaviour* (New York: Plenum Press).

ELMORE, R. (1987a) 'Choice in public education', in W. L. Boyd and C.T. Kerchner (eds.) *The Politics of Excellence and Choice in Education* (London: Falmer Press).

ELMORE, R. (1987b) 'Leadership and policy in education', unpublished manuscript.

ELMORE, R. and MCLAUGHLIN, M. (1988) 'Steady work: policy, practice, and the reform of American education', R-3574-NIE/RC (Santa Monica: RAND Corporation).

FREUD, S. (1937) 'Analysis terminable and interminable', *The Standard Edition of the Complete Psychological Works of Sigmund Freud, Volume 23* (London: Hogarth Press; Original work published in 1923).

FULLER, B., WOOD, K., RAPOPORT, T. and DORNBUSCH, S. (1982) 'The organizational context of individual efficacy', *Review of Educational Research*, 52(1), pp.7-30.

GOODLAD, J. (1984) *A Place Called School* (New York: McGraw-Hill).

GORMLEY, W. (1987) 'Institutional policy analysis: A critical review, *Journal of Policy Analysis and Management*, 6(2), pp. 153-169.

JOHNSON, S. (1983) *Teacher Unions in Schools* (Philadelphia: Temple University Press).

JOHNSON, S. (1988) 'Schoolwork and its reform', in J. Hannaway and R. Crowson (eds.) *The Politics of Reforming School Administration* (London: Falmer Press).

KERR S. and JERMIER, J. (1978) 'Substitutes for leadership: their meaning and measurement', *Organizational Behavior and Human Performance*, 22(3), pp. 375-403.

LEITHWOOD, K. and MONTGOMERY, D. (1982) 'The role of the elementary school principal in program improvement', *Review of Educational Research*, 52(3), pp. 309-339.

LIPSKY, M. (1980) *Street-level Bureacracy: Dilemmas of the Individual in Public Services* (New York: Russell Sage Foundation).

LORSCH, J. and MATHIAS, P. (1987) 'When professionals have to manage', *Harvard Business Review*, July-August, pp. 78-83.

LORTIE, D., CROW, G. and PROLMAN, S. (1983) 'Elementary principals in suburbia: an occupational and organizational study', final report (Washington: National Institute of Education).

LORTIE, D. (1986) 'Teacher status in Dade County: a case of structural strain?' *Phi Delta Kappan*, 67(8), pp. 568-575.

MARCH, J. (1978) 'American public school administration: a short analysis', *School Review*, 86, pp. 217-449.

MARTIN, W. and WILLOWER, (1981) 'The managerial behavior of high school principals', *Educational Administration Quarterly*, 17(1), pp. 69-90.

MCDONNELL, L. and ELMORE, R. (1987) 'Getting the job done: alternative policy instruments', *Educational Evaluation and Policy Analysis*, 9(2), pp.133–152.

MCNEIL, L. (1987) *Contradictions of Control: School Structure and School Knowledge* (New York: Routledge and Kegan Paul/Methuen).

MEIER, D. (1985) 'Retaining the teacher's perspective in the principalship', *Education and Urban Society*, 17(3), pp. 302-310.

MEINDL, J., EHRLICH, S. and DUKERICH, J. (1985) 'The romance of leadership', *Administrative Science Quarterly*, 30, pp.78-102.

MEYER, J. and ROWAN, B. (1977) 'Institutionalized organisations: formal structure as myth and ceremony', *American Journal of Sociology*, 83, pp.340-363.

MURPHY, J. (1988) 'The unheroic side of leadership: notes from the swamp', *Phi Delta Kappan*, 69(9), pp.654-659.

ORITZ, F., and MARSHALL, C. (1988) 'Women in educational administration', in N. Boyan (ed.) *Handbook of Research on Educational Administration* (New York: Longman).

PACKARD, J. (1988) 'The pupil control studies', in N. Boyan (ed.) *Handbook on Research in Educational Administration* (New York: Longman).

PETERS, T.J. and WATERMAN, R. H. (1982) *In Search of Excellence. Lessons from America's Best-Run Companies.* (New York: Harper & Row).

PITNER, N. (1986) 'Substitutes for principal leader behaviour: an exploratory study', *Educational administration Quarterly*, 22(2), pp.23-42.

PITNER, N. (1988) 'The study of administrative effects and effectiveness', in N. Boyan (ed.) *Handbook of Research on Educational Administration* (New York: Longman).

POWELL, A., FARRAR, E. and COHEN, D. (1985) *The Shopping Mall High School: Winners and Losers in the Educational Marketplace* (Boston: Houghton-Mifflin).

PURKEY, S. and SMITH M. (1983) 'Effective schools: a review', *Elementary School Journal*, 83(4),pp.427-452.

RAELIN, J. (1986) *The Clash of Cultures. Managers and Professionals* (Boston: Harvard Business School Press).

RAYWID, M.A. (1985) 'Family choice arrangements in public schools: a review of the literature', *Review of Educational Research*, 55(4),pp.435-467.

ROWAN, B. (forthcoming) 'The technology of teaching and school reform', unpublished manuscript. E. Lansing: Michigan State University.

SCHULTZE, C. (1977) *The Public Use of Private Interest* (Washington: The Brookings Institution).

SEDLAK, M., WHEELER, C., PULLIN, D. and CUSICK, P. (1986) *Sel'ing Students Short: Classroom Bargains and Academic Reform in the American High School* (New York: Teachers College Press).

WEICK, K. (1976) 'Educational organizations as loosely coupled systems', *Administrative Science Quarterly*, 21, March, pp. 1–19.

7   *Schoolwork and its reform**

Susan Moore Johnson
Harvard University

Educational policymakers are enthusiastic these days about the prospects for redesigning teaching – transforming 'creaky old jobs' into high-status, professional careers (The Holmes Group 1986: 7). Since 1982, many reform initiatives have worked their way out of blue ribbon commissions, through state legislatures, across governors' desks, and into the schools. Although the final results of these efforts are not yet in, it is clear that change has not been easy or quick (Olson 1987). Merit pay, career ladders, revised licensing standards, and proficiency testing often engendered disdain or encountered disregard among school people. Some plans have failed because of local opposition; others have collapsed under the heft of their own political and financial costs; yet others hobble along.

Recent proposals from the Carnegie Forum and the Holmes Group seem different from the so-called 'first wave' of reforms for they would *empower teachers rather than manage them*. Teachers would assume responsibility for licensing and supervising their peers; they would exercise control over their classrooms and schools. Through their National Board for Professional Teaching Standards, teachers would control access to and advancement in the profession. Lead teachers, selected for their expertise, would assume managerial roles in the schools, and executive committees of teachers might hire their own principals. In their classrooms, teachers would decide what to teach and how to teach it.

In addition to gaining control over their classrooms, schools, and profession, *teachers would expand the scope of their responsibilities*. In response to complaints that teaching is repetitive and confining, teachers could elect to assume a variety of curricular, supervisory, and administrative responsibilities. While their first commitment would be to their teaching, these teachers would benefit from the diverse opportunities offered by differentiated staffing.

Third, the Holmes Group reformers call for *staged careers* that would offer steps for professional advancement to be rewarded with higher pay, prestige, and influence. Decrying the 'flat career pattern, roundly condemned as teaching's "careerlessness" ' (p. 32), they advocate a three-tiered system of licensing that would permit outstanding teachers to advance to the level of the Career Professional.

Together, these proposals are intended to attract and retain competent and committed teachers. Even where the recommendations resemble earlier initiatives, as with career ladders or elevated standards for certification, the intent behind the new formulations seems different. Teachers are to be the agents rather than the objects of reform. The prospect of such a shift is attractive to many who work in schools, particularly given the restrictive, regulatory character of the initial reforms (McNeil 1987). One wonders, though, whether the 'new' reforms will be more fitting or potent than the prior initiatives. Are teachers discontent because they are confined to teaching or because they are prevented from teaching

*The research reported on here was supported by a grant from the Spencer Foundation and is part of a larger study to be reported in a forthcoming book, *Schoolwork*.

well? Are the problems that these reforms address the same ones that vex good teachers most? Are the proposed remedies appropriate and adequate?

Although the 'new' reform proposals have been prepared by informed and respected analysts, they are not explicitly based upon research findings (Ryan 1987, Jackson 1987). Because the proposals have been widely acclaimed, it is likely that many in the states and districts will set out enthusiastically to implement them. Since the recommendations are far-reaching – calling for the restructuring of teaching and schools as we know them – they warrant close attention, lest the moment for reform be lost, teachers' efforts be wasted, and the public once again become disillusioned with its schools.

This study explores such issues by examining how 25 high school teachers, identified as being 'very good' by their principals, respond to their workplaces. It begins with the assumption that before embarking on wholesale reforms, we must better understand how teachers whose work is valued experience teaching in their schools. What supports or compromises their best efforts? It is worth carefully studying this group of teachers because it is they who are likely to determine the course of school improvement. It is they who, under current working conditions, are most likely to leave teaching after several years (Kerr 1983, Weaver 1979, Schlechty and Vance 1981, 1982). It is these teachers for whom new roles as mentor teachers or lead teachers are being designed. It is they who are most likely to reform their schools from within. Finally, it is these valued teachers whose continued presence in the profession will draw others like them into teaching. If we care about our schools, we must attend to their views.

Methodology

Because there is little empirical research that directly addresses the school as a workplace, this study was intended to be exploratory and hypothesis-generating. A qualitative approach offered an appropriate method for examining the complexity of workplace issues. The study, therefore, has both the benefits and costs of gathering data intensively from a relatively small number of respondents. It sacrifices breadth for depth, telling a great deal about a few people, and does not permit statistical generalizations to a larger population. However, the rich and complicated data that emerge from intensive interviewing can offer valuable insights for teachers, school officials, and school watchers. The study can also offer direction for subsequent research with larger populations. In an effort to moderate the disadvantages of a small sample, I sought to ensure as much balance and diversity as possible.

In identifying the 25 high school teachers to be interviewed for this study, I selected an economically and demographically diverse group of school districts from eastern Massachusetts and wrote to 40 high school principals introducing the study and asking them to recommend three teachers whom they would 'consider to be "very good" teachers. These should be teachers whose work is respected by their colleagues and whose contribution to the school would be missed if they were to leave.' On a separate response sheet, principals recommended three teachers, noting their subject specialties and estimating the number of years that they had been teaching. From each list of three, I chose one, seeking to maintain as much diversity as possible in subject area, sex, and years of experience. In all, I asked 31 teachers who had been recommended by principals to participate in the study, and 23 agreed. Two additional teachers, whom I had selected for pilot interviews on the basis of their reputations as exemplary teachers, were included in the final sample of 25[1] representing 16 school districts.[2]

As with most qualitative studies, decisions about validity must rest with the insightful reader who is familiar with teachers, principals, and schools, and who weighs the data and subsequent analysis. There is, however, considerable evidence throughout the interviews that these teachers were committed to teaching, were respected by their peers, and had made special contributions to their schools. As a group, they were an impressive lot.

Along with a graduate research assistant, I conducted semistructured interviews with these teachers during the spring of 1986. Respondents were asked about many aspects of their workplace including the setting, provision of supplies, specialization of work, relationships with principals, colleagues, parents, and students, the supervision of their work, their roles in governance, wages and incentives, as well as opportunities for recognition, learning and growth. Questions ranged from those designed to gather facts: 'Are you involved in any formal policymaking?'; 'What administrative tasks or obligations do you have?'; 'Who evaluates your teaching?', to those that probed teachers' subjective judgments about their workplaces: 'Who provides leadership in this school?'; 'What about this school or district makes it possible for you to do your best teaching?'; 'Are you satisfied with the extent of freedom or autonomy that you have in your teaching?' At a minimum, 22 issues were covered in each interview; respondents often added more. The interviews, all of which were tape recorded, lasted between 1 and $2\frac{1}{2}$ hours.

Once the interviews had been transcribed, I coded them topically using the software program, *Ethnograph*, a filing system designed for analyzing large sets of qualitative data. The 92 codes that I used were drawn from a review of the workplace literature in other employment sectors (Kanter and Stein 1976, Terkel 1972, Richardson 1973, Biderman and Drury 1976, Duncan *et al.* 1980, Kanter 1983), relevant studies of schooling (Lortie 1975, Goodlad 1984, and Sizer 1984), and a preliminary analysis of these interview data. Because *Ethnograph* permits the use of multiple codes for any piece of data, I was able to systematically review printouts of all teachers' responses addressing a single topic, considering the range and distribution of those responses, and testing emerging hunches and conclusions against the data. In addition, I sent all teachers who participated in the study an early draft of this article and solicited their comments and criticisms.

The teachers' responses

These teachers were primarily concerned with, and sustained by, their classroom teaching. The policies and practices of the school or district commanded their attention to the extent that they supported or compromised their instructional efforts. Teachers valued their autonomy and were wary of any efforts to constrain it, but they also felt isolated and sought more purposeful interaction with colleagues. They were not bored with teaching and they actively varied their approaches in order to sustain their interest and enthusiasm. They believed that their best efforts as teachers went unrecognized by administrators and parents whom they wished would understand and appreciate their work more. Although few were involved in formal policymaking, having been discouraged by their lack of influence in the past, many continued to exert informal influence about things that mattered to them. There were important variations that seemed to result from differences in the circumstances of their work. This variation is as important to understand as the commonalities.

The current proposals for reform were only of modest interest to these teachers. Some, such as new roles for lead or mentor teachers, elicited more favorable response than others. However, the respondents emphasized that such changes in policy will not, in themselves, enable them to do well what matters most – to teach. They believed that the power to change their workplaces rested not in the hands of state-level policymakers, but in their schools and districts, with peers, principals, parents, and district administrators. They expressed little confidence that they, themselves, could be the agents of reforming their workplaces.

In order to understand these valued teachers' responses to the school as a workplace, it is important to start from the beginning, to consider first why they entered teaching, to what extent they believe their goals have been fulfilled, and what they plan for the future.

Why they entered teaching

As a group, these teachers are experienced, having taught an average of slightly more than 17 years. They said that when they began teaching, it was because they liked children, cared about their subject specialities, enjoyed teaching, or believed that they could change society through their work. One teacher reported, 'I just loved kids, always loved kids.' Another echoed, 'I liked working with young people.' An English teacher described his keen interest in literature and asked, 'What does one do with English in order to share that love? You go out there and teach it.' A foreign language teacher said, 'I love my field, and I really enjoy it when somebody has learned something he didn't know in it.' Similarly, a physics teacher who had taught at the college level and worked in industry before entering teaching said, 'I guess that when I started teaching, I remember high school teachers always saying, "I teach children, not biology." I thought, "No, I teach physics. And I teach it to some very interesting children."'.

There were a number of teachers who recalled an early interest in pedagogy. One told of attending a competitive public high school and deciding in his senior year that he would become a math teacher: 'You can blame it on some of the teachers. . . .There were some sharp teachers. They were sharp in that they knew their material, but whether they could get it across to students was another thing.' Similarly, a science teacher reported that she made her decision to teach before she entered high school:

> I think it was because I had a couple of very good teachers, one in seventh grade that I particularly remember, especially when I compared them to other teachers that I had. These people definitely did a good job, were well organized. I really learned a lot those years. I just felt that I could do as well as those two teachers. I could do better than the poor teachers.

Finally, there were those, many of whom began their careers in the late 1960s, who chose teaching for its larger social purposes. An English teacher explained: 'I entered teaching because I honestly felt that I could change the world singlehandedly.' Another said, 'I went into education because it was, well, my mission.' A social studies echoed, 'I was 22 years old and I was going to save the world.'

As a group, these teachers, like those interviewed by Lortie two decades before, had focused almost exclusively on the anticipated psychic rewards rather than the extrinsic rewards of teaching (Lortie 1975: 131). Their concerns centered on students, subject matter, and the classroom. Two teachers also mentioned the importance of the academic calendar and a predictable wage in their decisions to teach, factors that Lortie calls the 'ancillary rewards of teaching'; but these were secondary incentives. One said, 'I'm an unregenerate sixties liberal. I saw it as a way to do something useful and meaningful, have a moderately comfortable lifestyle, and have control of my life in terms of time.' A math teacher who entered teaching because he 'liked it' and eventually 'became good at it', said that he also valued the opportunities that his teaching schedule provided: 'It doesn't really restrict me. If I want to go to school in the summer, I can. If I want to travel, I can. If I want to work, I can.' These people began teaching to teach, to affect the lives of young people, and to contribute to the general social good.

Have these teachers' goals been fulfilled?

In considering whether their goals as teachers had been fulfilled, these teachers responded with an ambivalent 'Yes, but'. Although they had achieved much of what they had sought in teaching, most had been far less successful than they had hoped. They told of school practices that interfered with their teaching and of a society that discredits their efforts.

For these teachers, like those studied by Lortie (1975) and Goodlad (1984), success was apparent in the appreciation and accomplishments of their students. They described their pleasure in watching 'a kid get fired up', 'seeing the debate operation blossom', or reaching 'the kid that nobody else is able to or wants to'. One told of her pride in developing 'creative and challenging teaching strategies, getting the kids involved'. They recalled the satisfaction of hearing from 'the students who come back'. A chemistry teacher spoke with pleasure about having students eventually recognize the worth of what they had learned: 'Then, when they go on to college, they tell me, "Boy am I glad I studied those valences."' One expressed what was implicit in many others' remarks: 'I've touched a lot of kids' lives.'

For three teachers in this sample, work continues to be what they had hoped. One who teaches English in a suburban community that supports its schools well told of eager, well-prepared students, professional autonomy, interesting colleagues, and a school administration that encouraged good work: 'I can honestly say that I am really very, very happy with what I'm doing right now.' Another, who teaches English as a Second Language in a low SES community, described a very supportive principal and a program well-stocked with federally-funded materials. She spoke of her successes with individual students: 'I feel like I'm just born again with new ideas and seeing the way the kids respond. . . .I feel like I'm just starting to go and I've been teaching 20 years.' In each case, these teachers had autonomy in their classrooms, felt supported and appreciated for their efforts, and believed that their views were heard by responsive administrators.

Eighteen others acknowledged success in their work, but told of conditions that compromised their best efforts. Some spoke of small, but aggravating problems, that had accumulated over time. A home economics teacher from a large urban high school serving poor students recounted the difficulties of purchasing supplies for her work. Allotted less than $4.00 per student, per term, she shopped several times a week for perishable supplies and carried groceries to her classroom, often waiting months to be reimbursed for her expenses. She spoke angrily about the day when she had been thirty seconds late for school:

> It could be a function of a traffic light, or unloading groceries, or not finding a parking space, and they actually ripped the sign-in sheet down. Someone is standing there with a stop watch who rips it down at the exact second and you get a big red circle around your name. It's very demeaning. You have to sign in on a special sheet and if you have three a month, you get a special letter. It's like being treated like a child.

Although she had begun her teaching career with great enthusiasm and success, she had become discouraged by administrative practices such as these that discredited her efforts.

Three confronted more pervasive problems. An English teacher in a vocational school had decided to leave her job because administrators undermined instruction. When the head of the school created a rotating schedule, her new assignment included six preparations and 350 students, whom she met on alternate weeks. As an English teacher, she was required to de-emphasize literature in her classes and to give final exams that included 150 multiple choice questions. After teaching under this new system for five years, she was planning to leave: 'I think that I would never want to be anything else [but a teacher] if I hadn't been so abused in that school. I do feel badly thinking about leaving it, because I'm good at it.'

The large majority of teachers' responses fell between the extremes of contentment and despair. Their successes with individual students and classes were punctuated with annoyances and disappointments. Virtually all were pleased to have a great deal of autonomy in their teaching. Most spoke of competent, if not inspired, administrators, supportive colleagues, and adequate, though not sumptuous, supplies. But most also resented non-teaching duties, lamented relentless demands on their time, regretted the isolation of their work and felt unappreciated by administrators, parents, and the public.

Autonomy

Repeatedly, teachers spoke of the importance of being autonomous professionals. They thought themselves fortunate to be teaching in a state that does not mandate detailed curricula. In general, their instruction was not controlled by others and, where it was, they chafed under centrally imposed prescriptions. Most planned their classes as they thought best, keeping in mind the outlines of a formal curriculum, but not feeling bound by it. A science teacher explained that the curriculum 'is pretty much set up by the teachers who teach the subject along with the head of the department'. An English teacher who worked in a similar situation observed that it was ideal for 'competent people who are enthusiastic about what they're doing. If you take those teachers and allow them creative input so that they actually have an individual stamp, then I think that you're really going to support good teaching. It's self-motivating.'

In the extreme, four teachers said that they were totally unregulated, that no one paid attention to what they taught. One reflected critically on that lack of attention to their classroom teaching: 'I teach what I want. I teach the basic things, but if I didn't want to teach that and I wanted to teach something else, I could teach anything I wanted. No one would know.'

The appropriate balance between attention and undue regulation is sometimes hard to achieve. When professional discretion was tightly circumscribed, teachers complained bitterly. There were two teachers from a large, urban district whose autonomy had been severely restricted by school officials who sought to promote consistency and accountability among staff. One, who taught math at a technical high school, described a mandated curriculum and tests designed to ensure compliance:

> It's mind-boggling what they expect you to cover in a year with the type of students you have. They want us to cover trig and algebra II all in one year. We've told them that we could cover algebra II and then trig in another year. For two years, we fought the same battle. We kept recommending this, and they kept coming back with the same curriculum.

In the face of these demands, this teacher had chosen to pace his teaching according to his students' abilities, to exert the discretion of the street-level bureaucrat (Lipsky 1980): 'You can't really cover the whole curriculum. You've got to make a decision on what you think is the best.' Unlike certain teachers described by Corbett and Wilson (1988) elsewhere in this volume, this individual resisted the pressure of 'highstakes' tests.

A social studies teacher in the same district explained that in her American history classes she was obliged to use a required text and to proceed in lock-step fashion through the curriculum. She preferred her elective course to those with mandated materials and procedures:

> My best class is my Afro-American history class, a class where you don't have all this curriculum and objectives to follow – where you're a robot and it's an assembly line kind of thing, where you're not doing anything well. You're just on some kind of a schedule. You really don't have the time to do all those wonderful things that you want to do.

It's important to emphasize that these teachers did not seek to be free agents without responsibility to their colleagues or the larger instructional program. Rather, they endorsed establishing curricula by departments or schools and preferred maintaining a careful balance between prescription and license. Very few reported that they had adequate supervision of their work. One physics teacher who said, 'Nothing is prescribed, and that is marvellous' also thought that the department head should offer more supervision:

> The department chairman is not coming in saying 'You're lecturing too much.' 'Or you're not using the overhead enough – you're only using it 30% of the time or you're using too much chalk.' In fact, I wish he had more suggestions. 'Have you thought about trying this rather than what you're doing?'

Similarly, a social studies teacher in a vocational school spoke with pride about developing his own curriculum and designing the instructional schedule with his co-teacher: 'I like the control that the two of us have. If we want to extend a period or shorten a period we can do it. We can do anything we want, academically.' However, he also said, 'Nobody checks us. We should be checked. Nobody's ever checked me. . .' He, like other respondents, expressed concern about less able colleagues who abuse this freedom.

Isolation

Many of these teachers said that their work was isolating for a variety of reasons. Several spoke of the physical separateness of their classrooms. Others described buildings that promote departmental segregation. One teacher said, 'We're not only departmentalized, but compartmentalized.' Another, who blamed the lack of collegial interaction on a rigid schedule and heavy demands, complained, 'There are some people that I see on the first day of school and maybe five times throughout the year. And we work in the same building.' Some teachers observed that they contributed to this isolation by intentionally keeping to themselves in response to unfriendly, inhospitable work environments. One, who worked in a large, urban school explained, 'I was trying to figure out why I have been somewhat isolating myself, and the best that I can come up with is that it's peaceful where I am . . . When I go out into the halls, it's very stressful. There's craziness in the halls – yelling and sceaming and kicking and pushing. 'Another offered a similar explanation: 'I tend to isolate myself. I was at a junior high that had a lot of problems with discipline. But I found that I could just have my own little world and control that.'

In those schools where teachers said that they were not isolated, interaction was reportedly the result of deliberate efforts by faculty to overcome the distances between them. Some spent their preparation periods working in offices with other members of their departments, and in doing so, kept informed about their colleagues' interests and efforts. However, as Bird and Little's research (1984) demonstrates, efforts to maintain collegial interactions among teachers were often undermined by scarce time and conflicting commitments. Most of these teachers preferred to use non-teaching time to work with students in their classrooms. One English teacher whose school was very large, told of setting up a cluster program for ninth grade students and the challenge of maintaining daily faculty interaction:

> We just make it a point. We try to see each other before homeroom. Even though we're scattered all over. Might see each other at lunch. Might. We make it a point, if we have a free period, if it's important, to run over to the other teacher, and just say, 'did so-and-so show up for class?' or 'What's going on here?' or 'Don't forget the field trip coming up.' So, you just have to make the time to do it . . .

Peer observations in classrooms occurred very rarely, although many teachers thought that they would be useful. As Goodlad (1984) observed, the difficulty seemed to be less one of will than way: 'There are not infrastructures designed to encourage or support either communication among teachers in improving their teaching or collaboration in attacking schoolwide problems' (p. 188). Limited time, the egg-carton structure of schools, the absence of administrative expectations, and faculty norms that discouraged such initiatives combined to keep teaching a solo flight for these teachers.

Repetition

Contrary to conventional wisdom and some empirical evidence about elementary teachers (Boston Women's Teachers Group 1983), very few of those interviewed for this study considered their work to be repetitive or complained about being confined to the same set of unvarying tasks year after year. Most spoke of finding energy in the content of personally crafted curricula or the ever-changing composition of their classes. One foreign language teacher said, 'No other job could go so fast, be so different.' An English teacher said, 'I know that [repetition] is a common complaint, but . . . I always thought that the more I taught something, the better I understood the nuances of it. I would just find ways of going into it in more depth. I would find ways of teaching it better.'

Although they did not complain about repetitiveness in teaching itself, several teachers did report that they periodically needed to change courses or schools to keep themselves fresh and engaged. A social studies teacher had transferred from the junior to senior high school because he 'just wanted something new, something different'. Another social studies teacher who had traditionally taught courses with lower-ability students, had requested to teach an advanced-level class: 'I think that when you do the same thing for a number of years that you're ready for a change.' A physics teacher recalled that when he had been away from teaching doing research 'I got itchy to get back in the classroom. But being in the classroom 20 hours a week, year after year, has a grinding effect to it.' His solution, however, was not to substitute other work for teaching, but rather to move to another setting: 'I'd like something to spice it up a bit. Maybe just teaching at [the other high school]. I've seen this room for nine years now. Something a bit different might be fun.'

These teachers seemed to be seeking relief from excessive unremitting demands on their time and energy rather than from boredom. A few districts provided opportunities for paid leaves during which teachers could recharge their intellectual and professional batteries. One teacher described a program of short-term leaves during which teachers could spend one or two weeks on an issue of interest to them. However, under the pressures of fiscal constraints, most districts had eliminated such opportunities for leaves during recent years. Unless teachers returned to school or took a leave to raise children, they could not anticipate any sustained time off. More than one teacher observed that because of this, summer break had become increasingly precious.

Teachers who reported working in unsupportive workplaces suggested that it was not the repetition of their teaching, but the repetition of frustration that demoralized them. Inflexible schedules, curricula prescribed in detail, administrative rules that bound them to fixed procedures, and the repetition of demeaning non-teaching duties were said to interfere with good teaching. Therefore, although these teachers agreed that they would welcome changes that might lighten their load, vary the settings and circumstances of their work, and eliminate the repeated distractions and interruptions to good teaching, few suggested that what they sought was a substitute for the work itself.

Recognition

Despite the fact that these teachers had been identified by principals as being exemplary, the large majority said that their efforts and accomplishments went unnoticed. They believed that students were less likely to express appreciation for their teaching than in the past, and that parents were less involved in their children's education and more likely to blame them when the children didn't succeed. Furthermore, administrators were said to be preoccupied with managerial tasks and central office directives and, consequently, unable to pay close attention to classroom teaching.

These teachers were not seeking public or financial rewards. For them, recognition meant appreciation rather than reknown. In fact, several explicitly opposed awards that might single them out from other deserving colleagues. Because they were contending with difficult social and learning problems presented by students, and because they felt misunderstood and beleaguered by a public that discounts their talents and good intentions, these teachers were looking for some assurances that others knew of their work and valued their efforts. They sought recognition, not to motivate them, but to sustain them in difficult times.

Teachers who worked in high SES communities were more likely to report receiving parental thanks for their efforts than did teachers in poorer communities where student needs and working conditions often made good teaching even harder. One foreign language teacher in a wealthy school district said that 'parents out there are very appreciative of what they perceive to be good teaching and good work'. He said that he typically received '15 or 20 letters and cards from different parents at the end of the year. And it's almost embarrassing . . . but it's also really nice.' This teacher's experience was unusual, even for teachers from prestigious, suburban districts. The large majority of respondents reported that parents had become increasingly remote from the schools and that, therefore, they did not offer the levels of praise and support that they once had.

A few teachers reported that their principals regularly let them know that they were doing good work, but the majority said that there was little notice of their efforts and accomplishments. Three said that having been selected for this study was the first evidence they had that their principals regarded them as very good teachers. When asked whether she received recognition for her work, one teacher in a large, urban high school said, 'Nothing. Not a thing. Nothing. Excellent teachers do what they do because they love teaching. They love students. And they want to do things for students. [But] we need recognition, if no more than a "thank you" or a pat on the back or something.'

Several teachers observed that although their accomplishments weren't noticed, their shortcomings were. Rather than being credited for success with difficult subject matter or needy students, they were discredited for minor violations of bureaucratic rules. A foreign language teacher said, 'I don't even get a little pat sometimes. But I know right away when

I've done something wrong.' An English teacher said, 'In this city, not too many people appreciate anything. Any time you do something good around here, they want to find something wrong with it. It's a very negative city.' Teachers told of being criticized for failing to file reports on time, being late for hall duty, or permitting students to wear hats in their classes. One English teacher observed somewhat cynically, 'There's a real contradiction in attention. They say, "We'll trust you to make up the curriculum. We'll trust you to do a good job." On the other hand, "If you're not in your room at 2:30, Buddy, we know you're doing something wrong."'

Governance

These teachers varied in the extent to which they could and did influence matters of school or district policy. Very few were actively involved in any collective decisionmaking in their districts and many were cynical about administrators' sincerity in promoting teacher partici-pation on policy committees. Two teachers were adamant, however, that it was possible for colleagues to influence decisions of consequence through formal procedures. Most others relied on informal personal means of persuasion when they really wanted to be heard by a school official.

There were numerous reports of faculty who once had been active on committees only to find their reports and recommendations ignored by the administration or school board. One physics teacher's experience was like many others': 'Very often you would spend months working on a plan or a proposal for something and then nothing would ever come of it.' Few teachers suggested that school officials were intentionally misleading them in promoting participation that led nowhere. Rather, their accounts suggested that the complex organization of their schools and the political realities of their districts limited their influence over the outcomes. Too many people outside of their buildings had some stake in what happened. One teacher in a large, urban high school told of a decision to merge two schools. Many of her colleagues had been intently involved in plans for implementing change. After months of preparation, the school board voted to abandon the plan. 'So, essentially, we've been working under this merger for the past year and a half, developing special curriculum, going to meetings . . . That's been pulled out now. That's no longer going to happen.'

Faculty meetings provide the one regular forum where we might expect teachers to be heard, but scarcely any of those interviewed reported that important discussion took place there. Typically, principals used the time to inform staff about new regulations, to restate old expectations, or to sponsor formal presentations about instructional or social programs. One teacher observed that there were never any votes taken at these meetings. Another complained: 'Even when we have meetings, we never get to address educational issues . . . We end up talking about violence or crime or anything extraneous to education.' A third was resigned to having little influence at such meetings:

> We have a monthly faculty meeting with the principal, at which time, if the teachers wanted to bring something up, they certainly could. I hate to say it, but most of our major decisions are already cast. In other words, they come down as orders from high up, down to the principal. Once in a while, you fight them.

Although most teachers reported that they had little opportunity to effect meaningful change outside their classrooms or departments, teachers in several schools argued that such influence was available, but unused. The range of responses suggested that teachers' power to determine policies and practices varied considerably from school to school and depended largely on the principal.

A social studies teacher in a large suburban school spoke favorably of the principal there: 'the principal is a bright, alert, articulate administrator. I am just very pleased.' This teacher belonged to an informal faculty group, initially formed during a labor dispute several years before. The principal supported this group's efforts and frequently sought their advice. Recently, when members were dissatisfied with a proposed change in the instructional schedule, they prepared a position paper and met with the principal, who acknowledged the legitimacy of their complaints and urged them to draw up on alternative proposal, which they did.

Others told of different experiences. One math teacher recalled his principal's instituting an advisory committee in the school:

> You could go and talk with him and people liked him. Then all of a sudden after about a year or two, there was no more advisory council. We went to see him with a couple of suggestions and he became very defensive . . . There aren't really that many opportunities for [influence] to happen. Both the mechanism is not there and he's not responsive.

The formal authority of teachers in schools remains carefully circumscribed. They exert extensive control over teaching in their classrooms and departments, but their formal influence rarely extends beyond that. Faculty senates and principals' cabinets are explicitly advisory. Districtwide task forces issue reports and recommendations not edicts. It is the attitudes of principals toward teachers' roles in governance that determine how active and influential teachers can be. If principals take teachers' proposals seriously and incorporate their suggestions into the school's policies and practices, teachers, in response would likely commit more time to the task of improving schools. Where principals were closed to formal influence, teachers either withdrew completely behind their classroom doors or continued to exert their personal and political sway informally in an effort to right bad decisions that impinged on their teaching.

These teachers, some of whom had expected to shape instructional policy in their schools, had narrowed their sights and adjusted their expectations. They had accommodated to more passive roles. They wanted to ensure that they were supplied with appropriate books and materials, that their teaching time was protected from interruption, that they were able to teach as they saw fit, that they were treated fairly, and that they were not encumbered with distracting bureaucratic demands. But they did not expect to exert formal influence on policies.

Because many were convinced that administrators are not committed to improving classroom teaching, and in some cases, even impose practices that interfere with good teaching, they expressed little interest in what some school officials call the 'bigger picture'. For teachers, the center of schooling is the classroom and they are active at that center, making the important decisions about children and their learning. They were skeptical about long-term organizational planning, contemptuous of accountability devices. For them, as with Lortie's teachers, the classroom is 'the cathected forum' (1975: 131).

In summary, these teachers found their work demanding and personally rewarding, although their successes usually went unnoticed by others. Too often, they found that their schools' policies and practices interfered with their best teaching. They valued their autonomy, but would have appreciated more collegial interaction, meaningful supervision, and professional respect. They were seldom active participants in formal policymaking, but acted informally when they thought that conditions for good teaching might be jeopardized. Given these circumstances, will they remain in teaching?

What are their plans for the future?

Of the 25 valued teachers interviewed for this study, 14 reported that they will likely continue teaching in the same or similar positions. Three intend to leave for work in teacher training. Four others will probably seek administrative positions. Two are undecided, and two will likely leave for work outside of education. The loss of five or six valued teachers is regrettable, particularly when many of their respected colleagues had left before them in frustration. More important, though, is the likelihood that those who remain in teaching will not be as productive as they might be unless the conditions of their workplaces change significantly.

Some who intend to remain in teaching do so with enthusiasm and confidence. One math teacher who had worked for a time in business, said 'Gee, what do I really want? I think all the things I've been telling you are what I really want. I'll teach.' Others, like this English teacher, seemed resigned to making the best of a trying situation: 'If I have absolutely nothing to redeem my efforts, if I feel that every constructive avenue has been closed, if there is nothing to inspire me, I wouldn't hesitate to leave. But I have never gotten to that point.'

For several teachers who were the sole wage earners in their families, inadequate salaries compounded the problem. One explained that the financial demands of having two children in college might lead her out of teaching. For a social studies teacher, other reasons were prominent: 'It's not the money. [I'm seeking] more freedom, more flexibility and more appreciation from the people I work for.' As one teacher explained, 'I think that there must be other rewarding jobs out there, less frustrating, less stressful.' Many of these respondents had already made considerable compromises in their expectations for supportive, rewarding work environments, but they remained in teaching because they loved to teach.

One teacher told of a period when he had doubted his decision to stay: 'I was supremely naive up to that time. I really believed that the teachers were there to teach, and the parents were there to parent, and the politicians were there to see that the teachers could teach and the students could learn, and parents could parent.' He described his disillusion in discovering that 'Not everybody associated with the school system shares my idealism and my goals . . . not every parent shares my attitudes about what is best for young people, and . . . not every politician tells the truth.' He told of disputes about censorship, 'political leverage to maneuver grades', and administrators' 'questioning the validity of a teacher's standards in the classroom'. He said, 'I really questioned whether or not I had sacrificed far too much for far too little recognition.' Finally, he decided that he would be sustained by his own sense of accomplishment: 'It's like the tree falling in the forest. It does make a sound. I don't care if anyone's around to hear it or not. I make a sound – hell, I make a big boom. I think. So I'm going to go back to knocking over trees . . . '

Although three teachers said that they would likely apply for jobs as principals or assistant principals, most expressed little or no interest in pursuing administrative careers, noting that if they continue to work in schools, they want to teach. As one said, 'I just don't see people in administration boasting about the same kinds of goals that I have. I see them as people who are interested primarily in organization and in accountability, which has become an obsession.' A Latin teacher told of being approached by his principal about applying for a housemaster's job: '"Does that sort of thing appeal to you?" he said. It didn't and it still doesn't. I would terribly miss the classroom.'

Implications for reform

Having considered these teachers' views of their schools as workplaces, we can ask again whether the current proposals for reform address their concerns and are likely to sustain them in their work. Will the proposed changes reduce their isolation or increase the opportunities for recognition from students, parents and peers? Will they preserve autonomy without promoting ill-advised license? Will they increase teachers' formal authority over matters that affect their teaching? At first, these proposals for professional reform may seem tangential to the experiences of these teachers. To a teacher who is coping with a heavy instructional load, maneuvering through the requirements of mandated curricula, persisting despite scarce recognition, and feeling the sting of punitive rules, such proposals may promise only more work, less time, and greater distraction from teaching. But a closer consideration suggests a more complicated conclusion.

Empowerment

These teachers were not eager to become actively involved in formal policymaking, but they did want the power to protect their instructional autonomy and to command the attention of those who controlled resources in their schools. Most reported having influence in their departments, where the curricular decisions that mattered most were usually made. Many had found ways to informally influence their principals' practices without spending long hours in fruitless meetings.

In a very few schools, however, teachers reported feeling that their views on policy were afforded more administrative respect, that their time spent in meetings was productive. These teachers' accounts suggest that if teachers were truly permitted to set school policies, if formal authority over matters of consequence were truly granted, they would likely assume more active roles, particularly over instructional decisions. Most of those interviewed, however, did not anticipate that teachers would ever have such powers and they knew well the limits of advisory roles.

A Nation Prepared: Teachers for the 21st Century (Carnegie Forum, 1986) contains somewhat mixed messages about the authority that teachers should ultimately exercise. First, it proposes that teachers be granted formal authority over educational policy, but only provisionally: 'While it is important that teachers be invested with the authority and responsibility to exercise their professional judgment over a wide range of matters over which they currently have little control, that judgment . . . must be subject to certain constraints.' The reformers advocate trading 'a greater degree of accountability in return for increased discretion'. But what will the terms of that accountability be? Given the current trends in educational policy, it seems likely that the standards for such accountability would be set by states rather than by districts or schools. Teachers might well become responsible to politicians rather than parents. Moreover, test scores would probably be the primary, if not sole measure of success. One might expect these valued teachers to question whether such politically derived standards could be consistent with their best professional judgments. It is very doubtful that they would welcome active roles in policymaking if administrative and legislative support for their professional judgment were tentative or conditional.

The Carnegie Forum has also suggested that schools might be run by executive committees of lead teachers who would emerge from the ranks of teachers. There is a certain logic to arguing that pedagogical rather than managerial values should prevail in schools. And yet, without exception, the teachers interviewed for this study did not seek to run their schools. They did not advocate that the role of principal be eliminated, although some were critical of their current bosses. In fact, most of those interviewed emphasized the importance of the principal in enabling them to concentrate on their teaching. These teachers looked to principals to do what they have long done – manage buildings, satisfy the demands of central office, maintain discipline, deal with parents, and facilitate good instruction with few interruptions. In some cases, where individual principals were highly respected, these teachers believed that their building administrators could hold an organizational perspective and provide organizational leadership that teachers, invested as they were in their classrooms, could not. Therefore, although the promise of empowerment was attractive, the specific recommendations were not. Neither conditional authority nor wholesale responsibility would serve their interests or those of their students.

However, one could derive from this call for empowerment more appropriate recommendations for increasing teachers' roles in school governance. To ensure that their responsibilities are real rather than ceremonial, teachers could be granted authority, either alone or jointly with administrators, over specific matters that directly affect their teaching – the instructional schedule, the allocation of the supplies budget, the discipline code. In the past, teachers have withdrawn from advisory roles in school governance because their advice was so frequently ignored. The certainty of influence over decisions that matter to them would likely promote greater participation.

Differentiated staffing

It is worth restating that most of these teachers were not troubled by the repetition in the tasks of their teaching and, therefore, they were not eager to assume other responsibilities. Frequently, however, they did report feeling overwhelmed by the demands of heavy loads – 150 students and five courses. Also, they expressed concern about being isolated from the work and ideas of others. Differentiated roles which enabled teachers to substitute supervisory or curricular responsibilities for a class or two would, to many teachers' minds, lighten their loads by reducing the time required for preparation and grading. For many, the prospect of more time for better teaching would be very attractive. In addition, new roles that combined teaching and non-teaching responsibilities would extend teachers' values and expertise beyond their classrooms and into the larger school organization. One teacher, who was particularly dissatisfied with the conditions of her work, said, 'If there were some duties or responsibilities outside the classroom or ways of extending yourself beyond the classroom, that might be more satisfying certainly.' Other teachers expressed interest in such roles, provided their responsibilities supported rather than detracted from their teaching. A number were encouraged by the prospect of becoming mentor teachers and bestowing their pedagogical wisdom on others. As one social studies teacher explained, 'We could learn from each other. We really could.'

Several of those interviewed already had differentiated roles as department heads. They saw in these positions the opportunity to reduce professional isolation and to exert a broader influence on instruction. Therefore, although these teachers did not seek deliverance from their teaching through differentiated staffing, some could find in such positions the opportunity to make their teaching loads more manageable and to become more connected with their colleagues and schools.

One important finding of this research is that not only are teachers isolated from teachers, but they are also isolated from administrators. Many see little correspondence between their professional values and those of who supervise them. By creating differentiated roles, local districts would inevitably blur the distinctions between teachers and administrators as well as between classrooms and offices so that the professional values of teachers might have greater play in the formal decisions of school officials.

It is important in this discussion of differentiated staffing to emphasize that a number of these teachers expressed no interest in assuming new roles and responsibilities which might draw them away from their classrooms. They sought more time to teach well, to read, to work with colleagues, and to learn.

Staged careers

Many of these valued teachers knew that they were doing good work, that they put in long hours, taught well, and made a difference to students and colleagues. Several expressed interest in career ladders that would validate and reward their successes but, again, they were wary of reforms that would draw them away from their classrooms or implicitly diminish the status of teaching while elevating the status of teachers. They thought that staged careers could document professional progress and provide well-deserved financial compensation. Several suggested that career ladders might compensate them personally for the current lack of public and parental support for their work. One teacher, who was particularly dissatisfied with the absence of recognition for good teaching, welcomed the opportunity to distinguish herself, but her expectations were notably modest: 'Yes, yes, even if they just had different levels of teaching. A master teacher or – not necessarily in terms of money – just little things, like once you reach a certain level, there's no more lunchroom duty.' What mattered to her was not so much the particular rewards that each step offered, but the reassurance and recognition that accompanied advancement.

These teachers had little confidence that current evaluation systems could render fair appraisals of their practice. Moreover, they were wary of creating new hierarchies that would simply mimic the current administrative structures. They had watched the positions of principal and supervisor gradually come to serve administrative rather than instructional interests. They had observed the influence of politics and patronage in promotion. They could anticipate the organizational costs of a career plan that would produce bureaucratic annuities rather than professional engagement. If career ladders could be designed to overcome these problems and sidestep these hazards, this group of teachers would likely support them.

Therefore, although the Carnegie and Holmes proposals do not directly address many problems of the workplace that these teachers cited, there does seem to lie within their rhetoric and recommendations the opportunity for constructive change. Differentiated staffing may provide the slack that teachers need to think and pursue new ideas for their teaching. It may diminish isolation and promote collegial interaction. It may heighten the prominence of instructional values in the school. Granting teachers greater formal authority in school governance may empower them to make school policies and practices consistent with good instruction. Staged careers might improve teachers' pay and enhance their standing in the larger community.

It is important to aknowledge that repackaged responsibilities, new assignments for governance, or steps on a career ladder will not, in themselves, enable teachers to teach well. In fact, they might make things worse by diverting teachers' attention, wasting their time, or creating divisive distinctions among them. These are opportunities, not guarantees. By instituting different roles and career patterns and by redistributing authority, other changes might occur in schools that would improve them as workplaces. Isolation might diminish.

Expertise might be shared. Instructional values might gain a new currency. Groups of teachers might redirect school policies. Gradually, teachers might gain public recognition and respect. The current proposals are not sufficient, yet they do carry with them a message about the need for teachers to exercise greater control over their work and to make schools work on behalf of good teaching. It is this more general message from the Carnegie Forum and Holmes Group that deserves the attention of teachers and local school officials.

Embedded in the findings of this research are some messages for policy analysts who seek to professionalize teaching, for school officials who seek to improve their schools, and for teachers who want more productive and rewarding workplaces. First, policy analysts might learn from these teachers that to professionalize teaching is not to make it something other than teaching. The purpose of their reforms should not be to liberate teachers from their work, but to liberate them so that they can do their work well. This would suggest that differentiated roles should be in the service of better instruction, that teaching should remain at the center of staged careers, that teachers who participate in policymaking should be granted certain rather than conditional authority. Those who propose reforms should explore more fully the prospects for shared governance by teachers and administrators rather than expecting either to run the schools alone.

The findings of this research suggest that, if local districts are searching for ways to improve their schools as workplaces, they need not wait for outside plans, prescriptions, regulations, or incentives. Rather they would do well to understand what matters to their teachers whose work they value. If there is to be significant change in the school as a workplace, that change will occur school by school and district by district (Howe 1981).

School officials should think carefully about how to intoduce new roles and responsibi- lities in ways that will promote cooperation and interdependence, preserve creative autonomy for teachers, and incorporate teachers' values in school policies and practices. They can reorganize assignments and schedules to permit time for reflection and to promote interaction among staff. They can create forums where teachers' voices can be heard and develop new practices to ensure that those voices will not be ignored. They can select principals for their instructional competence and capacity to lead rather than for their managerial skill or political pull. They can engage parents in rethinking school purposes and practices so that teachers do not continue to feel isolated, unsupported, or unrecognized in their efforts. There are many possibilities, but they must grow out of local needs and local understandings.

There are, as well, important messages for teachers. Teachers in this study repeatedly suggested that they are successful despite administration. The increasing standoff between teachers and administrators during recent years has intensified teachers' isolation and has heightened their defensiveness. Over time, many teachers have concluded that it is safer to remain within their classrooms, to protect their autonomy, to conserve their energy, and to minimize to the impact of administration of their work. These interviews demonstrate, however, that such responses by teachers are counterproductive, that by withdrawing into their work, teachers surrender decisions about their workplaces to others. It seems likely that if teachers are to improve the conditions of their work, they themselves must step forward and initiate change.

In response to an earlier draft of this article, one English teacher concurred that teachers want to have their needs and views understood by responsive administrators: 'I, too, would like to go into my classroom and engage kids in fine talk about stories and ideas' while 'a group of powerful men and women somewhere down the hall make sure I could continue to do that in peace . . . But I don't think that it's likely that teachers are ever going to be so lucky.' Since his interview, he had been moved by the theme of self-governance in *A Nation*

Prepared and had initiated several reform efforts in his own school. He argued that teachers cannot leave decisions of professional practice to principals, superintendents, or school boards:

> It's awful, but it's true, I think. Those other folks just don't know enough about the job. It's also true that they often don't care enough about the job. And since it's the most important job there is, those people who know and care about it ought to be the watchful custodians of the conditions under which it is done.

Notes

1. The final sample of teachers, which includes 11 women (48%) and 14 men (52%), have been teaching an average of slightly more than 17 years. This purposive sample is roughly comparable to Louis Harris' random sample of 443 high school teachers, which was 56% male and 44% female with a median number of years of experience for all teachers in his sample being 15. (The total sample included 1/602 teachers from all levels. Harris does not compute the mean or the median for high school teachers' years of experience, although the raw numbers indicate that high school teachers were somewhat more experienced than either elementary or junior high school teachers [Harris, 1986].)
    The sample includes the following subject areas and special assignments:

    Regular English: 5
    Vocational School English: 1
    Alternative School English: 1
    English as a Second Language: 1
    Regular Social Studies: 6
    Vocational School Social Studies: 1
    Science: 3
    Mathematics: 2
    Foreign Languages: 2
    Home Economics: 1
    Music: 1
    Guidance: 1

2. Of the 16 school districts represented in this sample, nine are urban, eleven are suburban, three are small cities, and two are regional. They range in enrollment size from 57,461 to 900, the median being 3342. The 21 high schools also vary in size, ranging from 2390 to 286 students, the median having 1053 students. The 19 comprehensive high schools and two vocational schools are located in a range of socio-economic communities. According to the ratings of the Curriculum Information Center, an independent organization that publishes data about Massachusetts school districts, eight schools are located in communities of 'average' wealth (5 to 30% of school-aged children falling below the poverty line); six are in 'poor' communities (more than 30% below the poverty line), and seven are in 'rich' communities (less than 5% are below the poverty line).

References

BIDERMAN, A. D. and DRURY, T. F. (1976) *Measuring Work Quality for Social Reporting* (New York: Wiley).

BIRD, T. and LITTLE, J. W. (1985) *School Orgainzation of the Teaching Occupation* (San Francisco: Far West Laboratory).

BOSTON WOMEN's TEACHERS GROUP. (1983) 'Teaching: an imperilled profession', in L. S. Shulman and G. Sykes (eds.) *Handbook of Teaching and Policy* (New York: Longman).

CARNEGIE FORUM ON EDUCATION AND THE ECONOMY. (1986) *A Nation Prepared: Teachers for the 21st Century.* (New York: The Carnegie Forum).

CORBETT, H. D. and WILSON, B. L. (1988) 'Raising the stakes in statewide mandatory testing programs', in J. Hannaway and R. Crowson (eds.). *The Politics of Reforming School Administration* (London: Falmer Press).

DUNCAN, K. D., GRUNEBERG, M. M. and WALLIS D. (1980) *Changes in Working Life* (New York: Wiley).

GOODLAD, J. (1984) *A Place Called School: Prospects for the Future* (New York: McGraw-Hill).

HARRIS, L. AND ASSOCIATES, Inc. (1986) *The American Teacher 1986: Restructuring the Teaching Profession* (New York: Metropolitan Life Insurance Company).

HOLMES GROUP, THE (1986) *Tomorrow's Teachers* (East Lansing, MI: The Holmes Group).

HOWE, H. (1981) 'Education's centerpiece for the 1980s', *The College Board Review*, 120, pp.2–5, 26.

JACKSON, P. (1987) 'Facing our ignorance', *Teachers College Record*, 88, pp.384–389.

KANTER, R. M. (1983) *The Changemasters* (New York: Simon & Schuster).

KANTER, R. M. and STEIN, B. A. (eds.) (1979) *Life In Organizations: Workplaces as People Experience Them* (New York: Basic Books).

KERR, D. H. 'Teaching competence and teacher education in the United States', *Teachers College Record* 84, pp.525–552.

LIPSKY, M. (1980) *Street-level Bureaucracy* (New York: Russell Sage Foundation).

LORTIE, D. C. (1975) *Schoolteacher: A Sociological Study* (Chicago: University of Chicago Press).

McNEIL, L. (1987) 'Exit, voice, and community: magnet teachers' responses to standardization, *Education Policy*, 1, pp.93–113.

OLSON, L. (1987) 'Performance-based pay systems for teachers are being re-examined, *Education Week*, 6 (15 April), p.29.

RICHARDSON, E. L. (1973) *Work in America* (Cambridge, MA: MIT Press).

RYAN, K. (1987) 'The wrong report at the right time, *Teachers College Record*, 88, pp.419–422.

SCHLECHTY, P. C. and VANCE, V. S. (1981) 'Do academically able teachers leave education? The North Carolina Case, *Phi Delta Kappan*, 63, pp.106–112.

SCHLECHTY, P. C. and VANCE, V. S. (1982) 'The distribution of academic ability in the teaching force: policy implications, *Phi Delta Kappan* 64, pp.22–27.

SIZER, T. R. (1984) *Horace's Compromise: The Dilemma of the American High School* (New York: Houghton Mifflin).

TERKEL, S. (1972) *Working* (New York: Avon Books).

WEAVER, W. T. (1984), 'Solving the problem of teacher quality', *Phi Delta Kappan*, 66, pp.108–115.

8   *The teachers' political orientation* vis-à-vis *the principal: the micropolitics of the school*

Joseph J. Blase
University of Georgia

There is an organizational underworld, the world of micro-politics . . . It finds little place in organization theory and even less in management theory. It is rarely discussed in any formal context within organizations and it finds virtually no place in the teaching of educational administration. It is almost a taboo subject in 'serious' discussion, yet informally it is a favourite theme of organizational gossip as people talk about 'playing politics', 'hidden agendas', 'organizational mafias', 'Machiavellianism' and so forth . . . We know very little about this darker- or lighter-side of organizations. (Hoyle 1986 : 125)

During the first phase of a three-year (1983–1986) case study that I conducted of on-the-job socialization of teachers – of what teaching does to teachers (Waller 1932) – I learned, among other things, that teachers tend to develop what they call a 'political' orientation toward others with whom they routinely interact (for a complete explanation of the research procedures, see Blase 1986). In follow-up research in one high school setting, I probed what teachers meant by behaving politically, and it is the results of that probing that I report in this chapter. I specifically focus here on the political attitudes and behavior of teachers *vis-à-vis* school principals.

This research is part of a growing body of literature on political behavior within organizations or what is referred to as micropolitics (Bacharach and Lawler 1980, Ball 1987, Hoyle 1986, Mayes and Allen 1977, Pfeffer 1981). Although each of the writers cited defines micropolitics somewhat differently, in general, each refers to the use of power to achieve preferred outcomes in organizational settings. With a few notable exceptions (e.g. Ball 1987), little of this research has focused on everyday political behavior within school settings and even less on the particular political tactics teachers employ.

The description presented below is based on in-depth interviews, questionnaires, and observations of 40 teachers whom I had been investigating for two years prior to probing their political orientations. I was particularly interested in how their views of themselves changed over time and varied with different principals. Most of the teachers who participated in this study had worked under four different school principals during the preceding 12 years. The teachers I studied also worked without a union contract, because the state where the school is located prohibits collective bargaining.

Results

Overview

Teachers indicated that at the beginning of their careers they were preoccupied with developing competencies related to the instruction and control of students in the classroom. 'Strong' values and idealistic expectations of administrators, faculty, parents, and students dominated their views. Through direct experience, teachers became aware that political considerations were important in 'playing the game' and surviving at work ('Teaching is much more complex than I ever imagined').

Political changes in teachers appeared to stem primarily from their acquired sense of vulnerability to criticism and attack from others. They worked to manufacture a political self (to greater or lesser degrees) based on protectionist (reactive) and power (proactive) considerations. Many teachers, for example, felt that they worked in a 'fish bowl [and were] constantly being scrutinized' and that people associated with schools (particularly parents) 'react very strongly to little things'. They claimed their actions were frequently misunderstood and subject to dramatic distortion as personal and professional information about them was interpreted from diverse perspectives in the school and community. Such perspectives, teachers realized, were related to, among other things, the individual insecurities, hidden agendas, conflicting educational ideologies, and role responsibilities of other actors. The political behavior of the teachers was in response to these pressures.

The expectations and behaviors of many actors – including other faculty, parents, students, and administrators – contributed to the political changes in teachers. However, school principals and, indirectly, factors related to the external environment of the school were particularly significant. The political perspectives of teachers varied with the orientations of different school principals. In particular, they behaved differently with principals they trusted and viewed as participatory than with those whom they viewed as authoritarian and inconsistent (see Blase 1987 for a fuller discussion of these principal types).

The political perspective teachers took was based on a sensitivity to the power of principals and the development of strategies to deal with that power. Strategies of acquiescence and conformity were associated with a protectionist stance (e.g. job security) in teachers; they were reactive strategies. Other strategies – diplomacy, confrontation, passive-aggressiveness and ingratiation – although not unrelated to protectionistic considerations, indicated an attempt to influence the school administrator; they were proactive.

Teachers generally tended to be more straightforward with principals they considered participatory; they were less fearful of manipulation and reprisals. In dealing with such principals, teachers primarily employed acquiescence, conformity, and a great deal of diplomacy. In coping with principals viewed as authoritarian, teachers tended to be more closed. They were less honest (even devious) and more sensitive to the use of manipulation and punishment by principals. In addition to using higher levels of acquiescence, conformity teachers tended to be often passive-aggressive and ingratiating with authoritarian principals. There was noticeably less diplomatic behavior – indicating two-way exchange and reciprocation – with authoritarian principals. Direct confrontation was not used frequently with either participatory or authoritarian principals.

It should be emphasized that examination of both the political strategies and profiles discussed in this chapter suggests that teacher classroom and instructional processes were only slightly influenced by principals' expectations. For the most part, the data indicate, teachers' political orientations were tied more closely to the expectations of principals regarding investments of time and energy in the school and the community. Teachers explained that although these kinds of investments had several purposes, overall they functioned to assist principals in their efforts to create appropriate public images.

The remainder of this chapter describes dimensions of the teachers' political orientation specifically linked to interactions with school principals. Six categories that emerged from the data – acquiescence, conformity, diplomacy, passive-aggressiveness, confrontation, and ingratiation – and three profiles, derived from the data – extra involvement, visibility, and advocacy – are presented. The data also suggest systematic relationships between particular characteristics of principals and the teachers' political stance. The next section examines the conservative (passive) political perspectives of teachers in terms of the credibility of the school within the administrative hierarchy and, more importantly within the public arena. Finally, the data are discussed in terms of their implications for educational reform.

Six categories of teacher responses

Acquiescence: overt compliance

Acquiescence in teachers refers to overt behavioral compliance to the official policies, mandates, directives, and orders set forth by school principals in spite of disagreement and the questionable 'legitimacy' of the directives. Teachers reported that principals expected absolute and unquestioning obedience in a number of areas.

Most factors precipitating acquiescence in teachers were directly related to job security ('I'm afraid I'll be fired') and fear of sanctions for noncompliance. For example, principals could withhold basic resources, such as materials, space, funds, and time; assign teachers to unappealing schedules, higher class loads, extra duties, and slower students; enforce rules strictly; withhold support in conflicts with students and parents; and engage in personal and professional criticism. Although the threat of any sanction usually provoked apprehension in teachers, transfer to an undesirable school seemed to be most feared.

Acquiescence also resulted from the desire to protect one's reputation. Teachers explained that their 'reputations' were at risk if they tried to question or change the principal's directions; since hard data and teacher performance were not available, the principal was able to distort teachers' complaints in ways which made such teachers look bad.

The data suggest that parents and district office expectations frequently shaped the unreasonable and sometimes unethical demands of principals that contributed to teacher acquiescence. Parents, for example, demanded favoritism in class placement, special education referrals, gifted program admission, participation in class projects/activities, and the enforcement of disciplinary codes. Parents also often exerted power through the principal to lower standards and 'give away' grades.

Furthermore, central office expectations were often perceived as unrealistic ('unconnected with the real world'); uninformed ('Just because you're at central office doesn't mean you are knowledgeable'); authoritarian ('They treat us like cows . . . push us around like a herd', 'Any criticism and they will make you miserable'); conservative ('The front office is very hesitant to change'); overly concerned with standardization ('We need to be able to adapt at the school and class levels; they don't understand'); and, *more than anything else, preoccupied with public images* ('You don't rock the boat . . . don't criticize . . . gloss over the problems').

With regard to public image, teachers disclosed that administrative attempts to gain their compliance promoted some practices that were seen as negatively affecting the school's capacity to control and instruct students. For instance, to maintain an image of 'orderliness', teachers reported that they were required to 'handle [their] own discipline problems', regardless of how difficult or disruptive these problems were. Similarly, the principals' pivotal role in evaluation made teachers vulnerable and encouraged them to 'hide' problems and weaknesses related to classroom instruction.

As might be expected, acquiescence to school principals was associated with role conflict in teachers: This meant 'going beyond the point where you know in your heart you should take a stand as a professional'. However, most teachers seemed to rationalize their acquiescence to principals ('The school won't run unless there are a number of people willing to support the guy in the front office on his terms').

The interview responses of teachers strongly suggest that as the demands of principals for compliance increased (as was evident with authoritarian principals), teachers' political orientations tended to become more 'closed'. Teachers indicated less willingness to deal with issues openly and honestly. This negatively affected teacher morale and teacher involvement in work. Some teachers reported that after years of concessions during which 'the school sold the kids out', they wanted to leave teaching altogether. This was particularly true for special education teachers who failed to receive administrative support.

Although acquiescence represents only one dimension of the teacher's political orientation toward school principals, the degree to which this strategy dominated the perspectives of many teachers was striking. To be sure, the teachers' use of this strategy can be explained in terms of principal authoritarianism and the principals' willingness to employ sanctions. More broadly, however, the data indicate that this and the other political responses of teachers emerge, in part, because of the school's vulnerability as a public institution and the principals' sensitivity to maintaining a credible image of the school, especially in the local community.

Conformity

Teacher conformity was also a strategy anchored in protectionist considerations. However, in contrast to acquiescence, conformity was associated with compromises teachers made in responding to administrative expectations defined as relatively legitimate. Other important differences between this category and acquiescence were evident in the data. For example, feelings linked to conformity, while sometimes reflecting apprehension/anxiety, were seldom described as producing the deep-seated negative emotions commonly associated with acquiescence. In fact, although teachers commonly related conformity to political considerations (e.g., job security, resource acquisition), by and large they viewed its use less negatively. Finally, when conforming to the demands of principals, teachers reported exercising greater discretion in constructing their responses than when they were acquiescing to principal demands.

Specifically, teachers described conformity as a political response to legitimate formal organizational policies and rules and informal expectations for example, about the teacher as a role model for students.

Conformity to rules and regulations included such factors as arriving at work on time, faculty meeting attendance, presence in the classroom during periods, acceptance of responsibilities for supervision of students (hallways, cafeteria, parking lot), and overall adherence to formal procedures e.g., ('going through proper channels' for resource acquisition and planning field trips). In this respect, principals' expectations were seen as 'legitimate'; conformity reflected voluntary cooperation with principals.

Teachers explained that conformity to organizational norms was neither perfunctory ('You have to figure out what they want . . . there are a lot of mixed messages') nor transacted without concern about the image one produced for others. Teachers indicated a sensitivity to principals and a concern about reputational damage ('If the principal saw me not doing what I should be doing, that would be unwise . . . my indifference would stick in his mind').

Ironically, teachers reported that 'if you are a teacher who wants change . . . wants to improve things', it was politically important to conform (in varying degrees) to official organizational norms (e.g., working within the chain of command), particularly with non-supportive, authoritarian, and vindictive school principals. Conformity of this nature protected teachers from criticism and reduced the probability of alienating principals and other administrators 'overly concerned with their images'.

'Covering yourself'(C Y A) was discussed by teachers as an important protective dimension of conformity to formal organizational expectations. Teachers (and the school) were especially susceptible to blame and criticism from parents for problems related to the highly visible dimensions of their work, that is, classroom discipline, grading, extracurricular activities, and questions regarding instructional content and homework assignments.

The data show that teachers prepared to defend themselves against possible attacks from principals and parents. In reacting to discipline problems and grading, for instance, teachers found it politically important to 'build a case . . . document everything over a period of time . . . notify the right people on time'. When criticism resulted, teachers were able to support their position with 'objective' evidence. To protect themselves in other areas of their work (i.e., chaperoning, sponsoring clubs, coaching), teachers usually conformed to legal and organizational norms.

'Teachers also conformed to more informal expectations. They disclosed that to protect themselves from criticism they conformed to principals' (and the community's) expectations regarding specific aspects of their professional and personal lives. Professional-life demands covered such areas as dress, hair style, and language ('We don't use profanity'), and personal-life expectations encompassed drinking and dancing, dating, and membership in organizations. Since the expectations of principals were defined as conservative and traditional and were perceived to reflect the expectations of parents, they seemed to have a conservative impact on teachers' day-to-day political orientation.

The third area of conformity was associated with the use of controversial materials and the discussion of controversial topics (i.e., sex, abortion, drugs, religion, evolution, race). Teachers' data revealed that administrative (and parental) expectations tended to 'make [them] more conservative . . . careful . . . and paranoid sometimes' about subject-matter content. Confrontations with principals and parents usually required valuable time and 'resulted in bad feelings all around'. By projecting a conservative image in the classroom, teachers were able to reduce their vulnerability.

Although many teachers conformed to the expectations of principals and parents in this regard (by avoiding potentially controversial discussions altogether), others attempted to protect their discretion in such matters; they described their political orientation as 'guarded' and 'careful': 'I am careful about which books I assign. I scatter the ones I think might get a reaction from parents throughout the list I send home each quarter.' To avoid reprisals, teachers organized discussions in an objective manner: 'All views on an issue are presented . . . My view is one of several we explore.'

Diplomacy

Although the protectionism associated with acquiescence and conformity also served to some extent as a rationale for teacher diplomacy, diplomacy was also associated with proactive and positive forms of influence with principals. Consequently, the importance of maintaining one's professional and personal integrity ('There are certain compromises I don't make'), self-composure, and civility were emphasized: 'I'm not going to beat it over anyone's head . . . But . . . I want to get my point across').

The use of approaches consistent with norms of politeness, responsiveness, and empathy (awareness of another's needs, problems) was discussed in terms of diplomacy and defined as essential to the development of 'good rapport'. Friendliness, in the teachers' view, seemed to reduce the negative effects of administrator-teacher status differences and to increase the probability of bilateral (two-way) communication, influence, and collaborative problem solving: 'If you can see that person more as an individual, . . . it makes it easier to open up, to get along.'

Teachers emphasized the significance of using a positive approach. Questions and problems directed toward principals were therefore expressed empathetically ('You are sensitive to the principal's problems') and in a manner unlikely to engender defensiveness ('You try to be tactful . . . you don't challenge'). This, according to teachers, reduced their vulnerability to and increased their influence with administrators.

Diplomacy meant 'analyzing problems . . . offering solutions . . . not just criticizing'. By demonstrating forethought with regard to problems, teachers explained, they were perceived as 'serious and professional'. This orientation, along with the expression of empathy, encouraged problem solving and was viewed as reducing the 'chance that the administrators would take things personally' or that 'You [would] get into trouble'.

Teachers indicated that diplomacy required patience ('things change slowly'), tolerance ('understanding he can't always respond'), and skills related to nonaggressive forms of self-expression. On the other hand, teachers limited significantly the use of threats, gossip, and 'petty grumbling' ('complain too much . . . no one listens'). Clearly, powerful school norms, in large part reinforced by principals, ruled against such actions.

A few experienced teachers described themselves as 'real politicians' who were 'sophisticated in the art of diplomacy'. These teachers systematically analyzed the principal's expectations regarding key issues ('You take every opportunity . . . learn to read him'), listened closely, demonstrated awareness and appreciation of achievements, and carefully calculated and planned interactions

Generally speaking, diplomacy, as a dimension of the teachers' political orientation, was used to build interdependence and establish bases of partial reciprocation, that is, mutual assistance. Diplomatic political actions contributed somewhat to the development of two-way influence structures (i.e., bilateralism) and promoted limited exchange and reciprocation ('You help me, I'll help you') between teachers and principals. Again, much of this seemed to be related to the special sensitivity of principals to maintaining a stable, noncontroversial 'image' to satisfy central office administrators and the public.

Passive-aggressiveness

Passive-aggressive political strategies refer to teachers' attempts to sabotage principals through indirect, covert, and 'devious' means: 'Gossip and rumours helped to discredit him. I had my part there . . . I will do it again in certain situations.' Politically, a passive-aggressive orientation was designed to protect the self and discredit the administrator. Teachers using such strategies might criticize the principal with parents (especially a disaffected parental group) and important school officials, respond slowly to directives or respond 'differently enough to create problems' (e.g., completing forms), 'swamp the front office' with disciplinary referrals, or encourage parents to call principals (at home) to complain about policy.

Passive-aggressive strategies were only discussed as a means of dealing with authoritarian principals. Few teachers claimed to engage in passive-aggressive acts against principals. Such strategies violated norms reinforced by administrators and adhered to by teachers. Indeed, this political category was constructed indirectly – from teachers' observations of political tactics exhibited by other faculty.

Direct confrontation

Direct confrontation with principals refers to being 'blunt', 'straightforward', 'direct', and 'honest'. Quite often, any form of direct confrontation was viewed as 'abrasive' and 'antagonistic'.

Whereas some teachers viewed confrontational behaviors as political, others (usually those who identified themselves with diplomacy) considered confrontation to be 'unpolitical'. By this, they meant that confrontation was counterproductive in terms of protecting oneself and influencing the principal ('You open yourself up to criticism from all sides').

Teachers indicated that direct confrontation was seldom employed with administrators. Several teachers had used the strategy, but as one suggested, 'I was creamed by the administrator' and socially ostracized by some other faculty ('They're afraid to associate with you'). Once again, administrators' sensitivity to the expectations of superiors and others outside the school was reported by teachers as critical in accounting for the principal's unwillingness to deal openly with problems.

Ingratiation

In the perspective of teachers, ingratiation refers to political activities purposefully designed to 'flatter', 'appease', and 'brownnose' the school administrator to achieve one's purposes. Like diplomacy, the motivation to ingratiate oneself was grounded in both protectionistic and proactive influence aims of teachers. Activities such as volunteering for committee work, praising administrators, friendliness, invitations to social functions, 'openly supporting the administrator when you disagree', and 'say[ing] what the administrator wants to hear' were described as ingratiation.

Consistent with the dynamics of exchange and reciprocation, ingratiation was viewed as decreasing teacher vulnerability (e.g., criticism, punishment) and increasing opportunities to attain goals (e.g., resources, recognition). Some teachers seemed comfortable with ingratiation to advance personal careers ('It's part of them'). Others, however, reported that they were 'forced' to engage in such activities to secure programmatic support.

Several teachers reported that ingratiation was associated with the 'personalities' of some individuals ('they are always on'). However, a preponderance of the data suggests that factors associated with school principals were seen as most important in understanding the use of this strategy. Such factors included administrative (merit) evaluations of teachers (which produced teacher competitiveness), administrator insecurity (which encouraged teachers to feed the principal's ego), public relations pressures (which stimulated teachers' interest in developing personal and program visibility), lack of an objective teacher evaluation system, inconsistency in resource distribution (which promoted competition for resources and recognition), and the importance of impressionistic data for forming the teachers' reputation.

Without question, 'brownnosing' was considered 'offensive' and 'unprofessional' by most of the teachers studied. Despite this, many teachers believed that such tactics were essential to obtaining support from principals, particularly authoritarian types.

Three profiles

The following discussion shows how the categories of political orientation are frequently integrated into three typical profiles of teacher behaviour: 'extra milers', 'stars' and 'advocates'. The description of each profile reveals more fully what being political meant to teachers *vis-à-vis* their relationship with school principals. These profiles point out that teachers are not entirely passive political actors: they use political strategies proactively and constructively to increase their bargaining power with principals through the development of exchange (extra involvement), internal and external support (visibility), and expertise (advocacy).

Extra milers

Teachers claimed that it was politically expedient in terms of their relationship with the principal to work beyond contractual responsibilities – to 'arrive early and stay late', 'be accessible to students', and 'be active in community activities'. Teacher actions that focused on the initiation, supervision, and improvement of school problems, activities, and procedures – that is, involvements that 'help run the school' – were identified as especially important politically. These involvements protected them from criticism and influenced the development of relationships based on exchange and reciprocation. For these reasons, teachers reported that they sponsored clubs, chaperoned events, attended evening and weekend activities, worked with the school newspaper, and volunteered for committee work. Outside involvement was not unimportant. Teachers attended community functions, educational conferences, and workshops; enrolled in university course work; and were active in professional associations.

The data indicate that a positive disposition in teachers toward extra involvement was associated with working for an open, competent, and respected principal. With such a principal, many experienced teachers suggested, they were motivated to provide leadership in various areas of school life.

In the teachers' perspective, lack of involvement in the school and community was interpreted by administrators and parents as indicating 'lack of interest and caring about education . . . and kids'. In essence, to build a reputation, teachers claimed they were encouraged 'to do more than just teach'.

Although to some teachers extra involvement in work represented an acquiescent political response to principals, investments along these lines were seen by most as conformity and diplomacy. That is, although fear of punishment and criticism were major considerations, teachers were also motivated by satisfactions derived from meaningful commitments to students and community, particularly when the principal was characterized as participatory.

Teacher involvement appeared to be linked to increased awareness, knowledge, and responsiveness to students' interests and needs and served as the basis for a deeper understanding of the internal and external factors that influence school-community relationships ('the big picture'). For teachers, this acquired knowledge, coupled with more extensive responsibilities and effective performance, was associated with the exchange of 'credit' in the form of respect and prestige for their work. Moreover, teachers reported that their involvements built 'political clout' and increased administrator dependency ('they need your support as much as you need theirs'). In general, positive cycles of interaction with administrators seemed to precipitate further increases in teacher involvement.

Teacher involvement and influence were linked to the development of reciprocal relationships between teachers and principals. 'Playing the game' in this context seemed to promote an expansion of cooperative and collaborative networks of association throughout the school and community. Paradoxically, however, teachers claimed that as their involvement and visibility in the school and community increased, they became more conservative; they were more cautious, less willing to take risks, and less creative because of their increased susceptibility to public criticism.

'Stars'

Visibility as a political orientation refers to the display of one's involvements and accomplishments in the school and in the community ('putting on a show', 'mak[ing]) your successes public'). Attempts to increase visibility appeared to stem directly from principals' expectations supporting broad extracurricular and extraorganizational involvement and the teachers' interest in increasing their internal and external bases of support. As a result, teachers communicated their achievements through face-to-face interaction, school newspapers, letters, local newspapers, and attendance at meetings with parents and the local board of education. Quite directly, teachers explained that principals' expectations for visibility grew from a concern for public relations ('public image and support') and a desire to impress superiors 'controlled by the community'.

For most teachers who worked within an established curriculum and whose programs were regular budgetary items, the politics (and rewards) of visibility were regarded as valuable, but not essential, to program survival. However, to many music, art, reading, and special education teachers, developing visibility and credibility was considered necessary to the acquisition of material resources and symbolic support. Teachers from these groups typically utilized a mix of acquiescence, conformity, and diplomacy to achieve political ends. In presenting themselves and the work of their students, they attempted to promote understanding and appreciation in others.

To be sure, some fine arts and special education teachers resented the importance of visibility to the procurement of basic program resources. In fact, some teachers refused to engage in visibility politics. For others, resentment grew from the belief that 'this business of spotlighting every move you make' had been overdone. Teachers who were 'constantly in the limelight' were frequently defined as 'brownnosers'.

Advocates

Advocacy refers to political actions associated with the use of expertise: research ('reading to discover good ideas') and the development, implementation, and maintenance of programs, activities, and procedures. These actions were typically used to combat various forms of administrative resistance (e.g., ignorance, nonsupport). Fine arts and special education teachers were most closely identified with an advocacy perspective. Teachers from these groups involved themselves in long-term political activities to 'defend' and/or 'fight for' their programs and students, in other words, to secure 'symbolic and material support' from school principals. The data suggest that advocacy was linked to deep levels of personal commitment; such a perspective clearly contradicted the expectations of authoritarian school principals.

Although teacher advocates risked reprisals, protectionist concerns seemed to be less important to them than to other teachers. Two special education teachers reported that the importance of advocacy was first made apparent to them during their university training. In both cases, the teachers described a professor who had sensitized them to the problematic nature of support in the school setting.

For the few teachers oriented in this way, advocacy was linked to the acquisition of basic resources. This problem (as suggested earlier) was associated with working outside the guidelines of the traditional curriculum, the nonbudgetary status of some programs, and lack of understanding and appreciation ('they do not value the program') by school principals and among parents.

A few regular subject-area teachers were considered advocates. However, their advocacy appeared to be more intimately tied to a deep sense of personal and professional integrity: 'A belief in fairness forces you to challenge policies . . . actions of administrators'. These teachers fought against administrative actions that they believed 'demeaned' or 'ignored' the needs of students, teachers, and others. Although these teachers described long histories of advocacy, most reported that they had 'not won many of the battles against administrators'.

Teachers who engaged in advocacy worked arduously to persuade principals to support programs, individuals, and issues. Toward these ends, they invested much effort in planning and creating strategies to 'make a case' and develop visibility. As advocates, they relied primarily on the politics of diplomacy and occasional confrontation.

Summary and discussion

The data discussed in this chapter suggest that over the long term, teachers develop political values, purposes, and behaviors, partly as a result of their interactions with school principals. To be sure, becoming 'political' represents a significant expansion in the teachers' perspective toward their work. Conceptually, the six categories and three profiles derived from the data constitute what being political means to teachers *vis-à-vis* school principals. Taken together, these categories and profiles reflect a relatively 'conservative' (passive) political perspective dominated primarily by survival considerations. It must be emphasized that these categories represent the range of theoretical elements associated with the political phenomenon described. Any given teacher's political orientation, of course, would be described in terms of only certain specific response categories.

The findings reported in this chapter indicate that the teachers' political orientation stemmed from an acquired sense of dependency on and vulnerability to the expectations and actions of school principals. Over time, teachers worked to develop a political perspective, consisting of 'appropriate' behaviors and attitudes, and a reputation that they considered acceptable to principals. In the most fundamental sense, the political responses of teachers were associated with principals' manipulation of sanctions (e.g., resources, schedules, space, transfers, recognition, support) and expectations. The unavailability of 'hard' data regarding teacher performance (no objective systematic evaluation was used in the school) and a propensity for negative distortion of information within the internal and external environment of the school were also important factors in accounting for the conservative political orientations of teachers evident in the data.

Perhaps most important, teachers repeatedly attributed many of the expectations and actions of school principals to factors external to the school. Teachers indicated directly and indirectly that all the school principals for whom they had worked over the years were (in varying but significant degrees) influenced by their administrative superiors as well as by lay members of the local community, particularly parents. According to teachers, both sources of influence seemed to have the effect of making principals focus on maintaining an appropriate 'image' with the public. Indeed, the present data are valuable in suggesting linkages between the conservative external elements of the school environment that appear to shape the expectations of principals and the internal and quite intricate patterns of behavior and perspective that develop between teachers and principals. Thus, the present data describe some of the subtle, informal, but powerful linkages existing between the two environments that are frequently ignored in the micropolitical literature.

Further inspection of the political strategies and profiles presented earlier suggests that the teachers' political perspective – one that supports a stable, efficient, unproblematic, and noncontroversial 'image' of the school – may have been extremely helpful to school principals in their efforts to maintain public credibility with administrative superiors and community members.

First, analysis of most of the political strategies used by teachers reveals a fundamental concern on the part of administrators (and teachers indirectly) with the control of information and behavior that might threaten the external credibility of the school. For instance, in acquiescing to the principals' expectations (sanctioned by the principals' manipulation of resources and reputations), teachers kept discipline and instructional problems to themselves and, on occasion, changed standards for grades (for particular students) and homework, even though doing so violated their professional ethics. In conforming to principals' expectations, teachers followed rules, regulations, and policies and drastically limited attention to controversial instructional topics and innovative instructional methods. The teachers' professional orientation (e.g., hairstyle, dress) in the school and personal orientation (e.g., membership in clubs and activities) in the community were managed specifically to project an image consistent with conservative community norms.

Second, two of the profiles discussed earlier ('extra milers' and 'stars') provide additional evidence of the political centrality of the public to both principals and teachers. Analysis of these profiles underscores the 'political' concerns of the principals (and teachers' collaboration) with expanding the involvement of teachers more fully throughout the school and, to some extent, into the community. Expectations linked to extra involvement, for example, encouraged teachers to participate in events, clubs, and activities in the school and community. In responding to demands related to visibility, teachers worked to 'publicize' their involvement in curricular and extracurricular activities to gain recognition and support from school principals as well as from central office superiors and parents. Public visibility was also important to securing basic survival resources for certain teachers and programs (e.g., fine arts).

In essence, the political orientation of teachers seemed to indirectly assist school principals in their efforts to develop and sustain an image of the school that was considered acceptable to administrative superiors and the lay public. Two important functions were served by the behavior described in teachers' political strategies and profiles: The amount of negative or 'discrediting' information was reduced, and the amount of positive 'crediting' information was increased.

Conclusion

This chapter, based on data from a long-term socialization study of teachers, has described the political perspectives of teachers *vis-à-vis* school principals. Thus far, this and other aspects of micropolitical activity in schools have received little scholarly attention. The present data underscore the importance of micropolitical activity to understanding the complex nature of work in school settings.

Although the data appear to have important implications from several theoretical as well as practical standpoints, the most salient theme is the school as a 'public' organization. Here, of course, the data suggest that at least from the perspectives of those studied, principals and teachers are quite vulnerable to, and are in large part controlled by pressures emanating from the external environment of the school.

The sensitivity and vulnerability of schools to pressures originating in the environment and the significance of these pressures to the internal structures and dynamics of the school have been discussed by many (Callahan 1962, Chubb and Moe 1986, Dreeben 1973, March 1978, Ogawa 1984, Sarason 1982, Willower 1982). Some attention has been given to the boundary functions of the principalship, particularly the mediational role that school principals play in relation to the external and internal environments of the school. For example, Willower (1982), who described school principals as 'threshold guardians', explained that principals work to neutralize demands that challenge the normative structure of schools.

Other scholars have stressed the reactive responses of both principals and schools to forces in society. These writers have suggested that school principals are often 'captives of their environments' (McPherson *et al.* 1975); schools, in general, are viewed as conservative and reactive, as 'accommodating institutions' (Clark 1962, Green 1969, Waller 1932). The nature of the school as a public institution – its dependence on society for material and symbolic support and thus its constant struggle for legitimacy – are usually discussed as among the reasons for its reactive, conservative stance. These reasons, coupled with an understanding of the school principals' special sensitivity to conventional societal inputs (March 1978, Ogawa 1984), help explain the emergence of the teachers' conservative political orientation – an orientation that seems to help preserve the legitimacy and credibility of the school amidst remarkably conservative political pressures.

Thus, it seems reasonable to conclude that school principals in general will be especially sensitive to the demands of the new reform legislation currently dominating public education in the USA. Much of this new legislation proposes control of teachers through the extensive use of such bureaucratic mechanisms as standardized curriculum, evaluation, and testing. This legislation advocates a strong role for school principals (Brandt 1982): Principals are being encouraged to value control, predictability, and efficiency (Angus 1988), often in ways consistent with industrial management models developed earlier in this century (McNeil 1986). Indeed, the notion of control has been extended to 'school culture' and the direct management of values, norms, and language, among other things (Bates 1987).

The present data indicate that teachers are politically quite sensitive to the principals' use of power: Should principals become more control oriented as a result of recently imposed legislative demands and should they interpret these demands in narrow and rigid ways, one can anticipate teacher compliance, at least on the surface. At the same time, however, there is convincing evidence that teachers will reduce their overall involvement in work, in important quantitative (e.g., time, energy) and qualitative (e.g., commitment, caring) ways (Blase 1985; Blase 1986; Blase 1987). McNeil (1986) found that as administrators tightened control over teachers, they tended to become less engaged, less motivated, and less committed; teachers adapted to controls in ways that undermined educational processes in the classroom. In this volume, Johnson (1988) vividly describes the devastating effects of isolation, repetition, lack of recognition, and low levels of involvement in school governance – areas of school life over which principals have significant control. Goodlad (1983), who has suggested that satisfying schools can be distinguished from others by the quality of the school climate and by positive interpersonal relationships, which are characterized by openness, trust, and collaboration, believes that the school principal is the key to a school's climate.

Thus, the control ideology reflected in much of the new legislation may be misguided and may actually exacerbate the problems it is attempting to solve (McNeil 1986). Instead, it is recommended that school administrators work to empower teachers, that they provide the necessary material and symbolic support teachers need to teach. In part, this means substantial delegation of authority to teachers over instructional matters and much greater teacher involvement in school policy.

Democratic relationships between school administrators and teachers would promote not only the educational values and goals consistent with the future demands of a high-technology society, but also, as Guttman discusses in this volume, the intellectual independence necessary to promote viable democratic processes and structures in society (Gutmann 1988).

References

ANGUS, L. (1988) 'School leadership and educational reform' paper presented at the annual meeting of the American Educational Research Association, New Orleans.

BACHARACH, S., and LAWLER, E. (1980) *Power and Politics in Organizations: The Social Psychology of Conflict, Coalitions, and Bargaining* (San Francisco: Jossey-Bass).

BALL, S. (1987) *The Micro-Politics of the School: Towards a Theory of School Organization* (London: Methuen).

BATES, R. (1987) 'Corporate culture, schooling, and educational administration', *Educational Administration Quarterly*, **23**(4), pp. 79–115.

BLASE, J. (1985) 'The socialization of teachers: an ethnographic study of factors contributing to the rationalization of the teacher's instructional perspective', *Urban Education*, **20**(3), pp. 235–256.

BLASE, J. (1986) 'Socialization as humanization: one side of becoming a teacher', *Sociology of Education*, **59**(2), pp. 100–112.

BLASE, J. (1987) 'Dimensions of effective school leadership: the teachers' perspective', *American Educational Research Journal*, **24**(4), pp. 589–610.

BRANDT, R. (1982) 'Overview: the new catechism for school effectiveness', *Educational Leadership*, **40**(3), p. 3.

CALLAHAN, R. (1962) *Education and the Cult of Efficiency: A Study of the Social Forces that Have Shaped the Administration of the Public Schools* (Chicago: University of Chicago Press).

CHUBB, J. and MOE, T. (1986) 'No school is an island: politics, markets, and education', *The Brookings Review*, **4**(4), pp. 21–28.

CLARK, B. (1962) *Educating the Expert Society* (San Francisco: Chandler).

DREEBEN, R. (1973) 'The school as a workplace', in R. M. Travers (ed.), *The Second Handbook of Research on Teaching* (Chicago: Rand McNally), pp. 450–473.

GOODLAD, J. (1983) *A Place called School* (New York: McGraw-Hill.)

GREEN, T. (1969) 'Schools and communities: a forward look', *Harvard Educational Review*, **39**(2), pp. 221–252.

GUTMANN, A. (1988) 'Democratic theory and the role of teachers in democratic education', in J. Hannaway and R. Crowson, (eds.), *The Politics of Reforming School Administration* (London: Falmer Press).

HOYLE, E. (1986) *The Politics of School Management* (London: Hodder & Stoughton).

JOHNSON, S. (1988) 'Schoolwork and its reform', In J. Hannaway and R. Crowson (eds.), *The Politics of Reforming School Administration* (London: Falmer Press).

MARCH, J. (1978) 'American public school administration: a short analysis', *School Review*, **86**, pp. 217–250.

MAYES, B. and ALLEN, R. (1977) 'Toward a definition of organizational politics', *Academy of Management Review*, **2**, pp. 672–678.

MCNEIL, L. (1986) *Contradictions of Control: School Structure and School Knowledge* (New York: Routledge & Kegan Paul).

MCPHERSON, R. B., SALLEY, C. and BAEHR, M. (1975) 'What principals do: preliminary implications of "a national occupational analysis of the school principalship" ', *Consortium Currents*, 2(1), pp. 1–10.

OGAWA, R. (1984) Teachers and administrators: elements of the information processing repertoires of schools, *Educational Administration Quarterly*, 20(2), pp. 5–24.

PFEFFER, J. (1981) *Power in Organizations* (Boston: Pitman).

SARASON, S. (1982) *The Culture of the School and the Problem of Charge* (Boston: Allyn & Bacon).

WALLER, W. (1932) *The Sociology of Teaching* (New York: Wiley).

WILLOWER, D. (1982) 'School organizations: perspectives in juxtaposition', *Educational Administration Quarterly*, 18(3), pp. 89–110.

9   *Evaluation designs as political strategies*

George W. Noblit and Deborah J. Eaker
University of North Carolina at Chapel Hill

Introduction

Evaluation flourishes in eras of accountability such as that reflected by the recent reform movement in education. As Fuhrman's and Gutmann's chapters in this volume reveal, the school reform agenda is organized around the evaluation of the effectiveness of public education. And, as Corbett and Wilson's chapter shows, school reform has intensified the evaluation of individual student, school and district performance. In many ways, the reformers make the presumption that an evaluation process itself is objective and that its effects are direct and simple, rather than being a political act.

A similar notion is apparent in a recent article by Eleanor Chelimsky (of the General Accounting Office) in which she reviews the recent history of the politics of program evaluation. She speaks of the 'very difficult problem of *integrating* the *disparate* worlds of politics and evaluation research' (Chelimsky 1987: 200, emphasis added). We disagree, and will show that politics and evaluation research although giving the impression of disparate worlds, are instead inextricably linked. We argue that not only the outcomes of evaluation, but the evaluation process itself is political and the decision to subject a program and its participants to evaluation is a policy decision.

Policymakers and evaluators alike take a number of things for granted in evaluation. First, they assume that evaluation research does not have the characteristics of other social situations. That is they assume that all parties involved in an evaluation will suspend any vested interests and accord special status to the evaluation. As a result, they assume that the only salient outcome of the evaluation will be a report upon which they can base future actions. They seem to ignore the potential consequences of the evaluation for the parties involved. We suggest that these taken-for-granted assumptions of policymakers and evaluators have consequences which are in fact inherent in evaluation designs.

In this chapter, we examine evaluation designs and identify the inherent political strategy in each. Evaluation, as with any applied research, is 'inherently political because it wishes to establish the bases of judgement for others and moreover to replace those that might otherwise be employed' (Noblit 1984: 96). The Corbett and Wilson chapter, for example, shows how minimum competency testing changes social (and political) relations. We argue that all evaluation designs have the potential of realigning political power and re-defining what is credible knowledge. The choice of evaluation design, then, is more than a technical issue. To this end, we examine the alignment of political power and definitions of credible knowledge inherent in six evaluation approaches or designs: positivism, interpretivism, critical theory, aesthetics, collaborative research and action research. We believe that the issues of political power and credible knowledge take different forms in each of these evaluation designs. The power and credibility of those in charge (or the sponsor), the evaluator-researcher, the evaluatees and even the evaluation design itself are all at issue. We assert that each evaluation design implicitly presupposes and promotes patterns of social relations and particular knowledge bases and assumptions that facilitate the evaluator's access to the evaluation situation, develop commitment of participants to the evaluation and thereby enable the evaluation to be politically salient.

Nature of knowledge and social relations

The examination of evaluation designs as political strategies is appropriately a sociology of knowledge problem. The sociology of knowledge concerns itself with the social bases, construction and effects of forms of knowledge such as evaluations (Berger and Luckmann 1967). As Berger and Luckmann write:

> It is our contention, then, that the sociology of knowledge must concern itself with whatever passes for 'knowledge' in a society regardless of the ultimate validity or invalidity. And insofar as all human knowledge is developed, transmitted and maintained in social situations, the sociology of knowledge must seek to understand the processes by which this is done in such a way that a taken-for-granted 'reality' congeals for the man in the street.(p. 3)

The relative credibility of knowledge is evidenced in belief systems, variously conceptualized as culture, values, ideology and the like. This set of beliefs is what Collins (1982) refers to as the Durkheiman notion of 'precontractual basis of solidarity' inherent in social contracts. Durkheim has posited that every social contract, in this case that of evaluation, actually entails two contracts. The first is the agreed-upon contract, that of engaging in an evaluation using a particular approach. The second is the 'hidden contract' that rests on the implicit assumption that all participants agree to the rules of the first contract (Collins 1982). Thus, because of the political nature of evaluation, the 'hidden contract' brings the belief systems of the various parties to the evaluation into question.

Likewise, the social relations among the evaluation parties are also called into question. Evaluation situations generally involve relations among three parties: the evaluators, the evaluatees, and the sponsors to the evaluation, although in some designs the sponsors may be the evaluatees. To examine the social relations of evaluation design, we use ideas from social network theory, particularly 'political clientelism' (Schmidt *et al*, 1977). In its briefest form, political clientelism posits that networks are maintained by exchanges of favors in such a way that an obligation to reciprocate is engendered. Some (horizontal) networks can be more or less equals in power and status, and network relations maintain that equality. Other (vertical) networks consist of patrons and clients. In these networks, clients typically exchange deference and loyalty to the patron for the patron's protection and support. Again, network relations maintain this essential inequality.

Clearly, knowledge and social relations are interactive in evaluation as in all social processes. Evaluation designs are intended to establish the credibility of the knowledge the evaluation generates (House 1980). In so doing, evaluation challenges the belief systems of some parties and seeks to establish the dominance of the belief systems of others. As we will argue, some evaluation designs establish the credibility of local knowledge (Geertz 1983), although we use this in a more particularistic sense than Geertz. Local knowledge, as we use it, is simply the knowledge which considers the beliefs of *all* parties to the evaluation as credible. Alternatively, externally legitimated knowledge establishes the dominance of *one* set of beliefs, usually that of the sponsor or evaluator.

In what follows, we reconsider the evaluation designs of positivism, interpretivism, critical theory, aesthetics, collaborative research and action research as political strategies according to the nature of the knowledge and social relations each implies. The six designs are not always distinct. Collaborative researchers may employ interpretivist ideas, as may aesthetics. Action researchers may be rather positivistic. Critical theory is maintained to encompass and go beyond interpretivism and positivism. Research projects may be both collaborative and action research. Yet, since each evaluation design seeks to create a distinct set of social relations and beliefs, it is useful to examine the six approaches as discrete entities.

Evaluation designs: the meaning of 'policy'

Positivism

Knowledge discovered through a positivistic evaluation model is in service of patrons rather than clients with the design serving to promote the authority of scientific knowledge. Positivism extolls science as the superior way of knowing and the scientist as the expert, or credible agent. Knowledge is discovered through a reductionistic epistemology using a traditional scientific methodology. Human events are seen as part of the natural world and, therefore, lawful. Smith argues that 'these laws describe in neutral scientific language how . . . independently existing reality really operates' (1983: 11). As applied to educational evaluation, a positivistic design provides a utilitarian approach to solving evaluation issues 'to explain, and by extension to be able to predict, the relationship between or the invariant succession of educational objects and events (see figure 1).

	Positivism	Interpretivism	Critical theory	Aesthetics	Collaborative research	Action research
Credible knowledge	science	negotiated	dialogue and critique	connoisseurship and criticism	joint construction	practitioner expertise
Network relations	sponsor as patron	evaluator as broker	evaluator as patron	altruism	relative equality	evaluatee as patron
Political result	evaluator as co-patron	multiple perspectives	sponsor 'disappears'	sponsor 'disappears'	reification of collaboration	sponsor 'disappears'

Figure 1. Evaluation designs.

The evaluator-scientist role in this approach is one of the credible expert. His/her scientific expertise is used to legitimate this status as well as the evaluation design itself. Interpersonal skills are only minimally required and the relationship between the evaluator and evaluatees is often distant in the pursuit of objectivity. The evaluator-scientist relies on the authoritarian relations between the sponsor and the evaluatees to gain access to and maintain relations with the evaluatees.

The implementation of a positivistic evaluation design clearly assumes social relations which are defined according to carefully delimited patron-client networks. Initially, the evaluator-scientist is client to the patron-sponsor. He/she must show deference and loyalty during the careful negotiation of contract domains to gain access to the evaluatees and to assure power and credibility during the evaluation process. As this juncture, the evaluator-scientist theoretically becomes a competing patron to the sponsor. While the sponsor may maintain certain aspects of patronage, the evaluatees become clients to the evaluator-patron. This patron status is largely based in technical expertise and is reinforced by the access given to the evaluator by the sponsor.

The sponsor in this design is, in the end, also a client to the patron-scientist while continuing to be a patron to the evaluatees. If weak horizontal networks are present among the evaluatees, as might be expected in loosely-coupled educational organizations (Weick 1982), evaluatee clientelism is maintained by authoritarian relations previously established between the evaluatees and sponsor. However, if strong horizontal evaluatee networks exist or develop during the evaluation process, and these networks have an on-going basis of exchange, the evaluatee client networks can gain power and undermine the evaluation by playing off one patron against the other (i.e, the sponsor and the evaluator).

The belief system required by the positivistic design is one of reification of science. Credibility rests on the hidden contract by all parties that science is indeed an appropriate basis upon which to evaluate and make decisions. The utilitarian nature inherent in this model would seem to demand that knowledge gained would be instrumental or 'practical', presumably for the evaluatees. However, such knowledge may be instrumental only in terms of assuring a justification for sponsor decisions and reinforcement of science and the scientific method as the appropriate way to know (House 1980).

Interpretivism

Interpretivist evaluations are constructive of both belief systems and patron-client relations. They give 'voice' to the multiple perspectives revealed in the evaluation. Interpretivism, Patton (1980) has argued, is a dramatic alternative to positivism which focuses on putting the meaning of social situations into relevant contexts (Mishler 1979). In interpretive evaluations, the evaluator typically observes and interviews the parties to the evaluation to construct a 'reading' (Geertz 1973) of the 'multiperspectival realities' (Douglas 1976) of the situation being evaluated. While interpretivists often view their role to end with the completion of the research endeavor and its sharing, they will often propose that taking action based on the evaluation is not as straightforward as the sponsor or evaluatees may believe. As interpretivists will argue, the source of problems in an educational program may largely be the assumptions involved in creating the situation, and less so in technical deficiencies in program design or implementation.

Interpretivists see their evaluator role to be one of revealing such taken-for-granted assumptions. Since interpretivists are cautious about proposing an instrumental value to their evaluations, they focus more on developing relationships that first provide access to the situation and, over time, create trust in the evaluator. For interpretivists, though, the question of 'whose side are we on?' (Becker 1967) looms throughout the evaluation. This question is resolved either by consciously 'going native' (Wolcott 1977) or by providing a descriptive account that puts the case of each 'side' into an understandable context.

The social relations of an interpretive evaluation, thus, are complex and changing. The interpretivist usually negotiates for the unique status of a 'voyeur', a person who is able to watch universally but reserves the right to decide when participation is appropriate. In doing so, the interpretive evaluator maintains a distance from the normal authority structures present in the situation, carefully avoiding becoming an exclusive member of any network. The role, then is like that of a 'broker' between social networks. Yet, this broker, unlike most, witholds transmitting messages or facilitating social exchanges until the end of the evaluation, when credible knowledge is revealed in the words of those evaluated.

The evaluatees in an interpretive evaluation are expected to grant access of various sorts to the evaluator. However, they are not assumed to trust the evaluator or the evaluation, as interpretivists view trust as being earned through ongoing social interaction. In granting access, the sponsor-evaluatees in many ways are behaving altruistically. Access, then, is the result of a sponsor with sufficient authority and/or patron status *vis-à-vis* the evaluatee's clientelism, or of existing inter-network relations that include the evaluator prior to the evaluation. In any case, the evaluator avoids being either a patron or client, while the evaluatee becomes dependent on the good faith of the evaluator. In our experience, both sponsors and evaluatees resolve this by coming to believe that the evaluator's account will vindicate their position and actions (cf. Collins and Noblit 1978).

Unlike the other evaluation designs discussed here, interpretivism does not entail a prior belief concerning the legitimacy of the approach; rather only access is required. Interpretivists disavow the usual bases of legitimacy such as content expertise, instrumental utility, or authority. Yet it is expected that over time both trust and the legitimacy of the evaluation will be negotiated. That is to say, interpretivists seek to create a belief in the legitimacy of the evaluation in question, and interpretivism in general. In this way, interpretivists seek converts, and if the conversion is complete assume the role of a compassionate and even-handed patron to the evaluatees and sponsor. Loyalty and deference may be exchanged for the protection of a 'democratic' multiperspectival reality and the support of the evaluator-patron. If the interpretivist-evaluator cannot achieve this patron status, the evaluation may be rejected as biased and/or not useful.

Critical theory

Critical theory, as a mode of evaluation, is not as popular as the other approaches we discuss here (Bredo and Feinburg 1982). Yet we have seen its popularity increase in education in recent years (cf., Giroux 1981). An evaluation which uses the critical theory approach legitimates critique as the form of credible knowledge and the critical theorist as the expert patron. Nonetheless, the beliefs of the critical theorist-evaluator are potentially subject to the same critique as the beliefs of all other parties to the evaluation. Critical theory is essentially the critique of ideologies which justify domination. In Habermas' formulation, ideology distorts communication by masking social contradictions. Such distortion makes it difficult for individuals to discern the ideological content of the beliefs that structure their lives and their consciousness (Geuss 1981). The critical theorist would have people emancipated from ideological domination through a program of dialogue and discourse (dialogue about the nature of communication itself) designed to promote self-reflection and, consequently, enlightenment and emancipation. Such an evaluation program requires, however, that the evaluator can create an approximation of an 'ideal speech situation' which allows free and uncoerced discussion (Habermas 1970).

An evaluation based in critical theory is largely participative, trying to facilitate the evaluatees' free and uncoerced discussion of their situation. Yet, we see that the role of the evaluator-critical theorist is one of first among equals. The evaluator-critical theorist has expertise in critique as a genre as well as in the process of facilitating the ideal speech situation and the dialogue and discourse that ensues. Further, to the extent that such discourse must be based in evidence about social conditions, intersubjective meanings and the connections between the two, the evaluator-critical theorist also may have roles approximating those of the positivist or interpretivist.

The social relations involved in a critical theory are obviously delicate. The evaluator-critical theorist is in many ways a supreme patron, providing both content and process direction in the service of free and uncoerced dialogue. The evaluator-critical theorist must continually legitimate critique as a genre and reassure the evaluatees of the value of shedding their false consciousness. The evaluatees, at least initially, are clientele to the critical theorist's patronage, in the sense that they must commit to follow the patron to some enticing, yet unspecified, and in many ways, unpredictable end. They engage in the approximation of the ideal speech situation as equals among themselves, free to discern ideological distortions as they see them, and free even to decide not to proceed with a course of action once ideologies are revealed (Geuss 1981). Yet they are not equal to the evaluator-critical theorist in creating the content and process through which this occurs. An evaluation based in critical theory would be wary of an outside sponsor, since the interests of a sponsor may well perpetuate ideological distortions. Any outside sponsor would, of necessity, be more of a philanthropist, providing resources for others to do with as they wish.

A critical theory evaluation requires a set of prior beliefs to be credible. In critical theory, the agreed-upon contract about what is credible knowledge includes agreement concerning the need to shed delusions, a predisposition to critique as the genre in which to do so, and an interest in emancipation. Beliefs in the instrumental or technical value of the evaluation are not required and indeed may be exposed as ideology in the process. What is intriguing about the critical theory approach is that, while the evaluator is a strong patron, there is no suspension of belief in the vested interests of the evaluator-critical theorist. Indeed, since to critical theorists all knowledge has interests (Habermas 1971), the interests of the evaluator, as well as those of evaluatees, are subject to examination and reflection. Nevertheless, as part of the 'hidden contract', a critical theory evaluation in the end requires that the evaluatee believe the evaluator is serving their best interests.

Aesthetics

Aesthetic evaluations require that the evaluation be not a goal but an expression of key values that in the end reinforce the altruistic belief in aesthetics. Aesthetics is another type of qualitative approach to evaluation (Eisner 1979, House 1980). In Eisner's formulation, aesthetic evaluation involves both 'connoisseurship' and 'criticism'. Connoisseurship is the 'art of appreciation' (p. 14). The evaluator must have 'developed a highly differentiated array of anticipatory schema that enable one to discern qualities and relationships that others, less differentiated, are less likely to see' (p. 14). Connoisseurship is necessary to aesthetic evaluations in that ' . . . it provides that content for our knowing. It makes possible the stuff we use for reflection' (p. 15). Yet to Eisner, connoisseurship is private, not public. To make it public, it must be transformed into a form that others can understand. This is the role of criticism. Criticism entails first creating an artistic description so that others may 'vicariously participate' (p. 15) in the events at issue. Second, criticism includes rendering an interpretation by ' . . . applying theoretical ideas to explain the conditions that have been described' (p. 16). Third, criticism involves an appraisal. This appraisal is not in the form of an outcome-based evaluation. Rather it is to provide constructive criticism, ' . . . providing the conditions that lead to the improvement of the educational process' (p. 16).

Eisner and his students have conceived of the role of the evaluator to be one that provides 'a fresh eye' (p. 17). To do so, he argues that interpersonal skills and trust are essential between the critic and evaluatee: 'The teacher must be willing to have a critic in the classroom and must be willing to listen (but not necessarily heed) to what the critic says' (p. 17). In Eisner's view, this relationship is one of a dialogue between friends.

Yet on closer analysis, the social basis of aesthetics involves social relations that are not typically friendship relations. The evaluator-critic must have considerable expertise to be recognised as a source of credible knowledge, yet also be sufficiently independent of other power and authority relations so that the evaluatee is willing to participate in good faith and trust the evaluator-critic. The evaluatee must believe that improvement is so desirable as to seek a 'fresh eye'. Nevertheless, the evaluatee is dependent on the critic for insight and direction. Eisner argues that schools should provide 'structures' (p. 17) for observation and reflection; however, he is clear that connoisseurship and criticism concerns the particular not the universal, rendering aesthetic evaluation not amenable to bureaucratic ends.

The social relations between evaluator-critic and evaluatee involve a subtle dependency of the evaluatee on the expertise of the evaluator-critic without requiring compliance, much like the ideal speech situation in critical theory. Any sponsors outside of this dyadic relationship are simply to provide the opportunity for the evaluation, with the faith that improvement will occur. Intriguingly, the evaluator-critic is not in a patron status as he/she is unable to provide protection and support within the authority of the educational organization. The sponsor, on the other hand, is more like a patron of the arts than a direct supervisor to either party. He/she must believe in the value of aesthetics and sponsor its practice, but not be assured of any instrumental gain for the organization, except possibly in social status or in the evaluatee's internal motivations.

Aesthetics, like other designs, seem to involve a precontractual basis of solidarity (Collins 1982). The conscious contract is an expression of belief in the legitimacy of art criticism as applied to educational practice. Parties must believe that the pursuit of creative expression and its critique is valuable. On the other hand, the hidden contract requires a suspension of belief on the part of the evaluatee in the vested interests of the evaluator-critic and sponsor. Altruism for all parties is assumed. Trust and skills in interpersonal relations are to hold the relationships and beliefs together.

Collaborative research

There are no real 'results' in a collaborative evaluation as these evaluations can be considered ongoing 'experiments in practice' (Torbet 1981: 147). Certainly there is no search for instrumental knowledge. Rather, Torbet (1981: 151) states that collaborative inquiry is a seeking of 'valid social knowledge' for the participants to develop and apply to their everybody lives. Collaborative research assumes that research and action are inseparable, except in any analytic sense, and that knowledge comes through and for action. Collaborative inquiry diminishes some of the substantive differences that can be present among practitioners, sponsors and evaluators (Schlechty and Noblit 1982). In collaborative evaluation, all aspects are negotiated – the research design, the roles of all participants and the issues. The design of collaborative inquiry, then, is not pre-defined nor necessarily stable but is an evolutionary, developmental process (Torbet 1981).

The evaluator in collaborative inquiry must develop a 'shared reality' with all other participants in terms of belief in the collaborative process, role domains and evaluation issues. Thus, the evaluator's role must be or must become one of an interested agent within the evaluation process.

Collaborative inquiry in its 'purest' form requires relative equality of power. This requirement presupposes that social relations are in place prior to the evaluation and that socially enforced equality is maintained through negotiation and active bargaining. Networks within a collaborative design are, in essence, an alliance based on mutual trust and belief rather than one of patrons or clients. Thus, whether the participants are technically evaluator, sponsor or evaluatee, they must operate as a horizontal network with the interests of all parties given equal consideration. Yet if collaboration is to achieve an evaluation or a reevaluation of a setting, it must avoid 'group think' characteristics of groups together over time. This typically is the job of the evaluator (Schlechty and Noblit 1982, Newman and

Noblit 1982) who takes the role of representative. The evaluator in the collaborative endeavor represents perspectives from outside the evaluation situation as well as representing the collaboration's perspectives to wider audiences. The evaluator thus assumes an instrumental expertise as a translator. In social networks, this is akin to the role of a 'broker' who, in transmitting a message, also invariably alters its content (Lande 1977). Collaborative research creates a horizontal network and ideally avoids creating patrons. Yet the evaluator-as-broker is a boundary-spanning member of the social network and thus has a subtle, manipulative power upon which the fruits of collaboration are dependent.

It is also true that evaluations using a collaborative design require a precontractual basis of solidarity (Collins 1982). Legitimate knowledge is process knowledge, not substantive knowledge. The reification of this collaborative process is the basis of the conscious contract. In practice, however, the hidden contract requires a prior trust in the other participants that the negotiated social contract will not be violated. This social contract is definitive only in requiring collaboration and not in specifying a substantive knowledge base as credible.

Action research

Action research is as technical as postivism for its reifies practical knowledge. Unlike positivism, however, it does so in the service of the interests of the usual underdog in evaluations, the practitioner. Action research has several commonalities with collaborative research and, in fact, differences in the two may be virtually non-discernable in actual practice. However, we believe theoretically there are differences worth examining in the context of evaluation as political strategy.

Action research insists that the interests of the *practitioner* be primary. The particular method of the evaluation is not as important as its appropriateness to the environment, problem and participants (Nixon 1981). The action research approach is being adopted as a mode of evaluation and supervision in many situations, perhaps because it attempts to fill the gap between research and practice through a practice emphasis. In fact, action research uses evaluatee or practitioner world view as the most credible knowledge base.

The role of the evaluator within action research requires that he/she suspend all personal and professional beliefs about the evaluation issue(s) and setting and believe single-mindedly in the priorities of the practitioner. The evaluator must establish him/her as a credible technician to the practitioner as well as a trusted reporter at the conclusion of the evaluation.

This evaluation design is the only one in which the evaluator is ultimately the client to the evaluatees. Although this evaluator clientelism changes somewhat from the initiation to the conclusion of the process, the social networks remain relatively intact. Initially, the evaluator evidences deference and loyalty to the patron-evaluatee through his/her total attention to practitioner-defined issues. The evaluator may prompt action, but it must be justified in terms of practical knowledge as defined by the participants. At the conclusion of the process, the evaluator assumes a representative role, being charged with reporting the results obtained. However, any evaluation results would have been previously created and approved by the evaluatees (Sanford 1981: 178), reinforcing their patron status. Evaluatees would not feel the need to fulfill a clientele role of deference and loyalty to the evaluator since sponsor and evaluator power and authority do not exist within this design. Should a sponsor have a role in the process, generally in the initiation phases, the sponsor essentially 'disappears' as is the case in the aesthetic and critical theory designs.

The precontractual basis of solidarity (Collins 1982) in action research is predicated on the prior agreed-upon contract that the practitioner is the expert and that the process and results of action research are legitimate and credible. Practitioner knowledge, or local know-ledge, is the credible knowledge base. The knowledge gained is considered authentic *and* instrumental, unlike the more formal knowledge bases of positivism, interpretivism and critical theory. Like the aesthetic designs, the hidden contract in action research necessitates the suspension of belief by the evaluatees concerning the vested interests of the sponsor(s) and/or the evaluator. Any sponsor operates under the altruistic belief that the process and results will be valuable for the practitioner evaluatees and, therefore, that the action research evaluation is justified.

The political strategy of evaluation

We have made the case that evaluation is a socially-created 'reality' that alters social relations and beliefs. In this way, evaluation designs are actually political strategies. Corbett and Wilson, in their chapter, show how relations among teachers, students and what is taught have changed in the recent reform agenda. Johnson's chapter argues that teachers have not been empowered by this movement. As Fuhrman shows, the evaluation upon which the reform agenda has been based produced a new coalition of federal and state actors overcoming prior political coalitions. The essence of the political strategies of evaluation is to fashion a dominant coalition (Benson 1975). If we look at figure 1, we see that different evaluation designs result in dominant coalitions of rather different forms.

Positivism establishes a dominant coalition of co-patrons, the sponsor and the evaluator, enabling the evaluatees to, at best, play the co-patrons off against each other (Lande 1977). In any case, positivistic evaluation designs institutionalize the evaluatee's client status to some patron or patrons. Interpretivism negotiates a local definition of credible knowledge. The evaluator spans network boundaries between sponsor and evaluatee. The political result is less determinant than with positivism. However, an interpretivist evaluation that develops new understandings of what is credible knowledge through a broker role allows for con-siderable political bargaining. The political strategy of collaborative research, by comparison, is based in relatively equal political power between the parties. This reification of collabor-ative social relations also allows for considerable bargaining. Without a broker, however, the possibilities for new understandings of what is credible knowledge is considerably less than with interpretivism.

Critical theory, aesthetics and action research all result in a curious 'disappearance' of the sponsor from the dominant coalition that results from the evaluation design. Moreover, each has the sense that the sponsor 'volunteers' to disappear. What the disappearance means for the sponsor, however, varies. In aesthetic designs, the sponsor disappears because of an altruistic belief that the artistic is a valuable perspective to add to more instrumental per-spectives on education. Critical theory designs consider the sponsor's position to be (potentially) an ideological masking of raw power relations, undercutting any claims by the sponsor to legitimate and/or patron status. Inasmuch as the method is critique, the basis of new coalitions is in opposition to externally legitimated belief systems and patterns of social relations. As Everhart (1983) argues, however, opposition may well be reproductive of hegemonic social relations. Practical knowledge is reified in action research. The sponsor 'disappears' because this knowledge is the product of the practitioner. This reification of practical knowledge also reduces the credibility of evaluator to that of a technician. The dominant coalition in action research has the practitioners as the patrons.

If we combine this analysis of the six designs along the dimensions of relative power, and credibility of knowledge systems, the resulting table (see figure 2) suggests the conditions under which each of the six evaluation approaches would be successful as a political strategy to fashion a dominant coalition (Benson 1975).

	HIGH POWER IMBALANCE		LOW POWER IMBALANCE	
	Externally legitimated knowledge	*Local knowledge*	*Externally legitimated knowledge*	*Local knowledge*
Appropriate evaluation designs	Positivism	Action Research	Aesthetics	Interpretivism
	Critical Theory			Collaborative Research

Figure 2. **Fashioning a dominant coalition via evaluation.**

When there is a high power imbalance in favour of those in authority and an externally legitimated belief in science as a credible way to know, positivistic evaluation designs are most likely to fashion a dominant coalition. Under similar conditions, except that the externally legitimated knowledge base involves the process and substance of critique, critical theory is the effective strategy to achieve a dominant coalition. A high power imbalance (towards the evaluatees) coupled with locally legitimated knowledge are the conditions under which action research is an effective political strategy.

Under the conditions of a low power imbalance and an externally limited knowledge base that is personified in experts, aesthetic designs seem to be the appropriate mechanism by which to fashion a dominant coalition. Low power imbalance and a belief in locally legitimated knowledge indicate two appropriate designs. When multiple knowledge bases are legitimated, collaborative research is the political strategy leading to a dominant coalition. When the legitimated local knowledge is less based in practitioner expertise and more in a belief that what takes place 'here' is more worthy than knowledge bases external to the evaluation situation, interpretivisim is the political strategy of choice.

In the final analysis, however, it would be a mistake to consider the conditions and the resulting appropriate design as absolute. In practice, the choice of an evaluation design is recognized, we would argue, as a political strategy and, as such, the choice may alter the conditions themselves. We expect that politically successful (i.e., fashioning a dominant coalition) evaluations are iterative processes, a series of moves and countermoves that, in the end, produce a design or series of designs. This seems to require evaluators that are politically adept and methodologically flexible.

Conclusions

It is apparant from our analysis that a sociology of knowledge approach exposes many of the taken-for-granted assumptions in evaluation research. Evaluators seem to take a number of things for granted. First, regardless of the design they employ, they take-for-granted that evaluation research does not have the characteristics of other social situations. Our analysis shows that this is not fully the case. Evaluation situations have the same bases in patterns of social relations and beliefs as any other social endeavor. Evaluation designs are not only political strategies, but they must be considered as political as any other social design, plan or program. Second and related, (specific) evaluators take for granted that the evaluatees will suspend a belief in the vested interests of the parties to the evaluation. This is, they assume that evaluatees will accord evaluation a special status and treat it as an unusual social situation. Third, many evaluators take for granted a precontractual basis of solidarity (Collins 1982) in an evaluation situation. Positivists assume it emerges from the legitimacy of science. Action researchers, collaborative researchers, critical theorists and aesthetic evaluators all also argue that trust is a precondition. Only the interpretivists, as is consistent with their approach, view trust as something to be developed through the usual processes of social interaction. Fourth, evaluation researchers seem to take for granted that the salient outcome of the evaluation situation is a factual report and/or a set of values upon which future actions can be based. Our analysis suggests that another salient outcome is a new political arrangement between the parties to the evaluation situation. Further, we would argue that this arrangement may well be the primary basis of future action.

This reconsideration of evaluation should not be taken to imply that we believe evaluations designs are *only* political strategies; but we would argue that *at their base* they are political strategies. Further, it should not be inferred that because we see evaluations as political that evaluations are not worthy social processes. If anything, our analysis establishes that evaluations are recognizable processes through which values and, thus, worthiness are created.

Similarly, we can reconsider the recent reform movement as an attempt to improve American education through a political realignment. The 'crisis' evaluations made in the *Nation At Risk* report and elsewhere politicaly galvanized, as Fuhrman argues, state leadership and redefined state political contexts. As Corbett and Wilson demonstrate, the 'game' has changed for local systems. State responsibility to a national norm was established by the various reform reports. Local districts and teachers have been undercut in the process. This evaluation, like all evaluations, are well understood as a political strategy.

References

BECKER, H. (1967) 'Whose side are we on?' *Social Problems*, 14, pp. 239—247.

BENSON, J. K. (1975) 'The interorganizational network as a political economy', *Administrative Science Quarterly*, 20, pp. 229–248.

BERGER, P., and LUCKMANN, T. (1967) *The Social Construction of Reality: A Treatise in the Sociology of Knowledge* (Garden City, NY: Doubleday).

BREDO, E., and FEINBERG, W. (1982) *Knowledge and Values in Social and Educational Research* (Philadelphia, PA: Temple University Press).

CHELIMSKY, E. (1987) 'What have we learned about the politics of program evaluation? *Educational Evaluation and Policy Analysis*, 9 (3), pp. 199–213.

CORBETT, R. and WILSON, B. L. (1988) 'Raising the stakes in statewide mandatory minimum competency testing', in J. Hannaway and R. Crowson (eds.) *The Politics of Reforming School Administration* (London: Falmer Press).

COLLINS, R. (1982) *Sociological Insight* (New York: Oxford University Press).

COLLINS, T., and NOBLIT, G. (1978) 'Stratification and resegregation: the case of Crossover High School', final report of NIE contract # 400–76–009.

DOUGLAS, J. D. (1976) *Investigative Social Research* (Beverly Hills, CA: Sage).

EISNER, E. (1979) 'The use of qualitative forms of evaluation for improving educational practice', *Educational Evaluation and Policy Analysis*, 6 (1), pp 11–19.

EVERHART, R. (1983) *Reading, Writing and Resistance* (Boston: Routledge Kegan Paul).

FUHRMAN, S. (1988) 'State politics and education reform', in J. Hannaway and R. Crowson (eds.) *The Politics of Reforming School Administration* (London: Falmer Press).

GEERTZ, C. (1973) *The Interpretation of Cultures* (New York: Basic Books).

GEERTZ, C (1983) *Local Knowledge* (New York: Basic Books).

GEUSS, R. (1981) *The Idea of a Critical Theory: Habermas and the Frankfurt School* (New York: Cambridge University Press).

GIROUX, H. (1981) *Ideology, Culture and the Process of Schooling* (Philadelphia: Temple Univertisy Press).

GUTMANN, A. (1988) 'Democratic theory and the role of teachers in democratic education', in J. Hannaway and R. Crowson (eds.) *The Politics of Reforming School Administration* (London: Falmer Press).

HABERMAS, J. (1970) 'Toward a theory of communicative competence', in H.P. Dreitzel (ed.) *Recent Sociology No. 2: Patterns of Communicative Behaviour* (Basingstoke: Macmillan).

HABERMAS, J. (1971) *Knowledge and Human Interests* (Boston: Beacon Press).

HOUSE, E. R. (1980) *Evaluating with Validity* (Beverly Hills, CA: Sage).

JOHNSON, S. M. (1988) 'Schoolwork and its reform', in J. Hannaway and R. Crowson (eds.) *The Politics of Reforming School Administration* (London: Falmer Press).

LANDE, C. H. (1977) 'Introduction: the dyadic basis of clientelism', in S. W. Schmidt *et al.* (eds.) *Friends, Followers and Factions* (Berkeley, CA: University of California Press).

MISHLER, E. (1979) 'Meaning in context', *Harvard Educational Review*, 49, pp. 1–19.

NEWMAN, C., and NOBLIT, G. (1982) 'Collaborative research: a staff development experience', *The Journal of Staff Development*, 3 (2), pp. 119–129.

NIXON, J. (ed.) (1981) *A Teachers' Guide to Action Research: Evaluation, Enquiry and Development in the Classroom* (London: Grant McIntyre).

NOBLIT, G. W. (1984) 'The prospects of an applied ethnography for education: a sociology of knowledge interpretation', *Educational Evaluation and Policy Analysis*, 6 (1), pp. 95–101.

PATTON, M. Q. (1980) *Qualitative Evaluation Methods* (Beverly Hills, CA: Sage).

SANFORD, N. (1981) 'A model for action research' in P. Reason and J. Rowan (eds.) *Human Inquiry: A Sourcebook of New Paradigm Research* (New York: Wiley).

SCHLECHTY, P., and NOBLIT, G. (1982) 'Some uses of sociological theory in educational evaluation', *Research in Sociology of Education and Socialization*, 3, pp. 283–306.

SCHMIDT, S. W., SCOTT, J. C., LANDE, C. and GUASTI, L. (eds.) (1977) *Friends, Followers and Factions* (Berkeley, CA: University of California Press).

SMITH, J. K. (1983) 'Quantitative versus qualitative research: an attempt to clarify the issue', *Educational Researcher*, 12 (3), pp. 6–13.

TORBET, W. R. (1981) 'Why educational research has been so uneducational: the case of a new model of social science based on collaborative inquiry? in P. Reason and J. Rowan (eds.) *Human Inquiry: A Sourcebook of New Paradigm Research* (New York: Wiley).

WEICK, K. E. (1982) 'Administering education in loosely-coupled schools', *Phi Delta Kappan*, 63 (10), pp. 673–676.

WOLCOTT, H. (1977) *Teachers versus Technocrats: An Educational Innovation in Anthropological Perspective* (Eugene, OR: Center for Educational Policy and Management, Univerity of Oregon).

10   *Power and empowerment: the constraining myths and emerging structures of teacher unionism in an age of reform*

Samuel B. Bacharach
Cornell University
Joseph B. Shedd
Organizational Analysis and Practice, Inc.,
Ithaca, New York

Introduction

As collective bargaining in public education enters its third decade, and as recent efforts to 'reform' public schools pass the half-decade mark, policy makers and scholars are raising questions about relationships between the two developments and about their impact on the management of public school systems. Some observers insist that collective bargaining poses a serious threat to the management of school systems and to efforts to reform public education (Grimshaw 1979, Kearney 1984, Goldschmidt *et al.* 1984, Lieberman 1980). Others acknowledge that teacher unions have forced school boards and administrators to change the ways in which they manage, but claim that school management may have been strengthened in the process (McDonnell and Pascal 1979, Johnson 1983). Still others argue that teacher unions *and* school management are undergoing fundamental changes, as both struggle to adapt to the new public expectations reflected in the current 'reform' movement (Kerchner and Mitchell 1986, Johnson 1987, McDonnell and Pascal 1988).

Until recently, most observers seemed to agree on what unions and collective bargaining were like, even if they could not agree on their effects. But now an increasing number of policy makers, union leaders, school administrators, journalists and scholars are arguing that a new form of collective bargaining is actually emerging in public education, better adapted to the structures, processes and needs of the parties in that setting than the private sector practices that the parties initially borrowed. We agree with this basic argument.

Toledo. Hammond, Indiana. Rochester. Dade County. Philadelphia. Chicago. Cincinnati. Peer review. Mentor systems. Career ladders. School improvement programs. Quality circles. Labor-management cooperation programs. Teacher empowerment. School-based management. Trust agreements. The critical mass of accounts, reports and studies documenting a new era in labor-management relations in public education does not yet justify the assertion that the 'fight' is over, but is too substantial to be dismissed out of hand. Either a lot of people are fooling themselves – and their constituents – or something new is emerging in public education. Or perhaps, as we argue here, something new is emerging in public education and a lot of people are fooling themselves about what that 'something' might be.

Much of the speculation about what 'new' teacher unions will be like is still dominated by conventional images of the 'old' ones. Rather than being adversarial and concerned with preserving its own power, many people convinced that the new teacher union will be cooperative and non-confrontational; rather than opposing efforts to improve the quality of teaching, it will actually assume responsibility for the quality and quantity of its members' efforts; rather than negotiating rules that restrict flexibility, it will look for ways of relaxing restrictions on teachers and administrators alike; rather than insisting that teachers' rights and benefits be allocated equally or else on the basis of seniority, it will insist that the responsibilities and compensation of teachers be differentiated, ordered hierarchically, and allocated on the basis of professional competence.

Some of these assertions will prove to be accurate simply because people expect them to be. No doubt many policy makers, school board members, administrators, teachers, and their hired or elected representatives have *believed* that unions are necessarily adversarial, that they are invariably opposed to efforts to improve their members' performance, and so forth. As active metaphors or 'institutional myths' (Dowling and Pfeffer 1975, Meyer and Rowan 1977) such convictions have played an important role in shaping the behavior of unions and employers in public education, even if the evidence to support them has been ambiguous. There is no reason why a new set of myths should not have similar influence, even if some of them *have* been created by holding a mirror up to the old ones.

But such speculation says nothing about why a new form of labor-management relations might be emerging in public education; nor does it help predict which myths are likely to survive and which are likely to be modified or fade away. The purpose of this paper is to identify factors that appear to be influencing the evolution of union policy and labor-management relations in public education, and to speculate on where they might lead.

Drawing on the history of earlier forms of unionism in the private and public sectors, the authors argue that teacher unionism in the future will be grounded in the issues and kinds of power that are inherent in the labor and product markets, work processes and management systems of public education itself. The present system of collective bargaining in public education, we argue, was patterned largely after bargaining in the industrial sector of the economy, reflecting the top-down management ideology that was ascendant in education when teacher unions first won recognition. The basic dilemma for school managers and teacher unions, alike, is that there has never been anything but an imperfect match between that management ideology and the basic work processes and public expectations in most school systems. Frustration with this dilemma is one of the factors that has prompted teacher unions to abandon the reactive approach that industrial unions have typically followed and to join, as active participants, the debate over how school systems should be managed (NEA/NAASP 1986, AFT Task Force 1986).

The argument we develop supports or complements those of other recent scholars in many respects save one: it is both misleading and dangerous, we argue, to expect that 'cooperativeness' will be a defining characteristic of the new labor-management relations in public education. A bargaining system that is tailored to the markets, work processes and management systems of public education undoubtedly will remove some of the present sources of conflict in teacher bargaining. But such a system will almost certainly *expose* other sources of conflict that until recently have been sheltered behind assertions of 'management prerogatives' and 'professional autonomy'. Such a system is unlikely to emerge unless both union leaders and school managers are prepared to cooperate in the search for innovative solutions to these potential conflicts; such a system is unlikely to survive unless they and their constituents are equally prepared to accept conflict along the way.

The evolution of industrial unionism

To understand where collective bargaining in public education may be headed, we must understand where it came from. This section focuses on the private sector origins of the bargaining system in education. Our purpose is twofold: to show how the basic logic of that system reflected the markets, technologies and management structures of America's factories, and to illustrate why unions and employers invariably adopt or adjust bargaining systems to reflect the sector and settings in which they operate. Later sections will consider why policy makers, teacher unions and school districts apparently found the logic of that system to be attractive when they first began bargaining in the 1960s, and why the pressure to adapt their practices to the features of public education now leads them to question that same logic.

Except for restrictions on the right to strike and the substitution of various third-party impasse procedures, most of the features of collective bargaining in public education were borrowed from the private sector: district-wide bargaining units; the periodic negotiation of comprehensive agreements that last for fixed periods of time; legal restrictions that limit bargaining to so-called 'bread-and-butter' issues and that require the parties to negotiate 'in good faith'; multi-step grievance procedures for the resolution of disagreements that may arise during the life of an agreement; and the use of binding arbitration to resolve such mid-contract disputes, if the parties are unable to resolve them on their own.

These features are so common in the private sector today that it is easy to forget that most of them are only half a century old, that they were invented specifically for labor-management relations in America's burgeoning factories, and that the policy-makers, managers, and unions that invented them were actually thumbing their noses at an even earlier form of collective bargaining when they did so. In fact, sixty years ago, knowledgeable observers were proclaiming that another 'traditional' form of collective bargaining was obsolete and that workers no longer needed 'outside' unions. Scientific management and more sophisticated personnel practices were said to be ushering in a new age of industrial harmony, in which employers would willingly sit down with company unions and discuss problems rationally and openly, without workers having to use power tactics to get themselves heard (Taft 1964, Dulles 1966). Yet, only a few years later, America saw an explosion of militant unionism that turned the predictions of knowledgeable observers on their heads. In the short space of five or six years in the mid-1930s, the smokestack industries that experts thought were impenetrable were swiftly unionized and the number of American workers represented by unions more than doubled.

From the vantage point of history, it is easy to laugh at the observers in the 1920s who predicted that unions and collective bargaining were on the verge of extinction. But there was actually plenty of solid evidence, derived from nearly twenty years of failed organizing efforts, to 'prove' that unions would never establish a foothold in the smokestack industries. True, most American labor leaders showed only occasional interest in organizing those industries, but given the conventional wisdom about what made for a successful union, there were solid explanations to justify their pessimism.

Craft unionism, which was the 'traditional' form of unionism at the time, was based on principles that were fundamentally inconsistent with the factory system. It was based on the principles: (1) that workers had to be members of a union before they could be hired; (2) that it was the union's responsibility to train workers and to certify when they were ready to be employed; (3) that foremen or immediate supervisors had to be members of the union and subject to union discipline; and (4) that the union would control the work process through its unilateral specification of work rules. All four of these principles were fundamentally incompatible with the unskilled labor markets, standardized mass product markets, machine technologies and hierarchical managerial systems on which factory systems were based. As long as union leaders clung to those principles, the prediction that they could never break into the factory sector was absolutely well-founded.

What the observers of the 1920s were not counting on was that the workers in smokestack industries, with the help of some union leaders, would reinvent the concepts of 'collective bargaining' and 'union'. They abandoned the notion that a 'real' union must control hiring, training, immediate supervision and the work process itself, acknowledging that control of such processes was the prerogative of management. At first, that acknowledgement came grudgingly; soon, it was elevated to a set of principles, to be heartily embraced. What industrial unions got, in return for these concessions, were somewhat higher wages and increasingly detailed agreements, negotiated for fixed periods of time, with grievance procedures that culminated in binding arbitration for the resolution of disputes that might arise during the life of the agreement. Many of the provisions of these agreements established links between different jobs and pay rates and specified how employees were to be selected, either permanently or temporarily, for those jobs.

Management, in turn, got a stable workforce. The higher wages and benefit packages linked contractually to job ladders and seniority had the effect of lowering quit rates and tying workers with specialized skills to the employer, in what one scholar called a new 'industrial feudalism' (Ross 1958, also Block 1978). Seniority clauses governing reassignments, promotions and layoffs protected more-experienced workers from the threat of competition from junior workers, eliminating an obstacle to the informal sharing of job knowledge among workers (Thurow 1975). Lay off and recall procedures provided employers with a way of temporarily reducing employment in slack periods, without permanently losing the knowledge and skills of the workers who were laid off (Medoff 1979).

The stability that these various contractual provisions encouraged was an important asset to factory managers, and undoubtedly played a key role in enhancing worker productivity. Indeed, contrary to popular impressions, recent research indicates that unionized firms are almost always more productive than non-unionized firms in the same industries (Freeman and Medoff 1979). It is unlikely, however, that employers would have accepted industrial unionism if these stabilizing arrangements were all that a union had to offer. After all, an employer with sufficient resources could make most of these adjustments without collective bargaining, and many employers intent on avoiding unionization did precisely that.

Paradoxically, the most important concession that industrial unions could make to factory managers was to give them what conventional wisdom suggests unions took away: *authority* and *flexibility*. Although the tactics of industrial unions were militant and their leaders' rhetoric sometimes radical, the unionism they invented was essentially an accommodation to the basic features of the factory management system. To call their approach 'job control unionism', as some observers do, is both descriptive and misleading. The employee rights and benefits negotiated by industrial unions imposed restrictions on an employer's ability to direct the workforce, but actually complemented the factory system of management. The union's insistence on detailed specification of job duties (and the growth of technical personnel staffs to monitor the resulting job structures) complemented Frederick Taylor's system of 'scientific management', on which much of the design and management of industrial work processes depended (Nadworny 1955). Management flexibility was restricted by contractual guarantees that job assignments, promotions and layoffs would be governed partly by seniority, and by requirements that work rules must be published in advance before they could be enforced by discipline. But these were largely protections against favoritism and managerial abuse of authority. The actual *content* of job assignments, job descriptions and work rules, the structure of job ladders, and the actual decisions to fill jobs and lay off or recall workers were left to management.

The union's formal acknowledgement of management authority was embodied in several provisions of the parties' negotiated contract, and in the union's acceptance of what came to be called the 'reserved rights' principle. The discipline procedures in industrial union contracts established the principle that a worker's basic obligation to his or her employer was obedience: insubordination (not incompetence) was the primary grounds for discipline and/or dismissal. The grievance procedures in such contracts provided top management with information about shop-floor problems and first-line supervisory behavior that top managers would never have gotten through their own management hierarchies.

The key to these arrangements, however, was contained in the arbitration procedures of the parties' negotiated agreements, in the often-overlooked provision that specified that the terms of their agreement would remain in place for a fixed period of time, and in the union's promise not to call strikes during the life of the agreement. Together, these provisions helped establish the central principle of labor-management relations in the industrial setting, namely, that it is 'management's right to manage' and that any rights employers have not given up, either by express contract language or by mutually acknowledged past practice, remain rights which employers are free to exercise as they see fit for the duration of the agreement (Elkouri and Elkouri 1973).

The label 'job control unionism' is misleading, therefore, for industrial unions never presumed to control jobs as craft unions had done. Instead, they negotiated *limits on the employer's control* and acknowledged that workers would respect the employer's authority so long as it stayed within those limits. The structure of this deal reflected a different strategic relationship from the one craft unions and their management counterparts occupied. Craft unions, for the most part, dealt with employers who had no permanent workforces. In fact, they *provided* employers with their workers, using hiring halls, restrictions on membership, and apprenticeship programs to guarantee that those workers would be qualified to perform the work for which they were temporarily hired, In their dealings with an employer, craft unions occupied the position of a seller of labor; their basic 'deal' was an exchange of skilled labor of money.

But industrial unions never occupied such a position. Their members were permanently employed, were given any necessary training after they were hired, and were usually employees before they were members. Because the employer's products were standardized, produced in enormous quantities, and required relatively little decision-making by the workers who produced them, the employer could afford to separate the planning of work from its execution, giving managers and technical staffs the job of planning the work and giving each line employee a relatively fixed set of duties to perform. The seller of labor, in such a setting, is the individual employee. The control of labor is a management function. The craft union's two sources of leverage were never accessible to the industrial union.

What a unified industrial union could control (or could prevent the employer from securing) was the authority to make the whole elaborate system work. As Chester Barnard, one of the seminal theorists on the functions of the executive, noted in the mid-1930s, *authority is always delegated upward* (Barnard 1938). The right to direct workers, to give orders and to insist on obedience, must be acknowledged and respected by those workers or else it is an empty fiction. Managers, of course, always prefer to speak of authority being delegated downward. When they give credence to Barnard's assertion at all, they typically assert that individual employees 'gave' management the authority to direct them when they accepted employment; if workers want to revoke that authority, they can quit.

Industrial unions proved that workers need not accept that assertion. They took advantage of the fact that the effective operation of factory systems depended upon the willingness of workers to voluntarily accept directions from their supervisors. The systems were simply too complex, and their dependence upon large numbers of workers was too great, to pretend that obedience could be *coerced* from each individual, particularly if workers were prepared to act collectively in the face of coercion. The benefits and guarantees which soon began to fill industrial union contracts were the price an employer had to pay to secure that obedience.

The basic logic and structural arrangements of industrial unionism provided the starting point for teacher unions and school districts when collective bargaining began in public education in the 1960s.

The half-logic of industrial unionism

Industrial relations scholars have filled whole libraries documenting the basic premise of this paper: that the parties to collective bargaining relationships tend to adopt substantive and procedural rules that reflect the basic characteristics of their particular industries (Dunlop 1958, Kochan 1980). For some, that point is so obvious that the important question is not whether teacher unions and school districts will develop a system of bargaining that fits the features of public education, but why they haven't done so sooner.

Why would education bargainers have embraced a set of arrangements derived from a factory setting in the first place? The simple answer, we would argue, is that teacher unions adopted factory union strategies because the administrators and school boards they faced insisted on acting like factory managers. Indeed, one of the basic reasons so many teachers chose to join unions was that the prevailing logic of education *management* was itself patterned on the industrial model (Cole 1969, Callahan 1962). The structures, processes and myths of industrial unionism complemented and in some ways even supported the top-down managerial ideology that existed in most school systems when teacher unions first won recognition, just as they 'fit' the factory management systems of the 1930s. If there are grounds for believing that unions and employers in public education are now in the process of inventing a new form of collective bargaining – and we believe there are – it is because that management ideology itself is undergoing serious attack.

School boards and administrators have had an on-again, off-again love affair with industrial management models for most of this century, from the first two decades, when school reformers used 'scientific management' principles to give the new discipline of educational administration a body of supposed expertise (Callahan 1962), to the late 1950s when post-Sputnik reformers issued repeated calls to overhaul the structure and management of school systems. What, in most systems, had been collections of largely autonomous units dominated by building principals were now to be 'rationalized', by centralizing the control of educational policies and programs in the hands of district superintendents and central office staff experts (Tyack and Hansot 1982).

If schools were to be run like factories, with hierarchical controls and centralized planning, evaluation and policy-setting mechanisms, then teacher unions would necessarily have to act like factory unions, resorting to roughly the same sorts of strategies for protecting the interests of their members. Like their industrial sector counterparts, teacher unions often challenged particular management decisions and insisted upon reducing to writing policies that administrators might have preferred to leave to their own discretion. But, at least in the early years of bargaining, teacher unions played essentially the same

reactive role as their industrial counterparts, insisting that it was management's job to set
policy and manage; the union's job was to negotiate and then police protections against
abuses of that authority.

In fact, teacher unions have provided district central administrators with many of the
same benefits that industrial managers gained from collective bargaining: access to
information about school-level problems, orderly procedures for disposing of various
personnel issues, and grounds for insisting that school principals adhere to policies prescribed
or agreed to by central administrators. Indeed, case studies of school district power
relationships indicate that collective bargaining has provided central administrators with one
of their most effective tools for centralizing management authority and power in their own
hands. Not only has it helped them control their subordinate managers; it also has helped
them insulate themselves – and their staffs – from school board 'interference' in their day-to-
day decision-making, by insisting that board members and administrators must present a
'united front' in the face of union pressure (Bacharach 1981).

The features of industrial unionism that teacher unions did not seem to embrace were
the job ladders, pay hierarchies and detailed prescription of duties associated with different
jobs. Indeed, teacher unions have traditionally been strong defenders of 'unified salary
schedules', which provide pay increments for seniority and increasing levels of training but
which treat teaching as a single profession rather than a set of divisible tasks to be ranked in a
hierarchy (Bacharach *et al.* 1984). But even this seeming departure from industrial union
practice is somewhat deceptive. Teacher unions have generally maintained that the
compensation provided by the basic salary schedule is for a specified number of class periods
or class preparations, but in any event, only for duties associated with the classroom.
Additional classroom work (teaching summer school, covering classes for absent colleagues,
teaching classes that require more than the specified number of lesson preparations, etc.) and
duties performed outside the classroom (coaching, sponsoring extra-curricular activities,
serving on committees, etc.) are often considered 'extra', calling for additional
compensation. Teacher unions, in these respects, are just as wedded to the basic industrial
union principle of 'equal pay for equal work' – and its corollary, 'extra pay for extra work' –
as their counterparts in industry have always been.

School boards and administrators, for their part, sometimes complain about how
'unprofessional' it is for teachers to demand extra compensation whenever they are asked to
assume new duties, but their complaints have been muted. As in the private sector, such
union demands represent tacit acknowledgement that it is management's prerogative to
assign such duties in the first place.

Good reasons exist for questioning the logic of centralized, top-down management in
public education – reasons that we will discuss shortly – but there are also reasons for
supporting its application in school systems. As much as teachers would like to identify
themselves with independent professionals like attorneys or physicians, their situations are
substantially different. School systems are not like some service organizations where one
person provides one complete service to one client at a time. If they were, the issue of
management could be reduced to the (relatively) simple question of how to get the right
resources to the right teachers at the right time. But, in fact, no one teacher has complete
responsibility for teaching any one student, and students are not the only constituency a
school system serves. Students acquire 'a public school education' over twelve or thirteen
years of their lifetimes, as they move – individually and in groups – from classroom to
classroom, grade to grade, and building to building. If there is not some coherence and
consistency to a school system's educational programs – *if the efforts of individual teachers and
other members of a school system aren't effectively coordinated* – enormous amounts of resources

will be wasted, enormous amounts of confusion will be generated, and the likelihood that the system can meet the needs of its individual students or any of its other constituencies are relatively slim (Wynne 1981, Rosenholtz 1985).

Until recently, top-down models of factory or bureaucratic management were the only models that offered any coherent explanation of how school systems might meet this need for coordination. Since coordinating the flow of students through the system – and assigning teachers, specialists, support personnel, curriculum requirements, material resources, space and time schedules to serve students as they pass through – are jobs that have fallen to boards and administrators to perform, it is not surprising that so many boards and administrators would find those top-down models so attractive.

But if top-down models appear to make sense from the vantage point of the front office, they make much less sense from the front of the classroom. Most school systems are not the tightly-controlled organizations that many policy makers and managers would like them to be, but neither are they the collections of autonomous professionals that many teachers would prefer. As organizations go, they are remarkably complex combinations of 'loose' and 'tight' elements, with individual teachers isolated or insulated (depending upon one's point of view) from direct contact with administrators and each other (Weick 1976) yet constantly constrained by the decisions of others (Bacharach *et al.* 1986).

Time schedules, physical structures, one-teacher-per-class staffing patterns and high teacher/administrator ratios make day-to-day contact with other adults haphazard (Lortie 1975). Norms of 'non-interference' discourage the asking and offering of advice (Little 1982). Curriculum policies, if they do not square with a teacher's judgment of what his or her students need or are capable of learning, often go unobserved and unenforced.

These features – irrational to those steeped in the hierarchical tradition – are both consequence and cause of the demands that American school systems place on their teachers. American teachers are expected to be decision-makers (Mosston 1972, Conley 1988). They are individually responsible for making most of the decisions concerning what work they and their students will perform, how that work will be carried out, and how the results of their students' day-to-day efforts will be evaluated (Shedd and Malanowski, 1985; Conley 1988). Teachers must make a large number of decisions under intense time pressures, most of them while class is actually in session. (The average teacher in one study, for example, made over 200 pedagogical decisions per hour when classes were in session, or over three decisions per minute [Jackson 1968; also Mosston 1972]).

The decision-making pressures on teachers are intense, in part because there is no well-established or generally-accepted body of pedagogical knowledge that says how teachers should perform in any given situation. That is partly a commentary on the state of pedagogical research and on the training that teachers receive, but more a commentary on the kinds of situations they face in the classroom. Teachers must constantly interact with students whose needs and abilities vary widely, are constantly changing, and are often difficult to identify. The situations they confront are often unpredictable as a consequence, making it difficult to predict all the effects of any given teaching strategy (Lortie 1975).

Another factor that complicates teachers' decision-making is that they are expected to pursue a variety of different purposes, each reflecting a different set of public expectations and each implying somewhat different relationships with their students. Their students are future workers to be trained, scholars to be inspired and guided, clients to be served, subordinates to be managed, 'raw material' to be shaped, citizens to be socialized, captives to be controlled, and audiences to be entertained (Lampert 1985). Decisions that might be easy to make if all students were alike and if teachers had a single purpose to serve become extraordinarily complex when different groups and different purposes must be served simultaneously.

Job design experts recognize these different conditions – multiple purposes, work techniques with uncertain consequences, unpredictable situations demanding quick responses, constant interaction with others, and direct contact with organizational clients or customers with different needs – as conditions that require organizations to give their employees latitude to exercise discretion and judgment in the planning, execution and assessment of their own work (Perrow 1972, Mitchell 1986, Peters and Waterman 1982).

The problem is that many of the factors that generate the need for teacher discretion and judgment also generate the need for coordination *among* teachers as well. Indeed, debates over how school systems should be managed – and debates over how they should be 'reformed' – almost always turn on the relationship between the need to allow individual teachers discretion and the need to coordinate their individual efforts. Metaphors and strategies that focus on the former evoke images of autonomous professionals or craftspersons; those that focus on the latter evoke images of assembly lines and purposeful bureaucracies. *Neither* set of metaphors or strategies captures the truly demanding task of school management, which is somehow to satisfy *both* sets of needs simultaneously.

The top-down strategies which have ostensibly guided school management have never made more than partial sense in public education and have never been strictly observed. At one moment teachers are treated like workers on an assembly line, at another like bureaucrats executing general directives, at still another like independent professionals who are expected to figure out for themselves what it is they should be doing.

Observers who have styled themselves as realists have assumed that school systems must be satisfied with constant tension and watered-down compromises between two needs that are equally important and inherently in conflict with each other. Like a fitted sheet one size too small for the bed it is expected to cover, the management approaches employed by school systems could always be adjusted to fit one need or another but never (it seemed) the whole system. Researchers confirmed that teachers and administrators in most systems had informally negotiated 'zones of influence', each acknowledging each other's primacy within their respective zones. Teachers would agree to respect administrators' decisions over matters outside the classroom, and administrators would respect decisions that teachers made within their classrooms, so long as the latter did not cause problems for anyone else. The arrangement did not serve the need for coordination or the need for teacher discretion well, but it did allow both needs to be served (Lortie 1975).

School boards, administrators and teachers might be able to live with these laissez faire arrangements, but teacher unions have had a hard time doing so. Because school boards and administrators have seldom been very good at running their school systems like factories, teacher unions have had difficulty using factory union approaches to maintain their members' unity and commitment. The approaches provided a source of protection against arbitrary personnel decisions – protection that most teachers recognized was necessary – but they required union leaders to pretend that educational policy decisions were none of their concern.

In the private sector, decisions concerning 'the nature of the product' and 'the design of the work process' are defined as management prerogatives and therefore outside the scope of bargaining. Unions, in most cases, have a right to demand bargaining on the impact of such decisions on 'working conditions' but not on the 'substance' of the decisions themselves (Morris 1971). Those distinctions are relatively easy to draw in manufacturing settings; they are virtually impossible to draw in service settings, like public education, where the work of employees *is* the product the organization provides and where the most important 'working conditions' are those that affect a person's ability to do his or her job effectively. Yet, hemmed in by industrial sector precedent and by court decisions declaring educational policies to be management prerogatives and outside the scope of bargaining, teacher unions have often found themselves unable to affect those school and district decisions that have the greatest impact on their members' work lives (Edwards 1973, Shedd 1982).

The artificial distinction between 'union issues' and 'professional issues' has been a source of tension within teacher unions ever since they won bargaining rights in the 1960s. That tension has sapped the energies of NEA affiliates, in particular, which had to overcome a history of administrative domination before establishing themselves as teacher bargaining agents. Many teachers and staff persons in both the NEA and AFT still recall that boards of education and administrators often defined 'a professional' as someone who was cooperative and refrained from challenging the decisions of his or her superiors. For many teachers, the words 'professional' and 'cooperative' have been associated with servility and anti-unionism ever since. For many others – probably more – the words 'professional' and 'union' simply had very little to do with one another.

Reform

Until recently, most observers who have styled themselves as education reformers have ignored the tension between the need for teacher flexibility and discretion and the need for system-wide coordination, asserting that the key to strengthening public education lies *either* in giving school managers better tools for controlling what their teachers do *or* in freeing teachers from the top-heavy bureaucratic constraints to which they have been subjected (Bacharach 1988). For the first few years of this decade, it seemed that the most recent debate over education reform would follow this pattern. The teacher-related proposals that won attention in the first few years – those that raised minimum standards for teacher certification, required testing of already certified teachers, or set up competitions among teachers for limited numbers of 'merit pay' awards – were premised on the assumption that the foxes could not be trusted to guard the hen house: teachers had to be coerced or bribed into wanting to improve their performance; administrators and boards of education had to be forced to do the coercing or bribing. The rebuttal – that school systems needed to raise teachers' salaries and demonstrate greater respect for their 'professional autonomy' – sounded just as familiar and no more convincing.

Given the *laissez-faire* relationships between teachers and administrators in many school systems, it is not surprising that the first wave of recent school reformers would reach for top-down control techniques to force educators to swallow distasteful medicine. But neither is it surprising that many of their proposals merely reinforced the problem they meant to overcome: the tendency for people at each level – classroom, school and district – to seek better ways of insulating themselves from the 'unwarranted interference' of others. Cynics assumed that the storm would soon blow over.

But instead the winds shifted. A new group of reformers began calling for teachers to have 'a real voice in decision [making]', for developing 'school-site management' that would respect the professional judgment of teachers, and for developing certification boards and career ladders that would give teachers a measure of control over their own profession (National Governors' Association 1986, Education Commission of the States 1986, Carnegie Forum 1986, The Holmes Group 1986, California Commission on the Teaching Profession 1985). With remarkable swiftness, the debate over how to reform public education shifted from strategies that would have strengthened the bureaucratic controls over teachers to strategies meant to 'empower' them (Bacharach and Conley 1987).

'Empowerment' is such a vague term that it can be applied to anything from training school principals to be good listeners to restructuring the authority and power relationships of entire school systems. This ambiguity says a lot about the political stakes of education reform and about the kinds of pressures that are presently defining and sustaining it. The nation's governors deserve most of the credit for keeping education reform at the forefront of public attention. Teacher unions, which damned the first wave of reform proposals with faint praise or none at all, have played an important role in defining and supporting more recent 'second wave' proposals (McDonnell and Pascal 1988).

For governors, 'empowerment' has been a means to an end: their primary motivation has been to revitalize their states' economies and to forge an 'education strategy' for doing so (Osborne 1988). After several brutal episodes in Tennessee, Florida, Texas and elsewhere, state leaders realized that they would not be able to forge such strategies without the tacit, if not explicit, support of their states' teachers' associations. The unions, for their part, were concerned with fending off more objectionable reforms, capitalizing on the public's apparent willingness to provide more dollars for public education, and – least apparent but most important, at least for affiliates of the NEA – resolving the guerilla warfare between 'union' and 'professional' camps within their own organizations. For them, 'empowerment' was both means and end. As political animals, the governors and the unions both had a stake in seeing that the reform movement produced tangible results. Neither could afford to let the bloodletting continue between the advocates of top-down management and the advocates of professional autonomy.

The concept of 'empowerment' is vague, therefore, partly because it symbolizes the intersection of different sets of political interests. It is vague, as well, because it marks the crossroads between different avenues of research, all of which have contributed to the generation of 'second wave' proposals: research on schools; research on private sector white collar, technical and managerial occupations; and research on the management of manufacturing processes and blue collar occupations.

The school research that attracted policy-makers' attention during the late 1970s and early 1980s was the so-called 'school effectiveness' research. That research, which was designed to identify the characteristics of schools that are particularly effective, provided only ambiguous support for some aspects of the traditional top-down model (Rosenholtz 1985, Cuban 1984). School effectiveness researchers concluded that effective schools tend to have principals that provide strong instructional leadership and tend to make heavy use of a variety of sources of information for monitoring student performance. But the same research *also* suggested that teachers in effective schools sometimes provide instructional leadership as well as principals, that such leadership is needed at the school as well as district level, and that effective schools use student achievement data primarily for diagnostic and planning purposes rather than for drawing conclusions about the quality of individual teachers' performance (Edmonds 1979, Rosenholtz 1985). Such schools also placed heavy emphases on factors that the traditional management models have neglected or even undermined, like teamwork and collegiality, a clear focus on a limited number of academic goals, high expectations for all students, and student grouping policies that avoid the implication that less is expected of some students than of others (Brookover *et al.* 1982).

Studies of innovation in school systems generated conclusions that were even more at odds with traditional management models. Schools that are particularly innovative were found to have 'norms of collegiality' and 'norms of continuous improvement' that minimize status differences between administrators and teachers, engage all staff members in planning new programs, and cultivate an on-going critical dialogue on how school programs and every individual's performance might be improved (Little 1982). Other studies documented that new school programs have a much greater chance of success (judged by a number of different criteria) when teachers have been heavily involved in their initiation, development and implementation, as opposed to simply their implementation (McLaughlin and Berman 1975).

Studies of school systems as political and cultural systems have generated similar conclusions about the need for teacher involvement (Weatherley and Lipsky 1977, Wolcott 1977, McDonald 1988). Studies of schools as 'loosely coupled systems' concluded that over-reliance on a few adminstrators to serve as evaluators, as initiators of action and as conduits of information between staff members (among other things) was one of the causes of the very 'looseness' that the top-down model was supposedly so good at overcoming (Weick 1976, 1982).

These different strains of research all contributed to the vocabulary of 'empowerment' and 'school-based' management, but they might easily have been overlooked by policy-makers if they were not complemented by a wave of interest in the management techniques of 'excellent' private sector organizations, particularly those that rely heavily on white collar and technical employees to generate innovations responsive to the needs of clients and customers. Academic scholarship, as well as popular volumes like Peters and Waterman's *In Search of Excellence* (1982), were generating models of goal-oriented, participatory management remarkably consistent with the models that educators were beginning to discuss.[1] In terms of focus, they supplemented these other studies by stressing the need for organizations to involve those employees with direct, on-going contact with their clients or customers in the process of identifying those persons' needs and generating new products or services to meet them.

In addition to being explicit commentaries on the management process itself – and thus legitimating inferences that were being drawn from school research that was not, strictly speaking, on management – these studies were better known by the many private sector business leaders that served on the national and state task forces that were generating proposals for reform. Since the attractiveness of models of centralized, top-down management has always rested primarily on the insistence that they 'work' in the private sector, the emergence of a powerful strain of literature suggesting that they do *not* work in the private sector, at least in organizations that have to be continuously responsive to changing customer or client needs, provided an important justification for shifting the focus of the school reform debate.[2]

What is equally important is that school and private sector management research did not set the reform pendulum swinging back in the direction of autonomy for the individual teacher. Although many reformers stressed the importance of tapping the collective knowledge and wisdom of teachers (or other employees), few of them suggested that the information and knowledge of *individual* teachers was a sufficient basis for reform. Instead, they raised a possibility that no one had ever seriously entertained: that school systems might be able to give their individual teachers *more* discretion while achieving *closer* coordination of their separate efforts. By promoting agreement on ends, by involving teachers in the initiation and development of policies that they are expected to implement, and by promoting collegiality and closer working relationships among teachers, reformers argued, it should be possible to relax formal controls on *how* teachers perform their jobs (Bacharach and Conley 1986, Bailyn 1985).

While research on schools and research on the management of 'excellent' private sector organizations probably had the most influence in the development of this line of reasoning, there are reasons to pay particular attention here to yet another line of research that was producing somewhat similar conclusions about management in the manufacturing sector. Of all avenues of research, none reveals more clearly the dilemmas and opportunities that recent changes in thinking about management have generated for industrial unions.

While studies of white collar occupations have stressed the importance of employees' knowledge of client or customer needs, studies of changes in the management of blue collar occupations have stressed the importance of tapping workers' knowledge of the work process. As Michael Piore, an economist who has paid special attention to the relationships between product markets, work processes and models of unionism, points out, the logic that once dominated the design of manufacturing work processes – the logic of a detailed, explicit division of labor and of top-down control – rested on several assumptions. It assumed that it was *feasible* to separate the planning of work from its execution, to assign the planning function to managers, supervisors and staff experts, and to assign relatively fixed sets of routine duties to individual 'line' employees (Piore 1982, 1985).[3] These assumptions, Piore points out, are only likely to hold true in settings where large volumes of standardized products are to be produced, using production methods that are reasonably stable over long periods of time.

The more specialized an employer's products, the more rapidly they change, and the fewer of each product produced, the less feasible it is to draw a sharp line between the planning and execution of work. That, however, is precisely what is now occurring in large sections of the manufacturing economy. Increasingly stiff international competition and product specialization, enabled by improved transportation systems and new computerized production technologies, are undermining the economies of scale that America's mass production giants once enjoyed. The top-down management techniques that were sources of efficiency in an earlier era have grown increasingly inefficient in today's more specialized, varied and variable product markets (Rosenfeld 1988).

These changes are exerting two related but distinct pressures on the management of manufacturing firms. They affect (1) the design of individual jobs and (2) the planning and coordination of work across groups of workers. The more often products change – and the fewer of each product a manufacturer makes – the more frequently the tasks necessary to make those products change. As tasks change, so must the duties assigned to each employee, rendering jobs with fixed sets of responsibilities obsolete. The more rapidly job duties change, moreover, the less likely it is that staff experts at higher organizational levels will be able to anticipate and decide what all those duties ought to be. Employers, thus, have increasing need of employees who are willing and able to adapt to different work demands and who can determine for themselves what work needs to be performed (Rosenfeld 1988).

But granting individual employees more discretion increases the problems of coordinating their separate activities in manufacturing, just as it does in public education. Granting employees more independence restricts management's access to information about existing or anticipated problems in the work process, right when other developments are making it more and more imperative that such problems be anticipated and resolved before production begins. (If smaller batches of more specialized products are being produced, then the costs of each mistake can only be passed on to a limited number of customers.) In simpler times, manufacturers could resolve such problems by centralizing authority and tightening management control over individual workers, but it is their own efforts to *relax* such controls that are partially responsible for their current planning and coordination dilemmas. Like many ''effective schools'' that place heavy reliance on student achievement data, many manufacturers have shown growing interest in computerized information systems that help them keep tabs on the flow of materials and products through their systems. But manufacturers have also expressed interest in mechanisms like self-managed work groups and quality circles, that require employees to work cooperatively to identify and solve problems that once were the responsibility of managers to address.

All of these developments point to new forms of work organization and new kinds of management, as well as to changes in the kinds of training that workers receive.[4] Managers throughout the economy are attracted to job enrichment programs, 'pay for knowledge' compensation systems, and other strategies for breaking down narrow job definitions and assigning individual workers and groups of workers wider sets of responsibilities and more discretion over how they perform their work (Kochan 1985, Schonberger 1986). They are attracted, as well, to schemes for involving workers in decision-making beyond their immediate work assignments (Walton 1985).

As these developments take hold, industrial unions throughout the economy are having to reconsider strategies that have served them well for half a century. As Piore points out, the same factors which are forcing a reassessment of traditional management approaches are undermining traditional 'job control' unionism as well. A unionism that is premised on fixed job categories, close links between specific duties and compensation, and detailed rules on how job assignments are made – and on a 'common law' that prevents managers from holding workers accountable for mistakes in the organization and planning of work – is bound to be threatened by current economic changes.

If this thesis is right, then it would be a serious mistake for union leaders to assume – as some do – that the new management approaches are merely tools for busting or avoiding unions. Some managers certainly find them attractive for that reason, but the main reasons managers find such programs attractive are, first, they provide management with *information about production processes* that is becoming increasingly vital to their productive efficiency, and second, they provide management with needed *flexibility in the way work is organized and managed*. Union tactics that assume that what management expects of employees is blind obedience might well be undercut by such new management approaches, but such approaches also reveal new sources of management dependence on employees that might serve as the bases for new union tactics.

If these arguments apply in the manufacturing sector, where machine technologies still afford higher levels of management considerable control over the work process, they apply with a vengeance in the service sector, in public education and in teaching in particular. Few employers are more dependent than school boards and administrators on their employees' discretion, professional judgment and willingness to cooperate in translating general policies into concrete action. Few employees have as much responsibility as teachers for planning and evaluating the results of their day-to-day activities, much less for planning, directing and evaluating the activities of others. In most settings, those are still defined as management responsibilities, even if employees are being invited to share some of them. In public education, they represent the very core of the work of teachers.

The fact that teachers plan, direct and evaluate the work of others – that is, the work of their students – does not make them supervisors or managers in the traditional labor relations sense, because their 'subordinates' are not employees and the decisions they make are not, strictly speaking, 'personnel policies'. But teachers *are* supervisors and managers in the more generic sense of those terms: they are responsible for translating general policies into particular objectives; planning, supervising and adjusting work activities; securing needed resources; and evaluating both individual performance and the overall success of their work plans.[5]

In no other setting, then, does it make more sense for unions to seek a new model of labor-management relations than in public education. If teacher unions are threatened by the demise of top-down management strategies, they are also in a good position to take advantage of that demise. For one thing, they are not threatened by the declining employment base that is making it difficult for private sector industrial unions to convince their members to even think of 'cooperating' with management. For another, pressing for *collective* teacher involvement in school and district decision-making offers the possibility of overcoming the split between 'union' and 'professional' factions within their own organizations, by shifting the focus of thinking about 'professional' issues away from individual autonomy. Perhaps most importantly, such a shift might allow teacher unions to finally take advantage of a source of potential influence – or to put the matter more bluntly, a source of power – that industrial union principles have always required them to overlook: the fact that their members, as individuals, already manage much of what goes on in school systems themselves.

The prospect that a reassessment of union strategies might allow them to end the internal bloodletting, secure new monies for education, and build a stronger, more unified organization has provided union leaders with a powerful incentive to try.

Fading myths and emerging principles

Conceptually, the biggest obstacle to negotiating an end to teacher unions' internal friction has always been the myth that teachers' interests as union members and their interests as professionals were inherently incompatible. That observation is tautological, of course, but that is true of all myths: they are true because people who believe them to be true make them come true. What might we expect, then, if teachers' organizations were premised on the assumption that teachers' interests as union members and their interests as professionals are supportive or even identical?

The basic principles that future teacher unions are likely to follow are easier to discern than the specific arrangements that they and employers will work out. The first principle is that, in a setting like public education, *teachers' union and professional interests imply collective responsibility, not individual autonomy*. While teachers can always be expected to be sensitive to their need for discretion, the job of protecting that discretion is itself a collective responsibility and not one that entitles the individual to pursue whatever objectives he or she wants to pursue. Whatever more specific vehicles unions and employers choose for promoting closer ties and collective responsibility among teachers, the job of building them is likely to be a central concern of teacher unions in the future.

The second principle is that *teachers' 'working conditions' depend largely upon their ability to be effective teachers*. If curriculum or student grouping policies are inconsistent or poorly thought out, if needed time and other resources to plan and carry out one's responsibilities are not available, if opportunities to expand one's subject knowledge and pedagogic skills are not continuously available, or if students enter one's own classroom without the knowledge and skills they need to master the material to be covered, teachers' work lives are rendered more difficult as a consequence. For most teachers, there is nothing more exhilarating than to 'reach' students who were thought to be unreachable; there is nothing more humiliating than to 'bomb' in front of thirty trusting children or thirty hyper-critical adolescents. Whatever the mechanisms unions and school districts develop in the future for increasing teachers' collective participation in school and district policy and decision-making, the notion that a distinction either can or should be drawn between "educational policies" and "working conditions" is a patent fiction.[6]

The third principle is that *unions are neither inherently conflictual nor necessarily cooperative*, but are capable of either opposing or accommodating the interests of those with whom they deal, depending upon which best serves the interests of their members. As other observers of school labor-management relations have suggested, some conflicts in school bargaining have been provoked by frustration because restrictions on the scope of bargaining or other aspects of the existing system have prevented the parties from addressing serious issues, and other conflicts have been provoked by one or the other party's efforts to change the system of bargaining itself. A system more closely tailored to the public expectations, work processes and management systems of public education would undoubtedly serve to reduce such conflicts. But that argument would apply in any sector of the economy. To go farther, and to suggest that labor-management relations in public education will be especially cooperative and non-confrontational is not only misleading but dangerous.

Perhaps the greatest irony – and the greatest danger – in the current debate over the future of teacher unionism is that so many participants and observers have convinced themselves that the 'old' unions were inherently conflictual and that cooperativeness will be a defining characteristic of the 'new' ones. To the extent that many school boards, administrators, teachers – and their associations and hired representatives – have been wedded to the first conviction, they have undoubtedly acted on that conviction and *made* it seem accurate.

But the strength of industrial unions, as we have argued here, has always depended as much on their ability to accommodate management's interests as on their ability to threaten them. It is their ability to make their willingness to accommodate management interests *contingent on management's willingness to reciprocate* that has allowed them to play an independent, constructive role in the labor-management relationship. Myths – imposed or self-imposed – that force them to forgo one approach and that lock them into the other are the greatest threat to their viability.

Teachers will always be more aware of the need for flexibility and individual discretion, while boards and administrators will continue to be more sensitive to the need for coordination of programs and the flow of students through a school system. The parties will continue, in other words, to have different perspectives on what students and other school constituencies need, as well as what school systems can do to meet them. If their representatives are truly representative, then these differences will be reflected in the policies and strategies they pursue toward one another and in the agreements they work out.

Structures (likely and possible)

The basic structure of the agreements that education bargainers will negotiate can be expected to reflect the structure of the overall labor-management relationship in public education, just as the structures of craft and industrial union contracts reflect the relationships which produced them. While teachers will insist on playing a more active role in setting educational policies and programs, boards of education and administrators will almost certainly insist that fixed-term, fixed-length agreements are cumbersome and therefore inappropriate vehicles for addressing those issues. Teachers and their representatives, in turn, will demand guarantees that their involvement in policy-making is more than token. The result will probably be an increasing reliance on comprehensive negotiations to establish the *structure* and *ground rules* for joint decision-making that will occur away from the contract bargaining table. They almost certainly will continue to establish district and school committees to address educational issues.[7] They probably also will negotiate provisions that give building principals and their faculties the right to make exceptions to contract provisions that otherwise apply throughout a school district.[8] Both of these arrangements will provide system managers with additional flexibility and teachers with greater voice in the determination of educational policy.

What is more speculative but more intriguing is the possibility that some school districts and teacher unions might go farther and eliminate the provision that prevents one party from 'reopening' negotiations before the end of a contract without the other party's consent. That provision is a key element in the industrial sector deal that protects the employer's 'reserved right' to make management decisions unilaterally.[9] It is not clear that school districts either need or necessarily would want such protections, since they force unions to file grievances and arbitration appeals (or in some states, demands for single-issue 'impact' negotiations) over issues generated by the changing circumstances of school system management. Giving either party the right to reopen negotiations on any or all provisions of a district-wide agreement would provide managers with increased flexibility and would remove one of the principal objections to expanding the scope of bargaining.[10]

In addition to changes in the scope of bargaining, changes in the structure of agreements, and changes in the bargaining process itself, many observers expect teacher unions and school systems to negotiate changes in the structure of the teaching profession itself. Indeed, many of the recent debates over education reform have focused on the development of so-called 'career ladders' that draw distinctions between the duties of teachers at different 'career levels' and that pay teachers according to the level of the ladder that they occupy. We agree that such systems are likely to be discussed and experimented with over the next several years, but the line of argument we have developed here casts a different light on their prospects for success.

Drawing close connections between specific sets of duties and different levels of compensation is a basic feature of the top-down systems in industrial work settings. It is that feature, in fact, that managers in the manufacturing setting are now struggling to overcome and that is forcing unions in those settings to reassess some of the basic tenets of industrial unionism. To suggest that public education should move toward more formal differentiation of teaching duties would be to suggest that it should move closer to, not farther from, the industrial model, with its detailed rules on who has a right to bid on what duties, what career level gets what new duties, when the assignment of 'some' higher level duties requires a temporary promotion, and so forth.

Many of today's reformers characterize job differentiation as a way of involving more teachers in school and district decision-making that has typically been reserved for administrators. But the unified salary schedule that most school systems use is not an obstacle to such involvement, whereas a differentiated salary schedule would be: formal differentiation would mean that only a limited number of teachers could be involved in such activities, and any teacher would be entitled to refuse to accept responsibilities outside the job description for his or her career ladder level (Bacharach et al. 1986).

If there is any aspect of current salary practices in school systems that does represent an obstacle to increased teacher involvement in management, it is the ad hoc practice of treating formal assignments outside the classroom and outside the normal work day as 'extra' duties and of paying for each such set of duties separately. That practice is inevitable, of course, as long as the 'normal' teacher work day ends roughly when the normal school day ends and as long as the work year for teachers is approximately the same as the school year. Those practices are the real obstacles to developing a broader concept of teachers' basic professional responsibilities.

Most teachers, in our experience, devote much more than forty hours per week to their profession, but much of that time (primarily reviewing student work and planning lessons) is spent at home, in isolation, and goes officially unrecognized. If teachers' formal work day or work year were lengthened, without a corresponding increase in the school day or school year, the basis for a new 'deal' between teachers and their employer would be created. Boards and administrators would be in a position to insist that many duties that presently call for extra compensation would henceforth fall within the scope of teachers' basic responsibilities. Teachers would be in a position to demand assurances that they would have greater control over the additional time spent at the school-site, that is, assurances that administrators would not have the unilateral right to assign extra committee or administrative work to fill up all the extra time.[11] In return for such an exchange of assurances, both parties would be in a position to justify to taxpayers what virtually everyone says is needed: substantial increases in the basic salaries of teachers.

Beyond this possibility, some school systems – or perhaps entire states – might still experiment with systems that introduce some hierarchy to the compensation structure of teaching. But if such systems are developed and survive, they are likely to be more like the structures in craft settings (e.g., apprentice, journeyman, and master) or in higher education (e.g., assistant, associate and full professor), where pay levels are supposed to reflect different levels of skill or professional attainment, rather than like the hierarchies in manufacturing or bureaucratic settings where they are meant to reflect specific sets of duties. It is not yet clear whether school systems can draw such distinctions in skill or attainment level without sliding into a merit pay scheme that bases compensation on subjective assessments of performance. But it is worth noting that while some state teachers' associations have accepted 'master teacher' plans based on the extra-pay-for-extra-work model (e.g., California), the only state where the teachers' association has played a major role in initiating, shaping and supporting experimental career ladder legislation is Arizona, where it was the union (not management groups) that insisted on a skill-assessment model (see Conley 1986, Bacharach et al. 1986, McDonnell and Pascal 1988).

The willingness of teacher unions and employers in public education to entertain such radical departures from traditional practices probably says more about the pressures that school systems are under than it does about the specific formulas that the parties will agree to live by in the future. It undoubtedly will take some time for them to work out and finally accept new groundrules, just as it took employers and industrial unions time to work out all the details of what today is recognized as the 'traditional' labor-management formula.

But the historical parallel gives reason to have confidence in the basic argument outlined here. Economic developments, changes in public expectations, and changes in the ways in which organizations like school systems are being managed are once again undermining the bases of one form of unionism and are creating new forms of power in the employment relationship. Put simply, employers throughout the economy – but above all, in public education – are becoming increasingly dependent on their employees' detailed knowledge of work processes and client needs, on their individual willingness and ability to exercise discretion and judgment, and on their willingness to work cooperatively with one another in the face of constantly changing work situations.

The important question is not whether employers will try to make adjustments to these new forms of dependence – they must do so to survive – but whether unions will be able to develop strategies that allow them to marshall the power inherent in that dependence. If they can, they will have created a new form of union that has the potential of being every bit as vigorous and powerful and as appropriate to their setting as craft unions and industrial unions were to theirs. There are good reasons to believe that that is exactly what is happening today in public education.

It is remarkable but not altogether unprecedented that unions would play an active role in shaping the approaches of the managers they deal with. But no other unions have played such an important role in redefining the very concept of management – or in claiming, for their members, such an active role in the process of management itself – as today's teacher unions.

Notes

1. KarlWeick's studies of schools as loosely-coupled systems were cited by Peters and Waterman as one of the principal theoretical bases for these models of management.

2. Ironically, Weick's work has probably had more of an impact on thinking about school management by this round-about route than it has had as direct commentaries on schools.

3. The line of argument developed in this discussion of manufacturing jobs relies heavily on the work of Piore cited here.

4. In fact, it is these 'new kinds of training' that many governors have had in mind when they have issued their calls for education reform (see Rosenfeld 1988).

5. These features probably *would* make teachers 'management officials' under the Supreme Court's recent *Yeshiva* decision, which appears to deny bargaining rights to private sector employees who make or effectively recommend just about any kind of management decisions or policies and not just ones that pertain to personnel matters. Technically, that decision does not affect teachers and school districts, which bargain under separate public sector statutes that clearly anticipated that teachers would have the right to bargain. But the same logic does affect court and board decisions on what subjects are and are not bargainable in public education (Shedd 1982). We will discuss these legal issues in detail in a subsequent paper, but our basic argument should be obvious: the *Yeshiva* decision is the logical but absurd result of a case law that was originally meant to accommodate employees' bargaining rights to the hierarchical management structures in private industry. When laws which were meant to facilitate, encourage and (where necessary) require bargaining become basic *obstacles* to bargaining, it is time to change the laws themselves (or at least their interpretation.)

6. As our last footnote suggests, we recognize that this line of reasoning would require changes in the legal definition of what is bargainable in many states.

7. Boards of education may balk at union demands that these committees be given the right to make the final decisions in the policy areas they address, but the reservation of that formal authority may mean less than many assume. If boards and administrators insist on treating these committee arrangements as they sometimes have treated other committees in the past – manipulating agendas and arbitrarily deciding when they will pay attention to teachers' 'advice' – they may find that teachers will withdraw their cooperation altogether. Indeed, teachers' willingness to insist on reciprocal cooperation in such settings will probably be the most important test of their union's unity and strength. The assumption that school boards and administrators *need* their cooperation, of course, is fundamental to the entire argument of this paper.

8. Johnson's 1983 study of labor-management relations in school systems notes that many principals and school faculties already exercise the informal option of overlooking selected provisions of a contract, just as union stewards, work groups and supervisors do in other sectors of the economy (Kuhn 1961). The fact that the formal contract gives employees the right to file grievances and demand adherence to contract terms is a source of power in such "fractional bargaining", for it gives employees the option of falling back on what has already been negotiated if they do not accept the terms of the side-agreement being offered. Formally acknowledging the possibility of such side-agreements would allow the parties to specify that side-agreements do not create "past practices" that undermine the application of contract terms in *other* parts of the school system.

9. If a union were free to demand that negotiations be "reopened" at any time, the principle that management retains unilateral discretion over issues not covered by the contract would be meaningless.

10. Neither party would be likely to exercise the right to reopen negotiations cavalierly, since the other might insist on renegotiating provisions that were important to the one initiating negotiations. This would be the crucial difference between these kinds of mid-contract negotiations and the single-issue "impact" negotiations that are used in some states.

11. Boards and administrators would have to make some such assurances, because the planning and reviewing of student work that teachers presently perform away from the school site would still need to be done. The only way of really creating more time for teachers is to capitalize on their ability to *save* time by planning, exchanging information and performing other duties *together*.

References

AFT TASK FORCE ON THE FUTURE OF EDUCATION (1986) *The Revolution That is Overdue: Looking Toward the Future of Teaching and Learning* (Washington, DC: American Federation of Teachers).

BACHARACH, S. B. (1981) 'Consensus and power in school districts', final report under NIE Grant No. G780080 (Ithaca, NY: Cornell University).

BACHARACH, S. B. (1988) 'Four themes of reform: an editorial essay', *Educational Administration Quarterly* 24 (4) forthcoming.

BACHARACH, S. B. BAUER, S. C. and SHEDD, J. B. (1986) 'The work environment and school reform', *Teachers College Record*, 88 (2), pp. 241–256.

BACHARACH, S. B. and CONLEY, S. C. (1986) 'Education reform: a managerial agenda', *Phi Delta Kappan* (May), 67 (9) pp. 641–645.

BACHARACH, S. B. CONLEY, S. C. and SHEDD, J. B. (1986) 'Beyond career ladders: structuring teacher career development systems', *Teachers College Record*, 87 (4), pp. 563–574.

BACHARACH, S. B. LIPSKY, D. B. and SHEDD, J. B. (1984) *Paying for Better Teaching: Merit Pay and Its Alternatives* (Ithaca, NY: Organizational Analysis and Practice, Inc.).

BAILYN, L. (1985) 'Autonomy in the industrial R & D lab', *Human Resource Management*, 24 (2), pp. 129–146.

BARNARD, C. (1938) *The Functions of the Executive* (Cambridge, MA: Harvard University Press).

BLOCK, R. N. (1978) 'The impact of seniority provisions on the manufacturing quit rate', *Industrial and Labor Relations Review*, 31, pp. 474–81.

BROOKOVER, W. B. BEAMER, L. EFTHIM, H. HATHAWAY, D. LEZOTTE, L. MILLER, S. PASSALACQUA, J. and TORNATZKY, L. (1982) *Creating Effective Schools* (Holmes Beach, FL: Learning Publications, Inc.).

CALIFORNIA COMMISSION ON THE TEACHING PROFESSION (1985) *Who Will Teach Our Children?* (Sacramento: California Commission on the Teaching Profession).

CALLAHAN, R. (1962) *Education and the Cult of Efficiency* (Chicago: University of Chicago Press).

CARNEGIE FORUM ON EDUCATION AND THE ECONOMY (1986) *A Nation Prepared: Teachers for the 21st Century* (New York: Carnegie Forum on Education and the Economy).

COLE, S. (1969) *The Unionization of Teachers* (New York: Praeger).

CONLEY, S. C. (1986) 'Career development and labor-management cooperation', paper presented at the 1986 annual meeting of the American Educational Research Association.

CONLEY, S. C. (1988) 'Reforming paper pushers and avoiding free agents: the teacher as a constrained decision-maker', *Educational Administration Quarterly* forthcoming.

CONLEY, S. C. and BACHARACH, S. B. (1987) 'The Holmes Group report: standards, hierarchies, and management', *Teachers College Record*, 88 (3), pp. 340–347.

CUBAN, L. (1984) 'Transforming the frog into a prince: effective schools research, policy, and practice at the district level', *Harvard Educational Review*, 54 (2), pp. 129–151.

DOWLING, J. and PFEFFER, J. (1975) 'Organizational legitimacy', *Pacific Sociological Review*, 18, pp. 122–36.

DULLES, F. R. (1966) *Labor in American History*, 3rd edn, (New York: Thomas Y. Crowell).

DUNLOP, J. T. (1958) *Industrial Relations Systems* (New York: Holt, Rinehart and Winston).

EDMONDS, R. R. 'Some schools work and more can', (1979) *Social Policy*, 9, pp.28–32.

EDUCATION COMMISSION OF THE STATES (1986) *What Next? More Leverage for Teachers?* (Denver: Education Commission of the States).

EDWARDS, H. T. (1973) 'The emerging duty to bargain in the public sector', *Michigan Law Review*, 71, pp. 885–934.

ELKOURI, F. and ELKOURI, E. A. (1976) *How Arbitration Works*, 3rd edn, (Washington, DC: Bureau of National Affairs).

FREEMAN, R. B. and MEDOFF, J. L. (1979) 'The two faces of unionism', *The Public Interest* 57, (Fall) pp 69–93.

GOLDSCHMIDT, S. M. BOWERS, B. and STUART, L. (1984) *The Extent and Nature of Educational Policy Bargaining* (Eugene, OR: Center for Educational Policy and Management, University of Oregon).

GRIMSHAW, W. J. (1979) *Union Rule in Schools* (Lexington, MA: D. C. Heath).

THE HOLMES GROUP (1986) *Tomorrow's Teachers* (East Lansing, MI: The Holmes Group, Inc.).

JACKSON, P. (1968) *Life in Classrooms*, (New York: Holt, Rinehart and Winston).

JOHNSON, S. M. (1983) *Teacher Unions in Schools* (Philadelphia: Temple University Press).

JOHNSON, S. M. (1987)'Can schools be reformed at the bargaining table?' *Teachers College Record*, 89 (2), pp. 269–280.

KEARNEY, R. C. (1984) *Labor Relations in the Public Sector* (New York: Marcel Dekker, Inc.).

KERCHNER, C. T. and MITCHELL, D. (1986) 'Teaching reform and union reform', *The Elementary School Journal*, 86 (4), pp. 449–470.

KOCHAN, T. A. (1980) *Collective Bargaining and Industrial Relations* (Homewood, IL: Richard D. Irwin, Inc.).

KOCHAN, T. A. (1985) *Challenges and Choices Facing American Labor* (Cambridge, MA: The MIT Press).

KUHN, J. W. (1961) *Bargaining in Grievance Settlement* (New York: Columbia University Press).

LAMPERT, M. (1985) 'How do teachers manage to teach? Perspectives on problems in practice', *Harvard Educational Review*, 55, pp. 178–194.

LIEBERMAN, M. C. (1980) *Public Sector Bargaining: A Policy Reappraisal* (Lexington, MA: D. C. Heath).

LITTLE, J. W. (1982) 'Norms of collegiality and experimentation: workplace conditions of school success', *American Educational Research Journal*, 19, pp. 325–340.

LORTIE, D. C. (1975) *Schoolteacher: A Sociological Study* (Chicago: The University of Chicago Press).

MCDONALD, J. P. (1988) 'The emergence of the teacher's voice: implications for the new reform', *Teachers College Record*, 89 (4), pp. 471–486.

MCDONNELL, L. M. and PASCAL, A. (1979) *Organized Teachers in American Schools* (Santa Monica, CA: The Rand Corporation).

MCDONNELL, L. M. and PASCAL, A. (1988) *Teacher Unions and Educational Reform* (Santa Monica, CA: The Rand Corporation).

MCLAUGHLIN, M. and BERMAN, P. (1975) *Federal Programs Supporting Educational Change: Findings in Review* (Santa Monica, CA: The Rand Corporation).

MEDOFF, J. L. (1979) 'Layoffs and alternatives under trade unions in US manufacturing', *American Economic Review*, 69, pp. 380–95.

MEYER, J. W. and ROWAN, B. (1977) 'Institutionalized organizations: formal structure as myth and ceremony', *American Journal of Sociology*, 83 (2), pp. 340–363.

MITCHELL, S. M. (1986) 'Negotiating the design of professional jobs', working paper presented at the April 1986 annual meeting of the American Educational Research Association (Ithaca, NY: Organizational Analysis and Practice).

MORRIS, C. J. (1971) *The Developing Labor Law* (Washington, DC: Bureau of National Affairs, Inc.).

MOSSTON, M. (1972) *Teaching: From Command to Discovery* (Belmont, CA: Wadsworth Publishing Co.).

NADWORNY, M. J. (1955) *Scientific Management and the Unions* (Cambridge, MA: Harvard University Press).

NATIONAL EDUCATION ASSOCIATION/NATIONAL ASSOCIATION OF SECONDARY SCHOOL PRINCIPALS (1986) *Ventures in Good Schooling: A Cooperative Model for a Successful Secondary School* (Washington, DC: NEA/NASSP).

NATIONAL GOVERNORS' ASSOCIATION (1986) *Time for Results: The Governors' 1991 Report on Education* (Washington, DC: National Governors' Association Center for Policy and Research).

OSBORNE, D. (1988) *Laboratories of Democracy; A New Breed of Governor Creates Models for National Economic Growth* (Cambridge, MA: Harvard Business School).

PERROW, C. (1972) *Complex Organizations: A Critical Essay* (Glenview, IL: Scott, Foresman).

PETERS, T. J. and WATERMAN, R. H. Jr. (1982) *In Search of Excellence: Lessons from America's Best-Run Companies* (New York: Warner Books).

PIORE, M. J. (1982) 'American labor and the industrial crisis', *Challenge* (March-April), pp. 5–11.

PIORE, M. J. (1985) 'Computer technologies, market structure, and strategic union choices', in T. A. Kochan (ed.) *Challenges and Choices Facing American Labor* (Cambridge, MA: The MIT Press).

ROSENFELD, S. A. (1988) 'Commentary: educating for the factories of the future', *Education Week* 22 June 1988, p. 48.

ROSENHOLTZ, S. J. (1985) 'Effective schools: interpreting the evidence', *American Journal of Education*, 93 (3), pp. 352–388.

ROSS, A. M. (1958) 'Do we have a new industrial feudalism?' *American Economic Review*, 48, pp. 903–920.

SCHONBERGER, R. J. (1986) *World Class Manufacturing: The Lessons of Simplicity Applied* (New York: The Free Press).

SHEDD, J. B. (1982) 'An assessment of the duty to bargain in the public and private sectors', working paper (Ithaca, NY: Cornell University).

SHEDD, J. B. and MALANOWSKI, R. M. (1985) *From the Front of the Classroom: A Study of the Work of Teachers* (Ithaca, NY: Organizational Analysis and Practice, Inc.).

TAFT, P. (1964) *Organized Labor in American History* (New York: Harper and Row).

THUROW, L. (1975) *Generating Inequality: Mechanisms of Distribution in the US Economy* (New York: Basic Books).

TYACK, D. and HANSOT, E. (1982) *Managers of Virtue: Public School Leadership in America, 1820–1980* (New York: Basic Books).

WALTON, R. E. (1985) 'From control to commitment in the workplace', *Harvard Business Review*, pp. 77–84.

WEATHERLEY, R. and LIPSKY, M. (1977) 'Street-level bureaucrats and institutional innovation: implementing special-education reform', *Harvard Educational Review*, 47, pp. 171–197.

WEICK, K. E. (1976) 'Educational organizations as loosely coupled systems', *Administrative Science Quarterly*, 21, pp. 1–19.

WEICK, K. E. (1982) 'The management of organizational change among loosely coupled elements', in *Change in organizations*, ed. P. Goodman (San Francisco: Jossey-Bass).

WISE, A. E. (1979) *Legislated Learning: The Bureaucratization of the American Classroom* (Berkeley: The University of California Press).

WOLCOTT, H. F. (1977) *Teachers vs. Technocrats: An Educational Innovation in Anthropological Perspective* (Eugene, OR: Center for Educational Policy and Management).

WYNNE, E. A. (1981) 'Looking at good schools', *Phi Delta Kappan*, 63 (5) pp. 377–381.

11   *Alternative approaches to labor-management relations for public school teachers and administrators*

Douglas E. Mitchell
University of California, Riverside

Introduction

The unionization of public school teachers is one of the most important changes in public education in the last half century. The sweeping changes brought about through teacher unionization are matched in overall impact on education only by the desegregation decisions of the US Supreme Court and the development of categorical program budget mechanisms for controlling local school expenditures (Mitchell 1981; Kerchner and Mitchell 1988). Unionization has altered day-to-day working relationships between teachers and administrators, changed the conditions under which teachers are employed, and redefined school programs and services.

Some observers assert that the primary effect of collective bargaining has been to stimulate conflict and encourage self-servicing behavior on the part of teachers. A fair reading of the historical evidence demonstrates that this is not true, however. Teacher unions are the *result* of conflict in the schools, not its cause. Teacher unions were not organized to promote the self-serving interests of individual teachers – they were created by idealistic teacher organizers who saw them as the vehicle for needed reform in public education.

It may be hard to remember, given the avalanche of new programs and state laws adopted following the release of the National Commission on Exellence (1983) report, *A Nation at Risk*, but unionism among teachers was a reform movement long before the current movement burst on the scene. Teacher unions grew in power and prestige in the late 1950s and early '60s as teachers began an urgent, sometimes frantic, effort to generate stability and security in a period when schools were being held responsible for winning a global struggle for scientific and economic superiority and simultaneously singled out as the focal point of a national struggle to secure basic civil rights for minority citizens (ERIC 1987).

Teachers and administrators were, of course, deeply embroiled in conflict throughout the 1960s and '70s. To a substantial degree, however, these conflicts arose because neither group could control the problems of civil rights and economic development for which the schools were being called to account. Teachers felt abandoned and criticized by local school boards and administrators. They felt local leaders were too ready to embrace efforts aimed at developing 'teacher proof' curricula, imposing new programs and personnel practices without consultation, or equating poor school performance with poor teaching. Ordinary teachers came to believe the public, and to some extent their administrative superiors, were more interested in finding scapegoats than in solving problems. They adopted a defensive posture and pursued organizational power and political influence in order to promote change and defend themselves against charges that they were responsible for systematic failures.

Responding to workplace dilemmas and a sense of betrayal by administrators and local school boards, teachers adopted organizing strategies and goals reminiscent of the large private sector unions in such industries as steel, automobiles, rubber, textiles and coal mining. Working primarily in the nation's urban centers, the American Federation of Teachers led the way. Union locals were formed at the district level. Recognition of the right to elect exclusive representatives and bargain collectively over wages and conditions of employment were pursued with substantial success. The National Education Association, long dominated by administrators, continued to endorse individual teacher contract negotiations and a 'professional' approach to labor relations until forced to change direction at its Detroit meeting in 1968.

While it took about 15 years for unionization to become fully established as a national norm, the die was cast in the New York teacher strike of 1960. New York teachers drew national attention to their cause by demonstrating a willingness to risk their jobs and accept public criticism in order to establish their right to organized representation. Wisconsin had passed a collective bargaining law three years earlier, but the long standing power of organized labor in that state's political system led most observers to treat this law as a reflection of special circumstances rather than a national trend. In the New York strike, however, national battle lines were drawn and teachers with no prior union experience revealed that they were ready to demand recognition. By the end of the 1970s, 37 states adopted collective bargaining laws – most of them modeled after the National Labor Relations Act which had brought order to the chaos of private sector labor relations in the 1930s.

While teacher unionism has spread rapidly, it has not resulted in comfortable working relationships within the schools. Signs of turmoil and change abound. In a 1985 survey, for example, collective bargaining was cited as a 'major concern' by 29.3% of all school board members. This was more than three times the number reported just a year earlier (Institute for Educational Leadership 1986: 4). In 1985, California's prestigious Commission on the Teaching Profession encouraged change in the present pattern of labor relations, recommending that districts experiment with 'policy trust agreements' (CTP 1985). American Federation of Teachers' president Albert Shanker has endorsed this concept, and the California Federation of Teachers has supported experimental implementation. Within a year of the Commission on the Teaching Profession's report, the Association of California School Administrators commissioned a survey of its membership for the purpose of developing new approaches to the issue (Mitchell 1987). California is not alone, a number of school districts – most notably, Toledo, Ohio and Rochester, New York – have gained national recognition for trying innovative approaches to collective bargaining.

Meanwhile, observers of union development throughout the private and public sectors of the economy have begun to raise fundamental questions about the long term prospects of the labor movement. Overall union membership, it is widely noted, has declined significantly in the last two decades, despite its rapid growth in the public sector. While few analysts expect unions to disappear any time soon, an increasing number share Troy's (1986: 7) view that,

> The trends of union power and the factors responsible for its rise and fall show that the union movement is in a *permanent state of decline*. Yet decline does not mean extinction. (emphasis added)

Troy highlights the importance of economics and market forces in the declining fortunes of labor unions, but overt political challenges to the legitimacy of unionization, especially in the public sector, are frequently expressed by national leaders. The dramatic shift to avowedly conservative political philosophies found in the Reagan Administration in this country and the Thatcher government in Great Britain, for example, has been accompanied by a series of challenges to union organization throughout the economy. President Reagan's successful attack on the air traffic controllers union was based on a direct denial of the legitimacy of public sector unionism.

The time is ripe for a thorough reconsideration of the role of teacher unions in public education. Are recent changes a result of natural processes of maturation and development? Or do they presage fundamental change in the character and impact of teacher unions? Is the widespread search for alternatives to industrial unionism largely a matter of marginal adjustment to a well established model of labor relations? Or does it indicate that basic changes are needed to bring union organizations and labor relations practices into line with the real needs of the teachers and the public schools? Are the innovations and alternative practices found in various school districts merely cosmetic and idiosyncratic adjustments developed by naive or subversive interests? Or do they represent the beginnings of a truly new labor relations system?

Three lines of analysis

Three lines of analysis shed significant light on how these questions might be answered. First, a review of the historical processes by which contemporary union organizations were developed, beginning with their emergence from the medieval mercantile and craft guilds, reveals the processes of differentiation and change responsible for forming and transforming worker organizations over the last three centuries. In the modern period, this history reveals, worker organizations are of four distinctive types – industrial labor unions, skilled craft unions, creative artist unions, and professional worker associations. The four different union types organize in different ways, pursue different goals and provide very different services to their members.

A second perspective on the problem can be derived from an analysis of data collected in California school systems. These data, derived from the study sponsored by the Association of California School Administrators (Mitchell 1987), clearly demonstrates that significant innovations are already well developed in a large number of local districts. Additionally, these data reveal that attitudes toward teacher unionism are fluid, and the conditions under which labor difficulties arise can be clearly specified.

A third approach to the question of innovation and change in teacher-administrator relationships involves close scrutiny of the public policy implications of alternatives currently in use. This policy analysis indicates that, in addition to the widely recognized processes of accommodation and maturation, changes in labor relations policy and practice are of five basic types:

(1) bargaining process changes;
(2) changes in school budget and finance procedures;
(3) structural changes in the relationship between teacher organizations and management systems;
(4) development of improved due-process and fair treatment mechanisms for individual teachers;
(5) restructuring the scope and the nature of the agreements negotiated between teachers and school boards.

Each of these alternatives discussed in the concluding section of this chapter, after the historical and survey data have been briefly reviewed.

Labor relations alternatives in historical perspective

Investigation into the present state of unionization in education and identification of alter-natives to the current industrial union framework for labor relations begins with a review of the historical evolution of labor unions. In their present day form, unions are a relatively recent phenomenon. The National Labor Relations Act (NLRA) which set the national standard for union rights and practices was not adopted until 1935, and it has been significantly modified on several occasions since then.

Of course, labor unions were not created by the NLRA. They existed for nearly a century before gaining governmental support. As with the state laws supporting teacher unions, the NLRA was adopted to restore order to an economic system plagued by intense labor conflict. Intractable and sometimes violent conflicts had become frequent events in steel, coal mining, automobiles and other basic industries.

The pre-NLRA unions were very different from those of today. American unions, like the American economy, went through fluctuating periods of growth and collapse prior to passage of the NLRA. In the years between the Civil War and the First World War unionism was 'organized along craft lines. It foreswore reform and political action in order to seek the immediate improvement of the wage earner's status by economic methods' (Cox *et al.* 1981: 9). In Europe labor unions, adopting key elements of Marxist theory of class struggle, gave greater attention to political reform.

American unionism has its roots in eighteenth-century England, where medieval guilds were gradually transformed into modern craft unions. To understand the possibilities as well as the problems of reform in teacher unions, we need to go back and retrace the transition from guilds to craft unions. Once understood, this transition can be seen as the model for later movements from craft to industrial unionism. It also illuminates the relationship between these widely recognized union alternatives and the more specialized forms of worker organization found in artistic unions and professional associations.

Medieval guilds: organizing entire occupations

The most striking feature of medieval guild organization was its embrace of all workers in an industry, *both* laborers and their managerial superiors. The guild organization was originally motivated by problems related to the creation of modern money economies, *not* a need to protect workers from exploitation (Lambert 1891). Guilds were created jointly by owners and workers as a way of bringing stability and order to the processes of production and distri-bution of goods. As market systems developed, production was separated from mercantile trading. Price competition was substituted for the traditional personal relationship between craft workers and consumers. The resulting impersonal system of manufacture and marketing led producers and distributors alike to search for mechanisms capable of control-ling product standards and marketing arrangements.

On the production side, 'the self-perpetuating team of master, journeyman and apprentice, was a stable element in the violent decades as the old feudal world fell apart' (Lesson 1979: 23). These production teams formed the basis for production guilds known in England as the 'Yeomanry'. The establishment and enforcement of standards was necessary because workers moved from town to town to ply their trade. As the occupational groups spread to new towns and villages, 'the old ways and traditions would become diluted and distorted'. The guilds offset this degenerative tendency by creating a system of worker refer-ences and occupational rules. Letters of reference were carried by individual craft workers, and 'Rule books, passed from town to town, from trade to trade', and 'were altered and amended' (Leeson 1979: 275).

On the distribution side, the early guilds were developed to control the marketing process. Rights to trade were developed and agreements reached regarding both pricing and market access arrangements. Though they had the same original form as the yeomanry guilds, the mercantile guilds tended to become trade associations – dominated by owners and managers – rather than craft unions interested in protecting worker rights.

Unwin (1963: 13-14) summarizes the connection between the guild system and the development of early unions:

> whilst we may rightly insist on ... connecting the Trade Union with its sociological ante-cedents, it must be freely admitted that the story of the transformation of the guild is even more concerned with the organization of capital than it is with the organization of labour.

Early worker organization: the craft unions

The modern Trades' Union represented a distinctive break with the early guild organiza-tional structure because the Trades' Union was a combination of artisans, laborers, and jour-neymen among themselves and the employer of labor was outside the union (Lambert, 1891).

The seperation between workers and owners took place gradually.

> the first separation arose from the fact that as the master craftsman found more scope for his activity as a foreman, an employer, a merchant, and a shopkeeper, he left the manual labor entirely to his journeyman and apprentices ... As the interest of these journeymen was no longer represented by the master's guild, they sought to form an organization of their own ... (Unwin 1963: 11)

Craft unions grew strong during the period when division of labor was relatively low, especially in the construction and printing industries (Jackson 1984). By the beginning of the First World War, however, Jackson observes (p.3), 'these industries had grown tremen-dously; they had acquired a thoroughly capitalist organization; the major firms had achieved a considerable size; mechanization and increases in the division of labor had greatly changed the labor process.' These industries developed the strongest and most aggressive craft unions in the nation.

As markets expanded and the factory system developed, workers found they were converted from the dignified status of 'producer' to the common one of 'hired hand'. Beginning around the middle of the nineteenth century, the craft union movement gained international recognition as a potent vehicle for expressing the unique interests of wage laborers. Workers gradually shifted attention from concern about setting production standards to control over wages and benefits.

With the expansion of transportation and the development of new technologies, the years between the Civil War and the First World War witnessed the development of vast industrial empires. Fortunes were made in railroads, oil, timber, steel, coal and finally automobiles. By 1904, firms with annual product values in excess of $1 million employed about 25% of the wage earners in the United States and accounted for nearly 40% of the GNP. As affirmed by the courts in *American Steel Foundries v. Tri-City Council* (257 US 184, 1921), these economic changes eclipsed the capacity of individual workers to deal on an equal footing with their employers. Initially, these economic changes merely hastened the organi-zation of craft union. Eventually, however, they led to a worldwide restructuring of the labor movement.

The period of crisis in the American labor movement was signalled by the activities of the short-lived National Labor Union formed in 1866 and the Noble Order of the Knights of Labor, formed two years later. The National Labor Union was organized on the basis of an attack on the developing wage system that was replacing personal ownership of the products of labor with corporate ownership and marketing of mass produced goods.

The Knights of Labor, under the leadership of Terrence Powderly, grew successful by embracing a skilled craft approach to union organization, becoming this country's first large-scale labor organization. Membership in the Knights rose rapidly during the depression that followed the Panic of 1873. Powderly's ultimate objective was producer cooperatives. He was not wage conscious, and constantly emphasized the fact that strikes could not solve issues like apprenticeship, administration of justice, child labor, or laws of supply and demand.

By 1886 membership in the Knights' reached 700,000. They expanded the concept of union membership beyond the guild tradition of individuals closely associated with a particular trade, inviting anyone over 18, 'regardless of race, sex or skill', to join their ranks. Only such 'undesirables' as salesmen, bartenders, doctors, lawyers and bankers were excluded.

To Powderly's embarrassment, however, the Knights began engaging in strikes for higher wages, including a successful walkout and boycott against railroad financier Jay Gould. Powderly found himself heading an organization whose objectives – gains in the areas of wages and hours – and whose tactics – strikes – were not consistent with his own.

New unions emerged to embrace the self-interested, economic emphasis on wages and benefits expressed by the Knights' membership. The American Federation of Labor (AFL) was created in 1886 and flourished immediately under the leadership of Samuel Gompers. It was craft-oriented, pragmatic and nonrevolutionary. Its aims were probably best expressed by Cigarmakers Union president Adolph Strasser in testimony before a Senate committee: 'We have no ultimate ends. We are going on from day to day. We fight only for immediate objects – objects that can be realized in a few years.'

The movement from the Knights' to the AFL was more than just an organizational shift, however. It reflected a whole new generation of labor ideology. As Chamberlain *et al.* (1982) put it:

> The passing of the Knights reflected the emerging acceptance by workers of the wage relationship and the recognition that small workshops were rapidly being replaced by aggregations of capital and professionally managed enterprises. The AFL survived and grew because it came to terms with the capitalist, private enterprise system, adapting to it rather than seeking to destroy it.

This fundamental craft-oriented, pragmatic and nonrevolutionary ideology of the AFL was to remain strong through a half-century of contentious strikes, bloody battles, the Sherman Anti-Trust Act, yellow dog contracts, the socialist challenge of the IWW, and the prosperity of the 1920s.

Even as the labor movement was being formally legitimated by the Wagner Act of 1935, however, the AFL conception of craft unionism was being directly challenged. Major industrial complexes remained nonunion, and attempts to organize them were ineffective. In large part, this was because the techniques of mass production were rapidly eliminating craft work in manufacturing. Additionally, the unorganized firms used a very broad range of skilled workers, making it virtually impossible to organize the entire firm along craft lines.

From craft organization to the modern industrial union

John L. Lewis, whose mineworkers were dwindling in number, fought and lost a fight to have the AFL shift from craft unionism to industrialism. He argued, in essence, that unions should be organized by company across entire industrial sectors and floor sweepers, production workers, and skilled machine operators should all be included in the same bargaining unit.

Lewis had an essentially new idea of union organization. Where the craft unions, building on the legacy of guild organizations, sought control over the performance of various skilled tasks and insisted on the right to select and train new workers through the apprenticeship system, Lewis' mineworkers sought control over access to jobs, targeting employers rather than the tasks. Where craft unions assumed that their power rested on depriving employers of their special skills, the new industrial unions saw power in terms of shutting down the entire productive process.

Expelled from the AFL, a group of dissidents joined with Lewis to form the Congress of Industrial Organizations (CIO) and immediately launched major efforts to organize steel, textiles, rubber, and autos. By 1937, United States Steel recognized the steelworkers union; other major industries soon followed suit. The new industrial labor unionism was not easily accepted. Some strikes were bloody and protracted. By the end of 1937, however, the CIO had a membership of 3.7 million, about 300,000 more than the AFL.

As time passed, even the AFL began to organize along industrial lines, particularly the machinists and the electrical workers. Today, despite continuing tension between craft and industrial segments of the merged AFL-CIO, American unionism has taken on a decidedly industrial focus.

With the shift from craft to industrial union concepts, union organizing activity and contractual demands have shifted dramatically. Industrial unions seek control over access to all employment in the firm rather than the right to perform particular tasks. Where craft unions sought control over union membership, insisting that apprenticeships be served and separating journeymen from master craftsmen, industrial unions seek benefits for all workers equally. In addition to wages and benefits, workplace democracy became a dominant theme in industrial contract negotiations. Demands for health and safety protection were accompanied by insistence on effective mechanisms for adjudicating grievances. Eventually demands for participation in company policy were made – most notably in the Crysler Corporation restructuring under Lee Iacocca.

Industrial unionism represents a political philosophy as well as an organizational strategy. In recent decades the core concepts have shifted from wage increases to increased education for all, from job rights to civil rights, from organized workers to world organizations. Most of the new unions, as well as many of those that had previously existed, are now built on an inclusive, mass basis rather than on an exclusive, craft basis.

Organizationally, industrial unions accept management's right to control the means of production. They seek to control the *conditions* of work, not the specific duties assigned to individual workers. In this way, industrial unions are able to focus attention on the needs of unskilled workers, to concentrate on protecting them from exploitation, and to demand for them a larger share of the income produced by the sale of their labor.

As technology advanced, the change from craft to industrial unionism was probably inevitable. Though his words were controversial at the time, John L. Lewis was certainly right when in 1935 he said, 'The craft union principle has become fundamentally ineffective in the face of modern conditions.'

Industrial unions, with their emphasis on work rules and plant- or firm-based organization are not the only alternatives to the prevailing craft union model. Workers in the fine arts and the professions have also developed unique approaches to worker organization and labor relations. A brief look at developments in these occupations will further clarify the alternatives available to teachers.

Artist unions: a third worker organization

The development of artist unions differed from both craft and industrial unions in a number of important respects. First, like craft unions, artist unions generally embraced the idea that union organizations should ensure that their members would be able to perform competently. Rather than adopting the apprenticeship training model, however, artist unions tend to use a screening and selection strategy. The Screen Writers Guild, for example, does not accept anyone for membership who has not had a script accepted for production. Apparently it is assumed that artistic talent can be recognized and certified, but that it cannot be assured through training.

A second unique feature of the artist unions is their approach to salary setting. Craft and industrial unions have traditionally insisted on some version of 'equal pay for equal work', negotiating fixed wage rates for various job categories or the performance of particular tasks. Artist unions, by contrast, operate on the assumption that worker contributions have no standard value. While negotiating minimum rates of compensation aimed at insuring that individuals will be able to survive within the occupation, these unions expect individual artists to negotiate separate contractual agreements setting the value of specific products or performances.

A third unique feature of the artist unions is their insistence that ownership of the products of their labor does *not* pass into management hands as a result of wage payments. This aspect of the artist union concept is described in Schwartz's (1982) fascinating tale of the formation of the Screen Writers Guild. In reporting on the 1933 meeting at which the Guild was originally organized, she notes,

> The idea of royalties for screen writers was also enthusiastically endorsed, and it included not only a percentage of the gross but the right to audit studio books and circumvent cheating. The meeting ended with a few other exciting, enthusiastic proposals, including the determination of writer credits by writers instead of by producers . . . Today these sound like small, reasonable demands, but they were revolutionary at the time. (p. 18)

The long 1988 strike by the Guild has revisited these same issues – artistic control, continued crediting of work to the original authors, and control over royalties and residuals. The key to the artistic definition of work is that a performance is permanently a part of the artist's personal identity. It cannot be legitimately transferred to an owner or manager, and cannot be used or sold in the way ordinary work products are separated from the workers who produce them. Artistic work has its value as an expression of the artist's identity and the artist's worth is determined by the extent to which that work continues to be cherished and appreciated.

As organizations, artist unions have generally adopted the industrial union view that their function is to force owners and managers to recognize the value of worker *efforts* rather than their *skills*. They realize, of course, that artistic talent and skill vary widely. For that reason, individual contracts are endorsed as a means of letting individual artists identify and reap the benefits of their special skills and talents.

Professional associations: yet another alternative

The professional associations are the fourth type of worker organization to emerge from the medieval guild structure. While many observers treat professionals as unorganized, non-union workers, Steward and Cantor (1982: 173) frame the issue in terms appropriate to an analysis of labor relations alternatives. They assert that,

> In the United States there are two common types of workers' organization: the professional association and the labor union. Both types are outgrowths of nineteenth-century industrialization. The union is the result of those forces which centralized production in factories, the professional association is the result of having a class of free professionals who practiced independently of the workplace.

These authors acknowledge the philosophical and social status differences separating professionals from labor union members. Nevertheless, they insist that, 'Although the union and professional association were originally opposite in philosophy and orientation, as the work of both professionals and industrial workers converge, so do the philosophies of the organizations.'

The earliest and most powerful of all professional associations was the American Medical Association (AMA). Founded in 1847, the AMA eventually succeeded in acquiring the full range of powers sought by professional associations: control over training institutions, certification of workers, legal control over practice norms, privileged privacy in the doctor-patient relationship, confidentiality of records, even deference to professional judgment regarding possible cases of malpractice.

As Stewart and Cantor (1982: 174) put it,

> the purpose of the professional association was to protect its members from encroachment by the state and to secure status and economic privilege for its members . . . to create a monopoly over the skills and knowledge of the profession.

Comparing the four alternative worker organizations

Relationships among the four alternative types of worker organizations are depicted graphically in figure 1. As suggested by the figure, the shift from medieval guild to modern worker organizations is closely related to two critical features of advanced industrial economic systems: technological sophistication and the development of impersonal markets for both labor and finished goods. The combination of advancing technology and impersonal labor and commodity markets threatens all workers with loss of identity, economic exploitation, abuse by managers and owners, and destruction of standards of task performance. The organizational strategies adopted by various union organizations have been significantly influenced by how these two threats are experienced by individual workers.

Where workers see the primary issue as the substitution of capital for labor through technology, they respond with organizations aimed at controlling access to jobs. Using the techniques of organization and bargaining common to industrial labor and artist unions, these workers aim at establishing parity with management in the control of productive firms. They willingly defer to management on matters of direct supervision, but insist on limiting employment to union workers. By contrast, workers who feel that their skills cannot be undermined by capital investment tend to embrace the organizational strategies of the craft unions and professional associations. They demand control over who will be permitted to perform specific tasks, but are generally content to let workers performing unrelated tasks

Figure 1.   Alternative forms of worker organization emerging from medieval guilds.

SHARING CONTROL OVER ADVANCING
TECHNOLOGY

	Job access (employment)	Task definition (technique)
Worker control:		
Manager control:	Worker supervision (inspection)	Performance contracts (licensure)

Secure worker rights (autonomy, security, and dignity	**INDUSTRIAL LABOR UNIONS**	**SKILLED CRAFT UNIONS**
RESOLVING CONFLICTS ARISING FROM TRADE IN AN IMPERSONAL MARKET *Market place control* (ownership, appraisal and responsibility)	**ARTIST GUILDS**	**PROFESSIONAL ASSOCIATIONS**

Control the firm   Control the work

establish their own relationship with managers. Craft workers concentrate on defining and securing control over specific tasks through negotiations with owners and managers. Professional workers turn to public policy and law as the vehicles for establishing control over specific technologies. These workers tend to insist on licensure of workers (and denial of the right to practice to anyone not properly licensed).

When attempting to control the negative consequences of impersonal labor and commodity markets, union strategies are aligned differently. Industrial labor and craft unions adopt strategies that emphasize the importance of worker rights. The rights pursued are of three basic types:

(1)   workplace autonomy or independence from arbitrary and capricious managerial interference;
(2)   economic and job security, usually couched in terms of seniority, layoff and transfer rights;
(3)   the symbolic right to personal dignity or respect, a right that is difficult to articulate but widely held to be critical.

Artist unions and professional associations, by contrast, seek direct control over the marketplace itself. These organizations emphasize the importance of:

(1)   ownership of the products and services produced, refusing to relinquish control to owners or managers of the productive firms;
(2)   direct appraisal of the worth of each individual worker's productivity;
(3)   assignment of responsibility for performance to the individual worker.

In utilizing these different strategies, unions have very different effects on productivity and workplace relationships. The reshaping of the economic system that results can be seen in three distinct domains. First, the divergent union strategies produce very different effects on the underlying *character of the work* performed by union members. Second, the powers granted to unions and the ways in which they interact with employing firms is logically linked to the *organizational form of each industry* or economic sector. And third, each strategy of union organization develops a particular approach to the problems of *day-to-day interactions between managers and workers*.

There is a logical link between union strategies for coping with technological and marketplace conditions and their effect on the logic of the work performed, their impact on the organization of the workplace, and their ability to reshape on-the-job interactions. The linkage works in both directions. Thus, while medical doctors prefer the technical and marketplace control provided by professional associations, they have begun to join craft structured unions when they are employed by the state or hired as salaried employees in hospitals or other health maintenance organizations. Similarly, the internationalization of the automobile industry has generated tremendous changes in the character of autoworker unions. New approaches to technology control and worker rights are restructuring the relationship between the UAW and the big three auto producers.

A brief review of the logical connections between the organizational strategies of teacher unions, typical teacher work responsibilities, the nature of school organizations, and the day-to-day interaction between teachers and school administrators will help focus attention of potential targets of reform in the overall labor relations system.

Matching the logic of the work

While teachers have relied almost exclusively on the industrial labor model of union organization, this reliance is rather puzzling. The organizational strategy selected suggests that teaching is viewed by its practitioners as unskilled labor, threatened by technology and alienating individual workers through an impersonal labor market. Even a casual review of the literature on good teaching suggests that this view is not right, however. There is a widespread belief that effective teaching depends heavily on mastery of sophisticated instructional techniques that mark teaching as skilled craft. It is equally easy to find teaching theories that emphasize the development of intense artistic engagement or a strong sense of professional responsibility. Disregarding the apparent importance of craft, artistic and professional elements in teaching, however, the industrial union model tends to reinforce and protect the unskilled labor elements of teaching work (Mitchell and Kerchner 1983). In order to pursue the industrial labor model of employment control and protection of worker rights, teacher unions have tended to disavow responsibility for either the technical skill of individual teachers or the overall quality of the schooling process. Following the dictates of the industrial model means asserting that managers are responsible for task definition and worker supervision. It also means rejecting ownership of the final products of the school system.

Of course, not all teachers, not all union leaders, and certainly not all school policy makers endorse the strategic implications that flow from reliance on an industrial union model for teacher organization. Many educators continue to endorse teacher work role definitions that include craft, art and professional components. The language of professional responsibility is especially strong today. Recent reform efforts have echoed the language of the 1940s and '50s, calling upon teachers to embrace a professional self-image and organizational strategy. It is important to remember, however, that the earlier professionalization effort failed. Teachers were unable to secure either technical control over the way they work or marketplace control over who would be allowed to teach. Administrators secured control over the one dimension and state legislatures have maintained control over the other. It was not an accident that teachers turned to the industrial union model of today. Professionalism failed, despite its support for better teaching, because the professional association model is unable to deal with the harsh realities of contemporary school organizations and the alienation and vulnerability of teachers in their day-to-day interactions with parents, administrators and school board members.

Matching the power of employers

The industrial model of worker organization adopted by teachers is no more logically linked to the organizational structure of the school than it is to the logic of teaching work. Industries in which industrial labor unions grow and flourish share four basic characteristics:

1. the industry consists of large firms with strong owner/manager groups capable of defining productive goals and free to decide what combination of labor and capital investment will be used to pursue those goals;
2. managers with a fundamental interest in profits are willing and able to make hiring decisions based on the ability of workers to increase the profitability of the firm;
3. market structures control the distribution of products, enabling consumers to decide whether producers have been sufficiently economical in the use of various resources;
4. the production process relies heavily on unskilled labor, rather than skilled craft workers, talented artists or autonomous professionals.

It is not hard to see that public schools have none of these characteristics. Educational goals are established politically and access to capital funding for buildings or equipment is also subject to political review. Nor do school managers have a profit motive. Indeed, if public agencies do succeed in saving money political pressure for rebating it to taxpayers is almost irresistible. While market forces play some small role in the distribution of education (mostly by affecting real estate prices), poor school performance does not destroy its customer base. Most importantly, teachers are not unskilled workers to be replaced with the frequency of fast food service employees or assembly line workers.

In short, it can not be argued that industrial unionism was adopted by teachers in order to match union structure to the economic organization of schools. To the contrary, industrial unionism creates problems for schools, just because they do not have the appropriate economic organization.

Handling work place relationships

Teacher support for the industrial union model is understandable if we look at how it affects day-to-day relationships on the job. Industrial union strategies are based on four key assumptions about daily interaction between workers and their supervisors:

1. workers feel insecure and fear that their value in the productive process is poorly understood by their immediate supervisors;

2. economic or political conditions threaten job security which individual workers feel that they cannot control;
3. workers experience and become sensitive to arbitrary and capricious managerial decisions which are seen as based on organizational convenience or external pressures rather than interest in improved productivity or worker support;
4. workers, believing that they are powerless to cope on an individual basis with the substantial power and authority of their superiors in the firm, conclude that they must organize into a strong and cohesive unit.

These are, of course, exactly the feelings and problems identified by teacher union organizers over the last three decades. It was a near universal belief by ordinary classroom teachers that these conditions plague today's public schools which made it possible for teacher leaders to rapidly expand the influence of the American Federation of Teachers and to produce a dramatic re-definition of the goals of the National Education Association during the 1960s.

These working conditions are typical of relatively unskilled workers in large industrial firms and account for many of the organizing and bargaining strategies used by industrial labor unions. Their importance in the organization of teacher unions helps to account for the fact that militant teacher organizations were organized first and become strongest in urban centers where the conditions of alienation and abuse were most severe. Industrial unionism for teachers is, to put it in the simplest possible terms, the most logical tool for pursuing job security, personal dignity and rudimentary fairness in their daily working relationships with school administrators.

Alternatives as seen by school administrators

A recent survey of school administrators in California offers some interesting insights into the ways in which teacher unions are currently undergoing a period of adjustment and dynamic change. The survey project was a comprehensive study of administrator attitudes and experiences – using a questionnaire of some 98 items. A full review of the data is presented elsewhere (Mitchell, 1987), but three key findings highlight the overall direction of change.

Uncertainty about labor relations

The first indication of dynamic change in public school labor relations is the fact that, despite more than a decade of experience with legally sanctioned industrial unionism, California administrators hold very diverse opinions and attitudes about the nature and impact of collective bargaining in the schools. As expected, most administrators feel collective bargaining for teachers does not make a positive contribution to education. Fully a quarter of those surveyed, however, indicated they believe the overall effect has been positive. More importantly, large numbers of administrators are a bit confused about key elements of the labor process within their own districts. To cite a few examples:

— more than 20% of the respondents erroneously report themselves to be 'confidential employees';
— in 55% of the school districts represented in the sample, administrators from the same district disagree about who is the chief spokesperson for management during negotiations;

— in an even larger number of districts there is frequent disagreement about the
  number of grievances filed, whether particular clauses are found in the district
  contract, and other factual details about recent labor relations experiences;
— in about 50% of the districts reporting the use of alternative labor relations
  practices, administrators do not agree about whether the practices are actually
  different from ordinary industrial unionism.
— in a few districts (about 9% of the total), there is even disagreement about what
  union has been selected as the exclusive bargaining agent for teachers.

While these discrepancies are probably not serious enough to interfere with contract negotiation and administration, they do indicate that local school administrators lack a clear and
cohesive view about essential elements in the existing labor relations systems in public
education.

The lack of a clear view of the labor relations process cannot be attributed to a lack of
relevant experience. Substantial numbers of administrators are broadly experienced with all
aspects of labor relations:

— about 62% have helped prepare proposals;
— 55% have served on negotiating teams;
— 34% have personally been the object of worker grievances;
— 45% have been employed during a strike or other work stoppage.

The empirical evidence suggests instead that unionism in the public school is fluid and
confusing. The most likely explanation is that both teachers and administrators implicitly
recognize the mismatch between their own experiences and the assumptions of the industrial
union model. As a result, they are groping for a more meaningful and appropriate system.

The importance of trust

A second striking feature of this administrator survey is a reported linkage among three
broad factors, each covered in several questionnaire items:

— the frequency of objective labor relations problems;
— the level of trust and cooperation existing between management and the teacher
  organization;
— the belief that all parties are acting responsibly and in good faith.

In a statistically powerful way, administrators insisted that various types of labor problems –
tense negotiations, work stoppages, grievances, inability to establish multi-year contracts,
etc. – are clustered together in the same districts. Moreover, districts where these problems
have arisen share two other common experiences. They report low levels of trust and cooperation between unions and management groups. Further, they see teacher organization
leaders, managers and school board members as less fully committed to school improvement.

It is not clear from the data which of these problems might be the cause of this
unsettling pattern. Perhaps irresponsible action by local leaders erodes trust and results in
conditions that necessitate grievance filing and threats of work stoppage. It is equally
possible, however, that labor-management trust and cooperation is eroded by community
stresses not directly connected to labor relations and that reduced trust and cooperation lead
to both perceptions of irresponsibility and the invoking of the legal machinery for grievances
and work stoppages. It is even possible that the legal machinery created by California's
collective bargaining law makes grievances or strikes easier with the result that these actions

are, in turn, responsible for both the erosion of trust and the perception of irresponsible behavior. Whatever the causal system, however, this linkage between objective labor problems, inter-group trust, and the perception that actions are responsible is extra-ordinarily powerful, accounting for nearly 30 percent of the response variance in the related questions.

The search for alternatives

A third striking feature of the survey data is the extent to which administrators report widespread interest in the development of alternatives to the prevailing industrial union model of labor management relations. In 25% of the 503 districts represented in the sample administrators reported labor relations practices that are, 'significantly different from typical industrial unionism'.

Phone calls were made to follow-up on these reported alternative practices. The results of this follow-up survey are very illuminating. First, in about 20% of the districts reporting alternatives (i.e. about 5% of all districts in the state), no real alternative exists in the mind of the superintendent or personnel director. In another 30%, the reported alternative practice fits comfortably with the normal maturation of industrial unionism, a process leading to the reduction in overt conflict and the development of informal mechanisms of communication and contract settlement.

In about 50% of the cases (more than 12% of the State's school districts), however, the reported alternative practices were found to be real and quite substantial. Phone interviews and follow-up observations revealed that these substantial alternatives are of four basic types (see Glazer 1988):

(a) *bargain process changes* involving different time schedules, different participants, and/or different ways of handling proposed contract clauses;

(b) new *budget development procedures* involving the creation of financial formulas controlling teacher salary or benefit levels, new participants in the budget development process, and/or new mechanisms for exchanging budget and finance information among the parties;

(c) changes in the *ongoing working relationships between district managers and the local teacher organization* aimed at opening communication, creating trust, and/or solving troublesome issues;

(d) changes in the *nature of the agreement* reached at the conclusion of the negotiating process (this last alternative was not represented in the administrator data, but was gound in four school districts responding to a parallel survey of school board members).

The most prevalent form of alternative practice involves changing the bargaining process. Usually this involves expanding the number of people involved in the process, getting superintendents and board members (and sometimes community leaders) directly involved in discussions with teachers.

With remarkable consistency, administrators reporting the presence of alternative practices state that managers could and should accept responsibility for opening communications and establishing a cooperative and trusting relationship with teacher union leaders.

To summerize, substantial alternatives to the prevailing industrial labor union model are found in more than 10% of all California school districts. These alternative practices highlight the places where changes in labor relations policy and practice are most likely to facilitate a transition from current patterns of unionism inherited from private sector, unskilled worker organizations to new labor relations systems in the public schools. The concluding section of this chapter summarizes briefly a dozen policy options which might be considered by policy makers interested in encouraging movement into new ways of structuring the relationships between teachers, school administrators and school boards.

Policy options for changing labor relations

Can specific changes in labor relations policy or practice restructure the relationships between teacher unions and school organizations? In answering this question, the two simple answers – repealing state statutes legalizing teacher unionization and doing nothing – should not be forgotten. For a number of policy makers, repeal of collective bargaining statutes is ideologically supportable. It is probably politically impossible, however. More importantly, vital contributions have been made to conflict management and the creation of more rational ways of resolving labor problems. They have generally been addressed to real and pressing problems. Hence, changes in these basic legal structures should be carefully considered.

The second option – doing nothing – may have some appeal. It was, I think, Peter Drucker who said that the hardest thing to teach young managers is that some decisions should not be made. Some problems are best solved by evolutionary development of practice rather than through yet another round of abrupt policy change. School systems are already at work developing important labor relations alternatives. It is important that, whatever policy changes are adopted, the experience of those who are now experimenting with new practices be considered and honored.

There are a least twelve policy change options that might be considered. These options share a recognition of the important contributions made by the industrial union model to reducing labor strife and re-structuring day-to-day working relationships between administrators and teachers. Based on the changes already taking place, they represent promising ways of ameliorating the mismatch between the industrial union model and the work of teaching on the one hand and the public sector organization character of schools on the other.

Policy support for mature bargaining

Since the concern for due process protection has been the most important factor in motivating and sustaining strong teacher unions, public policy might recognize the importance of these concerns for teachers' sense of security and dignity. This would have the effect of reducing tension and creating a climate of greater openness and collaboration in the schools.

Policy Option 1: Mandate binding arbitration of specific teacher rights.
Of course, many teacher organizations have already won binding arbitration at the bargaining table. Keeping this issue on the bargaining table encourages teacher organizations to feel threatened, however, and therefore encourages unnecessarily aggressive behavior.

Policy Option 2: Expand and refine the security of employment concept originally embodied in teacher tenure laws.
It may not at first look like anything creative could be done with this policy which is frequently cited as one of the reasons that teachers do not need or deserve union protection. Job security is, however, only the flip side of performance accountability. It is quite possible to develop public policy strategies that strengthen the job security of teachers whose job

performance is meritorious while also strengthening accountability for all teachers. The trouble with most recent accountability systems is that they assume a skilled craft view of teaching by holding teachers accountable for personal performance of individual skills. To the extent that teaching is labor, art or professional work, current accountability systems create anxiety rather than either performance improvement or job security for high performance teachers.

> *Policy Option 3*: Clarify teacher evaluation, merit and promotion review
> procedures.

There is already a substantial body of state law addressed to the issue of teacher evaluation. It is not easy to see exactly what sort of changes in that law would provide the sense of professional responsibility and personal security that teachers need and desire. One thing is certain, however, the form of teacher evaluation assumed in existing law exacerbates conflict by assuming a power struggle between teachers and administrators. The problem is that when power struggles replace authority-based control systems the resulting anxiety damages the teaching performance of good teachers long before it produces the actions needed to eliminate poor ones. Whatever direction is taken, improved personnel practices in education cannot facilitate change in the labor relations system until a sense of collegial responsibility for peer-review and a sense of shared pride in the improvement of education are created to replace existing fears that teachers are being exposed to arbitrary and capricious scrutiny.

Negotiating budgets rather than demands

A second area in which policy changes might be contemplated springs from the experience some districts are already having with budget negotiations. In a number of alternative practice districts, teacher organizations and school managers have begun to negotiate the district budget – rather than teacher needs or demands. In some ways this is both the simplest and the most potent source of change in existing labor practice. The negotiating relationship can be shifted away from the bi-lateral conflict assumptions of industrial unionism by focusing teacher and administrator attention on the fact that school resources are generated through taxation rather than marketing of services. Substituting budget negotiations for the traditional negotiation of salary and benefit demands could help educators recover something of the long forgotten guild commitment to the goal of the entire occupational group.

There are two dimensions to this process, and policies might be formulated to support either one or both together. They are:

> *Policy Option 4*: Require that district and teacher negotiators frame their contract
> proposals as budget allocations.

This would undercut the tendency for management to hide resources and for teachers to insist that they are only responsible for making demands, not for understanding how those demands can be met.

> *Policy Option 5*: Require that district and teacher negotiators frame contract
> proposals as budget categories as well as setting budget allocation
> amounts.

It would be possible to create a policy system that separates the right to create budget categories from the negotiation of specific resource allocations among the various categories. Such a separation would maintain relatively stronger management/school board budget authority, if the right to create expenditure categories is reserved for their control while responsibility for distributing available dollars among the categories is brought to the bargaining table.

Reforming the bargaining process

A third set of policy options focuses on what might be done to streamline the bargaining process itself. The alternative practices already being utilized in some districts suggest three possible policy directions.

Policy Option 6: Restructure participation in the bargaining process.
It is not difficult to imagine ways in which restructuring participation in the bargaining process could alter the dynamics of contract development and settlement. One of the most cumbersome aspects of collective bargaining is the use of specialized advocates for both sides in a bargaining process that lasts for many months. Districts using so-called 'win-win' bargaining systems generally restructure participation so that top managers, school board members, a fairly broad cross-section of teachers, and sometimes even community leaders are involved in the process.

Policy Option 7: Foreshorten the timetable for bargaining.
Another feature of many existing alternative practices is the ability of district management and teacher leaders to set a timetable for decision making. Often the timetable is created by using some form of retreat or marathon bargaining process which keep the negotiators in close contact for a weekend or more with the commitment that a settlement will be reached before anyone leaves the scene. If this is to become a matter of public polcy, it is important that the timetable for bargaining not be pushed ahead of the state's budget setting process. It is unrealistic to expect short term bargaining to settle fiscal issues if the district budget is still unknown.

Policy Option 8: Create a cadre of trained professional neutrals and empower them to intervene in the bargaining process.
This could be a far more radical policy change than either of the first two proposals in this domain. The extent to which it would represent a radical change depends on how much authority the professional neutrals are given. A relatively high-profile model for this process is the Justice Department's Civil Rights Commission. The Civil Rights Commission is empowered to initiate action wherever federal funds are involved to secure the rights of minority citizens. Milder forms are found in the human relations agencies created in many communities. Typically members of these agencies can only enter a conflict situation if they are invited to do so by one or both parties.

Reforming the labor relations system

A fourth domain for policy adjustment involves restructuring the labor relations system by creating better mechanisms for ongoing collaboration and communication between teachers and school managers. Districts reporting alternative practices do this quite frequently on a voluntary basis. It would be possible to give public policy support to a wide variety of optional mechanisms for structured interaction. Two of the most obvious would be:

Policy Option 9: Create a system for appointing or electing teachers to serve as members of the superintendent's cabinet.
Many school districts have found it quite helpful to bring acknowledged teacher leaders into direct and regular contact with the superintendent's cabinet.

Policy Option 10: Establish a system of teacher representatives to engage in site-level or districtwide planning.

This approach would formally raise the overall level of participation by teachers in school program development and planning. It could also be used to structure participation more fully by identifying the specific decisions that could be referred to such a teacher council. This policy option is the one currently being given strongest support by the American Federation of Teachers.

Reforming the instrument of agreement

The last two policy options are focused on the underlying structure of the industrial union model itself. In that sense, these options may be considered quite radical. Kerchner and Mitchell (1988) argue that, if pursued together, they could lead to a positive restructuring of the overall labor relations process in the schools. The first structural reform is:

> *Policy Option 11*: Restructure the scope of negotiations provision of existing policy so as to insure that professional interests legitimately within the purview of a professional teaching staff are necessarily embodied in the bargaining process.

Perhaps the most pernicious feature of the current labor relations process is its effort to circumscribe the scope of negotiations and to limit teacher organizations to discussing only teacher self-interests. In making the assumption that the conflict between workers and managers is over the basic mission of the firm or the division of its profits, the industrial model makes it seem illegitimate for teacher organizations to adopt the professional attitudes appropriate to their work and their training. Narrowing the scope of bargaining is vitally important in private sector industries because that is the way the structure protects the private property interests of the owners and managers. The mission of the schools is publicly defined, however. And responsibility for implementing programs to pursue that public mission must be shared between teachers and administrators if they are to be successful. Where private industries rightly presume a fundamental economic conflict of interest between the owners and the workers in a firm, conflicts in education are about the appropriate way to pursue the goals of education. Current negotiating laws tell teachers that their only legitimate interest in coming to the bargaining table is to try to wrest material gain for their members from a presumably selfish management. This is the inevitable result of trying to limit the scope of negotiations to wages, benefits and terms of employment.

It is not, of course, immediately obvious that opening the scope of negotiations will eliminate teacher self interest. To be sure, teacher self-interest is not, however, made more difficult by simply expanding scope. Arguably, in fact, management would find it easier to reject self-interested demands because the broadened scope would elicit greater interest in teacher leadership from more professionally oriented teachers.

> *Policy Option 12*: Restructure the nature of the agreement reached through bargaining so that it is modeled after a trust agreement rather than a contract.

This option is the most complex and far reaching one proposed here. It is too complex for a full discussion, but is described at length in Kerchner and Mitchell (1988) and more briefly in Mitchell (1986). The concept is simple enough – there are two different legal mechanisms for formally allocating resources to the realization of future goals: *contracts* and *trusts*. Contracts bind the *behavior* of the parties to the agreement. By contrast, trusts are legal instruments explicitly designed to give formal expression to the *intentions* of those who create them. The legal traditions surrounding these two different forms of agreement are different in ways that appear to be quite compatible with the differences between school teaching and typical industrial labor work. Teachers and administrators routinely negotiate the goals and character of the work to be done (i.e., about their intentions). The teachers go to work inventing appropriate means of reaching the agreed upon goals. This contrasts sharply with the work of wage laborers who are typically prohibited from developing alternative means of pursuing work objectives. They are routinely expected to follow directions and apply standard operating procedures. Thus, while laboring work can be contractually specified, teachers and other professionals must be licensed to perform complex tasks and then given the freedom to apply their skills in accordance with the dictates of their own professional judgments.

Labor contracts are generally formulated and adjudicated on the assumption that they must specify the particular behavior required of workers and managers rather than the overall goals of the school. In the language of grievance arbitrators, the only rights and obligations created by a labor contract are those contained 'within the four corners' of the contract document. Intentions are held to be too vague to be enforced under contract law. Though it is not often recognized in the context of labor relations policy, however, the courts have developed very effective procedures for interpreting and applying trust agreements. Since litigation of intentions and purposes is basic to the enforcement of trust agreements, they may be seen as a promising mechanism for creating binding agreements in the schools that do not interfere with the development of professional teaching roles.

Conclusion

This chapter has reviewed the evolution of labor relations from the occupational organizations represented in the medieval guild system to the fluid and rapidly changing context of contemporary teacher unions. Along the way, we have examined the diverse and changing ideas of school administrators, and explored briefly a dozen policy options which might be utilized to guide and direct future developments in labor/management relations in public education. Perhaps the most important lesson to be drawn from this review is that the new forms of labor relations emerging in the public schools of the nation reflect the normal process of evolution. They should not be viewed as either corruptions of the one true system of labor relations or as the result of inexperience and ineptitude on the part of educators.

References

CALIFORNIA COMMISSION ON THE TEACHING PROFESSION (CTP 1985) *Who will teach our children?: A strategy for improving California's schools*, (Sacramento, CA: CTP).

CHAMBERLAIN, N. W., CULLEN, D. E., and LEWIN, D. (1980) *The Labor Sector*. 3rd edition (New York: McGraw-Hill).

COHEN-ROSENTHAL, E. and BURTON C. E. (1987) *Mutual Gains A Guide to Union-Management Cooperation* (New York: Praeger).

COX, A., BORK D. C. and GORMAN, R. A. (1981) *Cases and Material on Labor Law* (New York: The Foundation Press, Inc.).

COHEN-ROSENTHAL, E. and BURTON C. E. (1987) *Mutual Gains A Guide to Union-Management Cooperation* (New York: Praeger).

COX, A., BORK D. C. and GORMAN, R. A. (1981) *Cases and Material on Labor Law* (New York: The Foundation Press, Inc.).

ERIC CLEARINGHOUSE ON EDUCATIONAL MANAGEMENT (1987) *Collective Bargaining and Alternatives*. Value Search series; a collection of ERIC materials selected for relevance (Eugene, OR: University of Oregon).

GLAZER, J. P. (1988) 'Alternatives collective bargaining and labor relations practices in California public elementary and Secondary Schools'. unpublished doctoral dissertation (Berkeley, CA: University of California, Berkeley).

INSTITUTE FOR EDUCATIONAL LEADERSHIP (1986) *School Boards Strengthening Grass Roots Leadership* (Washington, DC: Institute for Educational Leadership).

JACKSON, R. M. (1984) *The Formation of Craft Labor Markets* (New York: Academic Press, Inc.).

KERCHNER, C. T. and MITCHELL, D. E. (1988) *The Changing Idea of a Teachers' Union* (London: Falmer Press).

LAMBERT, J. M. (1891) *Two Thousand Years of Guild Life* (London: A. Brown & Sons).

LEESON, R. A. (1979) *Travelling Brothers, The Centuries' Road from Craft Fellowship to Trade Unionism* (London: George Allen & Unwin).

MITCHELL, D. E. (1987) 'Labour relations in California as seen by members of the Association of California School Administrators', a White Paper prepared for the Center for Educational Policy at the Far West Laboratory for Educational Research and Development (San Francisco, CA: Far West Laboratory).

MITCHELL, D. E. (1986) 'A new approach to collective bargaining', Far West Laboratory of Educational Research and Development, *Policy Briefs* 3 (Winter).

MITCHELL, D. E. (1981) *Shaping Legislative Decisions: Education Policy and the Social Sciences* (Lexington, MA: Lexington Books).

MITCHELL, D. E. and KERCHNER, C. T. (1983) 'Collective bargaining and teacher policy', in L. Shulman and G. Sykes (eds) *The Handbook of Teaching and Policy* (New York: Longman), Chapter 8.

NATIONAL COMMISSION ON EXCELLENCE IN EDUCATION (1983) *A Nation at Risk: The Imperative for Education Reform* (Washington, DC: GPO).

SCHWARTZ, N. L. (1982) *the Hollywood Writers' Wars*, completed by S. Schwartz (New York: Alfred A. Knopf).

STEWART, P. L. and CANTOR, M. G. (1982) *Varieties of Work* (Beverley Hills, CA: Sage).

TROY, L. (1986) 'Why unions are declining', *The Letter* from The Institute for Contemporary Studies, 12(2); excerpts from *Unions in Transition* S. M. Lipset (ed.) (ICS Press).

UNWIN, G. (1963 [orig. pub. 1904]) *Industrial Organization in the Sixteenth and Seventeenth Centuries* (London: Frank Cass).

12   Democratic theory and the role of teachers in democratic education

Amy Gutmann
Princeton University

'There are two human inventions which may be considered more difficult than any others – the art of government, and the art of education; and people still contend as to their very meaning' (Kant 1900: 12). We can exercise the art of education, Kant argued, either unreflectively, 'without plan, ruled by given circumstances', (p.13), or theoretically, with the aid of principles. Must educational policy rest on a principled theory? Why not settle for making educational policy less reflectively, as we often have in the past? Without any principled plan, we could strengthen our science and math curriculum in reaction to Sputnik, desegregate some schools and fund more compensatory education in reaction to the Civil Rights movement, and go 'back to basics' in reaction to declining SAT scores.

Consider the back-to-basics movement in American education. In the absence of a theory, how might the call to go back to basics be defended? The most common and direct defense is that schools will better educate children by concentrating on reading, writing, history, mathematics, and science rather than on music, art, sex education, and so on. Having invoked the concept of a 'better' education, we must ask 'better' with respect to what purposes? Without a principled theory of education, an answer is not obvious. Neither, therefore, is the rationality of going back to basics.

This point is not simply academic. Consider the widely publicized recommendation by the National Commission on Excellence in Education (1983) for instituting the 'New Basics'. In making its recommendation, the Commission noted that 'If only to keep and improve on the slim competitive edge we still retain in world markets, we must dedicate ourselves to the reform of our educational system for the benefit of all – old and young alike, affluent and poor, majority and minority.' Although the tone of its – *A Nation at Risk* – report is set by this statement, the Commission also notes that our concern for education 'goes well beyond matters such as industry and commerce . . . [to include] the intellectual, moral, and spiritual strengths of our people which knit together the very fabric of our society' (p. 7). If our educational purposes are this broad, it is not clear why the new basics do not also include art history, sex education, racial integration, and the avoidance of academic tracking. A rigorous course in high school chemistry may not contribute more to the moral and spiritual strength of students than a racially integrated classroom or an equally rigorous course in art history. The problem is not that the reforms recommended by the Commission are necessarily wrong, but that we cannot judge them without a more principled understanding of our educational purposes.

The Commission may have had a political reason for not engaging in a more principled analysis: the desire to achieve public consensus. The 'basics' appear to provide a least common denominator for agreeing on a national agenda for education. If we agree on the basics, we can temporarily set aside our deeper disagreements on more controversial issues, such as racial integration and sex education, and get on with the work of improving our

This chapter is taken largely from Professor Gutmann's *Democratic Education* © 1987 Princeton University Press, with whose kind permission it is reprinted here.

schools. But do we agree on the basics? A greater proportion of citizens may approve of teaching American history than sex education in schools (although 82% of the American public approves of sex education [Spring 1985: 133], but *how* schools teach sex education and American history matters more to most citizens than *whether* schools teach these subjects, and there is no consensus on how either American history or sex education should be taught. There is, in this crucial sense, no consensus on teaching even the 'basics'.

Were there a consensus, it would not constitute a decisive reason for dispensing with a principled analysis of our educational problems. The charter of the Commission 'directed it to pay particular attention to teenage youth' (NCEE 1983: 2). The Report therefore focuses on high school education, yet it makes no mention (for example) of the educational problems created by a rapidly rising pregnancy rate among unmarried teenage girls, and therefore totally neglects the question of how schools might best deal with the problem. Although the teenage pregnancy rate has risen more rapidly in recent years than SAT scores have fallen, the Commission concentrated exclusively on the latter problem. If public commissions put avoidance of political controversy ahead of principled analysis, they are bound to fail in the task for which they are best equipped: improving the quality of American education not directly by changing school policy, but indirectly by improving the quality of our public deliberations over education.

In a democracy, political disagreement is not something that we should generally seek to avoid. Political controversies over our educational problems are a particularly important source of social progress because they have the potential for educating so many citizens. By not taking principled positions, commissions may avoid converting some of our disagreements into full-fledged political controversies. But we pay a very high price for their avoidance: we neglect educational alternatives that may be better than those to which we have become accustomed or that may aid us in understanding how to improve our schools before we reach the point of crisis, when our reactions are likely to be less reflective because we have so little time to deliberate.

Some members of the Commission may have had another reason for avoiding a principled analysis of our educational problems. They may have believed that the government's legitimate educational role does not extend to what might be called 'moral education'. On this view, the government should stay away from subjects such as sex education, since courses in sex education cannot possibly be neutral with regard to morality and moral education is properly a private not a public concern (*US News & World Report* 1980: 89).[1] Sex education should therefore be provided by parents, not by public schools. Whatever one thinks of this conclusion, it clearly presupposes a theory, a principled political theory, about the legitimate role of government in education. Unless the theory is articulated, citizens cannot assess its principled merits or its policy implications. Even a brief account of the theory suggests a problem with this rationale for the Commission's recommendations. If one embraces the principle that moral education is the domain of the family rather than the state, then the basics must not include the teaching of history or biology (insofar as it includes evolution) any more than sex education or racial integration. States cannot even support schools without engaging in moral education.

All significant policy prescriptions presuppose a theory, a political theory, of the proper role of government in education. When the theory remains implicit, we cannot adequately judge its principles or the policy prescriptions that flow from them. The attractions of avoiding theory are, as we have just seen, superficial. We do not collectively know good educational policy when we see it; we cannot make good educational policy by avoiding political controversy; nor can we make principled educational policy without exposing our principles and investigating their implications.

Why a democratic theory?

To defend the need for a theory of education, however, is not to defend any particular theory. Why a *democratic* theory of education? Although it would take an entire book to defend a democratic theory in detail, I can briefly explain the rationale for developing a democratic theory.

The most distinctive feature of a democratic theory of education is that it makes a democratic virtue out of our inevitable disagreement over educational problems. The democratic virtue, too simply stated, is that we can publicly debate educational problems in a way much more likely to increase our understanding of education and each other than were we to leave the management of schools, as Kant suggests, 'to depend entirely upon the judgment of the most enlightened experts' (1900: 17). The policies that result from our democratic deliberations will not always be the right ones, but they will be more enlightened – by the values and concerns of the many communities that constitute a democracy – than those that would be made by unaccountable educational experts.

The primary aim of a democratic theory of education is not to offer solutions to all the problems plaguing our educational institutions, but to consider ways of resolving those problems that are compatible with a commitment to democratic values. A democratic theory of education provides principles that, in the face of our social disagreements, help us judge (*a*) who should have authority to make decisions about education; and (*b*) what the moral boundaries of educational authority are.

A democratic theory is not a substitute for a moral ideal of education. In a democratic society, we bring our moral ideals of education to bear on how we raise our children, on who we support for school boards, and on what educational policies we advocate. But we cannot simply translate our own moral ideals of education, however objective they are, into public policy. Only in a society in which all other citizens agreed with me would my moral ideal simply translate into a political ideal. But such a society would have little need for politics as we now know it. The administration of persons would, as Engels (and later Lenin) imagined, be replaced by the administration of things. To create such a society, someone would have to establish an educational tyranny, a tyranny that would be unworkable without the simultaneous creation of a political tyranny as well. There is no morally acceptable way to achieve social agreement on a comprehensive moral ideal of education, at least in our lifetimes. We can do better to try instead to find the fairest ways for reconciling our disagreements, and for enriching our collective life by democratically debating them. We may even find ourselves modifying our moral ideals of education in the process of participating in democratic debates and of publicly reconciling our differences.

This defense of democratic education may seem to rest on a paradox: reasonable people disagree over what being well-educated entails, yet as citizens of the same society (state or school district) we have no more reasonable alternative than to agree collectively on how future citizens should be educated. Simply agreeing to disagree (as we do with regard to religion) is not a reasonable choice: education is not primarily a private good of parents (and public funding is incompatible with treating it as such) nor can parents be counted upon to educate their children in the public interest. Because schooling is a collective, publicly-funded good, citizens must agree on the kind of education that is worth publicly funding.

Which educational practices reflect our collective interest must be determined to some extent through democratic deliberations. If the politics of schooling does not leave room for such deliberations, we cannot say that public schooling reflects our collective interests. But neither can we say that public schooling is a collective good if it represses unpopular ideas, because a repressive education deprives future citizens of the capacity to think critically about, and to participate intelligently in, the politics that shape (among other things) school-ing in their society. For an educational system to be democratic, all children must be educated to participate intelligently in the politics that shape their society. Conscious social recon-struction is the core value of both democracy and democratic education: All adult members of a democratic society must be equipped by their education and authorized by political structures to share in ruling. Democratic education must not be rigged either to replicate existing institutions or to change them only in the interests of dominant groups.

To prevent education from being repressive, we must defend a principled limit on both political and parental authority, a limit that in practice require parents and governments to cede some educational authority to professional educators. The principled limit of nonrepres-sion prevents both majorities and minorities from using education to restrict rational deliberation of competing conceptions of the good life and the good society. Nonrepression is compatible with the use of education to inculcate those character traits – such as honesty, religious toleration, and mutual respect for persons – that serve as foundations for rational deliberation of differing ways of life. But nonrepression is incompatible with the use of education to prevent children from rationally evaluating differing ways of life. Rational deliberation remains the form of freedom most suitable to a democratic society. In a democracy, adults must be free to deliberate and disagree yet constrained to secure the intellectual grounds for deliberation and disagreement among children. The principle of non-repression prevents adults from using their present deliberative freedom to undermine the future deliberative freedom of children.

The ideal of democracy contains a principle of self-constraint. Citizens, public officials, and parents can use education to destroy democracy. One of the ways they can undermine the intellectual foundations of future democratic deliberations is by implementing policies that repress unpopular (but rational) ways of thinking. A democratic society must constrain itself – in the name of democracy itself – not to institute repressive educational policies. A demo-cratic theory of education therefore recognizes the importance not only of empowering citizens and their representatives (at various levels of government) to make educational policy, but also of constraining their choices among policies so as to secure the intellectual and social foundations of democratic deliberations in the future.

The democratic role of teachers

Democracy demands that citizens be authorized collectively to influence the purposes of schooling, but it also demands that they not be authorized to control the content of classroom teaching so as to repress reasonable challenges to dominant political and parental perspectives. Teachers who served simply to perpetuate the beliefs held by dominant majorities or minorities would be agents of political repression.

Without institutionalized challenges to political authority, governmental control over schooling could easily establish, as John Stuart Mill, in *On Liberty*, feared it would, a 'despotism over the mind'. At all levels of American government, political control over schools is challenged – and often shared – by other authorities: parents and parent-teacher associations, teachers and teachers' unions, accrediting associations, private foundations, civic groups and lobbying organizations (other than teachers' unions). Although all of these groups help shape what happens in American schools, the challenge posed by teachers and teachers' unions is by far the most significant in upholding the principle of nonrepression against majoritarian government. The division between majoritarian and nonmajoritarian control over schooling depends most crucially on the educational role we attribute to teachers and teachers' unions.

One way of conceiving of the division of educational authority between majoritarian governments (at federal, state and local levels) and teachers is as a complementary division of labor between popular authority and expertise: governments perpetuating a common culture, teachers cultivating the capacity for critical reflection on that culture. On this conception, the claim to educational expertise by teachers is both relative – to the role played by majoritarian governments in cultivating a common culture – and partial – it does not comprehend all of what matters in primary education. The professional responsibility of teachers is to uphold the principle of nonrepression by cultivating the capacity for democratic deliberation. Teachers serve to shed critical light on a democratically created culture.

The principle of nonrepression therefore not only constrains democratic authority, it also supplies democratic content to the concept of professionalism among teachers, requiring biology teachers, for example, to resist communal pressures to teach creationism instead of evolution (or even to give creationism equal time), and social studies teachers to develop their students' capacity to criticize popular policies from the perspective of mutually shared principles. More generally, nonrepression obligates teachers – at the same time as it authorizes them – to further democratic education by developing the preconditions for democratic deliberation among future generations of citizens. Prominent among those preconditions are two that Dewey defended as prototypically democratic – the recognition of common interests among citizens, and the related commitment to reconsider our individual interest in light of understanding the interests of others. To further these preconditions of democratic deliberation among their students, teachers must be sufficiently connected to their communities to understand the commitments that their students bring to school, and sufficiently detached to cultivate among their students the critical distance necessary to reconsider commitments in the face of conflicting ones.

Understood as the degree of autonomy – or insulation from external control – necessary to fulfill the democratic functions of office, professionalism completes rather than competes with democracy. On this prescriptive understanding of professionalism, the most prominent professions in our society have too much autonomy. Doctors and lawyers often claim, in the name of professionalism, authority over the rest of us far in excess of what their professional expertise warrants. Too much autonomy leads to 'the insolence of office' (Walzer 1983: 155). Too little autonomy, on the other hand, leads to what one might call "the ossification of office," from which, by almost all accounts, the teaching profession in the United States has long suffered. The rewards of professionalism – the pleasures of performance, high salary, status, and the exercise of authority over other people – are offered to a far smaller degree to far fewer teachers than in any of the other major professions in our society. The medical and legal professions suffer from a surplus of all but the first reward, while the teaching profession suffers from a deficit in all four categories.

The source of the first (and most serious) deficit – too few pleasures of performance – is surely not that teaching is an inherently unsatisfying or a socially unimportant profession. Even with its present problems, a majority of teachers say that they chose their career for its inherent satisfactions: they had a strong desire to teach, to serve society, or to be part of what they consider a worthy profession (Goodlad 1984: 171). Yet most teachers who begin with a sense of intellectual mission lose it after several years of teaching, and either continue to teach in an uninspired, routinized way or leave the profession to avoid intellectual stultification and emotional despair (Johnson 1988). A variety of recent studies support Seymour Sarason's findings that the structure of schools makes the daily work of most teachers so routinized that 'without exception, those who have been teaching for five or more years admitted that they no longer experienced their work with the enthusiasm, excitement, sense of mission, and challenge that they once did' (Sarason 1971: 163).

The salaries of teachers are also low, so low that many must moonlight in the summers when they (and their students) would be better off were they able to use summers to continue their education, to plan next year's courses, or to relax and thereby avoid the primary occupational hazard of teaching, early 'burn-out'. Teachers' salaries are far lower than those of comparably educated professionals. Relative to other salaried workers, teachers' salaries have increased very little in recent years although much more has been demanded of them: to cope with the effects of racial tensions and economic blight in our inner cities, an increased divorce rate among parents, the rise of drug use and unwanted pregnancies among teenagers, and so on.

Current salary levels attract more than enough applicants to fill teaching positions, but the quality of applicants is, by all accounts, low. The relatively poor pay of teachers discourages the best college students from entering the profession, and the slow rate of salary increases encourages the best teachers to leave (for two detailed descriptions – and excellent discussions – of the dimensions of this problem, see Boyer 1983: 165-174 and Sizer 1984: 183-187). Low salaries coupled with little autonomy on the job all but guarantee low social status. The recent increases in teachers' salary in some states do not come close to addressing the magnitude of this problem.

The ossification of office, like the insolence of office, therefore has structural sources: little control over work, low pay, and low social status. The teaching conditions in most public schools make it all but impossible for teachers to develop a positive sense of professionalism: 'an ethical code, a social bond, a pattern of mutual recognition and self-discipline' (Walzer 1977: 155; for the 'negative' senses of professionalism, see Larson 1977). Instead, most public schools encourage ossification by discouraging intellectual creativity:

> In the worst schools, teachers are demeaned and infantilized by administrators who view them as custodians, guardians, or uninspired technicians. In less grotesque settings, teachers are left alone with little adult interaction and minimal attention is given to their needs for support, reward, and criticism (Lightfoot 1983: 334).

Even in many of the best schools, the work load of full-time teachers is so great as to require them continually to compromise their judgment of what constitutes good teaching (see Sizer 1984: 9-21, Goodlad 1984: 193-195, and Boyer 1983: 155-161). Far more than doctors or lawyers, teachers make compromises in their professional standards for causes that are often entirely beyond their personal control: too many students, too little preparation time for teaching, too much administrative work, too little money to support their families. Some of these causes, however, may be within the collective power of teachers – organized by teachers' unions – to change.

Teachers' unions

Democratic authority stands between teachers and the insolence of office, but it also often promotes the ossification of office, by saddling teachers with heavy teaching schedules, crowded classrooms, low salaries, little time for collegial consultation, threats to their intellectual independence in the classroom, and/or rigid rules governing what and how to teach. The failure of democratic communities to support conditions under which the teaching profession would suffer neither from the insolence nor the ossification of office legitimates the organization of teachers into unions. The principle of nonrepression defines the democratic purpose of teachers' unions: to pressure democratic communities to create the conditions under which teachers can cultivate the capacity among students for critical reflection on democratic culture. It does not follow that all claims to educational authority or challenges to democratic control by teachers' unions are legitimate. We still need to ask how much authority unions should be granted over what school policies.

There is surely not a single correct answer to this question, but the democratic conception of professionalism provides principled guidance in avoiding two theoretically elegant but politically dangerous answers, which reflect alternative visions of democracy. One vision, of what one might call 'directed' democracy, sanctions the authority of unions above democratic communities to the extent that unions better represent educational expertise, even if unions thereby control the form and content of public schooling. The other vision, of 'strong' democracy (Barber 1984), sanctions all policies that result from negotiations between democratic communities and unions, even if the policies leave teachers with little or no autonomy in the classroom. The democratic conception of professionalism offers a critique of both visions and an alternative. The alternative is that teachers' unions be granted enough educational authority to overcome ossification of office but not so much as to convert teaching into a profession that, like medicine or law, is characterized by insolence of office. Union claims of educational expertise cannot in itself carry sufficient moral weight to override democratic authority. Being an expert in education is neither a necessary nor a sufficient condition for claiming authority over education in a democracy. The more compelling claim available to teachers' unions is that greater professional control over schooling is a necessary condition for upholding the principle of nonrepression. When democratic control over primary schools is so absolute as to render teachers unable to exercise intellectual discretion in their work: (1) few independently-minded people are attracted to teaching; (2) those who are attracted are frustrated in their attempts to think creatively and independently; and (3) those who either willingly or reluctantly conform to the demands of democratic authority teach an undemocratic lesson to their students – of intellectual deference to democratic authority. A democratic conception of professionalism supports those union claims to educational authority necessary to cultivating a democratically-tempered sense of professional mission among teachers.

The strongest rationale for the earliest demands of teachers' unions – for greater teacher participation in the administration of schools and the determination of educational policies – was this need to cede teachers more control over their work. When most of these demands were denied, the newly formed AFT directed its efforts toward establishing rights of collective bargaining with school boards, rights that they used to demand better pay and pensions for teachers on grounds that 'their professional and social standing is far too low to enable them to produce effective results in teaching' (Spring 1985: 215). This rationale for better pay still makes sense. Paying elementary and secondary teachers more is a necessary (but not sufficient) way to raise their quality, not because income is the sole measure of the status of teachers, but because the average salary of teachers today is *so* low as to discourage college graduates who have other options from choosing teaching as a career.

The pressing need to pay all teachers more is not good grounds for unions to oppose policies that would pay some teachers more than others on the basis of their better teaching. The institution of merit pay is another way of mitigating the ossification of office among the best teachers. If teaching is a profession, it must have a set of standards by which teachers can be judged better and worse. Unions can play an important role in preventing merit pay from becoming a political tool of administrators by elaborating those standards and insisting on their use in the evaluation of teachers. But to oppose merit pay on the ground that all teachers should be paid more or that no teachers should be subject to external evaluation is a form of professional insolence: an attempt to shield teachers from legitimate external evaluation. As long as the standards used to judge some teachers better than others are relevant to their social functions, the institution of merit pay can support the professionalism of teachers. Unions threaten to abuse their authority when they oppose the institution of merit pay, although they use it well in demanding better pay for all teachers.

Substantially raising teachers' salaries – across the board and on the basis of merit – is an obvious (probably even a necessary) means of supporting the professionalism of teachers, but certainly not a sufficient means. Democratic education depends not only upon attracting intellectually talented people with a sense of professional mission to teaching, but also upon cultivating and sustaining that sense during their careers as teachers (for the problems of sustaining a sense of professional mission among experienced teachers, see Jackson 1968: ch. 4, Brenton 1970, Sizer 1984, Lortie 1975, and Goodlad 1984). Unions therefore do not fulfill their democratic function just by demanding more money for teachers. They must also demand that schools be structured so as to sustain teachers in cultivating the capacity for critical deliberation in their classrooms. The limitations on democratic authority over schools suggested by this professional purpose are significant. To support professionalism among teachers, democratic communities must delegate a substantial degree of control over what happens in classrooms. Although a school board may establish the curriculum, it must not dictate how teachers choose to teach the established curriculum, as long as they do not discriminate against students or repress reasonable points of view. Although a school board may control the textbooks teachers use, it may not control how teachers use those textbooks (within the same principled constraints).[2] The rationale for so limiting democratic authority is straightforward: if primary school teachers cannot exercise intellectual independence in their classrooms, they cannot teach students to be intellectually independent.[3]

Too much independence, however, can be as bad as too little. If one thinks only of the best teachers, those with high intellectual standards and humane values, it may be hard to imagine the dangers of granting teachers too much 'academic freedom'. When one thinks less selectively of public primary school teachers, who now number about 2.5 million, the dangers of too much freedom are less difficult to discern. In the early years of public schooling in New York City, teachers resisted pressure by the Public School Society to abolish corporal punishment. After several unsuccessful attempts at abolition, the Public School Society managed to convince teachers not to cane children on the head (Kaestle 1973: 180-181). Although the United Federation of Teachers in New York City has never championed the cause of corporal punishment, it has championed – and won – a form of tenure for teachers that makes it extremely difficult for schools to dismiss incompetent or ineffective teachers: 'principals . . . shift a teacher to another school rather than go through the time-consuming dismissal procedure, which involved formal charges, substantiated evidence, and professional witnesses (Ravitch 1974: 318). The union's tenure rules have protected not only good teachers against punitive transfers or dismissals, but also incompetent and ineffective teachers against legitimate sanctions by local school districts. If there is a solution to this problem, it does not lie in giving school boards the authority, claimed by the demonstration districts in New York City in the late 1960's, to dismiss teachers without cause or review. A solution is more likely to lie in the institution of impartial review procedures, dominated by neither union nor school board.[4]

Although professionalism among public school teachers does not require absolute authority within the classroom, it requires more authority outside the classroom than most teachers now have. 'Good schools' treat teachers with what Sara Lightfoot (1983) calls 'respectful regard'. Principals of such schools invite teachers to participate as members of a profession – not only individually in the classroom but collectively in the school as a whole – in shaping the curriculum, disciplinary codes, graduation requirements, and their own working conditions. Teachers in good schools exemplify an important aspect of the democratic ideal of professionalism: the primary reward of their work is not high pay or social status, but the pleasures of performance and the satisfactions of social service. Their work is demanding but undemeaning, other-regarding but not other-directed.

The ability of unions to create these conditions of 'respectful regard' for teachers may be limited both by their self understanding and their legally sanctioned operation as collective bargaining agents of employees with management. If the democratic ideal of professionalism suggests that school boards and principals treat teachers as partners in determining school policy, then it also suggests that unions demand fewer fixed policies regarding curriculum, discipline, and work schedules, and more participatory structures within which teachers can join administrators and members of school boards in shaping these policies. The law may create a substantial disincentive to such a reorientation of union demands. Were unions successful in elevating teachers to the status of sharing in the 'management' or 'ownership' of schools, courts might rescind the right of unions to represent teachers in collective bargaining over salaries and other working conditions. Although there has never been a test case with regard to public schools, the Supreme Court in 1980 ruled (in a 5-to-4 decision) against faculty members who were organizing a union at Yeshiva University on grounds that they were not employees but managers, who were 'substantially and pervasively operating the enterprise'.[5] Were public school teachers ever to participate as extensively as college professors in shaping their work, such a decision would be a much bigger blow to unionism than to professionalism.[6] The gain in professional autonomy and status among public school teachers would overwhelm the loss in union bargaining rights. But the prospects of such a (premature) loss may deter unions from fighting as hard for structural changes as they do for economic improvements in the status of teachers.

Teachers' unions are ideally an interim solution to the problem of professional ossification, but the interim is likely to last a long time given the obstacles now standing in the way of teachers gaining a greater role in shaping school policy. Many of the most difficult obstacles to overcome have been erected not by local communities but by city, state, and federal governments in the form of regulations governing (among other things) curriculum, hiring and firing standards, salary and workload of teachers, the academic calendar, and the education of handicapped and other disadvantaged children. Some of these obstacles – such as the federal requirement to provide adequate schooling for all handicapped children – should not be overcome until local educational authorities can be trusted to carry out the educational purposes that the requirements are intended to serve. Other obstacles ought not to be so considered: regulations concerning minimum graduation requirements are appropriately set by more centralized political authorities and interfere very little, if at all, with the ability of teachers to exercise substantial control over their work. At John F. Kennedy High School in the Bronx, for example, 'it is not the numbers of state or city required courses that cause rancor among teachers and administrators. They seem to be perceived as relatively neutral guidelines shaped by a convincing intellectual rationale . . . ' (Lightfoot, 1983: 112). Most good schools, like Kennedy, supplement the state and city requirements.

Other requirements, however, are unnecessary barriers to achieving an appropriate degree of autonomy for teachers. At Kennedy High School, 'the complaints surrounding external regulation tend to be focused on the requirements of staff responsibilities . . . ' The city requires monthly departmental and faculty meetings, teacher supervision and evaluation of written lesson plans. The union has successfully resisted some of these requirements; its contract gives teachers the right not to comply with requests for written lesson plans, for example. By its regulations, the city tries to prevent teachers from shirking some of their duties. By its resistance, the union tries to prevent the city from overworking teachers or imposing unreasonable requirements on them. The city's regulations call for the union's resistance, but without externally imposed regulation or resistance, teachers would be better able to achieve a sense of professional autonomy and probably more willing to work harder. As one teacher at Kennedy High put it: 'Somehow the edict from on high makes us all respond like resistant children who would rather go out and play' (Lightfoot, 1983: 113).

Edicts from the federal government elicit the most criticism. The criticism is often too sweeping, since some federal requirements – such as those that prevent schools from excluding disadvantaged children from an adequate education – have the compelling democratic rationale of overcoming discrimination. The criticism is well directed, however, at other federal regulations, such as the *Lau* Remedies and the 1978 Amendments to the Bilingual Education Act of 1968 (Title VII of the Elementary and Secondary School Act of 1965). Although neither repressive nor discriminatory, the *Lau* Remedies and the 1978 Amendments put the federal government in a doubly inappropriate position, first, of dictating a pedagogical approach of disputed and unproven efficacy to teachers and, second, of superseding the diverse views of ethnic communities on the value of bilingual education (versus alternatives such as more intensive English instruction) in public schools. If bilingual education is valued as means of teaching English to non-English speaking children, but bilingual techniques have not been proven generally more effective than other techniques (such as intensive English instruction), then teachers should play a substantial role in determining which pedagogical methods are used for different groups of students.[7] If bilingualism also is valued for enabling ethnic communities to preserve their cultural heritage and identity, then those communities – rather than the federal government – should be empowered to decide whether and how they wish to preserve their culture through bilingual education.

The *Lau* Remedies and the 1978 Amendments signaled a shift of federal involvement in bilingual education from financially supporting all pedagogical programs that met 'the special language skill needs of national origin-minority group children'[8] to requiring public schools to educate all groups of limited English-speaking students bilingually as a condition of receiving federal support. In the course of this shift, the federal government limited the autonomy of teachers without furthering the self-determination of ethnic communities. The *Lau* Remedies and the 1978 Amendments left teachers with considerably less collective influence over the shape of schooling and ethnic communities with little (if any) more.

While the conflict over community control in New York City illustrated the tension between teachers' autonomy and local democratic authority, the controversy over bilingualism illustrates the tension between centralized authority and *both* teachers' autonomy and local democratic control. The latter tension is more pervasive today than the former, and probably more destructive of professional autonomy. As school districts in the United States have consolidated over the past fifty years (from over 127,000 in 1932 to under 17,000 in 1982), the size of schools and their administrations have grown. Layers of administrative decisions now insulate the policies of school boards and the preferences of ethnic communities within local school districts from the potentially critical perspective of teachers, and vice versa, overwhelming a potentially creative tension within democratic education between communal and professional authority, whereby communities and teachers are encouraged to take each others' educational priorities and programs seriously.

We cannot return to the small schoolhouse of the nineteenth-century nor would we be wise to abolish educational administration. Large schools districts have some significant advantages over small ones, such as the ability to offer a broader curriculum and therefore to meet the needs of a wider variety of students. And administrators perform some valuable functions, not the least of which include lightening the administrative burdens of teachers. But the advantages of large administrations are often offset by more significant disadvantages, such as the insulation of school policies from public scrutiny, the demoralization of teachers, and the alienation of students. One way of combining the advantages of bigness with those of smallness, suggested by Ernest Boye, is to organize large schools into several smaller 'schools-within-a-school' (1983: 235). It is important to recognize, however, that the smallness of the subunits themselves would be insufficient to overcome the problems of professionalism created by large administrations, unless those subunits were also to a significant extent professionally self-governing and accountable to a public for their educational policies. So conceived, schools-within-a-school can prevent educational bureaucracies from destroying professional autonomy while creating the potential for more local participation in the making of school policy. By empowering both teachers and concerned citizens in local communities, schools-within-a-school can preserve the democratically healthy tension between professional and communal judgment.

Democracy within schools

The professionalism of teachers, properly defined, serves as a safeguard against repression and discrimination. But professionalism, even on this democratic definition, erects another obstacle to democratic education. The professional autonomy of teachers stands in tension with democratic education to the extent that teachers invoke their professional competence to deny students any influence in shaping the form or content of their own education. The solution to this problem cannot be to give students equal control over the conditions of their schooling. Students lack the competence necessary to share equally in making many decisions. Ceding them equal control on all issues would mean denying teachers even a minimal degree of professional autonomy. The problem of authority within schools, therefore, does not lend itself to the democratic solution of political equality. Yet neither does it lend itself to the most apparent alternative to democratic rule: professional autonomy based upon competence. Insofar as professional autonomy teaches deference to authority, it teaches a lesson in conflict with the conditions of democratic deliberation.

Whether professional authority teaches deference to authority or respect for high intellectual standards is partly an empirical question concerning the effects of different methods of teaching, partly a normative question of what professionalism requires. One way of answering the empirical question is to investigate the extent to which schools that are more internally democratic support the development of more democratic values among students. This investigation runs up against the obvious empirical difficulty of controlling in a non-experimental setting for the many other variables that also distinguish more from less democratic schools or students who choose to participate in more democratic schools within a school from those who do not. A student from Brookline's School-Within-a-School (SWS) – where students share authority with teachers over a remarkably wide range of decisions – comments that 'In SWS people care about learning. There is a real sense of community.' Although this sentiment is widely shared among SWS students, one cannot assume that it is a product of SWS schooling. SWS students tend to be 'a much more homogeneous group than the diversity reflected in the school at large' (Lightfoot, 1983: 187). They probably enter SWS with a commitment – or at least a predisposition – to participation.

Students who are predisposed neither to participation nor to learning present the greater challenge to a democratic conception of teaching because their negative attitude toward schooling can readily reinforce a purely disciplinary method of teaching: teachers assert their authority, first, to produce order and, then, to funnel a body of knowledge into students. Some teachers who are not otherwise committed to the disciplinary method use it when they teach students in the lowest academic tracks.[9] The disciplinary method may be the easiest way to educate students who do not want to be educated. Perhaps more importantly, if education fails, disorder does not ensue (at least not in the classroom). A disciplinary approach therefore recommends itself over 'nondirective guidance, which, in gist, means copping out – abdicating the teachers' responsibilities and leaving pupils to work out their own "development" '. But, as Harry Eckstein points out: 'One style will hardly shape democratic character; the other will not shape anything at all'(Eckstein, 1984: 122).

In practice, however, teachers' options are not this stark even in classrooms of unmotivated students. Teachers committed to a more participatory approach appear to be more successful both in getting their students to work and in increasing their commitment to learning than teachers who take a more disciplinary approach.[10] Participatory approaches aim to increase students' commitment to learning by building upon and extending their existing interests in intellectually productive ways.[11] To the extent that a participatory approach builds upon students' interests and elicits their commitment to learning, it may be considered more democratic than a disciplinary approach.

By the same criterion, school practices outside the classroom may be considered more or less democratic. The day after Martin Luther King was assassinated, one desegregated junior high school in Berkeley held an assembly exclusively under faculty initiative and planning, while a second, with a similar student body, turned over the plans for its assembly primarily to the students. In the first school, the program was largely nonparticipatory. Most of the students on stage were white and almost exclusively from the high academic tracks. The program in the second school, by contrast, 'provided for more audience participation. It was universally praised as a moving experience, even by the "old guard" teachers. The usually restless and noisy assembly audience was attentive and quiet even through a period of silent meditation' (Metz, 1978: 231). The participants, chosen by the students, were a more diverse group. Although the second school was less orderly, even its lower-track students were more engaged in its life. The students generally seemed 'more independent, reflective and insightful about their education, and in many cases more directly responsive to the activities and conditions which support the fulfillment of the school's educational goals'. But they were also (according to one sympathetic observer) more disorderly and 'arrogant' than students in the first school (p. 228).

The choice of a participatory approach may not bring all good things in its wake. Ideally, students in the second school would also be orderly and humble. A participatory approach gives priority to cultivating self-esteem and social commitment over humility and order, a priority presumed by the democratic goal of educating citizens willing and able to participate in politics. But because not all good things go together in education any more than in life, this priority is not absolute; it should be overridden when disorder and arrogance are so great as to threaten the very enterprise of education within schools.[12]

Existing studies are by no means definitive in their findings of the educative effects of more democratic methods. More empirical data would help us judge the effect of democracy within schools on cultivating participatory virtues – a sense of social commitment, political efficacy, a desire to participate in politics, respect for opposing points of view, critical distance from authority, and so on. Were teachers to discover that more democratic methods better stimulated the development of these virtues, they would still have to consider how much emphasis to give to developing them. The purposes of primary education – even the democratic purposes – are not exhausted by the successful cultivation of the participatory virtues. The disciplinary virtues – the imparting of knowledge and instilling of emotional along with intellectual discipline – are also among the purposes of democratic education, and apparently they are not always most effectively taught by the most democratic methods, especially among those students least committed to learning. The question of how much democracy within schools is democratically desirable remains doubly difficult to answer, therefore, because we have incomplete data on the educative effects of more democratic methods and because we rightly value the disciplinary as well as the participatory purposes of primary education.

Without more empirical evidence, we cannot say precisely how much democracy in schools is desirable, but we can say something significant about the way the professional standards of teachers should and should not be defined. Many teachers conceive of teaching the participatory virtues as lying beyond – or at best on the periphery of – their professional obligations, the core of their professional obligation being to teach what I have called the disciplinary virtues. This understanding is based on two misconceptions, one related to the means and the other to the ends of democratic education. Students generally learn best when they have a prior commitment to what they are being required to learn.[13] Many, perhaps most, students enter school lacking such a prior commitment.[14] Permitting students to participate in determining aspects of their education generally serves to develop a commitment on their part to learning.[15] Among the least motivated students, however, a participatory method can entail compromising what many teachers consider the demands of professional competence. In the study cited above, teachers committed to the participatory approach occasionally allowed their lower-track students to engage in some classroom activities that were 'not officially acceptable' (but harmless) in order to elicit concentrated effort for those academic activities the teachers deemed educationally most important. The additional work and concentration that such teachers thereby elicited from lower-track students was, according to Mary Metz, 'modest, not miraculous.' Yet the participatory teachers, Metz comments, 'got their students to work seriously for a larger proportion of their time in class than did teachers who officially required them to work all the time but were pushed by constant disruptions into using up their resources for control on matters other than directly academic effort.'[16] Metz's study suggests that more democratic methods may be a means of motivating students to develop even the disciplinary virtues.

The ends of democratic education are, of course, not limited to teaching disciplinary as distinct from participatory virtues. Even the ability to think critically about politics is an incomplete virtue from a democratic perspective. If primary schooling leaves students with a capacity for political criticism but no capacity for political participation or sense of social commitment, either because it fails to cultivate their sense of political efficacy or because it succeeds in teaching them deference to authority, then it will have neglected to cultivate a virtue essential to democracy.[17] Although we lack enough evidence to say how much internal democracy is necessary to cultivate participatory virtues among students, the low levels of political participation in our society and the high levels of autocracy within most schools point to the conclusion that the cultivation of participatory virtues should become more prominent among the purposes of primary schooling, especially as children mature intellectually and emotionally, and become more capable of engaging in free and equal discussion with teachers and their peers.

How much internal democratization of schools is desirable in a democracy? Dewey conceived of an ideal, democratic school as a 'miniature community, an embryonic society' (Dewey 1956: 18), but he never specified which structures of a democratic school correspond to those of a democratic society. If the Laboratory School at the University of Chicago under Dewey's leadership from 1896–1903 is evidence of the structures he would support, then Dewey's characterization of school as a miniature democratic community is misleading.[18] Dewey treated teachers at the Lab School as colleagues: they met with him weekly to discuss curriculum and other educational matters. Teachers also had a free period daily to discuss their work with other teachers. Students did not have the same freedom, authority or influence as teachers over the curriculum or the structure of their schooling, but they too were encouraged to engage in far more collective deliberation and decision making than is common in most primary schools. Classes at the Lab School often began with 'council meetings' in which teachers discussed past work and planned future work with students. The youngest students were given the daily responsibility of collectively distributing and carrying out important tasks. Judging by its efforts to teach participatory virtues, the Lab School was more democratic than all but a few American elementary and secondary schools. It was an embryonic democratic society because it elicited a commitment to learning and cultivated the prototypically democratic virtues among its students, not because it treated them as the political or intellectual equals of its teachers. The most internally democratic schools typically balance the participatory and the disciplinary purposes of education, leaving some significant educational decisions – such as the content of the curriculum and the standards for promotion – largely (but often not entirely) to the determination of teachers and administrators.[19]

That an ideal democratic school is not as democratic as an ideal democratic society should not disenchant us either with schooling or democracy, since democracies depend on schools to prepare students for citizenship. Were students ready for citizenship, compulsory schooling – along with many other educational practices that deny students the same rights as citizens – would be unjustifiable. It would, on the other hand, be remarkable if the best way to prepare students for citizenship were to deny them both individual and collective influence in shaping their own education. The most democratic schools, like Dewey's Lab School and Brookline's SWS do not look like miniature societies, at least not like miniature democratic societies: teachers have much more authority, both formal and informal, than democratic legislators have, or ideally should have. But these schools do come close to living up to the educational standard dictated by democratic values: democratize schools to the extent necessary to cultivate the participatory along with the disciplinary virtues of democratic character. If, as Dewey argued (1966 [1916]: 99), a democratic society requires that citizens have 'a personal interest in social relationships and control, and the habits of mind which secure social changes without introducing disorder' then a substantial degree of democracy within schools will be useful, probably even necessary (although undoubtedly not sufficient), to creating democratic citizens.

It is up to principals and teachers, taking upon themselves the considerable burdens of professional obligation, to foster this degree of democracy within schools, along with the disciplinary virtues that are also essential to democracy. But it is up to democratic citizens and their representatives to create the working conditions under which principals and teachers, mere mortals like the rest of us, can be reasonably expected to live up to their professional obligations, which will be extremely demanding even under the best of possible circumstances. The vast majority of teachers and principals must now cope with far from the best.

A detailed program of democratic reform is beyond the scope of this essay, but it may be helpful to suggest some directions for change, other than the obvious ones of decreasing (often counterproductive) centralization and bureaucratization of school systems. Several essays in this volume describe in detail other, less obvious obstacles to the development of democratic professionalism that are within the power of educational authorities to overcome. The regulation of teaching often stifles rather than encourages responsibility and creativity among teachers. Democratic professionalism does not encourage teachers to take over (or eliminate) the jobs of school administrators and educational policymakers. Rather it recommends a goal more in keeping with the aspirations of most teachers: that 'teachers be granted authority, either alone or jointly with administrators, over specific matters that directly affect their teaching – the instructional schedule, the allocation of the supplies budget, the discipline code' (Johnson 1988). Democratic professionalism does not recommend that competency testing be abolished, but rather that such tests not be used as surrogate standards for good teaching. If states implement competency testing in a way that takes responsibility for good teaching out of the hands of teachers, teachers and teaching will simultaneously suffer, with little likelihood of long-term improvement in anyone's education.[20] A democratic theory of education of course cannot substitute for practical thinking about the design and implementation of educational policies, but it can alert us to the hypocrisy of holding teachers up to demanding standards of professional responsibility while denying them working conditions conducive to the satisfaction of those standards.

Notes

1. Q: Why shouldn't schools teach about sexual choices?
A: Because such choices pertain to values, and schools should leave the teaching of values to the family and the church.
2. Although democratic communities *may* unilaterally select textbooks, they would be wise to consult with teachers and leave them with a considerable range of choice, for the sake of both choosing better texts and retaining good teachers. 'It's fine to talk about getting new and talented people into teaching through higher salaries or other means', Saul Cooperman, the New Jersey Commissioner of Education commented. 'But unless you can also get these teachers more involved in choosing curricula, selecting textbooks and shaping grading policies, they may not stay around very long' (*The New York Times*, Sunday, 27 April 1986).
3. 'Teachers must feel inspired and committed to educational goals in order to be in a position to light the fire in students' (Lightfoot 339).
4. The 'Yeshiva Plan' outlined such a procedure for empowering local school boards in New York City to fire teachers while protecting teachers against arbitrary dismissal. The plan was initially approved by union and community representatives, but the UFT withdrew their approval when the central Board of Education decided not to give the demonstration districts any additional funds to support improvements in educational services (smaller classes, a new reading program, a training program for community leaders by teachers and one for teachers by community leaders, and additional professional services [see Ravitch 1974: 313-319].
5. *National Labor Relations Board v. Yeshiva University*, 444 U.S. No. 78-857, pp. 679-691 (1979), see Angell 1981.
6. In ruling against unionism at Yeshiva, the Court found that professors determined curriculum, grading systems, graduation standards, academic calendars and course schedules, and were consulted in all hiring, tenure, firing, and promotion decisions.
7. For a review of the evidence on the effectiveness of bilingualism compared to intensive instruction in English among different types of students, see Rotberg, 1982: 155–163.
8. Samuel Pottinger, 'Identification of discrimination and denial of services on the basis of national origin', memorandum, Office of Civil Rights, US Dept. of Health, Education, and Welfare, 25 May 1970, quoted by Rotberg 1981: 151.
9. Metz (1978) calls this method 'proto-authority' (see pp. 59-62, 101–110).
10. See Metz (1978: 115–116). What I call the participatory approach is similar to what Metz calls the developmental approach.
11. Metz can be compared here with Whitehead 1967 [1929]: 29–41.
12. This priority is overridden even in the most self-consciously democratic of schools, such as Summerhill. 'For example, one safety rule is that kids under a certain age may not possess matches or knives. These safety rules are arbitrary, and are not subject to change by the weekly General Meeting' Popenoe 1970: 28.
13. The Coleman Report, for example, found that 'of all the variables measured in the survey, the attitudes of student interest in school, self concept, and sense of environmental control show the strongest relation to achievement' (Coleman, *et al.*: 319).
14. For the problems of getting students involved in their work, and additional evidence of the relationship between involvement and learning, see Jackson 1968: 85–111; see also Metz 1978: esp. 91–144.
15. 'For apart from the fact that fruitful suggestions may develop from such discussions [between students and teacher], there is at least one thing that is known about learning, which is that it tends to improve if the learners begin to feel involved in and responsible for their learning situation' (Peters 1973: 49).

16. Metz's analysis (pp. 115–116) suggests that the results in the lower tracks might have been less modest than it appeared, since once students were successful they were moved into the next higher track. Her further observation fuels the case against tracking: those who might have become leaders and exemplars for the rest of the class were 'drawn upward and out leaving the bottom tracks always populated with the slow or unwilling' (p. 116).

17. Richard Peters makes a similar argument (1973: 51–52).

18. For a detailed description of the 'Dewey School', see Mayhew and Edwards 1966; see also Sarason's favorable discussion, (1971: 195–211).

19. Cf. Metz 1978: 118–19: 'This attraction of competent teachers to roughly similar [developmental] styles suggests that competent teaching may require an assumption that teacher and student share goals – or perhaps better it may require the creation of such sharing in actuality. It may also require that a middle ground be struck between total dominance of the teacher and predominance of the student.'

20. See Corbett and Wilson (1988) for a detailed account of these and other problems in implementing competency testing.

References

ANGELL, G. W. (1981) *Faculty and Teacher Bargaining: The Impact of Unions on Education* (Lexington, MA: D.C. Heath).

BARBER, B. (1984) *Strong Democracy: Participatory Politics for a New Age* (Berkeley, CA: University of California Press).

BOYER, E.L. (1983) *High School: A Report on Secondary Education in America* (New York: Harper & Row).

BRENTON, M. (1970) *What's Happened to Teacher?* (New York: Coward McCann).

COLEMAN, J.S. *et al.* (1966) *Equality of Educational Opportunity* (Washington, DC: GPO).

CORBETT, H.D. and WILSON, B.L. (1988) 'Raising the stakes in statewide mandatory testing programs', in J. Hannaway and R. Crowson (eds.) *The Politics of Reforming School Administration* (London: Falmer Press).

DEWEY, J. (1916) *Democracy and Education* (New York's Free Press, 1966).

DEWEY, J. (1956) 'The School and Society', in *The Child and the Curriculum and the School and Society* (Chicago: University of Chicago Press).

ECKSTEIN, H. (1984) 'Civic inclusion and its discontents', *Daedalus*, 113(4), p. 122.

GOODLAD, J. (1984) *A Place Called School: Prospects for the Future* (New York: McGraw-Hill).

JACKSON, P.W. (1968) *Life in Classrooms* (New York: Holt, Rinehart & Winston).

JOHNSON, S.M. (1988) 'Schoolwork and its reform', in J. Hannaway and R. Crowson (eds.) *The Politics of Reforming School Administration* (London: Falmer Press).

KAESTLE, C. F. (1973) *The Evolution of an Urban School System: New York City, 1750–1850* (Cambridge, MA: Harvard University Press).

KANT, I. (1900) *Über Pädagogik/On Education*, trans. Annette Churton (Boston: D.C. Heath).

LARSON, M.S. (1977) *The Rise of Professionalism: A Sociological Analysis* (Berkeley, CA: University of California Press).

LIGHTFOOT, S.L. (1983) *The Good High School* (New York: Basic Books).

LORTIE, D. (1975) *Schoolteacher: A Sociological Study* (Chicago: University of Chicago Press).

MAYHEW, K.C. and EDWARDS, A.C. (1966) *The Dewey School* (New York: Atherton).

METZ, M.H. (1978) *Classrooms and Corridors: The Crisis of Authority in Desegregated Secondary Schools* (Berkeley, CA: University of California Press).

NATIONAL COMMISSION ON EXCELLENCE IN EDUCATION (1983) *A Nation at Risk: The Imperative for Educational Reform* (Washington, DC: GPO).

PETERS, R. (1973) *Authority, Responsibility and Education* (London: Allen & Unwin).

POPENOE, J. (1970) *Inside Summerhill* (New York: Hart).

RAVITCH, D. (1974) *The Great School Wars, New York City 1805–1973: A History of the Public Schools as Battlefields of Social Change* (New York: Basic Books).

ROTBERG, I. C. (1982) 'Some legal and research considerations in establishing federal policy in bilingual education', *Harvard Educational Review* 52, pp. 155–163.

SARASON, S.B. (1971) *The Culture of the School and the Problem of Change* (Boston: Allyn & Bacon).

SIZER, T. R. (1984) *Horace's Compromise: The Dilemma of the American High School* (Boston: Houghton Mifflin).

SPRING, J. (1985) *American Education: An Introduction to Social and Political Aspects* (New York: Longman).

US News & World Report (1980) 'Sex Education in public schools? Interview with Jacqueline Kasun', *USN & WR*, 89 (14), p. 89.

WALZER, M. (1983) *Spheres of Justice* (New York: Basic Books).

WHITEHEAD, A. N. (1929) 'The rhythmic claims of freedom and discipline', in *The Aims of Education and Other Essays* (New York: Free Press, 1967).

Commentary

Scott D. Thomson
National Association of Secondary School Principals

> No duty the executive had
> to perform was so trying as
> to put the right man in the
> right place

THOMAS JEFFERSON

Finding the right man or woman to lead schools today would challenge the veracity of anyone, even Solomon. That wise king, at least, understood clearly the problem to be resolved when facing the two women and single child. He also possessed no qualms about his role or political authority.

As the authors of this *Yearbook* point out, however, consensus today is limited on the responsibilities and political relationships of school administrators. Generally it's a muddle 'out there' in the public arena where principals and superintendents attempt to exercise their roles under the mandate of school reform. Almost every interest group is calling for effective school leadership, but often the messages are contradictory.

Some clear thinking is essential to focus upon the major issues and to sketch solutions. Fortunately, important strides are made in this document toward that end. The forces of school reform, from national report to state mandate to school site politics, are all recorded, along with thoughtful analyses of their impact upon school administration and its reform.

For example, principals and superintendents would agree with Corbett and Wilson that state-mandated testing is a high stakes game that increases the political significance of measurement at the local level. Furthermore, the rigorous state-mandated graduation requirements of the mid-1980s diminish the political significance of local standards as Fuhrman points out. Looking more directly at the school site, Bacharach and Shedd clearly express the dilemma of principals who balance the expectations of teachers as autonomous professionals against the broader requirements that the school be a 'purposeful bureaucracy'.

Perhaps the influence of two major players, the local school boards and the national foundations, is too lightly examined. Since the 15,600 school boards located across the nation are the actual employers and terminators of principals and superintendents, their political leverage is substantial. As elected representatives of the community, they exercise far more immediate power than can any other player in public education. Furthermore, given the proclivities of human nature, many individual school board members exercise direct political influence on school administrators across the full spectrum of school affairs, from the length of the school year to textbook selection to interscholastic athletics.

As both policy formulator and employer, local school boards wear large boots. Their decisions are implemented by school administrators. For public schools, as with other public agencies, the elected layman has the last word unless recalled by the electorate. Sometimes board decisions are unpopular, but unpopular or not, the school administrator is expected to implement those decisions. Sometimes board decisions draw the ire of teachers, with principals the immediate object of that criticism.

We can argue for a more democratic profession, as does Gutman. Teachers, as professionals, should influence school boards. Educational problems should be 'publicly debated'. The bottom line in public schools, however, is the board vote. Professional educators may disagree with that vote, but the decision is accountable – not by 'educational experts' – but to the local public and its various taxpaying constituencies. In private schools, professionals may have stronger leverage. Certainly the university professional is largely untouched by the immediate impact of public opinion. Public schools face that opinion consistently and directly.

National foundations possess formidable political power. They don't govern schools, but their prestige, their access to the national media, and their funds combine for major influence. For example, foundations have bankrolled all of the major reforms except *A Nation At Risk*. Beginning with Ernest Boyer's *High School* in 1984, continuing with the three volumes of Ted Sizer's *A Study of High Schools* and the Carnegie Forum's *A Nation Prepared*, and including the many current volumes on 'at risk' youth, foundations have been the initiators of major political agendas for the public schools.

Traditionally it has been almost unAmerican to criticize foundation initiatives in public education. After all, the Ford Foundation created the curriculum reforms of the 1960s before it retired to other quests. A black hole of inattention to secondary education followed during the 1970s. Now, in the 1980s, schools are again important enough for the major foundations to become involved.

Foundations are probably this nation's best example of a lay church. Their motives supposedly are almost sacramental. They contribute concepts and conversation and funds to the public good. Many school administrators, however, believe that some foundation work of late falls below those expectations. For example, practitioners question the Carnegie Forum's proposal to lead schools with executive committees of teachers. How is this proposal substantiated by leadership theory or by practice in large institutions, they ask? Are foundations doing sufficient homework before launching proposals?

Meanwhile, the 'movement' has been launched, and school administrators feel the political pressure to respond knowledgeably and with an open mind. Foundations do demonstrably alter the political landscape for school professionals.

A deluge of political forces

The past three decades have brought successive wave of change to the school campus, all with political impact. The era began with Sputnik and the major curriculum reform which followed. It will be useful to describe briefly the major forces as they washed against the school door, and to examine their implications for the current policies of school reform.

Sputnik decade, 1958–1967

The national response to Sputnik spawned a remarkable effort to reform the curriculum and organization of schools. Major elements of that reform included a complete recasting of the science curriculum (PSSC physics, BSCS biology, Chem Study chemistry) and of the mathematics curriculum (SMSG mathematics). The entire foreign language program was revamped with the electronic language laboratories. Thousands of teachers and administrators attended programs funded by the National Defense Education Act to master the new programs.

Public pressure to make schools better places to learn reflected the views of progressive school administrators. For example, the National Commission for the Utilization of Staff was launched by the National Association of Secondary School Principals to recognize schools for instruction (Trump 1958). This effort focused first upon 'team teaching' with small group and large group instruction, and then evolved into the flexible scheduling movement with new computer-generated scheduling programs developed simultaneously at Stanford University and at the Massachusetts Institute of Technology. Some prominent secondary schools, for example Evanston Township High School in Illinois, completely renovated their buildings to accommodate flexible groupings and time periods. About 300 new schools were constructed, as well, on the flexible template.

School administrators were in the middle of planning and inplementing efforts to recognize schools for instruction in other concurrent programs, as well, to include the Kettering Foundation's IDEA program which focused upon designing sub-units of teachers and students. Analysts today who conclude that principals have never been involved intimately with the instructional program simply ignore the Sputnik era in public schools. The political pressures of the early 1960s required principals to make curriculum and instruction their central priority.

Political–legal decade, 1968–1977

Student activism hit high schools like a thunderbolt in September 1967. In a matter of months, schools were immersed in the politics of Vietnam up to their mortarboards. Students, under new schemes for open scheduling, began to use their independent study time for guerrilla theater instead of chemistry projects. Sylvia Hoyt Williams, a teacher in Palo Alto, California describes a typical incident in the book, *Hassling*:

> At a regular meeting of the large and active Palo Alto-Stanford Democratic Club, the scheduled subject was 'Student Power', and the scheduling was a good topic which should have commanded considerable community interest, but attendance from the Club's membership was light that Monday evening, November 25. The radical young were there in full force, however. The word had been passed to come and they were there, smoking up a storm, most of the girls in jeans, a few boys looking a little stoned.
>
> Perhaps it was unfair for the *Catamount* reporter to call the meeting 'one-sided' or 'stacked', for the topic was student power, why shouldn't the speakers be student power advocates or participants? Who better could 'tell it like it is'? Furthermore, the panel included (besides Chris Menchine, Tim Wise and a Stanford graduate student) Dr Scott Thomson and Mrs Agnes Robinson, a liberal board member whose five sons had attended or were attending another Palo Alto high school.
>
> Mrs Robinson spoke first and came out foursquare for student power and more of it. 'Student power doesn't exist yet in our schools but it ought to', she declared, recommending less authoritarianism in the schools so that they could develop responsible citizens. 'Our country will sink or swim, depending on how well this age group can handle responsibility', she concluded.
>
> If she had not spoken first but had been able to listen to the three students and Dr Thomson, possibly Mrs Robinson would have modified her remarks. I doubt it, even though she clarified them later. She spoke with sincerity and intelligence and said what

she believed. The difference was a matter of semantics: she meant something different by 'student power' from what the student speakers meant, as was clear when they went on to attack 'top-down thinking', 'bureaucratic decision-making', the schools as 'training centers', lack of student control over their own lives, the 'dehumanizing' act of signing attendance slips, and finally, inevitably 'the group of people who are there to contain change – the administrators'. It should be noted that Mrs Robinson and the students agreed absolutely that there must be changes in the public school system.

When Dr Thomson spoke, he was as frank as he had ever been about student power. He had had some difficult and illuminating experiences, and it appeared as though he had chosen this forum, where he undoubtedly expected to address a group made up principally of adults, to express some of his doubts about the student power movement. I attended the meeting with Ray Fleming, the black social studies teacher whose son was on the student cabinet; Bill was there that night too. As Dr Thomson stepped to the microphone, he appeared every inch the successful young high school principal – dressed conservatively in a dark suit, his hair carefully groomed, and a definite air of confidence and control in his straight, easy carriage and his intelligent face. Yet the moment he began speaking, the open scorn and hostility of the young people present were evident. They moved around, snickered, blew out smoke ferociously and contemptuously, laughed openly when he spoke of the range of activists 'from anarchists and Maoists to leftist socialists to traditional liberals', and hissed when he suggested publicly for the first time that some students were 'being used' by adults outside the schools 'for ulterior motives'.

While he declared his sympathy with their desire to have 'their share in the decision-making', he openly admitted that he had come to feel 'some disillusion' with the activists as a group; he was 'apprehensive of their tactics of confrontation, intimidation, and contempt for majority rule in government'. This last remark brought a howl. Flushing slightly, tight-lipped, Dr Thomson sat down. Ray Fleming and I exchanged looks, probably appearing as tight-lipped ourselves, and when Chris Menchine spoke next, Ray scribbled out a note – three words in his big sprawling hand: 'Garbage! I'm sick!' (Williams 1970).

Principals clearly were facing a brand new political landscape. Some survived and some did not adjust quickly enough to survive.

Partisan politics had become more prominent in school board elections by 1970, as well. For example the non-partisan, neighborhood-based caucus system used by many suburban Chicago school districts to nominate school board members was replaced by a two-candidate system, each with thinly disguised support from the local Democratic or Republican organization. Schools, traditionally screened from partisan political activity as 'consensus institutions', became jousting grounds for the major political issues of the decade; military draft and military service, racial integration, the war in Southeast Asia, rights of minors, legalization of drugs, Cuba and Che Gueverra, and trimming the power of 'The Establishment'.

These powerful political movements constitute two of the many factors which pushed principals suddenly to understand that the public had dropped the old agenda of better instruction for the new agenda of social change. This message came most clearly from Supreme Court decisions, such as *Tinker*, that restricted the authority of local school boards and their school administrators to monitor student First Amendment rights. Additionally, litigation against schools became commonplace. For example, two attorneys in 1970 handled all of the legal work of all school districts in northern Illinois. By 1974, three law firms in Chicago were devoting their major attention to school litigation.

Collective bargaining for teachers and programs for racial integration were other major political forces of the day. Schools were viewed as vehicles for change, and change was coming at a furious pace. Principals and superintendents became the point men on this march. Blase is accurate about the vulnerability of schools to pressure. Few principals, however, expected 'absolute and unquestioning obedience' during that era or since.

Academic decade, 1978–1988

Angry political hyperactivism waned during the Bicentennial celebrations of 1976, and by 1978 had been overshadowed by the omnipresent 'smiley' buttons on everyone's lapels. Schools became happier places; students and adults declared a truce; civility made a comeback.

New political pressures, now academic once again rather than social and legal, appeared with the passage by Oregon of minimum competency test legislation in 1978. Soon a dozen states had approved similar bills. Meanwhile the dropoff in SAT scores became a national issue while voices of concern were raised about the diminishing flow of graduates with engineering degrees.

Many school administrators, still adjusting to the social demands placed on schools by American society during the prior decade, uncertain of their own legal authority, and caught by a values conflict that undermined the consensus tradition of public schools, played it safe. Having seen their colleagues go down when some of the experiments in modular scheduling went stale, and other of their colleagues crumble under the idealogical heat of the early 1970s, principals began to keep their heads down and play safe. Master contracts with teachers further circumscribed their inclination and authority to initiate. They became reactors.

President Reagan's press conference on *A Nation At Risk* abruptly ended that posture. Once again, after a decade of benign neglect, schools were expected to focus upon student achievement. Priorities for teaching and learning were re-established by public politics as abetted by international economic competition.

In the meantime, the older principals had become rusty as educators, and the younger principals had graduated from educational administration programs that now featured courses on collective bargaining and school law rather than on curriculum and instruction. It would be necessary to play 'catch up' again.

Quite unanticipated by anyone, another circumstance had transformed schools over two decades. As categorical programs were administered by the Department of Education, as special education became a major movement, as school districts sought protection from litigation through control of practice as well as policy, schools became increasingly bureaucratized. Principals, as well as teachers, lost independence and flexibility at the school site. New state requirements intensified the trend. Certainly principals as well as teachers have been involved in the implementation of state-mandated reforms, as Odden and Marsh point out. System leadership at the school site was not dead, it had simply been placed on a short leash.

Restructuring: leader or managers?

Most observers agree that the core purpose of schools is teaching and learning. Few observers agree, however, on the role of the principal in making schools effective institutions for learning. Is the principal manager or educational leader?

The authors in this Yearbook tend to favor the notion that schooling is too important to be left to the occasional principal with sufficient vision and talent to shape educational programs for students. Blase views principals as hypercritical of teachers. Gutman votes for a democratic theory of school policy formulation. While Bacharach and Shedd acknowledge the need for system coordination as well as teacher involvement, Sykes and Elmore dismiss the possibility that principals can be educators rather than managers.

Principles as managers is actively advocated, as well, by the American Federation of Teachers. Consider the antecedents of this advocacy, however. The AFT brought collective bargaining to public education 23 years ago in New York City. That movement created a breach between teachers and administrators. Hostility replaced collegiality in many schools, especially if bargaining was aggressive or a strike occurred. Now today, the collective bargaining movement is spent. It is no longer an avenue to gain power; it must be replaced by another strategy. Hence a new promise was made to the AFT constituency to gain power by executive committees of teachers providing leadership in schools. It's a neat maneuver if you create a problem – distrust between teachers and principals – then blame principals for the problem, and then also propose a solution that gains the objectives of the earlier strategy under the pretense of improving schooling!

A more constructive solution is suggested by Bacharach and Shedd. They predict an increasing reliance on comprehensive negotiations to establish the structure and ground rules for joint decision-making. A cooperative publication of the NASSP and the National Education Association, *Ventures in Good Schooling*, (NEA/NASSP 1986) accomplishes that objective. *Ventures* defines the professional responsibilities of teachers on the one hand, and of principals on the other hand, for the educational program. It provides specific guidelines, emphasizes collaboration, and recognizes that principals are accountable to superintendents and school boards for final decisions.

The micropolitics of the school campus are complex and changing. Calls for the restructuring of schools can improve the workplace, especially in large districts weighted down by regulations and layers of central office personnel. But school site management and teacher involvement is already common in those districts with one or two high schools. Given that 78% of the school districts in the United States operate only one high school, teacher involvement is significant nationwide.

What concerns principals and superintendents the most about calls for restructuring, however, are the inaccurate observations of some authors. For example, Sykes and Elmore report that given the demands of a tough workload, principals often construct 'seemingly important roles for themselves in such areas as facilities, transportation, and food service management . . . ' Since these functions are typically managed by district office supervisors of maintenance, transportation, and food service, it is somewhat difficult for principals to identify with the argument. It appears to most practitioners that some critics have become increasingly removed from the schoolhouse.

Even data have become suspect, as school administrators understand with Noblit and Eaker that 'All evaluation designs have the potential of realigning political power and redefining what is credible knowledge'.

Feistritzer's recent profile of school administrators conducted for the Education Department illustrates the point. The narrative report focused upon the homogeneity in outlook of principals and other administrators. A 'similarity of views' and 'old boys club' were featured points made at a national press conference. Yet, principals report their political affiliation to be 43% Democrat, 25% Republican and 23% Independent. Is this homogeneity? Twenty-four percent of principals are women, about one in four. Women are doing pretty well in school leadership positions, better than in most professions. When principals were asked what grades they would give public schools nationally, 5% said 'A', 55% said 'B', 32% said 'C', 2% said 'D', and 5% gave no grade. This is not a mindlessly monochromatic report card. Other data displays show a similar variety of opinions on most issues (Feistritzer 1988).

Critics aside, the key to the successful restructuring of schools is effective leadership within the context of the central demands placed upon schools for student achievement and low dropout rates.

Dimensions of school leadership

The talented inventor and successful corporate executive, George Land, believed that institutions progress through three phases: (1) *formation* – a period of trial and error as the organizational is founded and takes shape, (2) *monitoring* – an age of standardization when functions are solidified requiring careful management, and (3) *death or rebirth* – a time when the old ways fail to work resulting in gradual strangulation or else major new innovation and rebirth.

The nature of leadership in each phase differs significantly. In phase 1, an idea person willing to take risks becomes the leader. In phase 2, control and management skills are required. Phase 3, however, requires transformational leadership, the ability to understand a changing environment and to energize the institution to achieve new goals and to utilize new procedures.

Transformational leadership involves more than modification of old ways. It requires the acceptance of new goals that transcend the normal boundaries of an institution and the recognition of new challenges in the broader environment. Transformational leadership clarifies the conditions necessary for success. Leaders may not possess all the answers, but they motivate personnel in the organization to reframe their thinking, reorganize priorities, and direct their energies toward challenges caused by emerging conditions.

Public schools today are entering phase three of Land's framework. Major shifts in the world environment suggest that incremental improvements in school leadership will not be sufficient. The growing contribution of education to economic growth, the need for better academic achievement and stronger thinking skills, the revolution in information technology, major demographic trends, dramatic shifts in family patterns, and the social impact of drugs are but a few of the watershed changes facing schools and their educational leaders.

Significant change requires the collective wisdom of an institution to solve. Leaders must motivate individuals to reach for, and succeed, with emerging tasks. Motivation is best achieved by giving people the understanding that they can make a difference, that they have a stake not only to attain institutional goals, but to accomplish personal goals as well. Transformational leadership fits the two together. It frees people to make a difference for themselves as they make a difference for the institution.

A particular challenge for school leaders is to strengthen student mastery of content and thinking processes in the face of a rising tide of 'at risk' students. This will require schools to acquire a greater depth of understanding of the teaching/learning process than is needed with self-motivated students. It will require efforts to motivate students, to develop values in students for achievement, and to gain insight about the ways that individual students process information. In other words, schools to be successful in the future must acquire more pedagogical muscle to meet the changing, transformational demands of today.

Effective staff development plans include two components: (1) provision for an individualized program; and (2) provision for development on the job rather than elsewhere. Summer courses, for example, are less beneficial than job-immersed assistance at the school site.

The requirements for effective staff development, therefore, cause the principal to be more centrally involved with this function than under older systems. In fact, the principal should begin to see staff development as perhaps the prime leadership responsibility, given the changing conditions facing schools today. If staff are adequately prepared for change as individuals, if they are helped to meet challenges, then collectively the school as an institution will be successful in meeting the broader social and economic challenges as they emerge. If staff members use technology effectively, then schools will use technology effectively. If staff members adjust their professional skills to demographic trends or to new skill requirements facing students, then the schools will have met successfully the challenges posed by growing minority populations and by international economic competition.

Leadership and school inprovement

Unfortunately, the role of leadership in school improvement has been largely ignored by the national reports. One notable exception, the National Governor's Association's *Time For Results*, includes a section on leadership. While acknowledging the importance of effective leaders to school success, few guidelines are offered for achieving effective leadership beyond general prescriptions to improve the preparation and in-service programs for principals.

Ironically, a decade of research, culminating in recent data by Professor Richard Andrews of the University of Washington, affirms the relationship between effective leaders and effective schools. Evidence is reasonably conclusive that an able principal is a central component of a productive school.

Clearly, if schools are to become transformational institutions, more attention must be focused on the leadership role in schools. Without this attention, the potential for school effectiveness will be severely limited given the full range of challenges poised to deter learning.

The leadership role

John W. Gardner, former Secretary of Health, Education and Welfare, and founding chairman of Common Cause, reminds theorists and the American public alike that even the best institutions – those with a clear sense of mission, excellent internal communications, and spectacular technical capabilities – will fall short in the long run without effective leadership.

Gardner defines leadership as 'judgment in action', certainly a description that applies to principals who must make dozens of decisions daily affecting as many as 3000 students, 150 faculty and staff, and 5000 or more parents. True leadership involves action, not authority or position. Status alone does not convey leadership; any large bureaucratic organization can confirm that fact. Countless persons with impressive credentials may hold a 'position' requiring their initials on memoranda to maintain the paper flow. But that function is not an expression of leadership.

Leadership and power

Democracies make grants of power for specific purposes. A person elected to chair a meeting that goes badly is resented if he fails to exercise sufficient authority to conduct the business at hand. Appointed leaders, including principals, carry a clear expectation to utilize the power necessary to accomplish the tasks of the organization. Serious problems develop when this power is not exercised.

While all leaders possess some power, many powerholders – a loan officer or a police detective, for instance – do not fill leadership roles. Money, property, and knowledge are all expressions of power, but not necessarily of leadership. Even proximity to power can be a source of power, as demonstrated by White House aides or the superintendent's administrative assistant. Do not, however, confuse this 'power' with the leadership role.

Americans tend to be suspicious of power; some even prefer the exercise of minimum leadership. A diverse, heterogeneous institution such as a secondary school, however, requires sufficient leadership power to join together the fragments into a working whole. The proposal for executive committees of teachers to oversee the school clearly runs counter to the theory and practice of leadership in complex organizations. There is nothing bland about horizontal relationships. The hazards of peer pressure and the tendencies towards group coercion are well documented. Power lodges somewhere, and it is more tolerable in the hands of a visable, accountable leader than it is in the hands of invisible and unaccountable personages.

Douglas McGregor, an industrial psychologist, was known for his view that people should be given maximum opportunity to exercise initiative. After a tour of duty as a college president, however, McGregor wrote:

> I believed . . . that a leader could operate successfully as a kind of advisor to his organisation . . . I couldn't have been more wrong . . . I finally began to realize that a leader cannot avoid the exercise of authority . . . It is a major function of the top executive to take on his own shoulders the responsibility for resolving uncertainties that are always involved in important decisions . . . He must also absorb the displeasure, and sometimes severe hostility, of those who would have taken a different course.

Unstructured settings can be devastating to morale as well as to productivity. Staff members operating in limbo crave a clear definition of expectations, orderly planning, adequate coordination, and feedback about performance. Furthermore, a loose organization will create internal coalitions and conspiracies to fill the power vacuum.

Barbara Tuchman, the eminent historian, makes the point: 'If power corrupts, weakness in the seat of power, with its constant necessaity of deals and compromising arrangements, corrupts even more.'

A pragmatic, working world requires leaders. Principals, as leaders, move schools toward the goals and expectations of society. Certainly students, to develop cognitively and socially as young people, need effective expressions of leadership in a school setting. Principals are granted power for specific purposes. They must exercise that power to achieve those purposes. for their constituents.

John Gardener underlines the point: 'For leaders, invisibility is not an opinion . . . Leaders, provided we have effective means of holding them accountable, can serve as checks on unseen players. When accountable leaders are stripped of power, the people lose power.'

Teaching: the school's central task

Skillful leadership is essential to effective schools. A paper entitled 'Attributes and Context' includes a summary of attributes Gardner considers essential to leadership. Included near the top is, 'Task Competence' (Gardner 1987):

Researchers on leadership use the phrase 'task competence' to mean the knowledge a leader has of the task at hand. Columbus was not just a man with a burning mission; he said of himself with considerable modesty, 'The Lord hath blessed me abundantly with a knowledge of marine affairs.' At the other extreme Winston Churchill's father, Randolph, was appointed Chancellor of the Exchequer for the most political of reasons. He did not increase his standing when once, on being shown a balance sheet, he waved a finger at the decimal points and said, 'I could never make out what those damned dots meant.'

Clearly, this observation relates directly to the principalship. If the person charged with the leadership for a school does not know the environment in which the school functions month by month, how can this leadership be exercised? The question is not, can the principal teach math or music or whatever, but rather has he rubbed shoulders sufficiently as a teaching colleague to understand circumstances so that later as a leader he and the faculty can communicate effectively. This experience also allows principals and teachers jointly to anticipate issues and opportunities, and be mutually familiar with the 'corporate culture' of the school. Effective leadership requires more than bringing administrative efficiency to specific tasks.

Last year, John Roueche and George Baker III completed an analysis of schools cited for the Education Department's Secondary School Recognition Program. They found that the principals in these nationally recognized schools were typically committed both to instuctional leadership and to participative decision-making. On a more specific level, the authors concluded that these principals 'contribute to organizational health through strong leadership, staff involvement, systematic evaluation of instruction, and recognizing their faculty and staff'. These findings corroborate with research conducted in 1978 by NASSP on 60 'effective' principals. If the principal as leader devotes time and attention to the educational program, then the faculty and students take notice and the quality of schooling improves. Only a leader can have this kind of pervasive impact.

Recently, the Clearinghouse on Educational Management published, as part of their series on *The Best of ERIC*, an annotation of ERIC literature entitled, 'Improving the Quality of Teaching' (ERIC 1987). A clear message coming from the eleven articles cited from various sources was the key role principals play in developing and maintaining top-notch teaching. For example, Raymond Calabrese in an article entitled 'Effective schools and classroom instruction' (Clearing House, February 1986) contends that a principal must surely be an educational leader if his purpose is to upgrade the quality of education in school. Furthermore, citing Good and Brophy's book, *Looking in the Classroom*, the author stated that instructional leadership is possible only 'when principals clearly understand classroom evaluation and staff evaluation'.

This past summer, the Southern Regional Education Board, probably the most active group nationally for responsible school reform, published a *Progress Report and Recommendations on Educational Improvements*. Their section on School Leadership and Organization focuses upon personnel assessment programs, leadership training, and educational leadership. For example, they note that 'States are agreeing that effective principals have knowledge about supervising and evaluating instruction and a common set of skills such as the ability to communicate well, analyze problems, and organize work efficiently.'

Instructional leadership

Schools today are returning to an old and basic premise: that the principal should be an instructional leader. This trend in no way diminishes the principal's responsibility for managing school resources. Rather, it extends the management function beyond the commonplace daily operations of the school.

If current educational issues reflect social change, as many observers contend, the focus of the schools and the role of the principal require a new look in this transformational setting.

Instructional leadership is the principal's role in providing *direction*, *resources*, and *support* to teachers and students for the improvement of teaching and learning in the school. This role includes four broad domains: formative, planning, implementation, and evaluation. It has nothing to do with the notion advanced by some that an instructional leader must be expert in a dozen subject areas.

Formative: The principal must operate from a firm and secure knowledge base. An effective instructional leader knows the trends in school curriculum, the new approaches to organizing schools, and the state of the art in instructional media and methodology.

Planning: Instructional planning involves helping teachers organize for instruction: Assessing current student and program needs, establishing goals for the school, helping teachers see the relationship of goals to the instructional program, developing goals for the various areas of instruction, translating goals into operational objectives, formulating a plan for school improvement, and securing appropriate resources to support the program are all required. Goals and objectives are the framework, in turn, for organizational, programmatic, and budgetary decisions.

Implementation: The planning process leads naturally to activities for enhancing the quality of teaching and learning. The process begins with the selection and employment of first-rate teachers. It goes forward with the proper deployment of resources, setting high expectations for teachers and students, and instructional supervision. The principal needs to know the attributes of quality instruction to validate effective practices and to assist teachers find better ways to reach students.

Research into school effectiveness shows that academic emphasis, the quality of student–teacher interactions, and the type of incentives and rewards all make a difference in student outcomes. The school's climate for learning is the product of the collective efforts of the principal, the teachers, the parents, and the students.

Evaluation: If the school really helps students to learn and grow, it will be evident from a number of vital signs: student test scores, average daily attendance, library and media usage, number of students participating in curricular activities, number of incidents of vandalism caused by students, number of students referred for discipline, percentage of students receiving passing and failing marks, percentage of students from all socioeconomic backgrounds electing advanced courses, success of the graduates.

Evidence collected systematically can serve as the basis for program improvements and community support. Basing educational decision-making on carefully gathered information establishes a professional posture that wins public respect and support.

Principals who understand the formative, planning, implementation, and evaluation dimensions of instructional leadership are well on the way to affecting the educational quality of the school. This role is key to school improvement. This role, more than any other, positions the principal for success in a transformational era. Most other tasks should be delegated, including most of those which demand routine decisions. The key is not to separate the principal from the instructional program, but to sharpen professional skills as required. Don't let the tail wag the dog.

The purpose of schools remains to school students. This task will be tougher in the years ahead. The principal might be distracted by the changing contexts, viewing them as central. Rather, they are implementing factors, supporting actors for the main show. A good batter accommodates for dust or wind, and keeps his eye on the ball. So does a good principal, where the game is to get every student to home plate.

Refocusing preparation programs

Almost everyone agrees that the preparation of school administrators requires a drastic overhaul. Calls for reform come from higher education, from professional associations, from governers and state departments of education, and from individual school executives across the nation.

For example, the American Association of Colleges for Teacher Education in a recent report entitled, *School Leadership Preparation: A Preface for Action*, argues that, 'Dramatic changes are needed in programs to prepare school administrators if they are to lead their schools and faculties rather than just manage them' (AACTE 1988). Another voice from higher education, the Holmes Group, proposes that member institutions make the professional education of administrators compatible with the requirements of the profession of teaching.

The most comprehensive proposal for reform comes from the University Council for Educational Administration, sponsors of the National Commission on Excellence in Educational Administration and its report, *Leaders for America's Schools* (NCEEA 1987).

Public school administrators welcome these calls for stronger, more contemporary programs. Repeated surveys by the National Association of Secondary School Principals and by the American Association of School Administrators confirm that principals and superintendents believe their preparation to be seriously deficient. This view has led to a growing conviction that practitioners must begin to play a larger role in defining professional standards and designing preparation programs that express these standards.

While school administrators and university personnel agree on the need for reform, only marginal consensus exists on the central causes of the deficiences or on steps for improvement. Indeed, perspective among the university community also vary, with major research institutions arguing to maintain the theory movement of the 1960s, and the 'comprehensive' institutions focusing more upon developing professional skills.

School administrators and their professional organizations have been generally uninvolved in debates about preparation and certification during the past decade. Meanwhile, the traditional stream of superintendents and principals moving to the professoriate has become smaller. In retrospect, a lack of direct participation by professional associations representing the viewpoint of elementary and secondary educators in the design of preparation programs was a serious policy omission for these groups. The kingdom was ruled by professors.

More recently, however, the natives have become restless over criticims of school leadership that principals and superintendents consider uninformed as well as unfair. For example, school administrators were astonished when the Tomorrow's Schools Group, a task force of the Holmes Group, expressed the need to 'make a pointed and explicit critique of the field of educational administration, its failure to take its central purpose from teaching and learning . . . ' (TSG/Holmes Group 1987) Such statements, practitioners believe, reflect a misreading of the values of school administrators and a gross simplification of contextual factors surrounding today's operating schools.

Struck by this charge, and marginally aware of the attrition of deans who were former school administrators, the NASSP surveyed the education deans of 26 major research universities, both public and private. The results are dramatic in contrast to the backgrounds of earlier deans who led the major schools of education during their formative years, pioneers like Elwood P. Cubberley of Stanford Univeristy, Frank Chase of the Univeristy of Chicago, and Paul Hanus and Henry W. Holmes of Harvard University. All these educators had extensive backgrounds as school administrators.

Of the 26 deans contacted, 22 responded to our requests for information on their area of professional preparation, their experience as educators, and their major contributions to the field. Of the group, only five deans indicated any preparation in educational administration or in leadership. The professional experience of the deans surveyed indicates an even lower level of commonality with practicing school administrators. While 14 deans have served briefly as teachers at the elementary or secondary school levels, only one has any experience as a principal or superintendent.

The frayed connections between deans of research universities and school leaders constitute only one facet of a troublesome two-world syndrome plaguing the field of school administration. The problem extends to departments of educational administration, as well. A recent study of Martha McCarthy and colleagues on departments of educational administration in 297 universities entitled, *Under Scrutiny: The Educational Administration Professoriate*, reports that only 23% of these professors were appointed directly from the position of superintendent or other K-12 administrator. (McCarthy *et al.* 1988) The balance had transferred from other university assignments. Perhaps this phenomenon reflects an in-house bias, since McCarthy also finds that, 'professors with strong research orientation believe that former practitioners do not make the best professors'.

Furthermore, McCarthy observers that, 'the more research-orientated the university, the less likely its faculty members are concerned about practical problems in the field or developing ties with practitioners. Faculty at research institutions were more concerned about the need to secure external support for their scholarship.'

The public school superintendents and principals of the nation find this posture alarming as well as unacceptable. It constitutes professional narcissism, a focus upon personal agendas rather than providing knowledgeable service to the public and its schools. It rejects accountability to the working profession and to the electorate for outcomes. Furthermore, if W. K. Hoy's view is valid that 'not only is research theoretically barren, it also has little or no practical value', a clear need exists for professional associations to assume a more prominent role in preparation and professional development programs for school administrators (Hoy 1982).

Superintendents and principals believe that research can make contributions to the profession of educational administration. They are not, however, blind devotees to inquiry for its own sake. Research can be scholarly or it can be pedestrian. It can also be routine, repetitive, or irrelevant to the life of the school. Some investigations may be elegant in form, but produce petty outcomes. Too much research in education reflects these deficiencies. Too much is unrelated to practice.

The profession of school administration, unlike the professions of medicine, engineering, law and the rest, has failed to rely sufficiently upon practice to generate theory. Empirical observations form the building blocks of theory for most professions, which in turn gives shape to practice. While theory provides context, its authenticity depends upon giving meaning to practice. Confident theorists welcome this interchange and build upon its inherent power. These are the theorists that contribute to the building of a profession.

When deans and departments of educational administration emulate the values of the arts and sciences faculty on campus, problems arise beyond that of producing a chasm between professors and school administrators. A single-minded focus on research in the university reward system, when applied to professional education, causes a benign neglect of curriculum development and program innovation within the institution. Professional progress stalls. Vitality is lost.

Professional interests are narrowed, not broadened. Contact is lost with the full range of activities at work in the profession. For example, of the four most frequently read journals by professors of educational administration, three are aimed exclusively at higher education: the *Educational Administration Quarterly*, the *Journal of Higher Education*, and *Administrative Science Quarterly*. Only the fourth, the *Phi Delta Kappan*, provides a solid link between practitioner and research-orientated professor. Similar gaps occur in professional association memberships and at professional conferences held at the national level.

In sum, we have created two cultures in educational administration, with incompatible perspectives, divergent reward systems, and little agreement about the root causes of current deficiences in the preparation and development of elementary and secondary school leaders. School administrators are considered successful by boards of education when they exercise effective leadership, defined by John Gardner as 'judgment in action'. National quality rankings of university preparation programs as voted by the professoriate, on the other hand, 'reflect institutional prestige and scholarly productivity rather than excellence in the preparation of educational leaders' (McCarthy 1988).

Unfortunately, these circumstances generate a regressive 'doom loop' which further divides the two cultures, each peering apprehensively from behind defensive lines. As perspectives diverge and suspicions rise, the loop becomes embedded. Relationships then continue to deteriorate unless strong counter initiatives are taken.

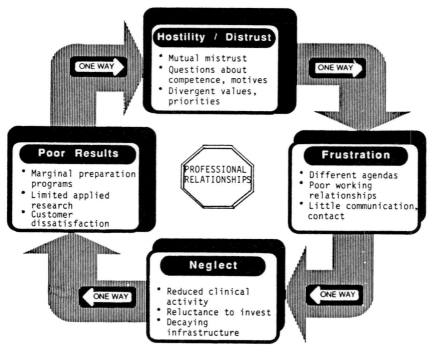

Figure 1. Doom Loop.
Research professors and school administrators.

Fortunately a few initiatives are emerging to reverse the loop's downward spiral. Some of the most encouraging proposals come from higher education while others reflect school and college partnerships.

For example, the Texas Education Administration Advisory Committee, co-chaired by Thomas J. Sergiovanni of Trinity University and Jane H. MacDonald of New Braunfels Independent School District, calls for 'a new balance to be struck among academics, the professional community, and the State in the governance of programs for school administrators as a significant step in reducing bureaucracy and inefficiency, the raising of standards, the promotion of professionalism, and the enhancement of accountability'. (EAAC [Texas] 1987).

Florida is implementing a new design for preparing principals based upon similar formulae, initiated by Cecil Golden of the State Department of Educuation. The state superintendent's Task Force on Leadership, Training, and Licensure for the State of Wisconsin is recommending an annual exchange of small numbers of professors of educational leadership with school administrators. They further propose that, 'professors who teach and supervise practicums, internships, and other field based experiences should have at least three years of regularly licensed administrative experience in elementary and secondary education' (State Superintendents Task Force 1988).

The AACTE supports this general direction in the document, *School Leadership Preparation* by recommending that programs in educational administration be modeled after 'professional programs' rather than replicating a liberal arts model of graduate education. Also recommended: 'Faculty should have leadership and/or teaching experience in schools' (AACTE 1988).

The new National Policy Board for Educational Administration, representing three groups from higher education, five administrator professional associations, and the National School Boards Association will be a major national player in bringing together the values of practitioners and the values of departments of educational administration in a common quest to improve professional standards. The Board's work is partially funded by the Danforth Foundation.

These initiatives all reflect a positive start toward constructing a common agenda for school administrators and those who prepare them for practice in the schools. They mark only a beginning, however, because resistance from the research 'industry' remains at hand, well-funded and connected.

Old habits are not easily buried. New programs, to reach their required potential, must reflect more than a firm handshake among the participants. Rather, some bold new perspectives must be applied to preparation programs for school leaders. The elements include:

1. Research programs should be accountable, focussing upon a demonstrable improvement in educational outcomes. If the learning environment is excluded by the investigation, how do students benefit from the work? How do schools benefit, and their communities? How does the economy benefit?

2. Conceptual frameworks must be broadened to reflect modern social science research. Important elements here include assessment center protocols to identify and counsel promising candidates since some key leadership behaviors can be gained by recruitment and selection, and a recognition that effective school leaders require more than analytical training and content knowledge. For example, the National Commission on Professional Standards for the Principalship sponsored by NASSP has identified on a preliminary basis, twenty professional skills essential to success as a principal, including organizational competence, interpersonal skills, oral and written expression, and specific leader-

ship behaviors. Most current preparation programs ignore these dimensions of the principalship.

3. Instructional methodology for future school leaders needs to reflect modern adult learning theory, including the use of simulations, coaching and mentoring, and employing occupational environments.

4. Concepts of leadership and organization must be extended to include the best research methodologies utilized by schools of management and industrial psychology. For example, more attention is required of inductive strategies utilizing task analysis in the identification of professional 'knowledge, skills and abilities' essential to perform these tasks, and the development of procedures to evaluate the acquisition of the knowledge or skill. The traditional focus of educational research on matrices based deductively on logical models is useful, but not complete. The models may look, even sound brilliant, but in practice they seldom fulfil expectations.

5. Knowledge of management theory and practice needs strengthening. Far too many authors in education ride the latest hobby horse, adding to a notorious 'trendy' profession. Some rather superficial pieces have been written recently about teacher empowerment and the role of principals. These authors reflect a shallow understanding of modern management, ignoring the central requirement that workable empowerment depends upon a common outlook by all participants. Since Peters and Waterman popularized the concept, they provide a good reference point: 'A set of shared values and rules about discipline, details, and execution can provide the framework in which practical autonomy takes place routinely . . . Too much overbearing discipline of the wrong kind will kill autonomy. But the more rigid discipline, the discipline based on a small number of shared values . . . in fact, induces practical autonomy and experimentation throughout the organization' (Peters and Waterman 1982). Any teaching staff at loggerheads with the board of education or its superintendent fails to meet these criteria. Decentralized decision-making requires a substantive context, not simply a new organizational framework.

6. The education departments of major research universities, in particular, should refocus priorities. Their professional education programs for school administrators and teachers need to be placed on par with research efforts. The Arts and Sciences model cannot dominate if professional education is to thrive. In addition, a bachelor's degree in the liberal arts should be expected for advanced degree candidates to eliminate the redundancy of foundation courses unrelated to an educational setting. What other profession places its professional preparation so squarely upon general education at the graduate level rather than upon clinical experience and applied general knowledge? Marginal candidates should not be intellectually subsidized by weakening the professional dimensions of their graduate program with general education coursework.

7. Finally, the reward system for research activity should emphasize its application in a practical, real-world context.

Looking ahead

Superintendents and principals believe, as do a growing number of professors of educational administration and state officials, that the present preparation model for school leaders reflects the deficiencies of a fragmented profession. Programs, therefore, should be redesigned, with the redesign effort providing a catalyst for devleoping a more positive partnership between higher education and the public schools.

Old ways should be replaced by a coherent professional studies model that is more intellectualy rigorous on the one hand and less inclined to unlinked research on the other hand. Key to this approach is applying the yeast of rigor to school practice. Also required will be the development of new competencies in leadership, and systematic clinical study.

This approach recognizes that professional knowledge is created when unique and changing problems are faced in applied settings, requiring appropriate, informed courses of action. As Sergiovanni and MacDonald note, 'Professionals rely heavily upon *informed* intuition as they create knowledge in use . . . ' (Texas Educational Advisory Committee 1987).

Pursuing a professional studies approach holds great promise for developing a new partnership among university faculty and talented professionals in the field. The outcome will be a strong and vital kingdom to serve the schools of the land. Given that 40% of the school administrators will retire by 1995, now is the time to act with conviction and force.

Reprise

No one view can accommodate all the nuances affecting the politics of reforming school administration. Probably no single observer enjoys a full vision, given the range of American politics, the complexities of the school, and the many interfaces between school and their publics at the local and state levels.

Considering the central contribution of schools to economic growth and to national well-being, however, it becomes essential to understand the political framework within which school leaders operate, and to sketch some promising approaches to making that leadership effective in accommodating the external and internal forces which play upon public schools.

This volume provides some worthy insight, and offers some provocative proposals, toward this end.

References

CARNEGIE FORUM ON EDUCATION AND THE ECOMONY (1986) *A Nation Prepared: Teachers for the 21st Century* (Washington, DC: CFEE).

CLIFFORD, J. C. and GUTHRIE, J. W. (1988) *Ed School* (Chicago: University of Chicago Press).

CLINTON, B. (1987) *Speaking of Leadership* (Denver: Education Commission of the States).

EDUCATIONAL ADMINISTRATION ADVISORY COMMITTEE (1987) *Preparing Tommorow's School Administrators in Texas* (Austin, TX: Coordinating Board, Texas College and University System), p 3.

ELMORE, R. F. and MCLAUGHLIN, M. W. (1988) *Steady Work: Policy Practice, and the Reform of American Education* (Santa Monica, California: The Rand Corporation).

FEISTRITZER, C. E. (1988) *Profile of School Administrators in the US* (Washington, DC: National Center for Education Information.

GARDNER, J. W. (1986–1988) *Leadership Papers*, 1 to 10 (Washington DC: Independent Sector.)

HEATON, H. (1977) *Productivity in Service Organizations: Organizing for People* (McGraw-Hill, Inc., New York).

HOY, W. K. (1982) 'Introduction: recent developments in theory and research in eductional administration', *Educational Administration Quarterly*, 18, p. 5.

HOYLE, E. (1986) *The Politics of School Mangement* (London: Hodder and Stoughton).

INSTITUTE FOR EDUCATIONAL LEADERSHIP, INC. (1986) *School Boards* (Washington, DC: IEL).

KEEFE, J. W. and JENKINS, J. M. (1984) *Instructional Leadership Handbook* (Reston VA: National Association of Secondary School Princpals).

MCCARTHY, M. M., KUH, G. D., NEWELL, L. J. and IACONA, C. M. (1988) *Under Scrutiny: The Educational Administration Professoriate* (Columbus, Ohio: University Council for Educational Administration), p. 51.

MURRAY, F.B. (1987) 'Holmes Group pursues reform agenda' *The School Administrator*, February, 44 (2), pp.29–34.

NATIONAL COMMISSION ON EXCELLENCE IN EDUCATIONAL ADMINISTRATION (1987) *Leaders for America's Schools* (Columbus OH: University Council for Educational Administration).

NATIONAL GOVERNORS' ASSOCIATION (1986) *Time For Results. The Governors' 1991 Report on Education* (Washington, DC: NGA).

NATIONAL GOVERNORS' ASSOCIATION (1988) *Results in Education: 1988. The Governors 1991 Report on Education* (Washington, DC: NGA).

PETERS, T. and WATERMAN, R. H. (1982) *In Search of Excellence* (New York: Harper and Row).

SARASON S. B. (1971) *The Culture of the School and the Problem of Change* (Boston: Allyn & Bacon).

SCHEIN, E. N. (1985) *Organizational Culture and Leadership* (San Francisco: Jossey-Bass).

SOUTHERN REGIONAL EDUCATIONAL BOARD (1988) *Program Report and Recommendations on Educational Improvements* (Atlanta: SREB).

STATE SUPERINTENDENTS TASK FORCE ON LEADERSHIP TRAINING AND LICENSURE (1988) *Draft Recommendations* (Madison, WI: Wisconsin Department of Public Instruction), p.33.

STRIKE, K. A., HALLER, E. J. and SOLTIS, J. F. (1988) *The Ethics of School Administration* (New York: Teachers College Press).

SUBCOMMITTEE ON THE PREPARATION OF SCHOOL ADMINISTRATORS (1988) *School Leadership Preparation: A Preface for Action* (Washington, DC: American Association of Colleges for Teachers Education), p. 1.

THOMSON, S. D. (1986) 'Strengthen, don't diffuse, school leadership', *Education Week*, 28 May, p. 28.

THOMSON, S. D, (1986) 'School leaders and the Carnegie agenda', *The American School Board Journal*, September, p. 32.

THOMSON, S. D. (1988) *Uncertain Images: Deans and School Administrators* (Reston, VA: National Association of Secondary School Principals).

THOMSON, S. D. (1988) 'The principalship: ingredients of programs to prepare effective leaders', *Bulletin*, May 1988, pp. 72, 508.

THOMSON, S. D. (1988) 'The parting of deans and administrators', *Education Week*, 7 (16), pp. 48, 36.

TOMORROWS SCHOOLS GROUP (1987) unpublished paper (Lansing, MI: The Holmes Group).

HOLMES GROUP (1986) *Tommorow's Teachers* (East Lansing MI: The Holmes Group).

TRUMP, J. L. and BAYNHAM, D. (1961) *Focus on Change* (Chicago: Rand McNally).

NEA/NASSP (1987) *Ventures in Good Schooling* (Washington DC: National Education Association and the National Association of Secondary School Principals).

WATERMAN, R. H. (1987) *The Renewal Factor* (New York: Bantam Books).

WILLIAMS, S. B. (1970) *Hassling* (Boston: Little, Brown & Company).

Index